Kamisama Kiss

Story & Art by

Julietta Suzuki

Kamisama Kiss

Volume 15
CONTENTS

CHARACTERS

Tomoe
The shinshi who serves Nanami now that she's a tochigami. Originally a wild fox ayakashi. He controls powerful kitsunebi.

Nanami Momozono
A high school student who was turned into a kamisama by the tochigami Mikage. She likes Tomoe.

Onikiri
Onibi-warashi, spirits of the shrine.

Kotetsu
Onibi-warashi, spirits of the shrine.

Mamoru
Nanami's shikigami. He can create a spiritual barrier to keep out evil.

Mizuki
Nanami's second shinshi. The incarnation of a white snake. Used to be the shinshi of Yonomori shrine.

Mikage
A kamisama who ran away from home. He turned Nanami into a tochigami and left his shrine in her care.

Yukiji
A human woman from more than 500 years ago who was somehow connected to Tomoe.

Akura-oh
A great yokai and Tomoe's partner more than 500 years ago. He committed every evil act he possibly could.

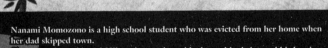

Nanami Momozono is a high school student who was evicted from her home when her dad skipped town.

She meets the tochigami Mikage in a park, and he leaves his shrine and his kami powers to her.

Now Nanami spends her days with Tomoe and Mizuki, her shinshi, and with Onikiri and Kotetsu, the onibi-warashi spirits of the shrine.

Nanami has been slowly gaining powers as a kamisama by holding a festival at her shrine, attending a big kami conference, and getting embroiled in the succession fight at the tengu village.

But mysterious marks have appeared on Tomoe's body, causing him to go into a coma. Mikage explains that the marks are part of a curse cast by a fallen kami.

So Nanami goes back in time to search for clues to break the curse, but the past has some surprises in store for her!

Story so far

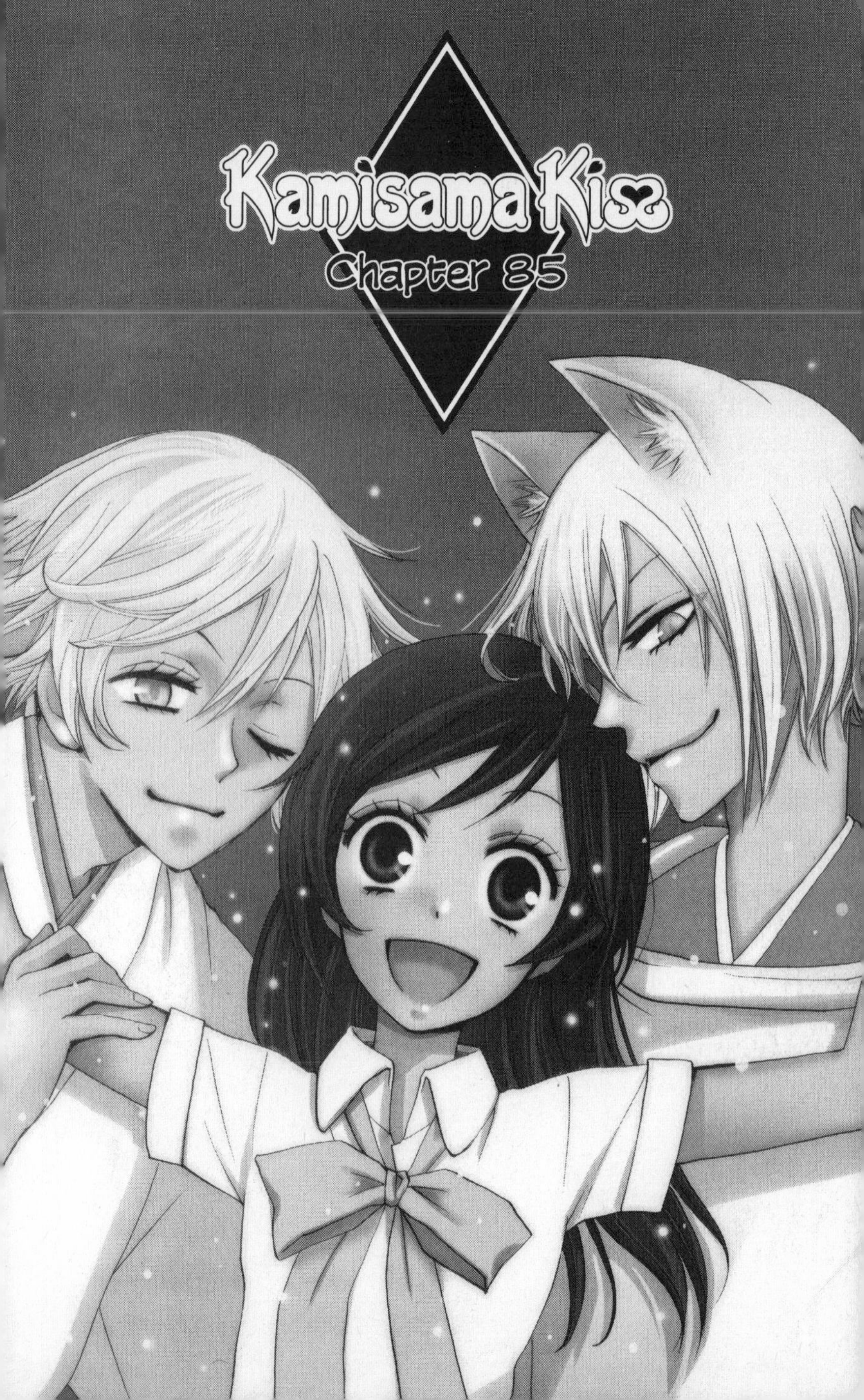
Kamisama Kiss
Chapter 85

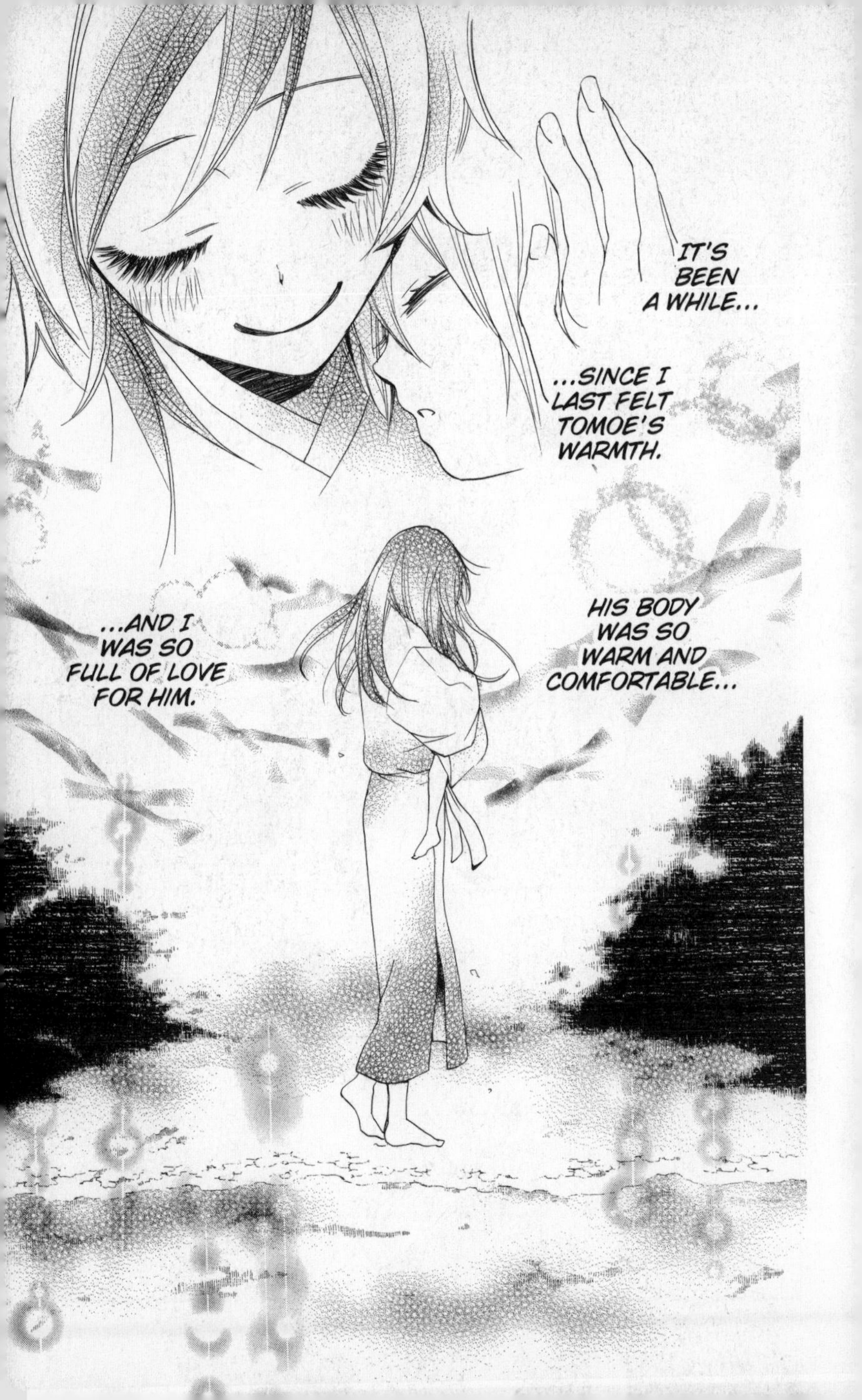
IT'S BEEN A WHILE...
...SINCE I LAST FELT TOMOE'S WARMTH.
HIS BODY WAS SO WARM AND COMFORTABLE...
...AND I WAS SO FULL OF LOVE FOR HIM.

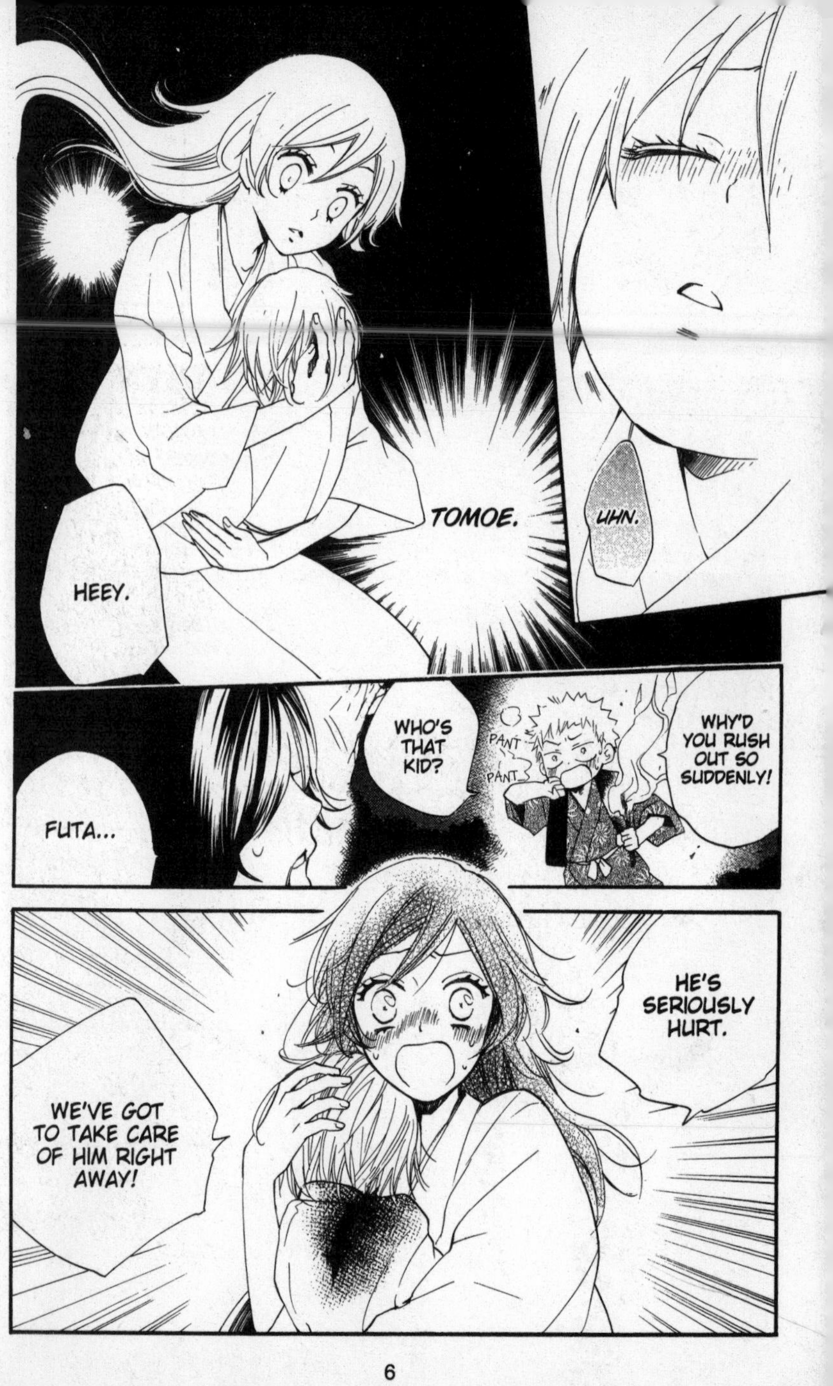
UHN.
TOMOE.
HEEY.
WHY'D YOU RUSH OUT SO SUDDENLY!
PANT
PANT
WHO'S THAT KID?
FUTA...
HE'S SERIOUSLY HURT.
WE'VE GOT TO TAKE CARE OF HIM RIGHT AWAY!

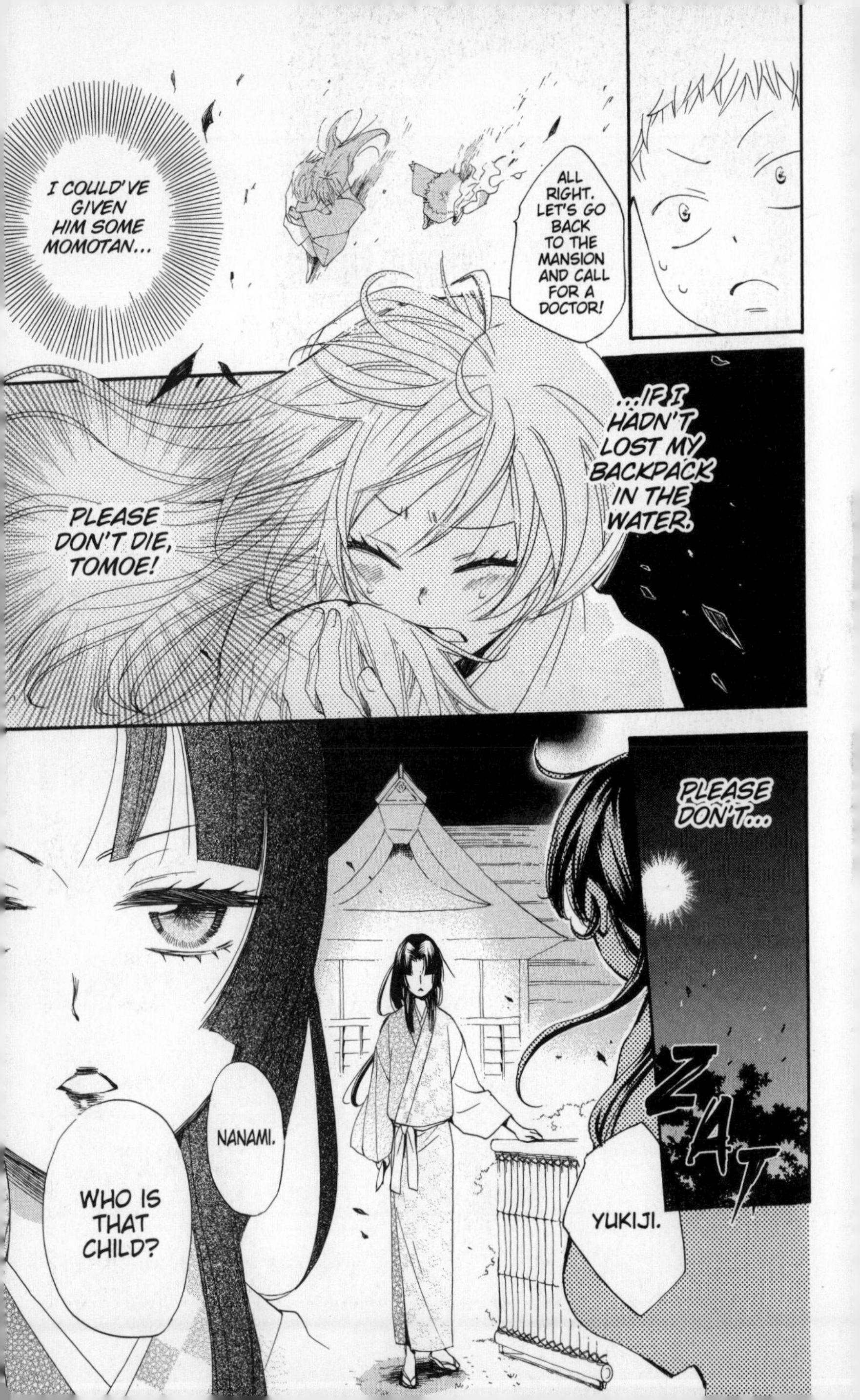
ALL RIGHT. LET'S GO BACK TO THE MANSION AND CALL FOR A DOCTOR!
I COULD'VE GIVEN HIM SOME MOMOTAN...
...IF I HADN'T LOST MY BACKPACK IN THE WATER.
PLEASE DON'T DIE, TOMOE!
PLEASE DON'T...
ZAT
YUKIJI.
NANAMI.
WHO IS THAT CHILD?

GET AWAY FROM HIM, NANAMI.

HE DOESN'T LIVE HERE.

I DON'T RECOGNIZE HIM.

WAIT.

I FOUND HIM BY THE RIVER. HE COLLAPSED FROM HIS WOUNDS!

WE HAVE TO GET A DOCTOR RIGHT AWAY—

WE'LL HAND HIM OVER TO THE MEN IN TOWN.

I'VE HEARD FOXES CAN TRANSFORM INTO HUMANS.

THAT BRAT MAY BE THE FOX YOKAI EVERYONE'S LOOKING FOR.

I...

...KNOW THIS CHILD.

HE'S FROM MY VILLAGE.

I THINK HE FOLLOWED ME HERE... SO...

I WON'T HAND HIM OVER TO THOSE MEN...

BUT.

I...

I WON'T HAND HIM OVER.

I...

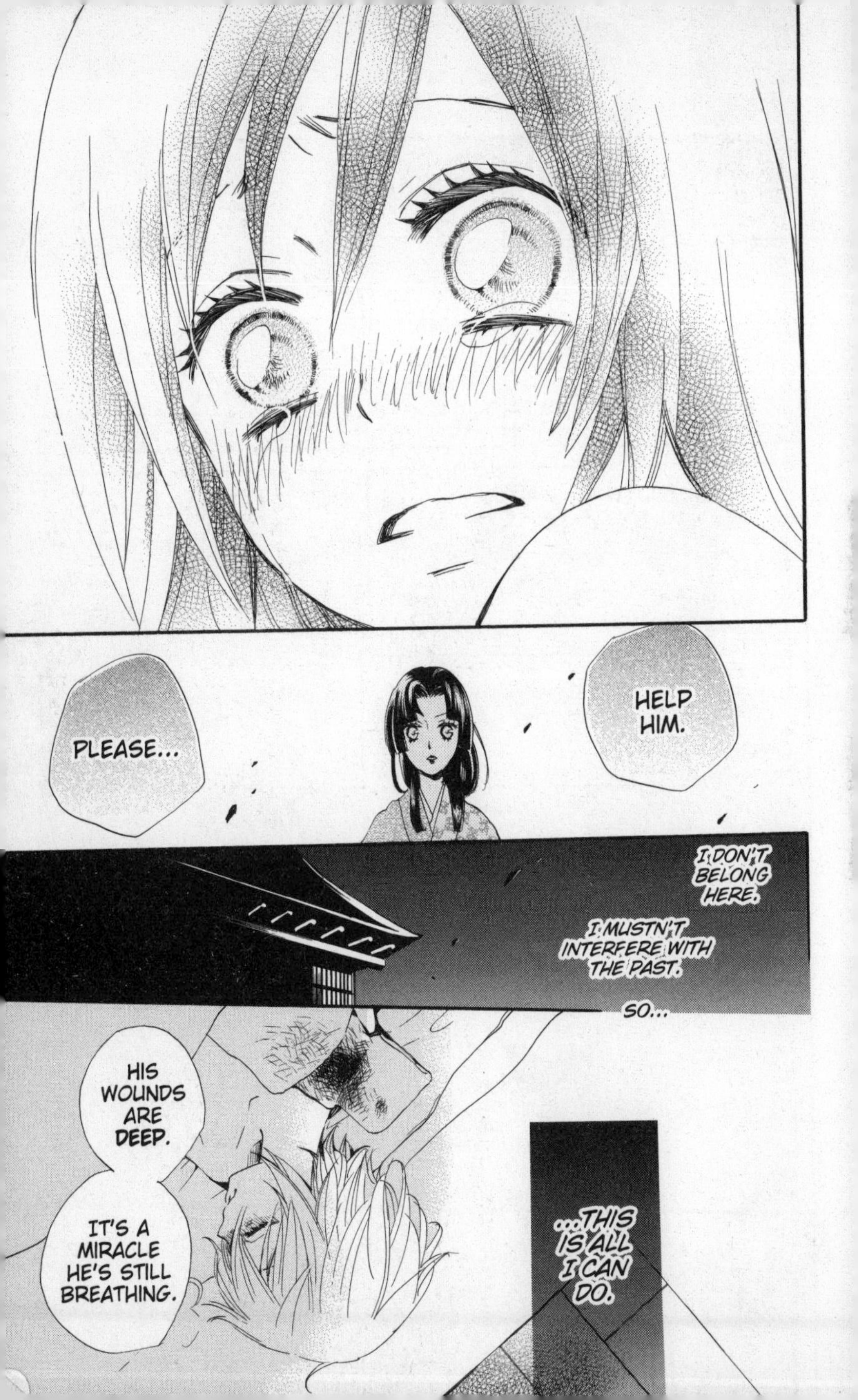
HELP HIM.
PLEASE...
I DON'T BELONG HERE.
I MUSTN'T INTERFERE WITH THE PAST.
SO...
...THIS IS ALL I CAN DO.
HIS WOUNDS ARE DEEP.
IT'S A MIRACLE HE'S STILL BREATHING.

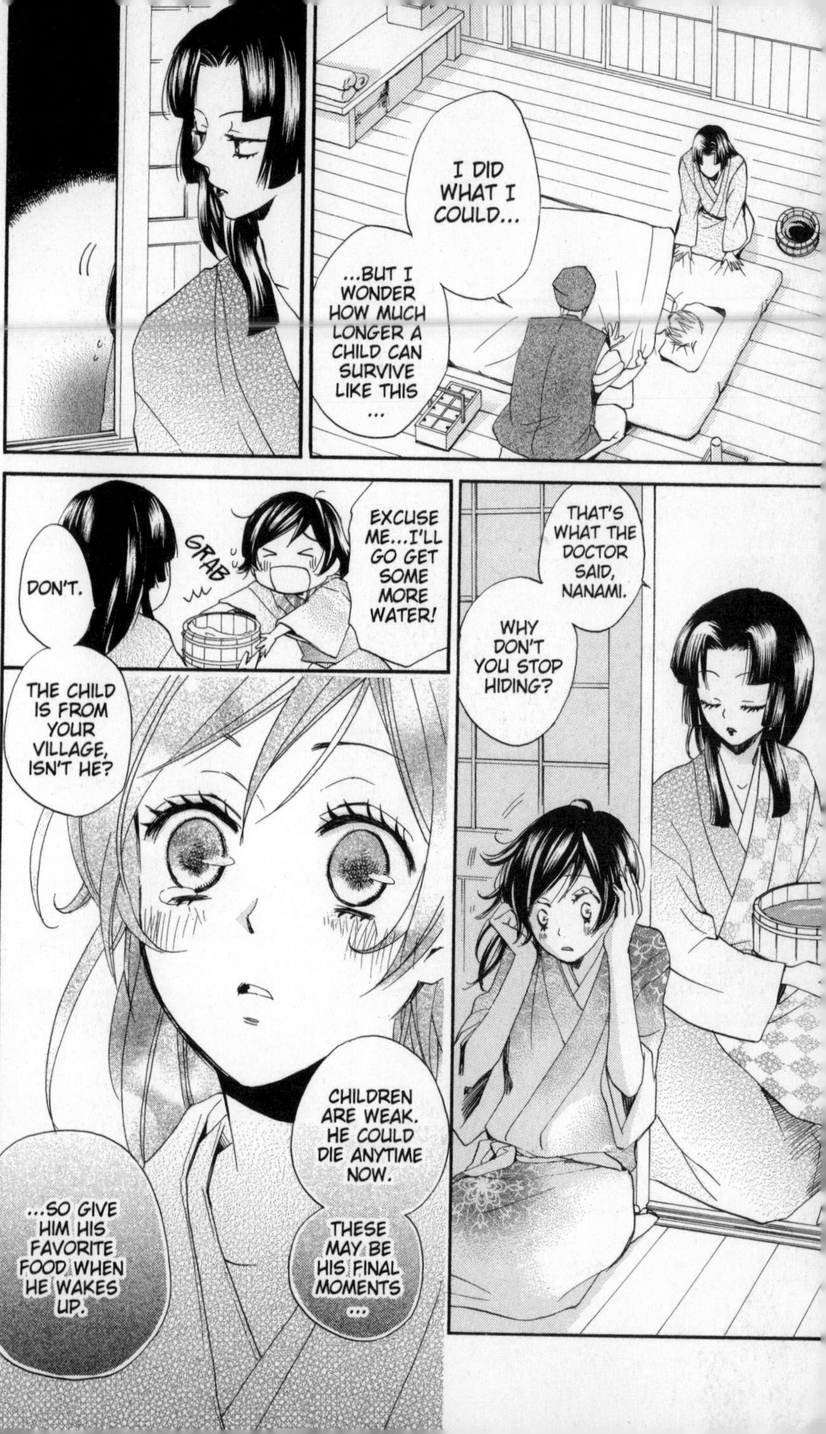
I DID WHAT I COULD...
...BUT I WONDER HOW MUCH LONGER A CHILD CAN SURVIVE LIKE THIS...
THAT'S WHAT THE DOCTOR SAID, NANAMI.
WHY DON'T YOU STOP HIDING?
EXCUSE ME...I'LL GO GET SOME MORE WATER!
GRAB
DON'T.
THE CHILD IS FROM YOUR VILLAGE, ISN'T HE?
CHILDREN ARE WEAK. HE COULD DIE ANYTIME NOW.
THESE MAY BE HIS FINAL MOMENTS...
...SO GIVE HIM HIS FAVORITE FOOD WHEN HE WAKES UP.

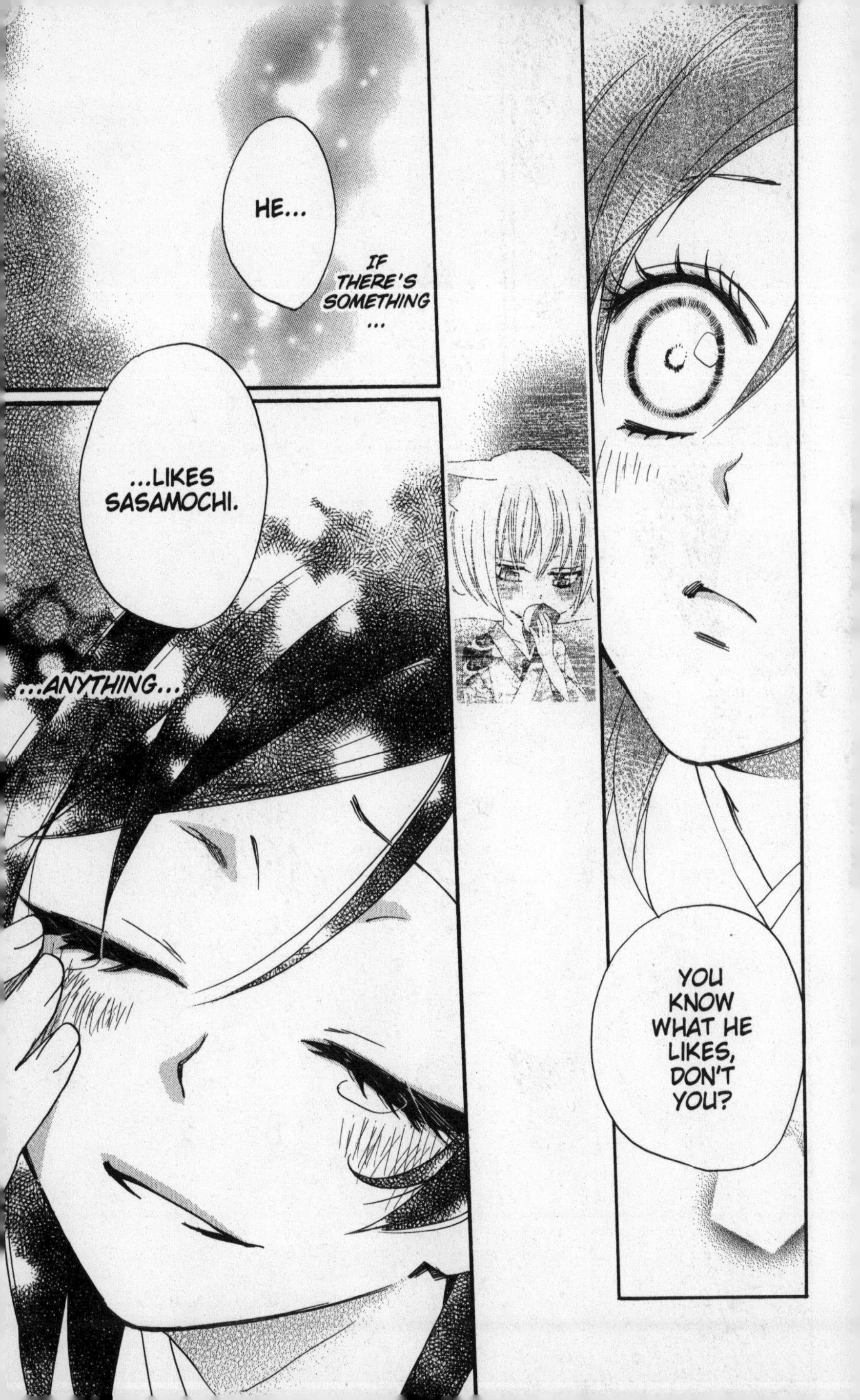
YOU KNOW WHAT HE LIKES, DON'T YOU?
HE...
IF THERE'S SOMETHING ...
...LIKES SASAMOCHI.
...ANYTHING...

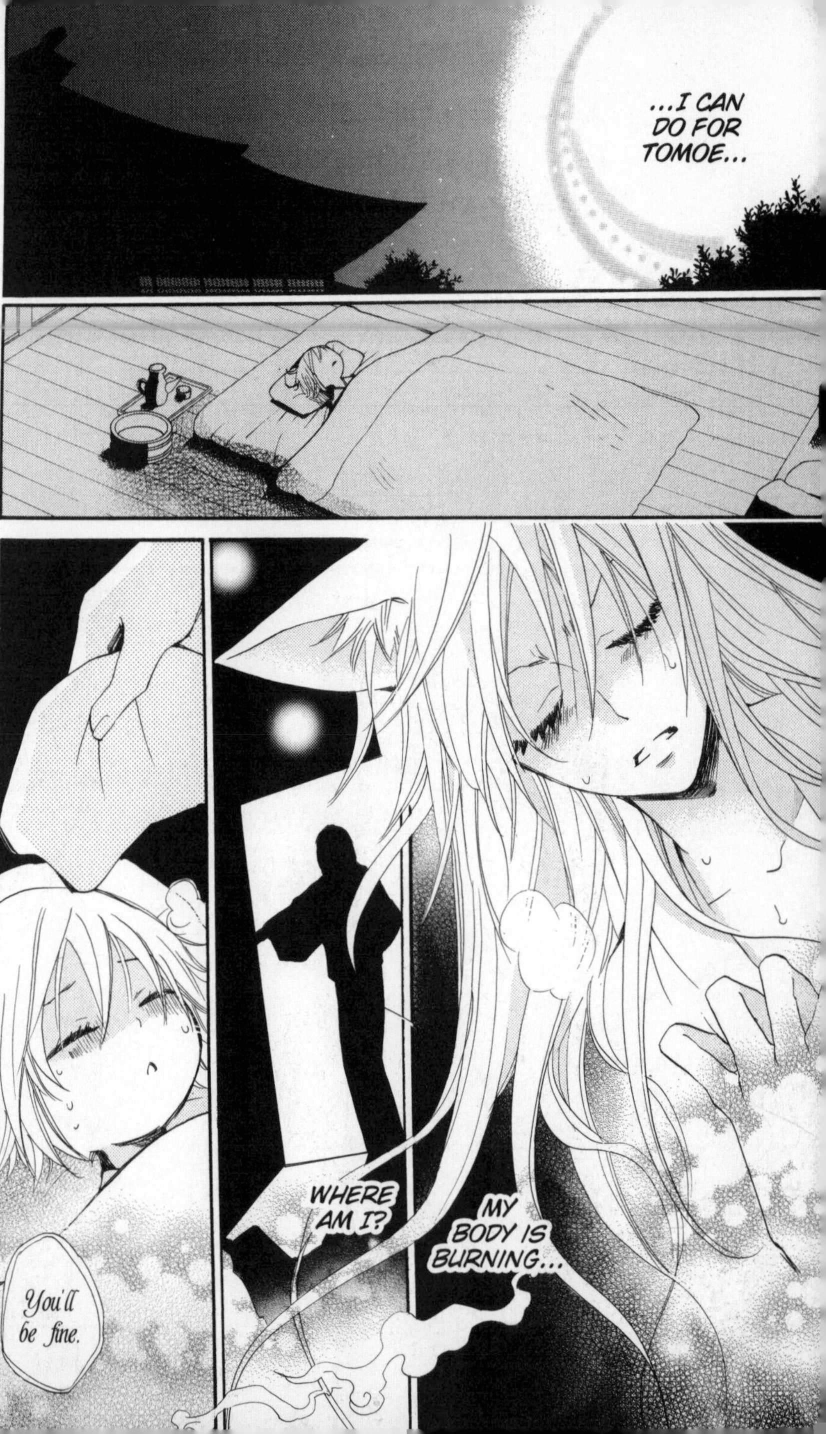
...I CAN DO FOR TOMOE...
MY BODY IS BURNING...
WHERE AM I?
You'll be fine.

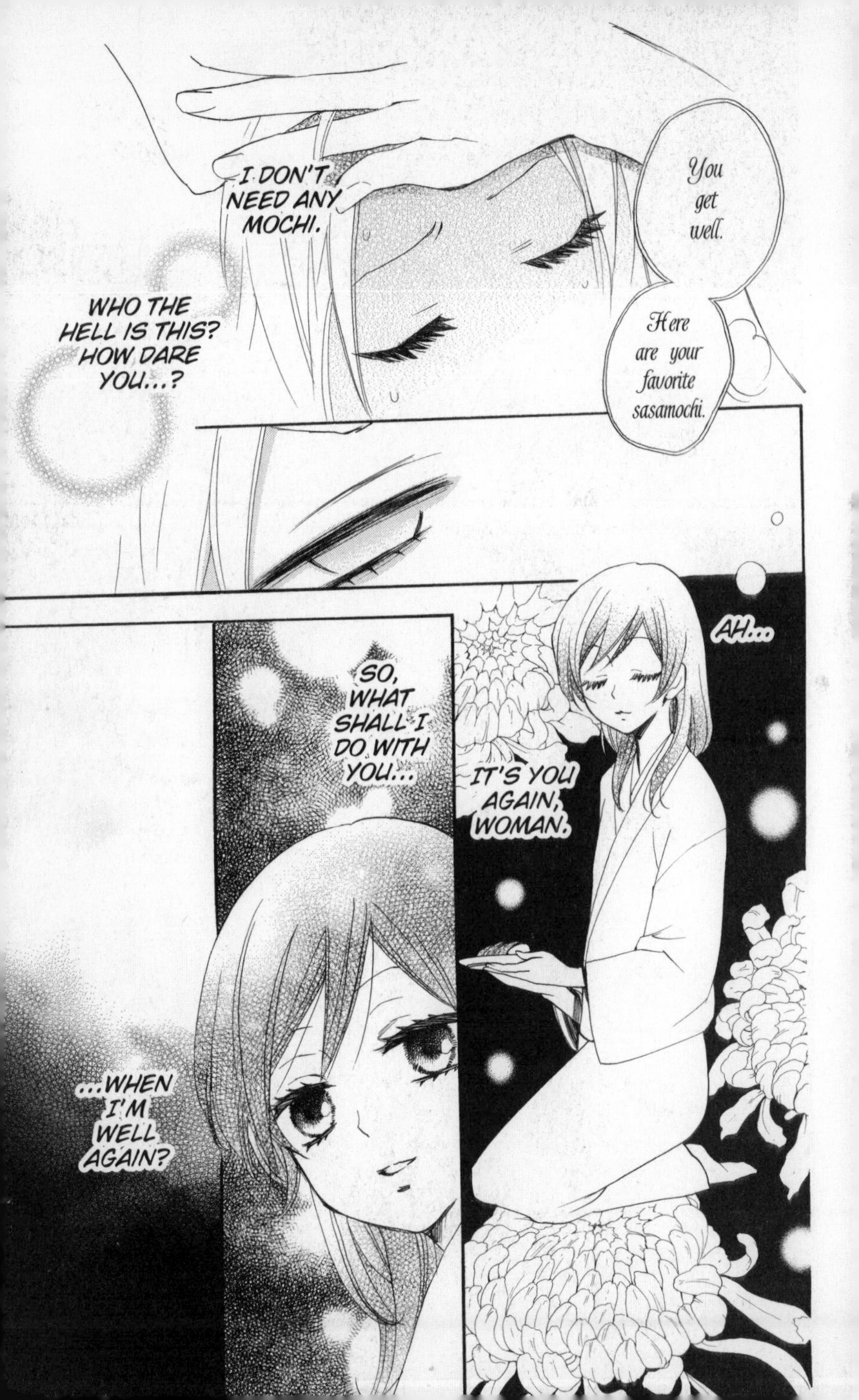
You get well.
Here are your favorite sasamochi.
I DON'T NEED ANY MOCHI.
WHO THE HELL IS THIS? HOW DARE YOU...?
AH...
IT'S YOU AGAIN, WOMAN.
SO, WHAT SHALL I DO WITH YOU...
...WHEN I'M WELL AGAIN?

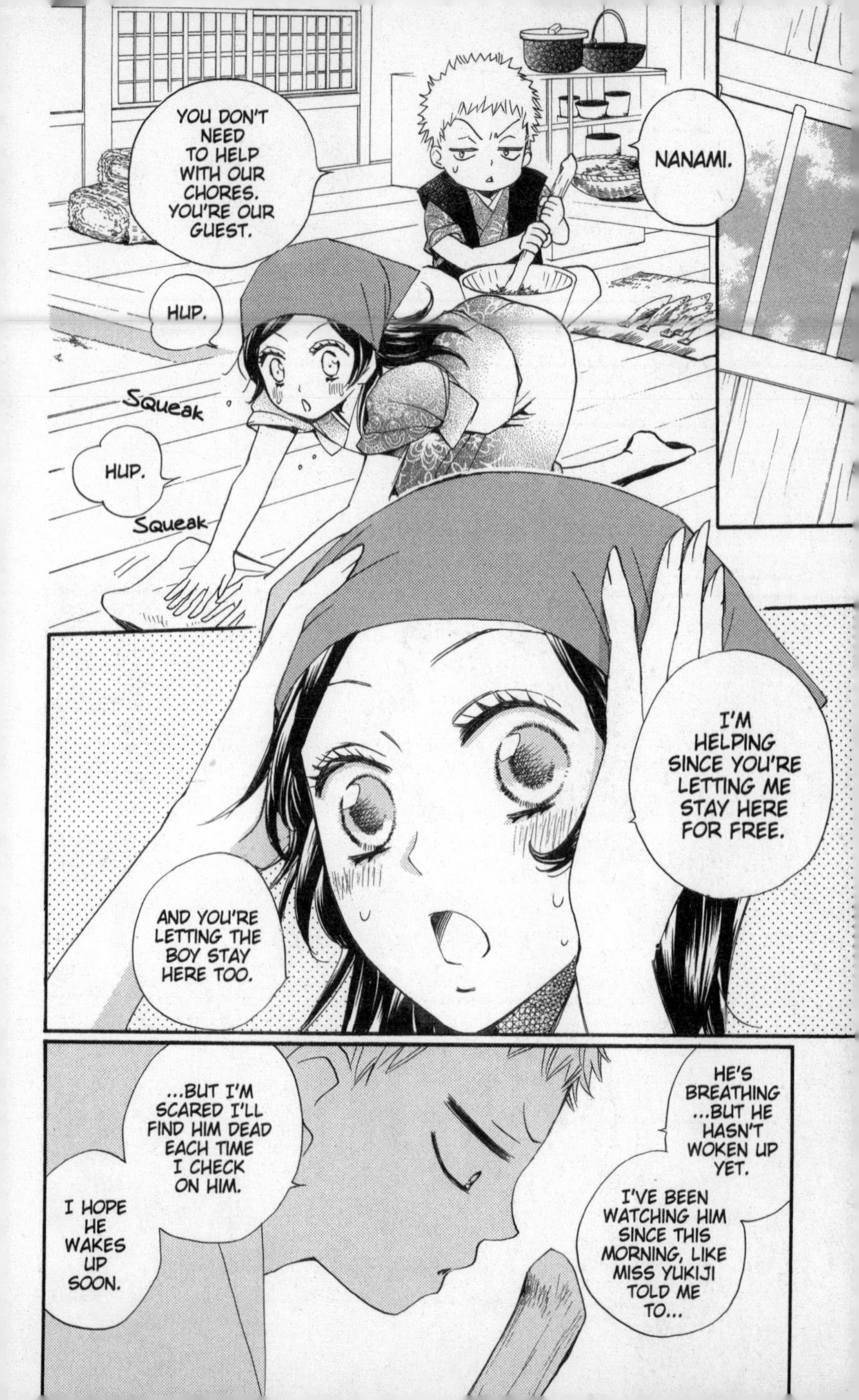
NANAMI.
YOU DON'T NEED TO HELP WITH OUR CHORES. YOU'RE OUR GUEST.
HUP.
Squeak
HUP.
Squeak
I'M HELPING SINCE YOU'RE LETTING ME STAY HERE FOR FREE.
AND YOU'RE LETTING THE BOY STAY HERE TOO.
HE'S BREATHING ...BUT HE HASN'T WOKEN UP YET.
I'VE BEEN WATCHING HIM SINCE THIS MORNING, LIKE MISS YUKIJI TOLD ME TO...
...BUT I'M SCARED I'LL FIND HIM DEAD EACH TIME I CHECK ON HIM.
I HOPE HE WAKES UP SOON.

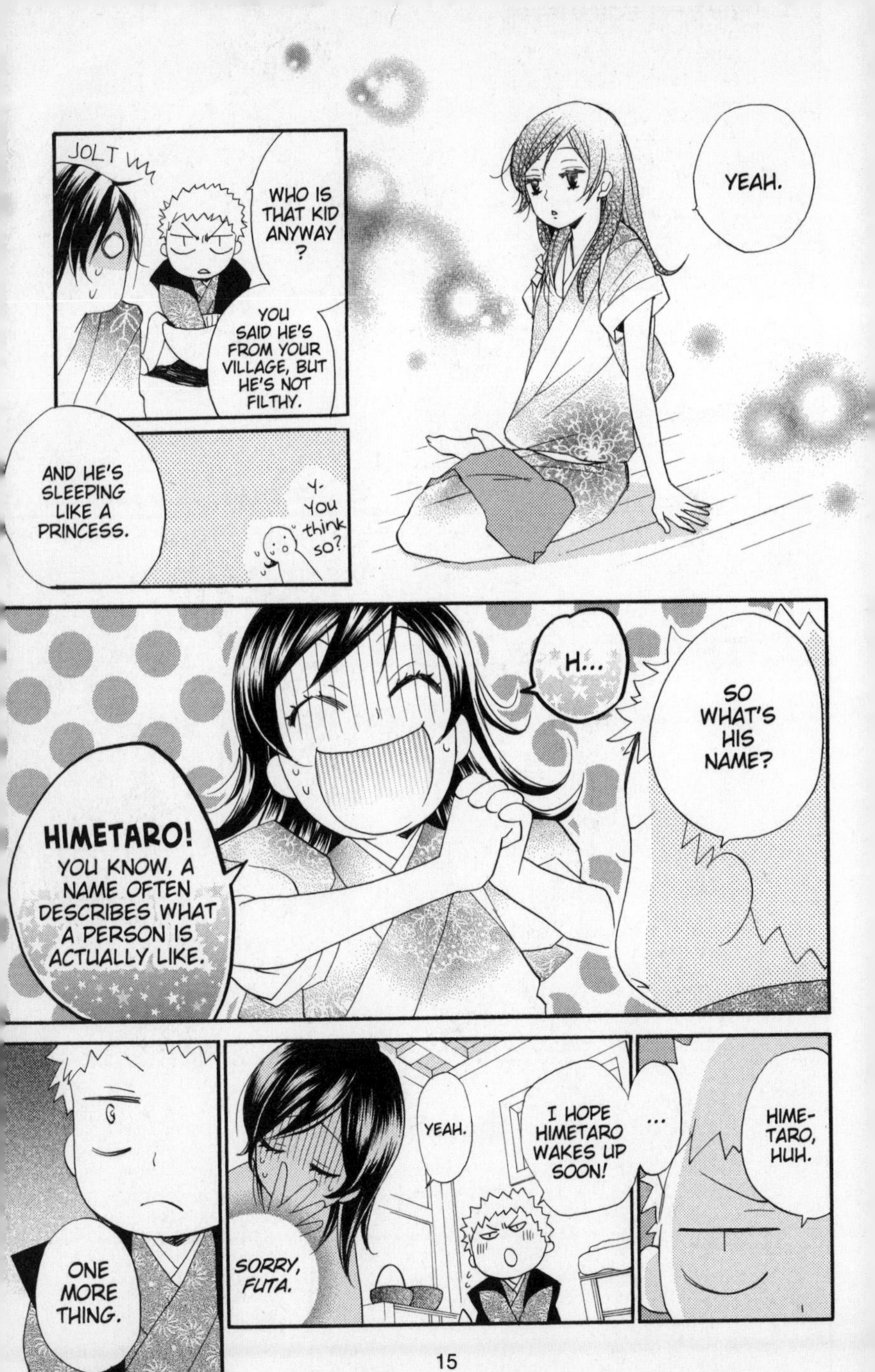
YEAH.
JOLT
WHO IS THAT KID ANYWAY?
YOU SAID HE'S FROM YOUR VILLAGE, BUT HE'S NOT FILTHY.
AND HE'S SLEEPING LIKE A PRINCESS.
Y-You think so?
SO WHAT'S HIS NAME?
H...
HIMETARO! YOU KNOW, A NAME OFTEN DESCRIBES WHAT A PERSON IS ACTUALLY LIKE.
HIME-TARO, HUH.
...
I HOPE HIMETARO WAKES UP SOON!
YEAH.
SORRY, FUTA.
ONE MORE THING.

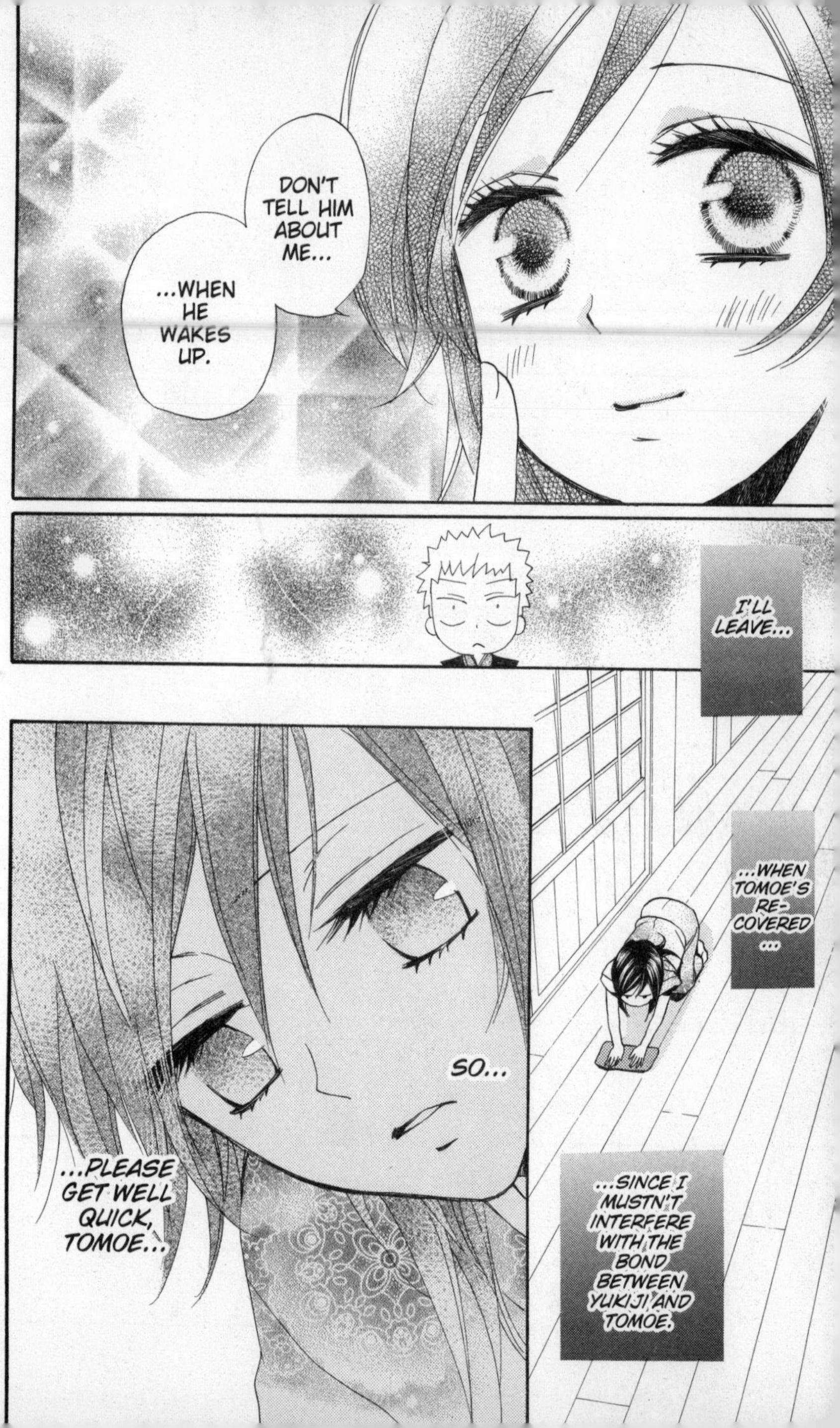
DON'T TELL HIM ABOUT ME...
...WHEN HE WAKES UP.
I'LL LEAVE...
...WHEN TOMOE'S RE-COVERED...
...SINCE I MUSTN'T INTERFERE WITH THE BOND BETWEEN YUKIJI AND TOMOE.
SO...
...PLEASE GET WELL QUICK, TOMOE...

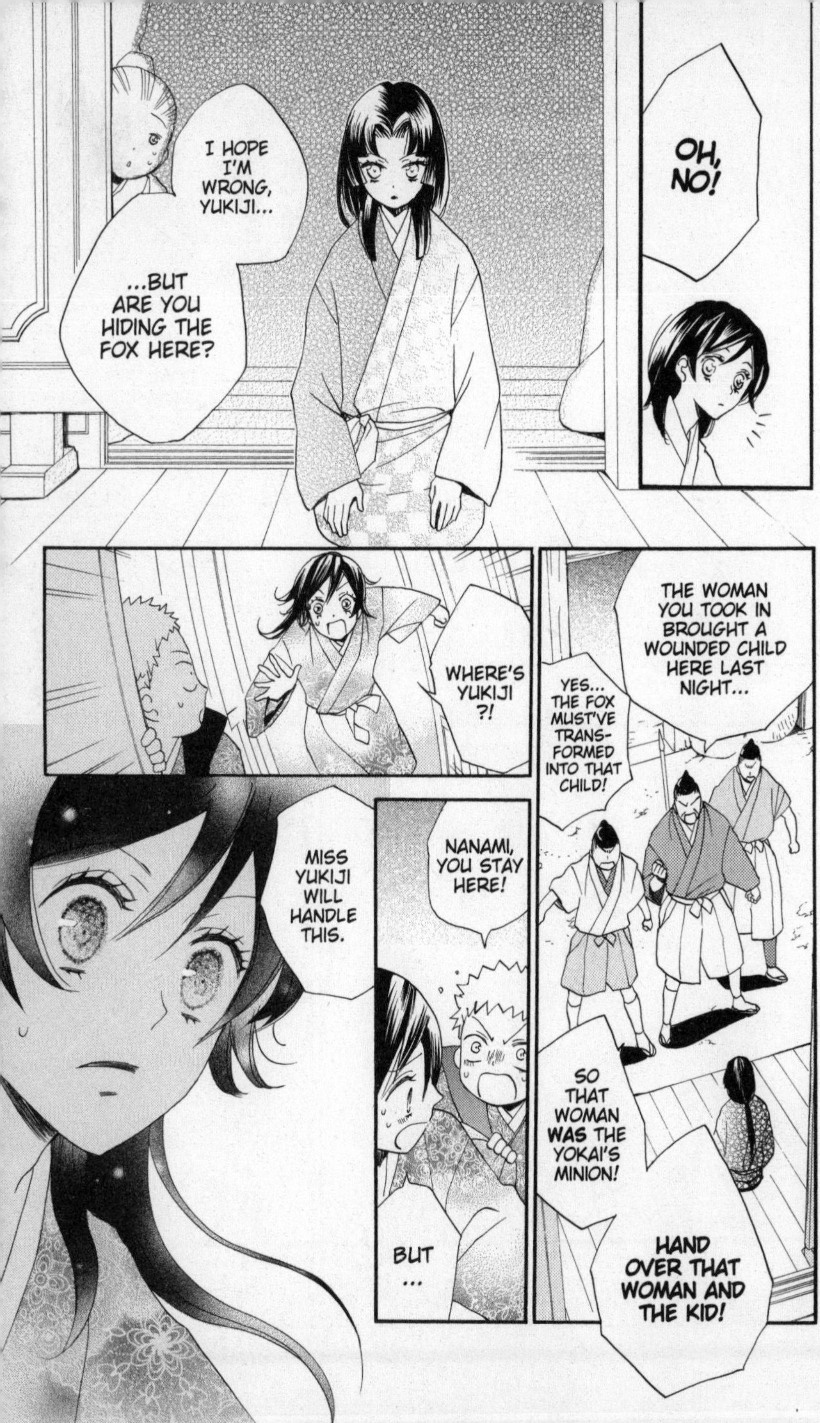
OH, NO!
I HOPE I'M WRONG, YUKIJI...
...BUT ARE YOU HIDING THE FOX HERE?
THE WOMAN YOU TOOK IN BROUGHT A WOUNDED CHILD HERE LAST NIGHT...
YES... THE FOX MUST'VE TRANS-FORMED INTO THAT CHILD!
SO THAT WOMAN WAS THE YOKAI'S MINION!
HAND OVER THAT WOMAN AND THE KID!
WHERE'S YUKIJI?!
NANAMI, YOU STAY HERE!
BUT ...
MISS YUKIJI WILL HANDLE THIS.

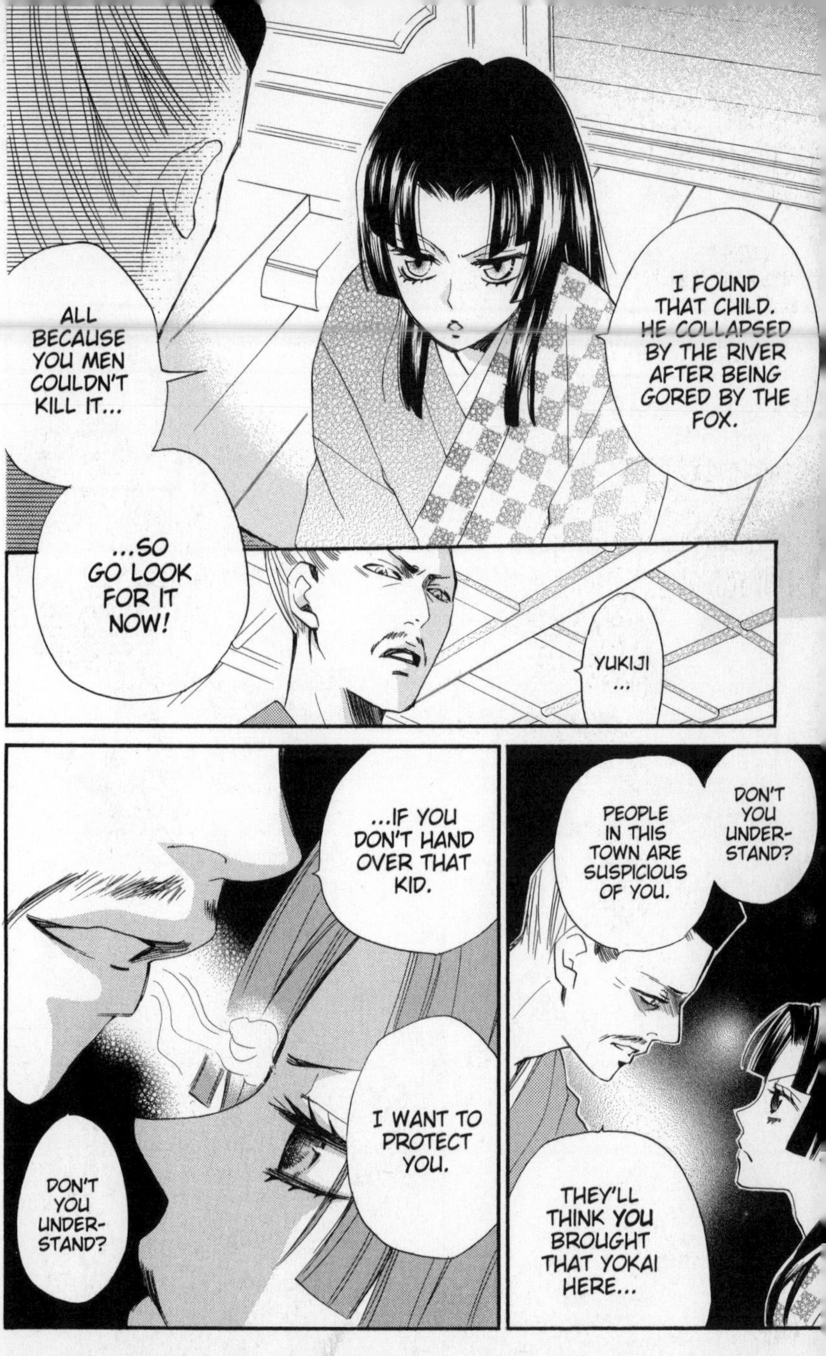
I FOUND THAT CHILD. HE COLLAPSED BY THE RIVER AFTER BEING GORED BY THE FOX.
ALL BECAUSE YOU MEN COULDN'T KILL IT...
...SO GO LOOK FOR IT NOW!
YUKIJI...
DON'T YOU UNDER-STAND?
PEOPLE IN THIS TOWN ARE SUSPICIOUS OF YOU.
THEY'LL THINK YOU BROUGHT THAT YOKAI HERE...
...IF YOU DON'T HAND OVER THAT KID.
I WANT TO PROTECT YOU.
DON'T YOU UNDER-STAND?

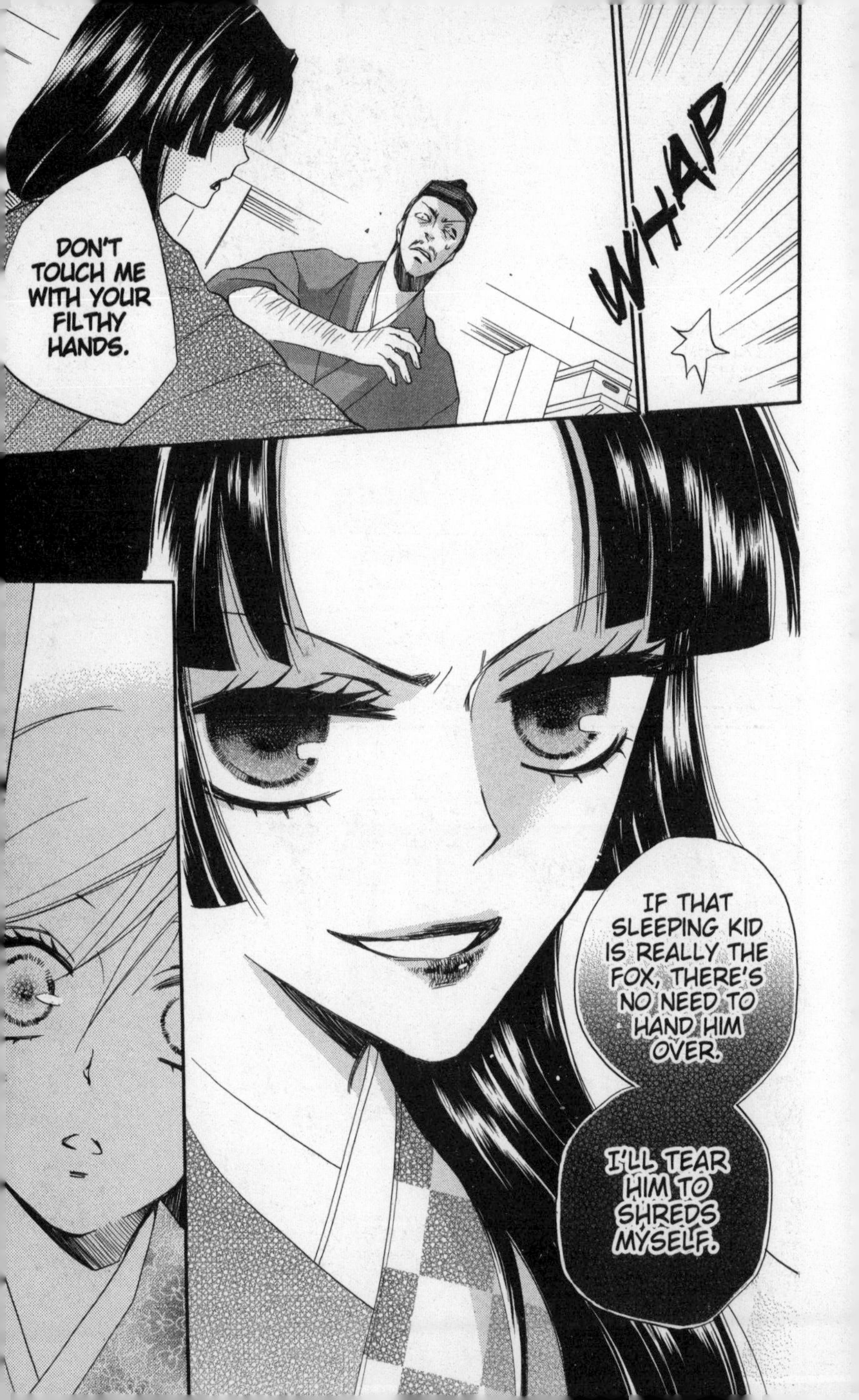
WHAP
DON'T TOUCH ME WITH YOUR FILTHY HANDS.
IF THAT SLEEPING KID IS REALLY THE FOX, THERE'S NO NEED TO HAND HIM OVER.
I'LL TEAR HIM TO SHREDS MYSELF.

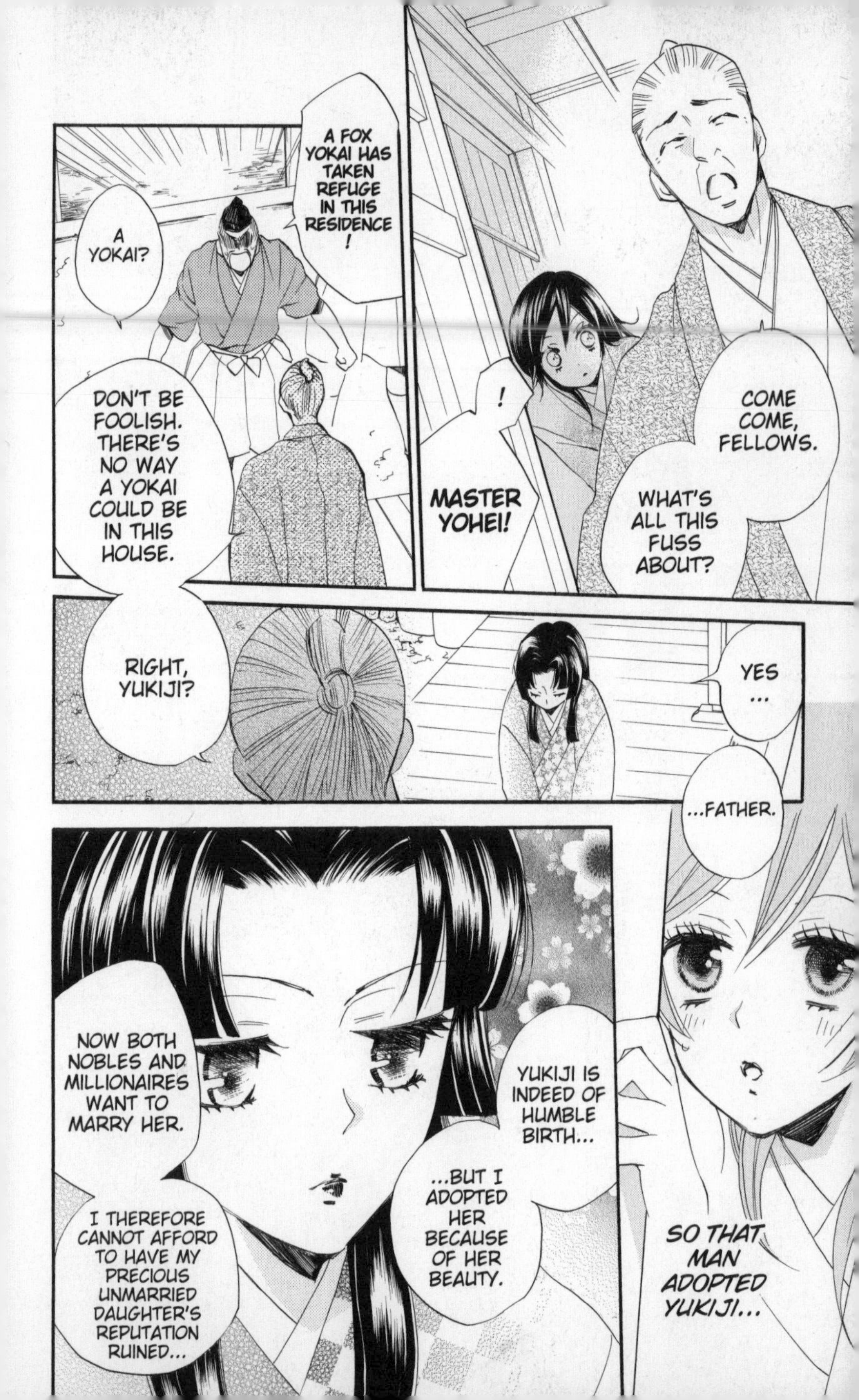
COME COME, FELLOWS.
WHAT'S ALL THIS FUSS ABOUT?
!
MASTER YOHEI!
A FOX YOKAI HAS TAKEN REFUGE IN THIS RESIDENCE!
A YOKAI?
DON'T BE FOOLISH. THERE'S NO WAY A YOKAI COULD BE IN THIS HOUSE.
RIGHT, YUKIJI?
YES...
...FATHER.
SO THAT MAN ADOPTED YUKIJI...
YUKIJI IS INDEED OF HUMBLE BIRTH...
...BUT I ADOPTED HER BECAUSE OF HER BEAUTY.
NOW BOTH NOBLES AND MILLIONAIRES WANT TO MARRY HER.
I THEREFORE CANNOT AFFORD TO HAVE MY PRECIOUS UNMARRIED DAUGHTER'S REPUTATION RUINED...

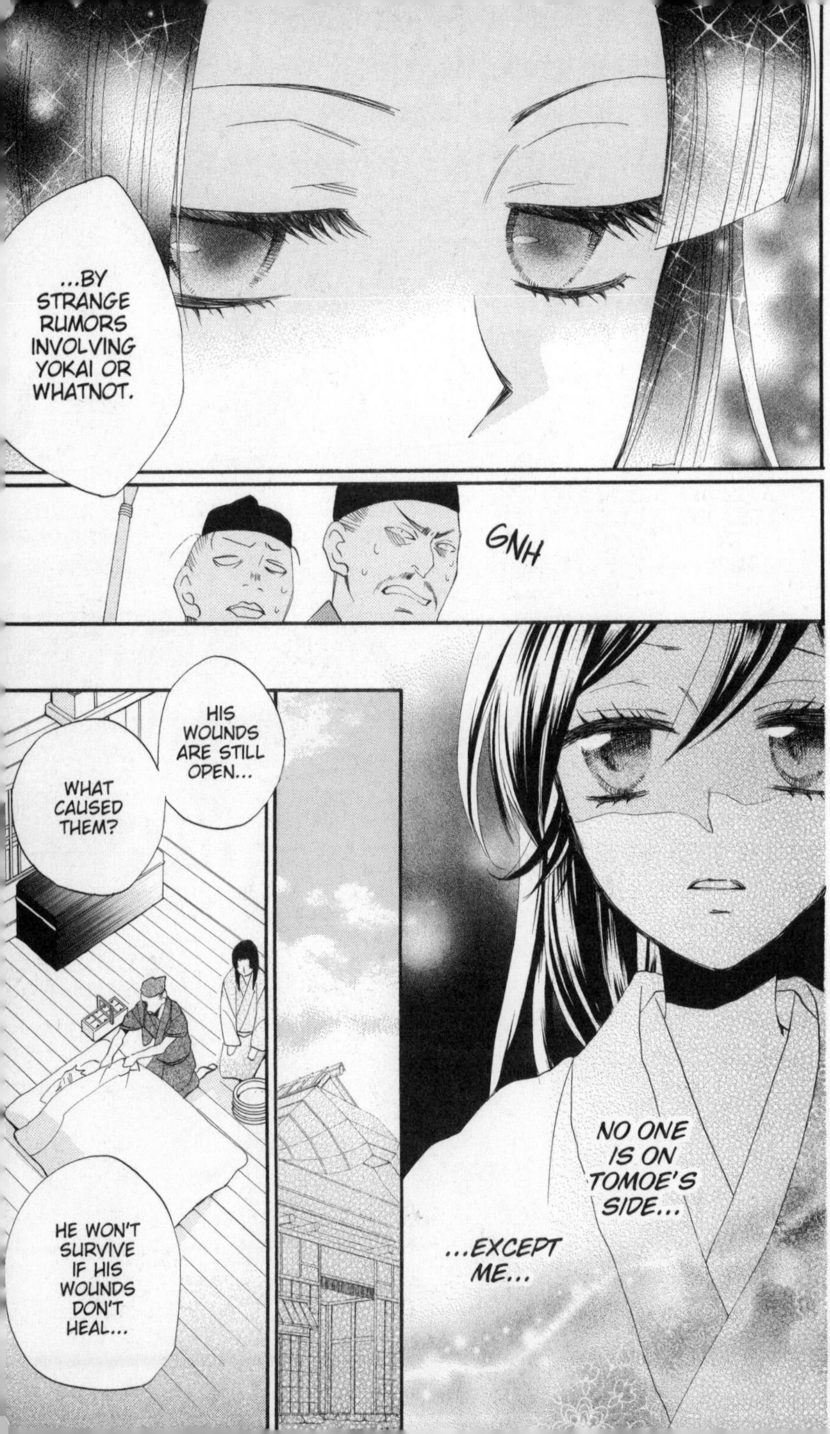
...BY STRANGE RUMORS INVOLVING YOKAI OR WHATNOT.
GNH
NO ONE IS ON TOMOE'S SIDE...
...EXCEPT ME...
HIS WOUNDS ARE STILL OPEN...
WHAT CAUSED THEM?
HE WON'T SURVIVE IF HIS WOUNDS DON'T HEAL...

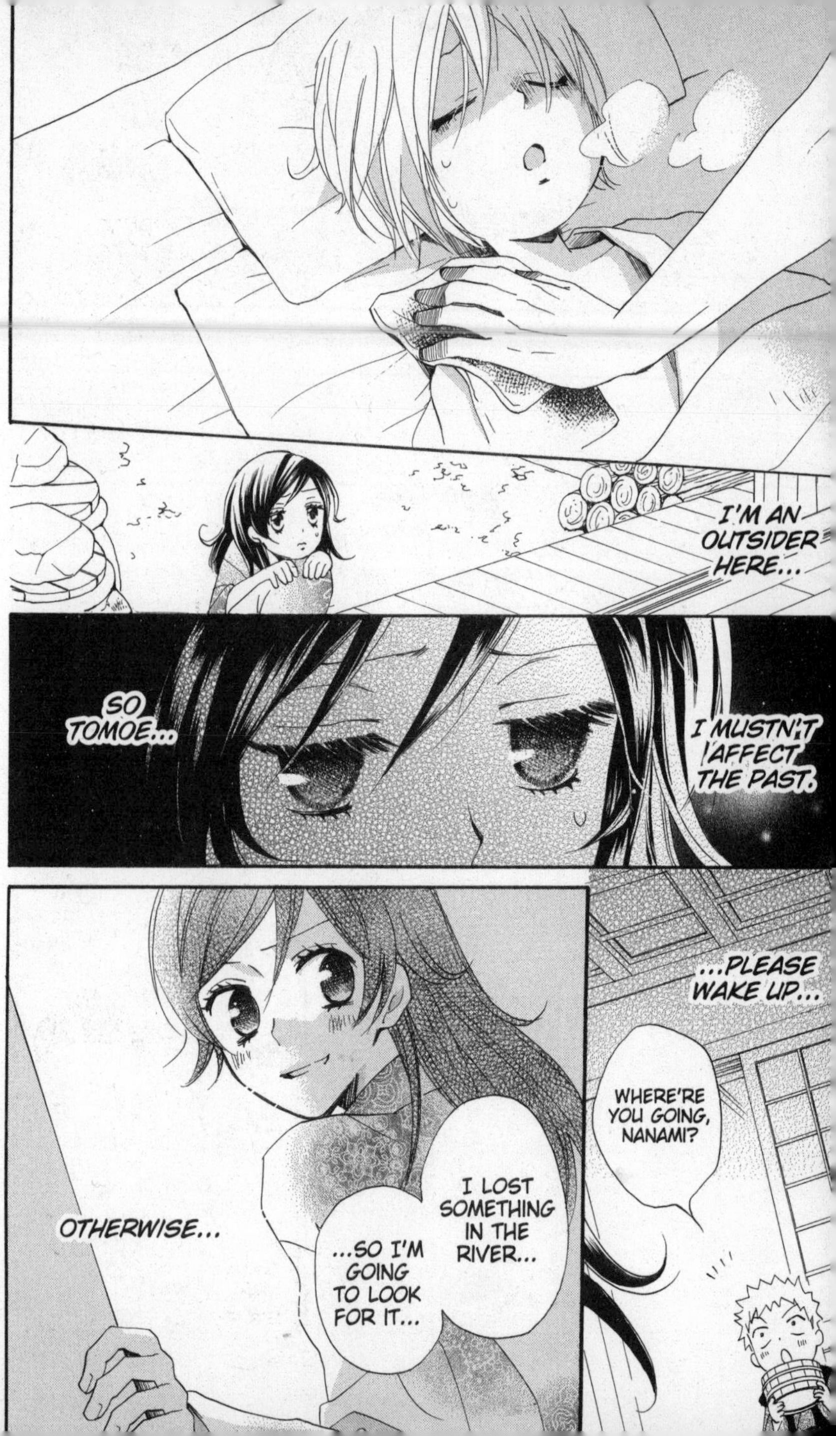
I'M AN OUTSIDER HERE...
I MUSTN'T AFFECT THE PAST.
SO TOMOE...
...PLEASE WAKE UP...
WHERE'RE YOU GOING, NANAMI?
I LOST SOMETHING IN THE RIVER...
...SO I'M GOING TO LOOK FOR IT...
OTHERWISE...

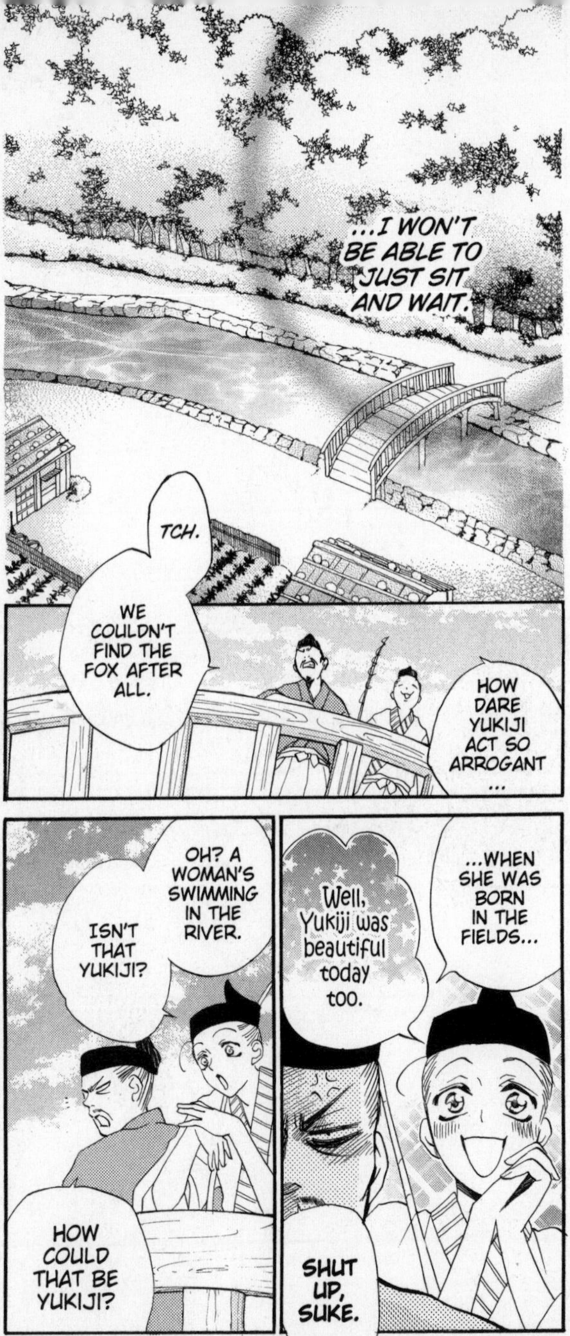
...I WON'T BE ABLE TO JUST SIT AND WAIT.
TCH.
WE COULDN'T FIND THE FOX AFTER ALL.
HOW DARE YUKIJI ACT SO ARROGANT...
...WHEN SHE WAS BORN IN THE FIELDS...
Well, Yukiji was beautiful today too.
SHUT UP, SUKE.
OH? A WOMAN'S SWIMMING IN THE RIVER.
ISN'T THAT YUKIJI?
HOW COULD THAT BE YUKIJI?

Thank you for picking up volume 15 of Kamisama Kiss!

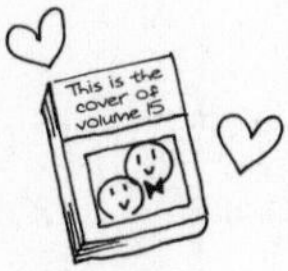
This is the cover of volume 15

I hope you enjoy reading it!

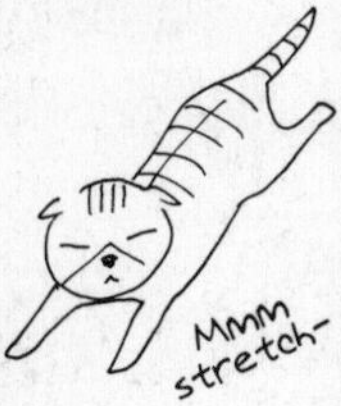
Mmm stretch-

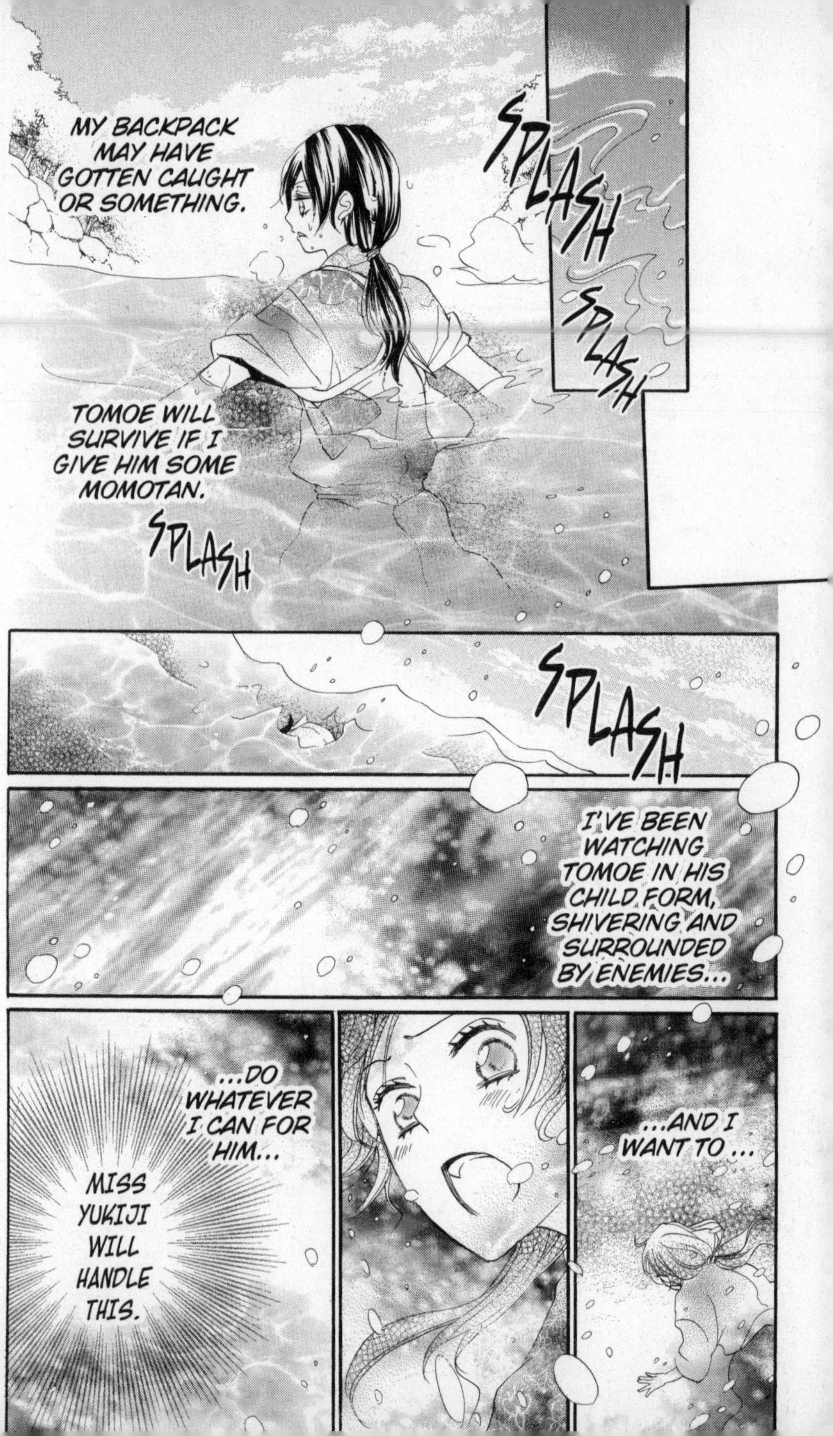
SPLASH
SPLASH
MY BACKPACK MAY HAVE GOTTEN CAUGHT OR SOMETHING.
TOMOE WILL SURVIVE IF I GIVE HIM SOME MOMOTAN.
SPLASH
SPLASH
I'VE BEEN WATCHING TOMOE IN HIS CHILD FORM, SHIVERING AND SURROUNDED BY ENEMIES...
...AND I WANT TO ...
...DO WHATEVER I CAN FOR HIM...
MISS YUKIJI WILL HANDLE THIS.

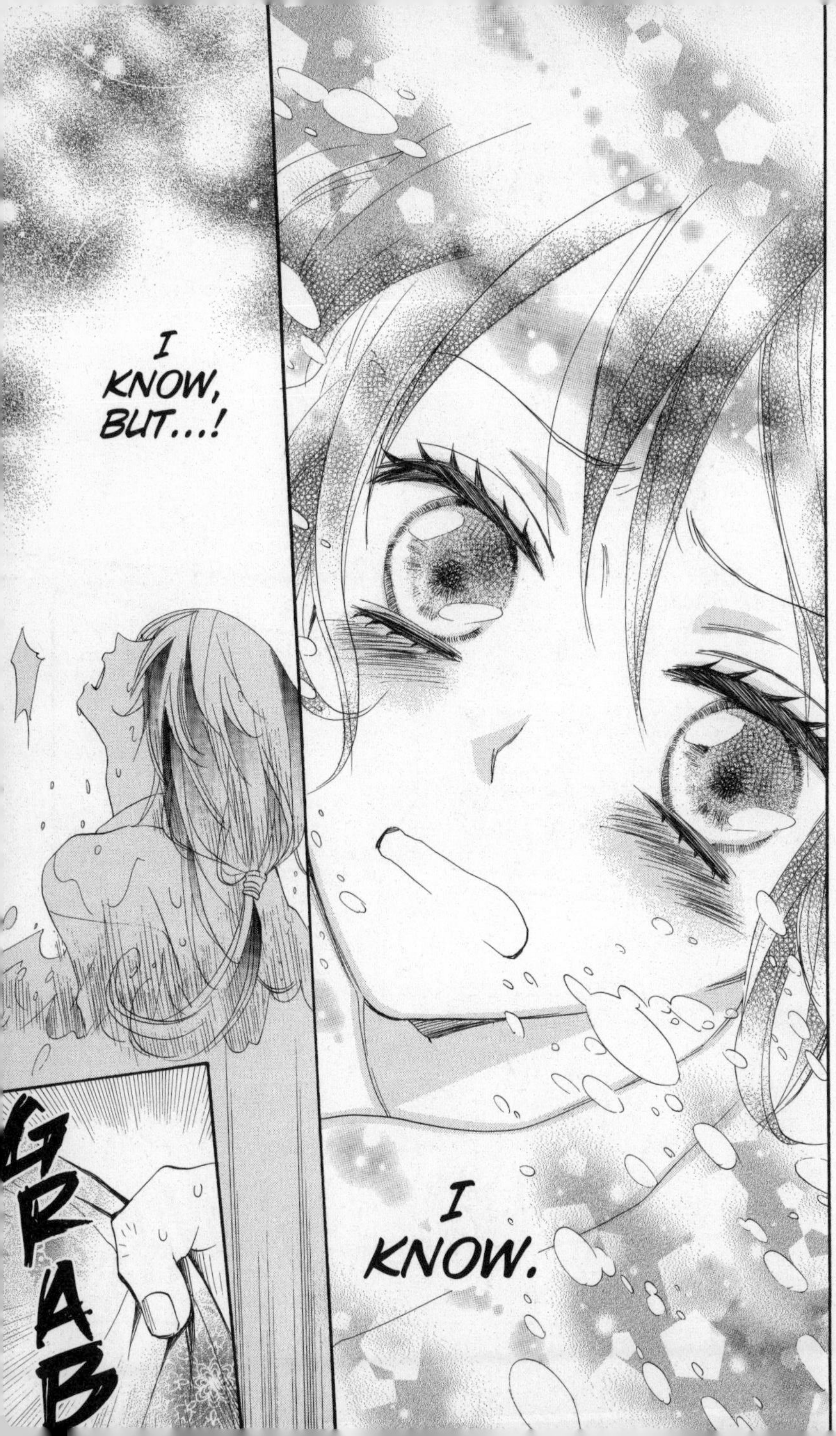
I KNOW.
I KNOW, BUT...!
GRAB

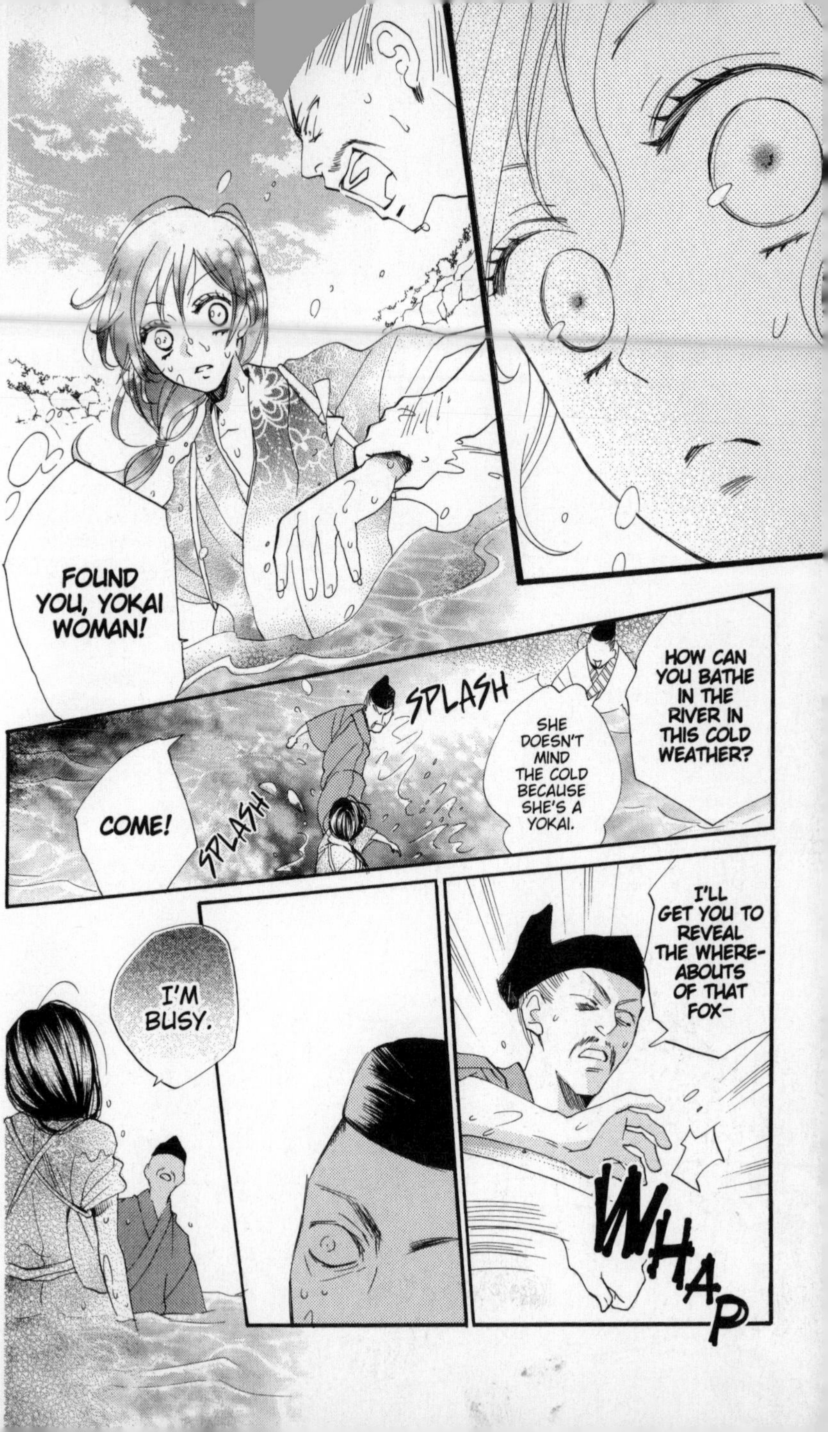
FOUND YOU, YOKAI WOMAN!
HOW CAN YOU BATHE IN THE RIVER IN THIS COLD WEATHER?
SPLASH
SHE DOESN'T MIND THE COLD BECAUSE SHE'S A YOKAI.
SPLASH
COME!
I'LL GET YOU TO REVEAL THE WHERE-ABOUTS OF THAT FOX-
WHAP
I'M BUSY.

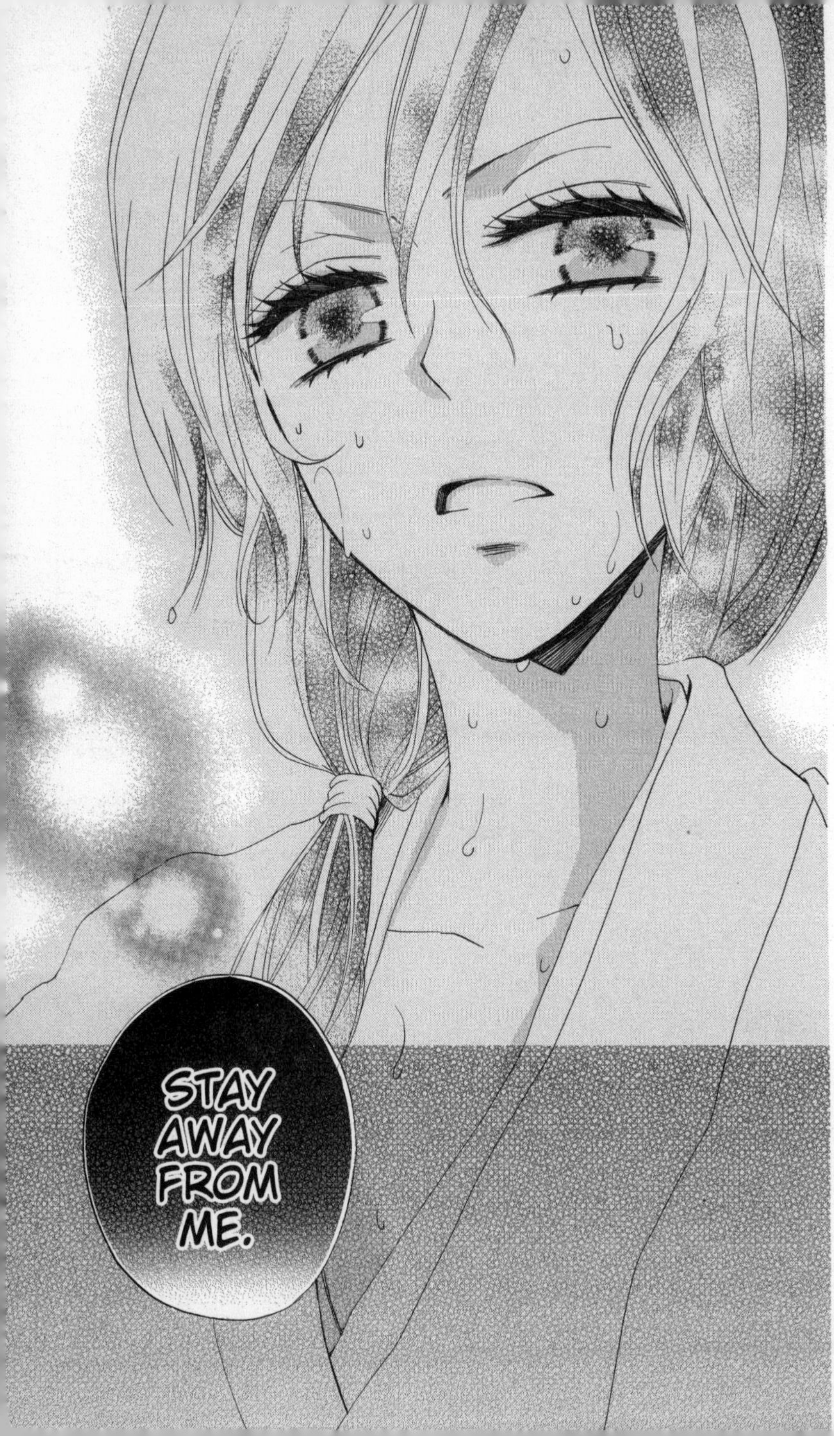
STAY AWAY FROM ME.

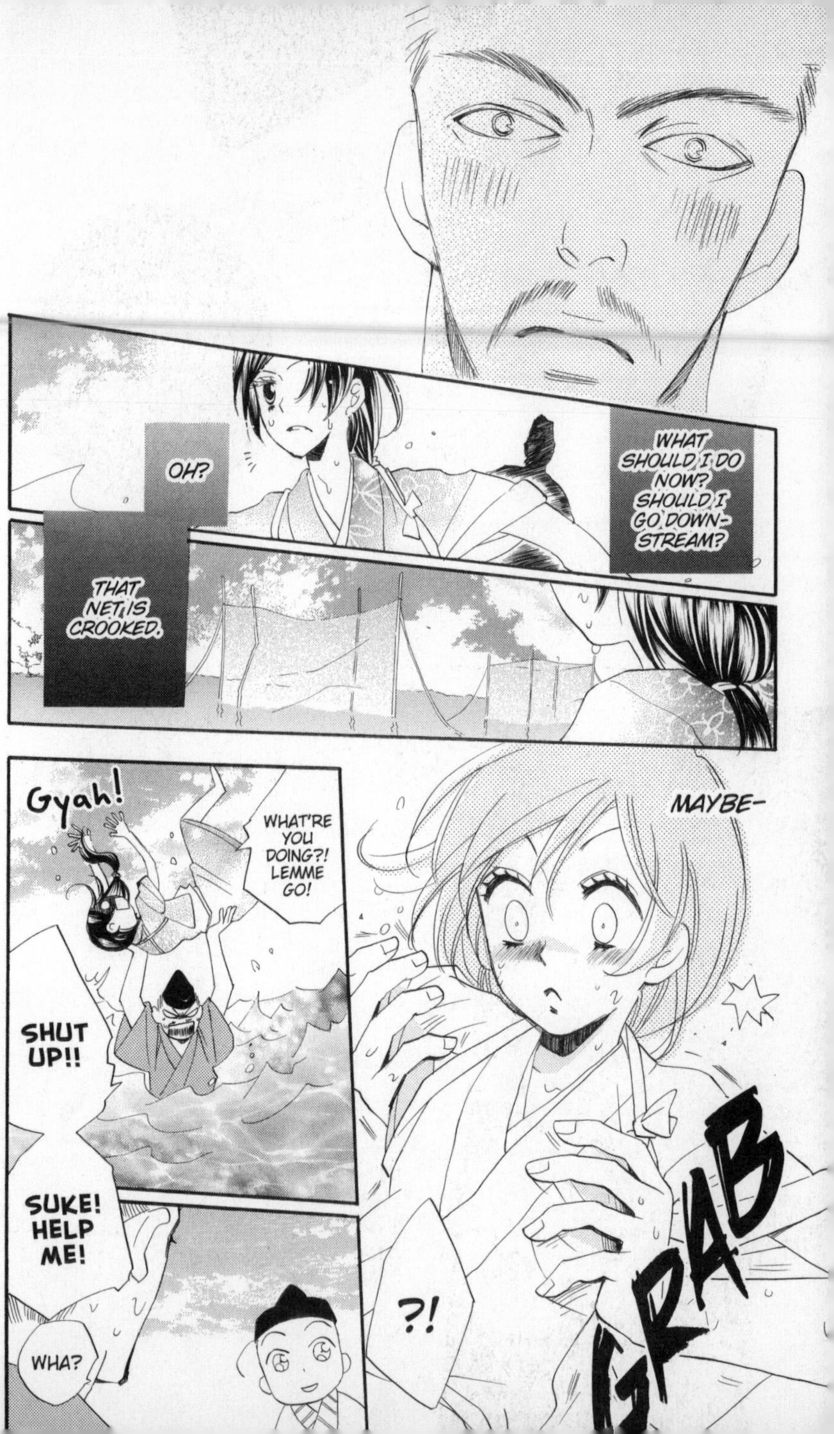

WHAT SHOULD I DO NOW? SHOULD I GO DOWN-STREAM?
OH?
THAT NET IS CROOKED.
MAYBE-
?!
GRAB
Gyah!
WHAT'RE YOU DOING?! LEMME GO!
SHUT UP!!
SUKE! HELP ME!
WHA?

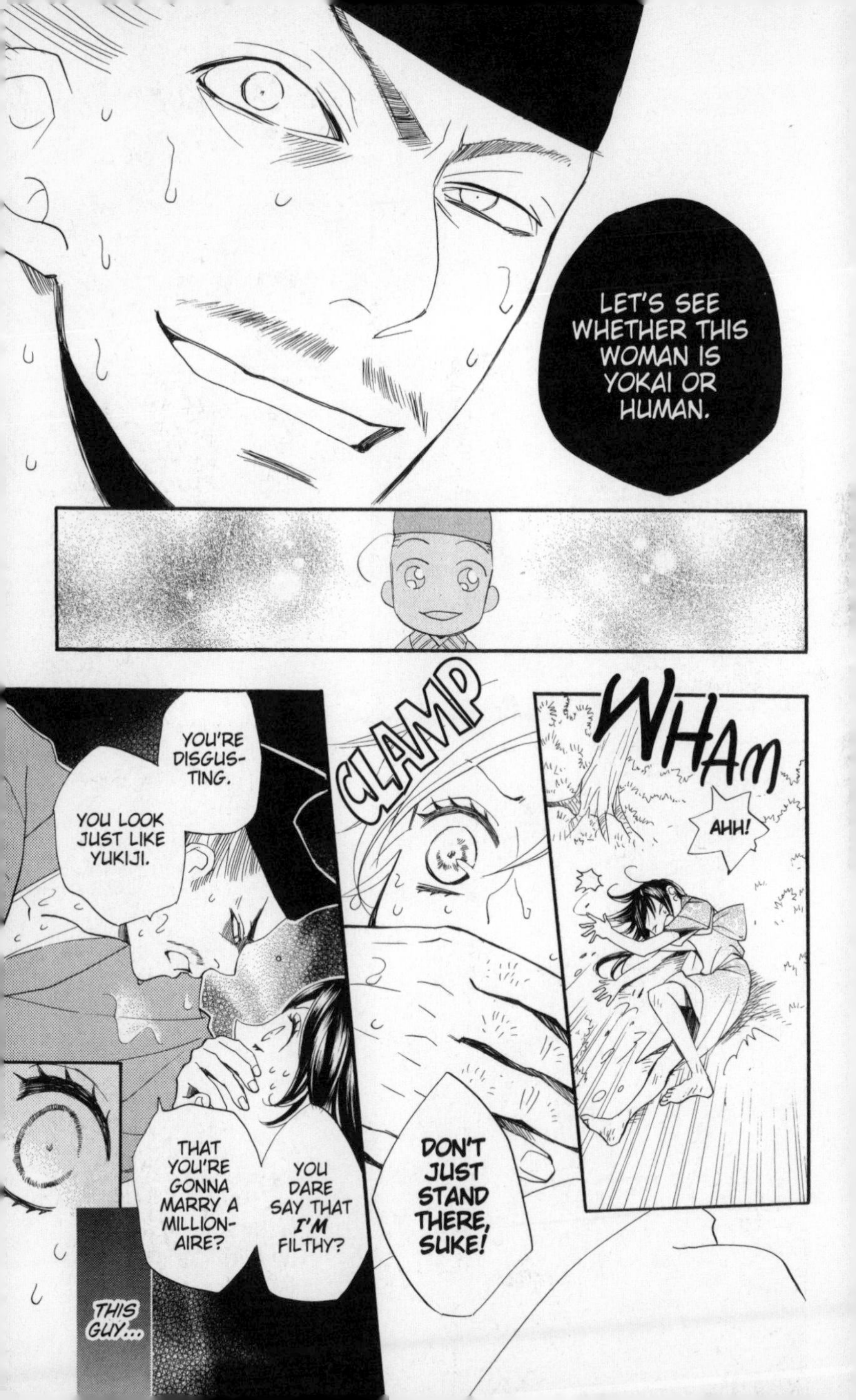

LET'S SEE WHETHER THIS WOMAN IS YOKAI OR HUMAN.
WHAM
AHH!
CLAMP
DON'T JUST STAND THERE, SUKE!
YOU'RE DISGUS-TING.
YOU LOOK JUST LIKE YUKIJI.
YOU DARE SAY THAT *I'M* FILTHY?
THAT YOU'RE GONNA MARRY A MILLION-AIRE?
THIS GUY...

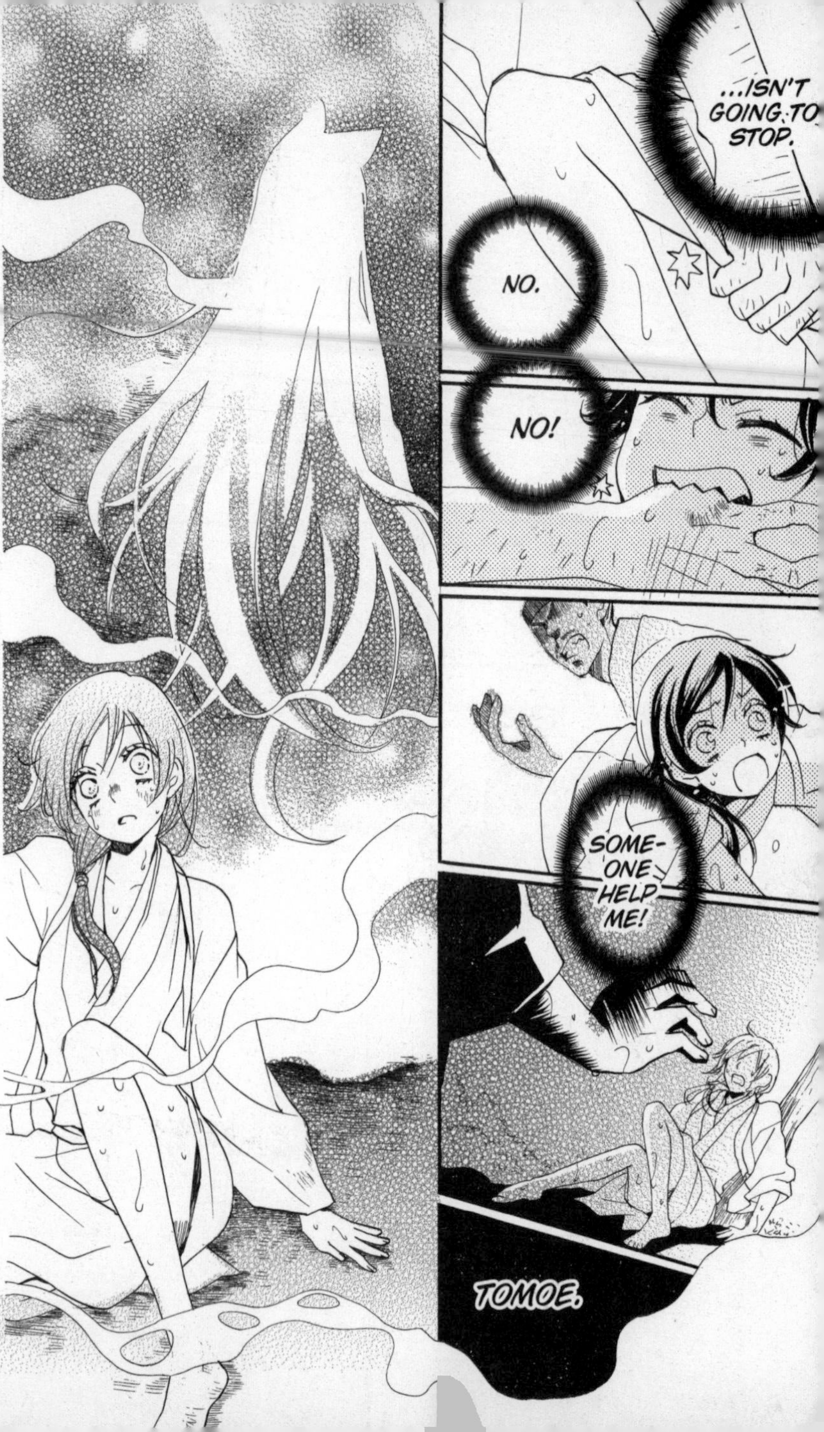
...ISN'T GOING TO STOP.
NO.
NO!
SOME-ONE HELP ME!
TOMOE.

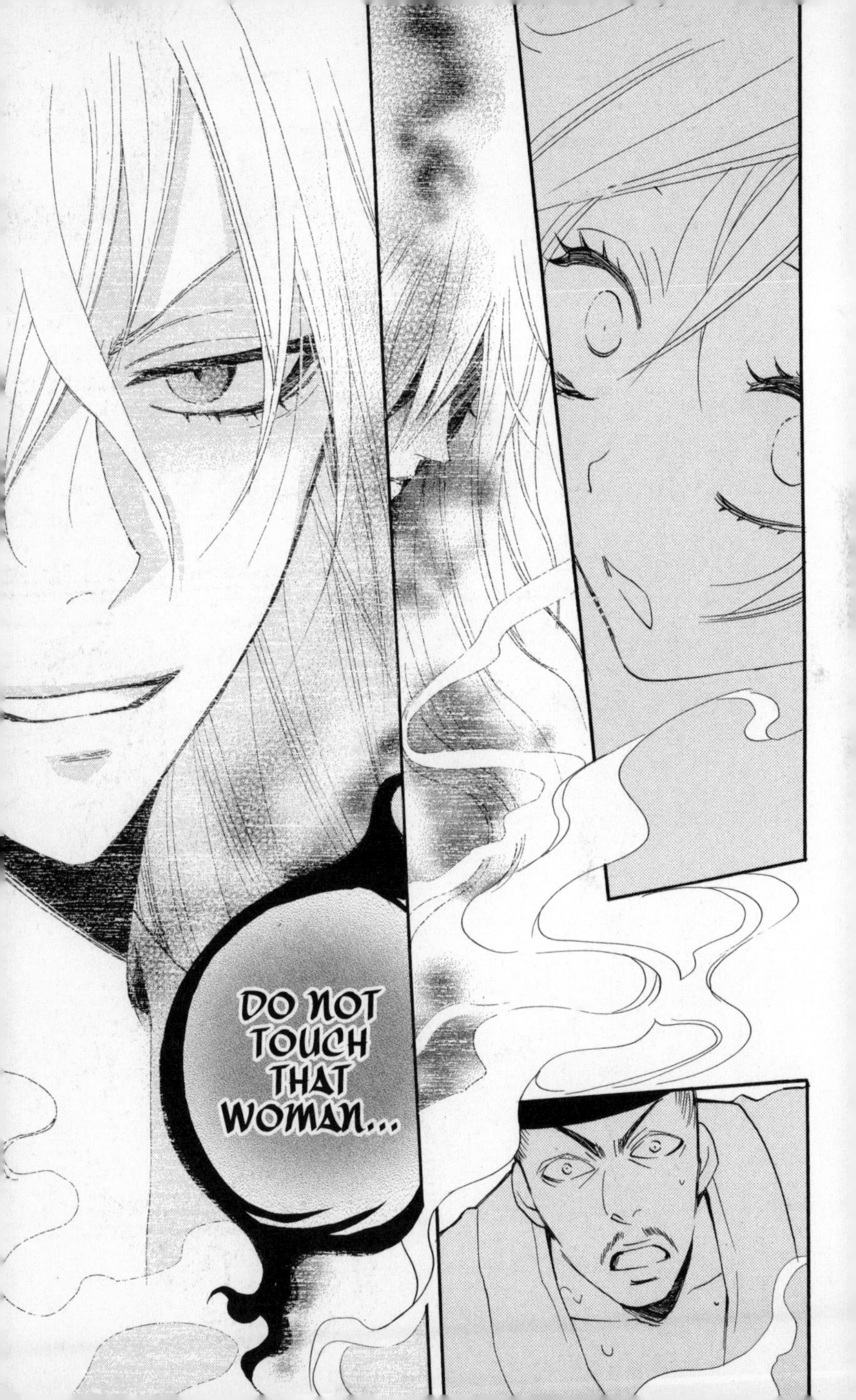
DO NOT TOUCH THAT WOMAN...

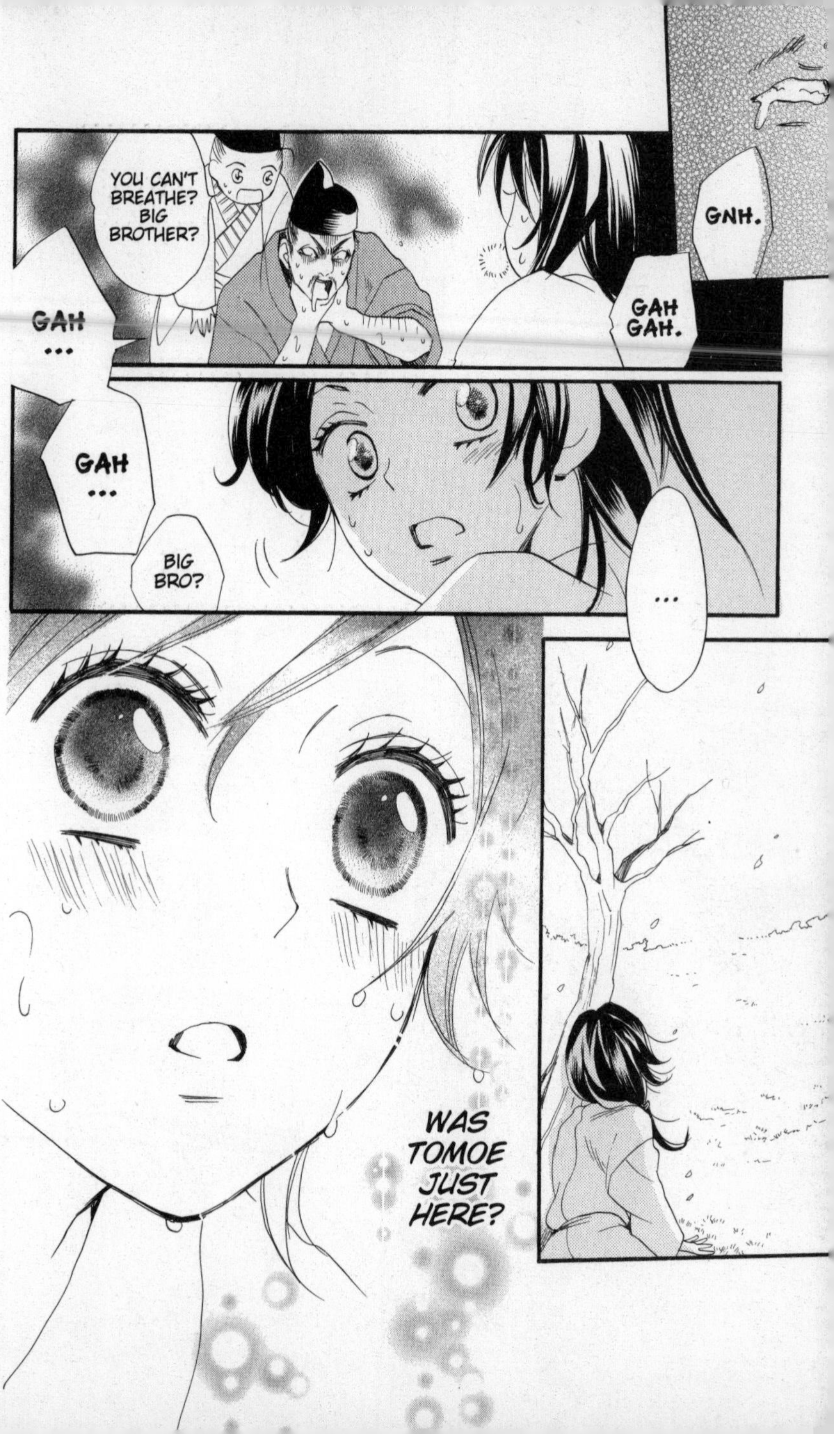
GNH.
GAH GAH.
YOU CAN'T BREATHE? BIG BROTHER?
GAH ...
...
GAH ...
BIG BRO?
WAS TOMOE JUST HERE?

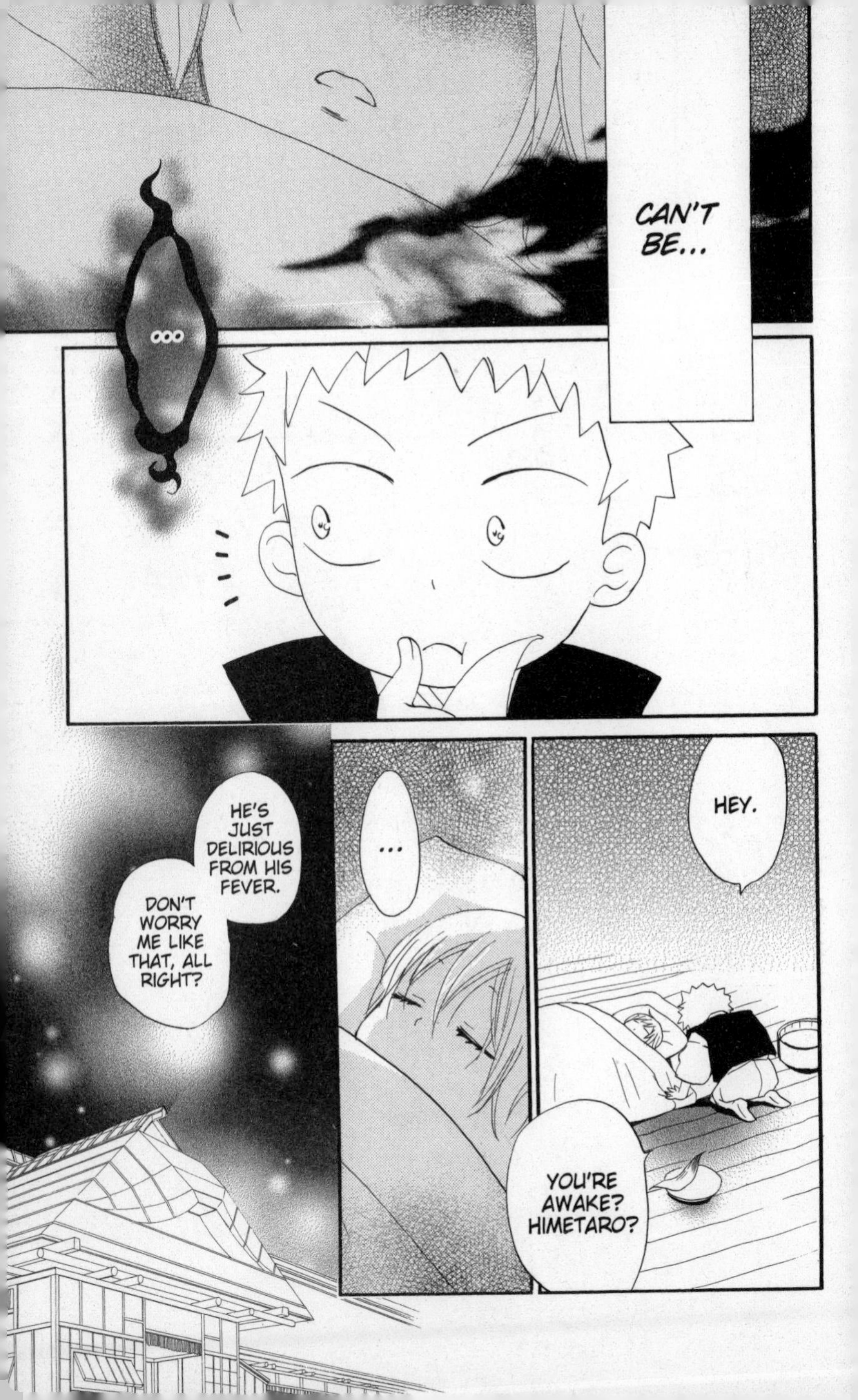
CAN'T BE...
HEY.
YOU'RE AWAKE? HIMETARO?
...
HE'S JUST DELIRIOUS FROM HIS FEVER.
DON'T WORRY ME LIKE THAT, ALL RIGHT?

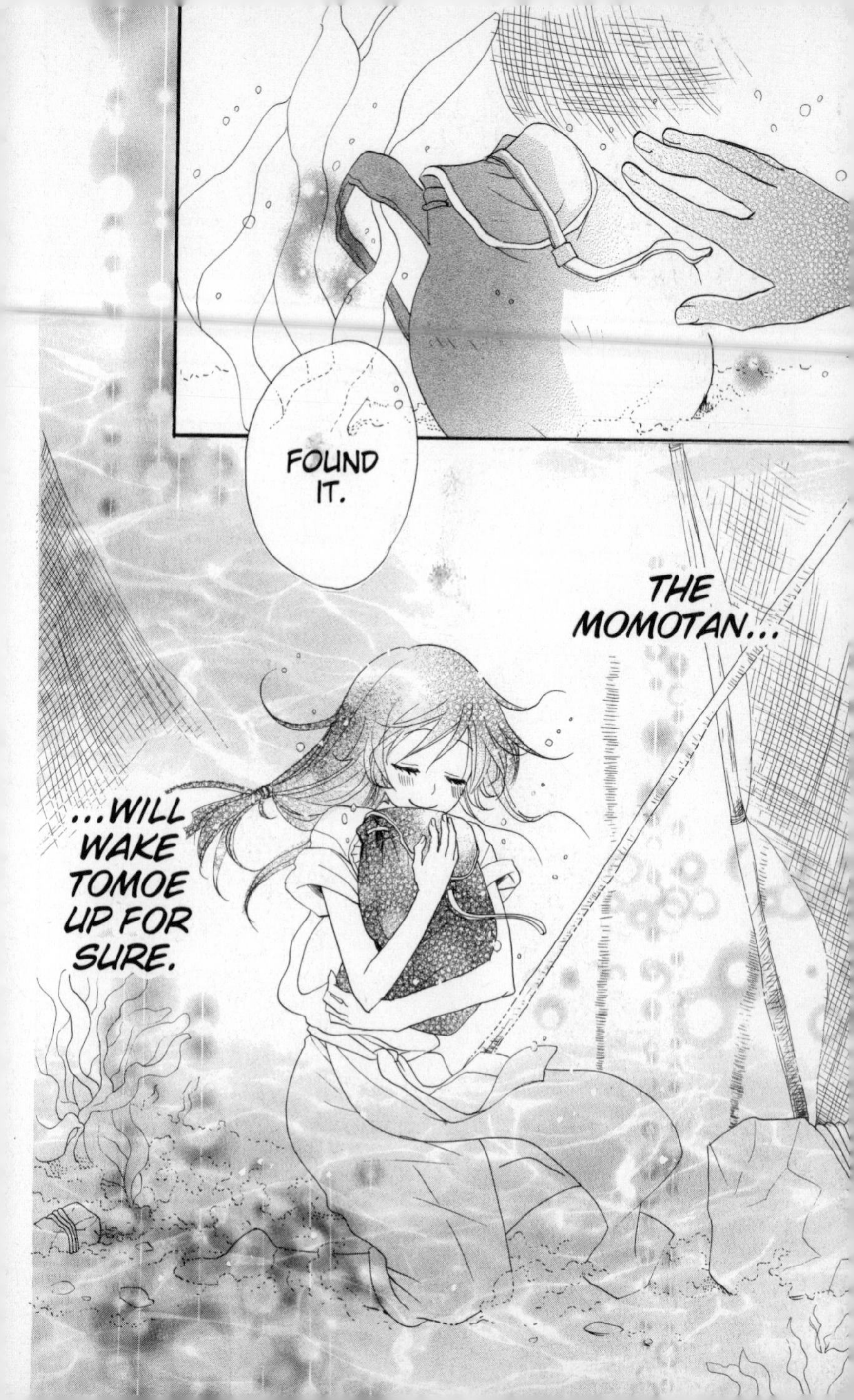
FOUND IT.
THE MOMOTAN...
...WILL WAKE TOMOE UP FOR SURE.

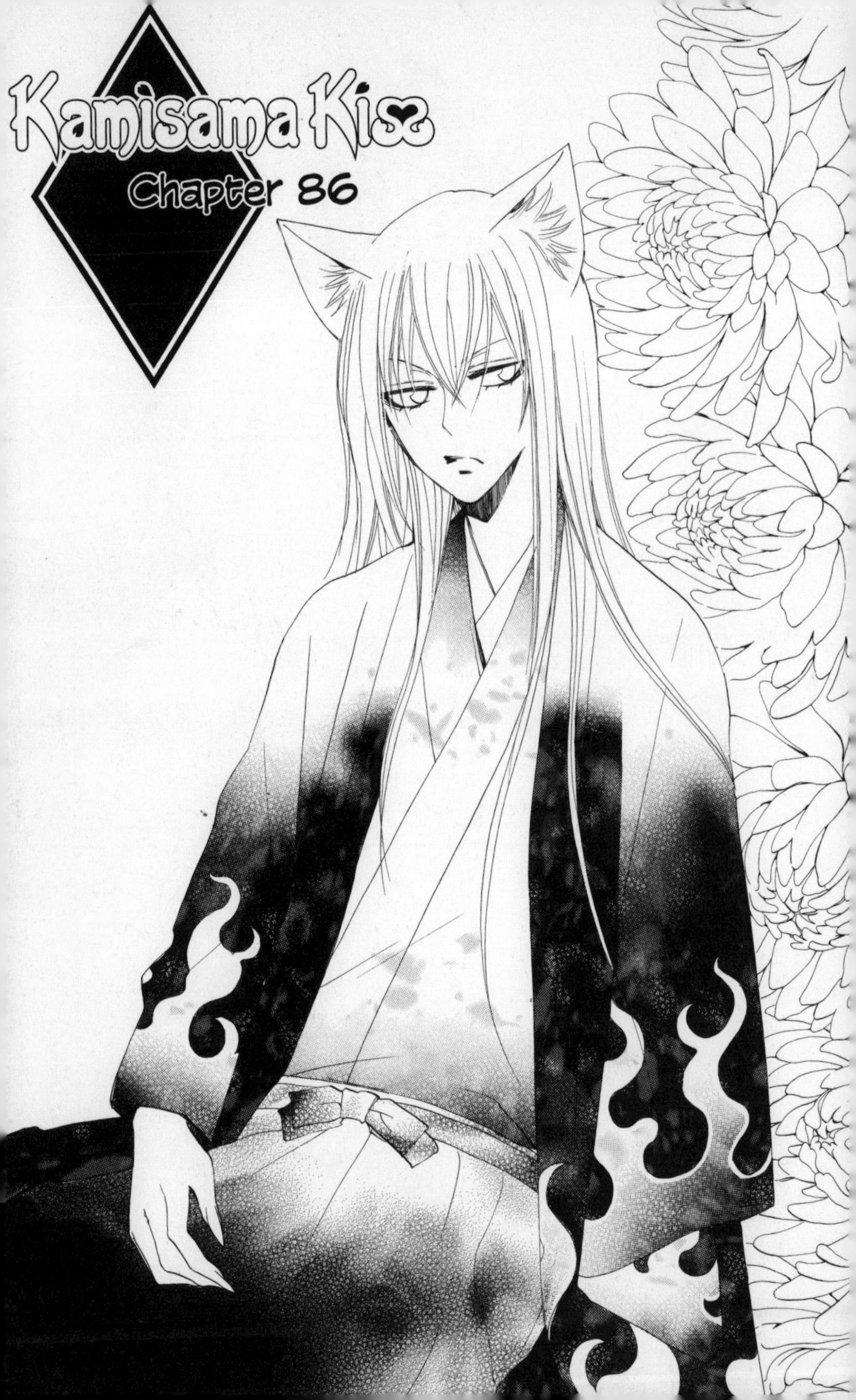
Kamisama Kiss
Chapter 86

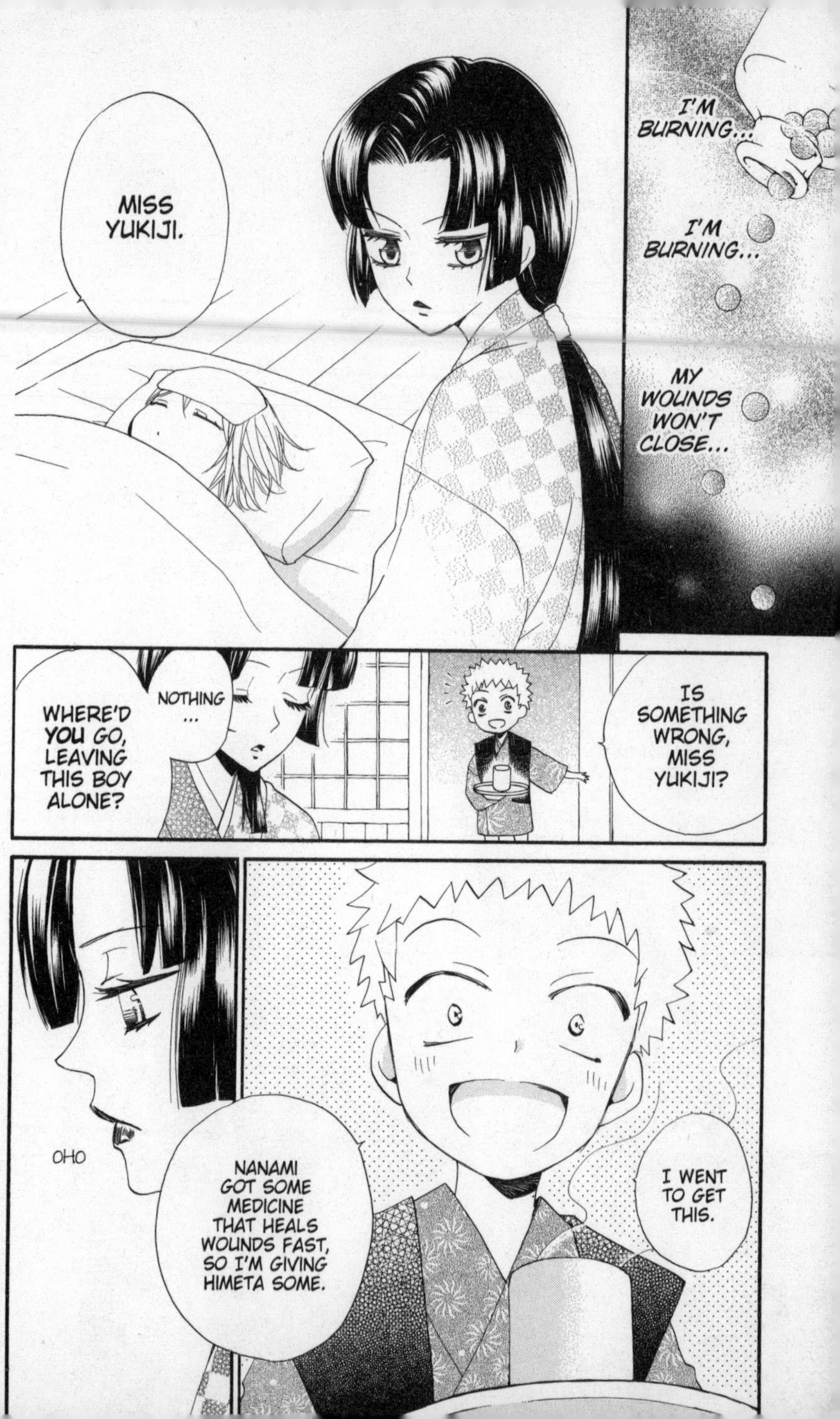
I'M BURNING...
I'M BURNING...
MY WOUNDS WON'T CLOSE...
MISS YUKIJI.
IS SOMETHING WRONG, MISS YUKIJI?
NOTHING...
WHERE'D YOU GO, LEAVING THIS BOY ALONE?
I WENT TO GET THIS.
NANAMI GOT SOME MEDICINE THAT HEALS WOUNDS FAST, SO I'M GIVING HIMETA SOME.
OHO

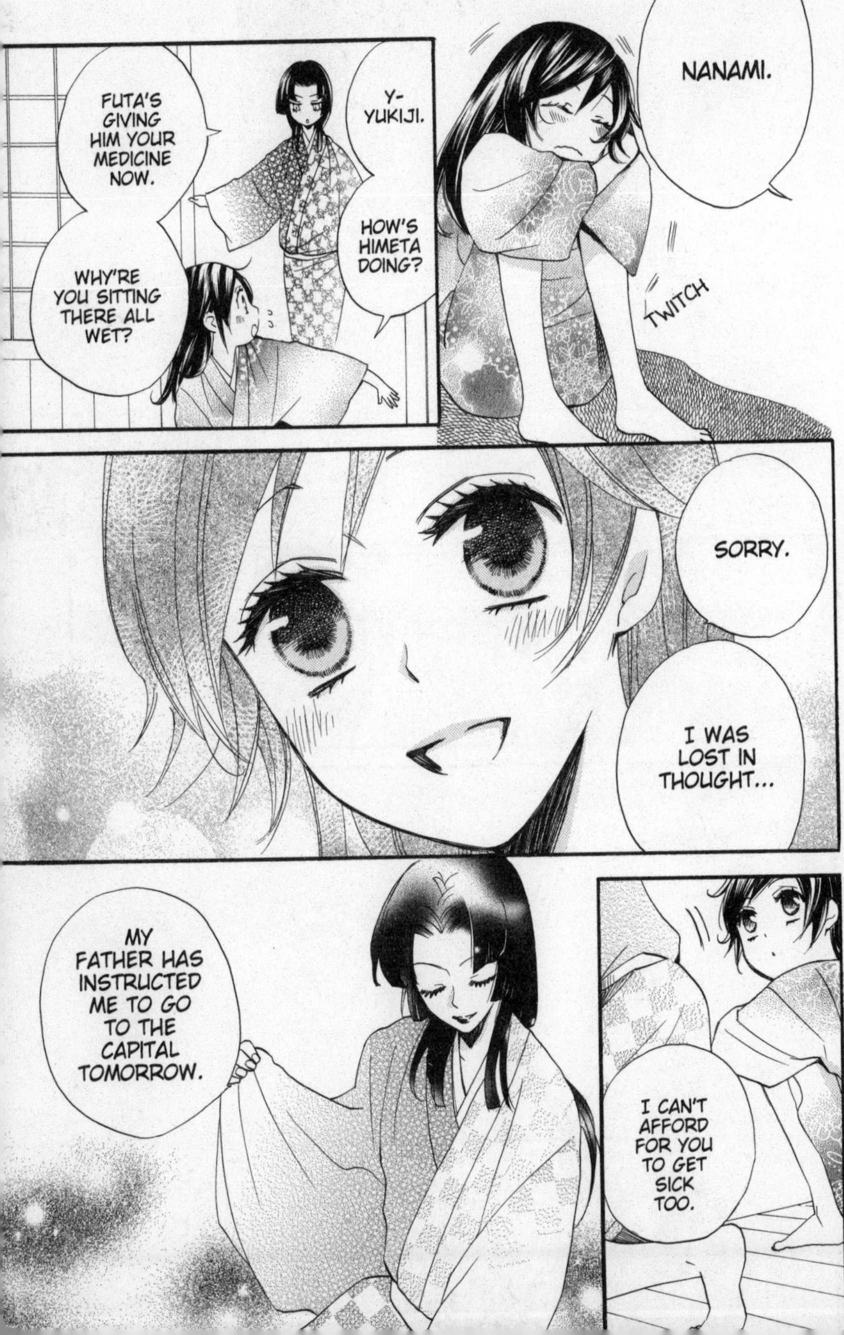
NANAMI.
TWITCH
Y-YUKIJI.
HOW'S HIMETA DOING?
FUTA'S GIVING HIM YOUR MEDICINE NOW.
WHY'RE YOU SITTING THERE ALL WET?
SORRY.
I WAS LOST IN THOUGHT...
I CAN'T AFFORD FOR YOU TO GET SICK TOO.
MY FATHER HAS INSTRUCTED ME TO GO TO THE CAPITAL TOMORROW.

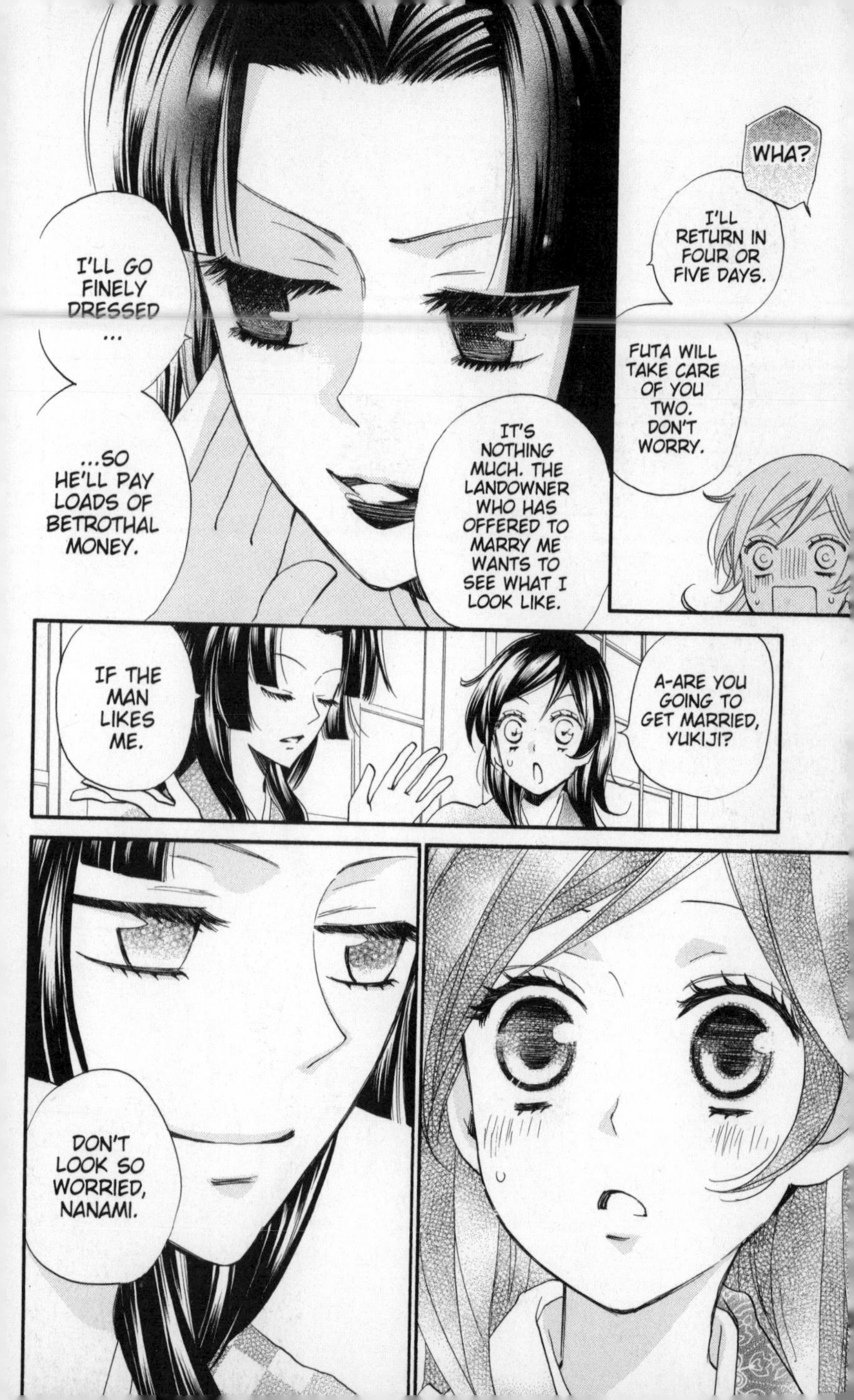
WHA?
I'LL RETURN IN FOUR OR FIVE DAYS.
FUTA WILL TAKE CARE OF YOU TWO. DON'T WORRY.
IT'S NOTHING MUCH. THE LANDOWNER WHO HAS OFFERED TO MARRY ME WANTS TO SEE WHAT I LOOK LIKE.
I'LL GO FINELY DRESSED...
...SO HE'LL PAY LOADS OF BETROTHAL MONEY.
A-ARE YOU GOING TO GET MARRIED, YUKIJI?
IF THE MAN LIKES ME.
DON'T LOOK SO WORRIED, NANAMI.

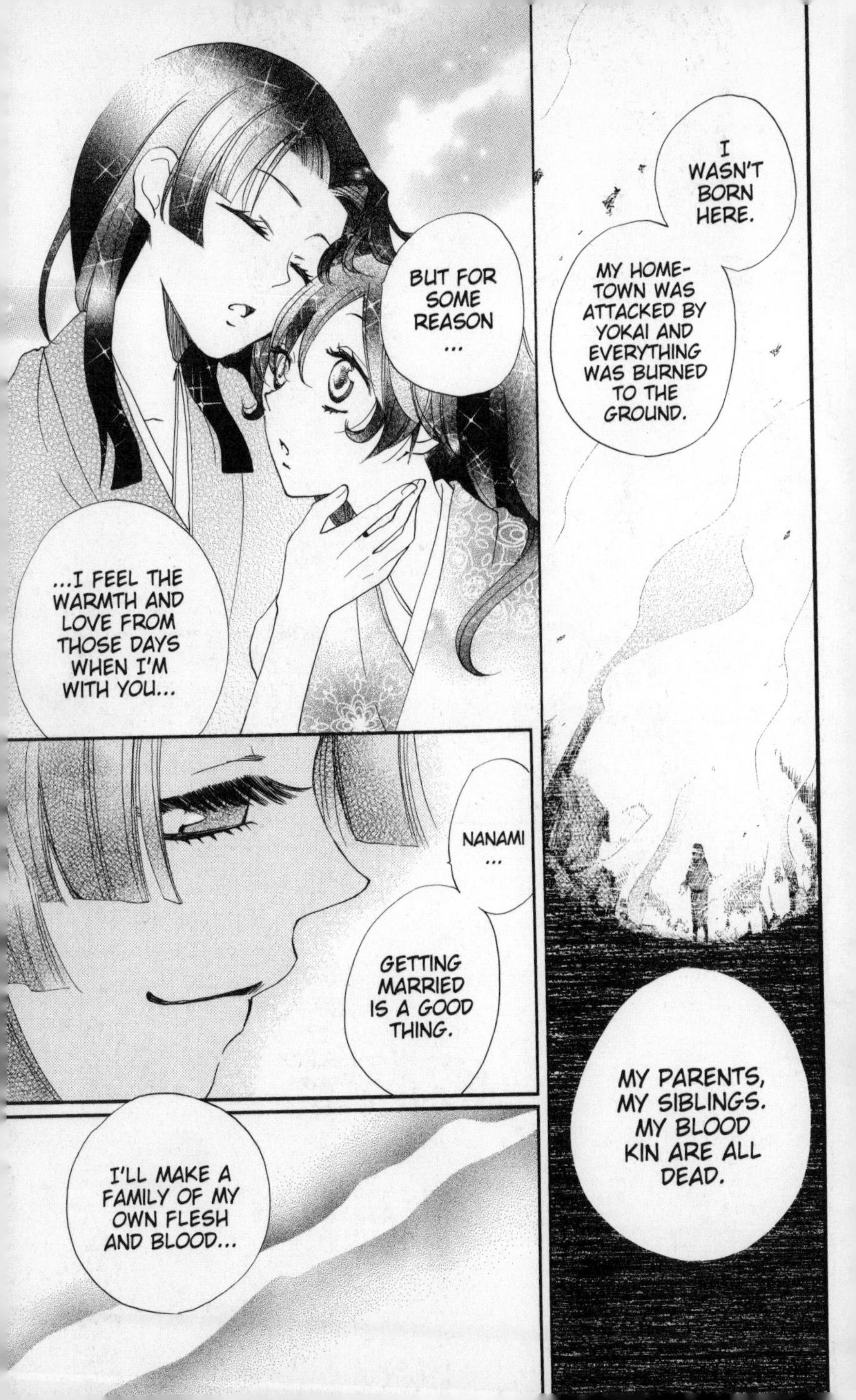
I WASN'T BORN HERE.
MY HOME-TOWN WAS ATTACKED BY YOKAI AND EVERYTHING WAS BURNED TO THE GROUND.
MY PARENTS, MY SIBLINGS. MY BLOOD KIN ARE ALL DEAD.
BUT FOR SOME REASON ...
...I FEEL THE WARMTH AND LOVE FROM THOSE DAYS WHEN I'M WITH YOU...
NANAMI ...
GETTING MARRIED IS A GOOD THING.
I'LL MAKE A FAMILY OF MY OWN FLESH AND BLOOD...

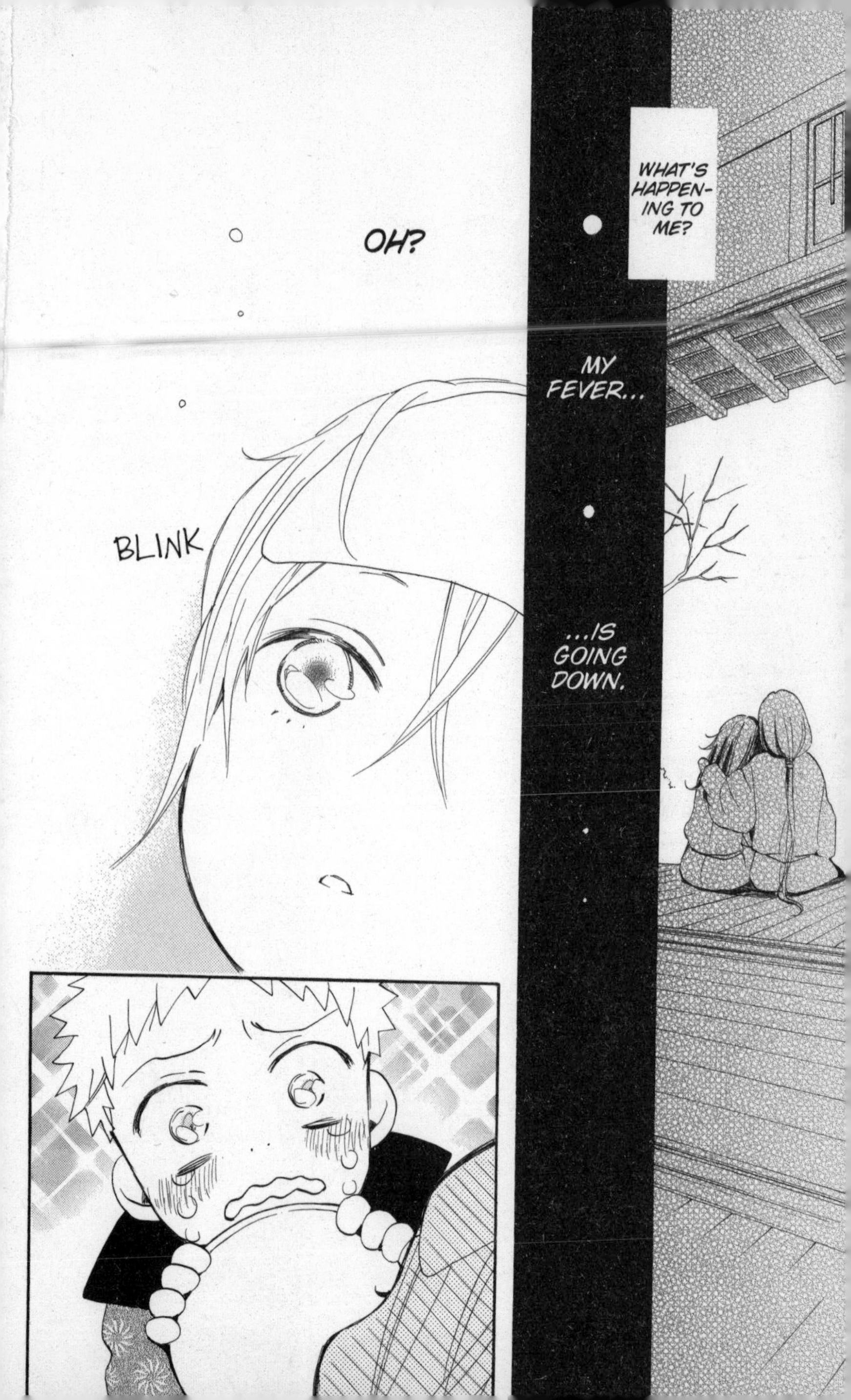
WHAT'S HAPPEN-ING TO ME?
MY FEVER...
...IS GOING DOWN.
OH?
BLINK

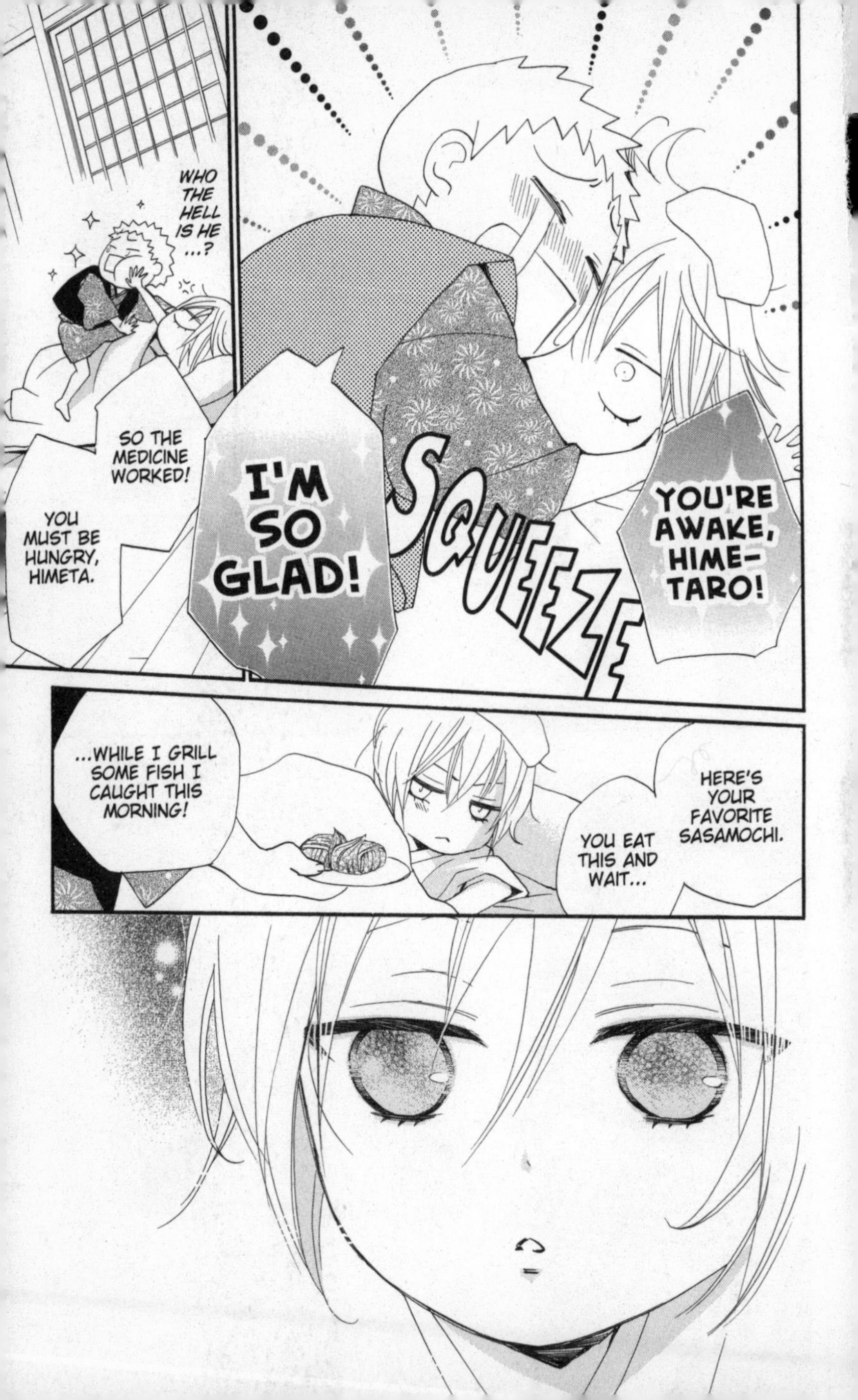
YOU'RE AWAKE, HIME-TARO!
SQUEEZE
I'M SO GLAD!
WHO THE HELL IS HE ...?
SO THE MEDICINE WORKED!
YOU MUST BE HUNGRY, HIMETA.
HERE'S YOUR FAVORITE SASAMOCHI.
YOU EAT THIS AND WAIT...
...WHILE I GRILL SOME FISH I CAUGHT THIS MORNING!

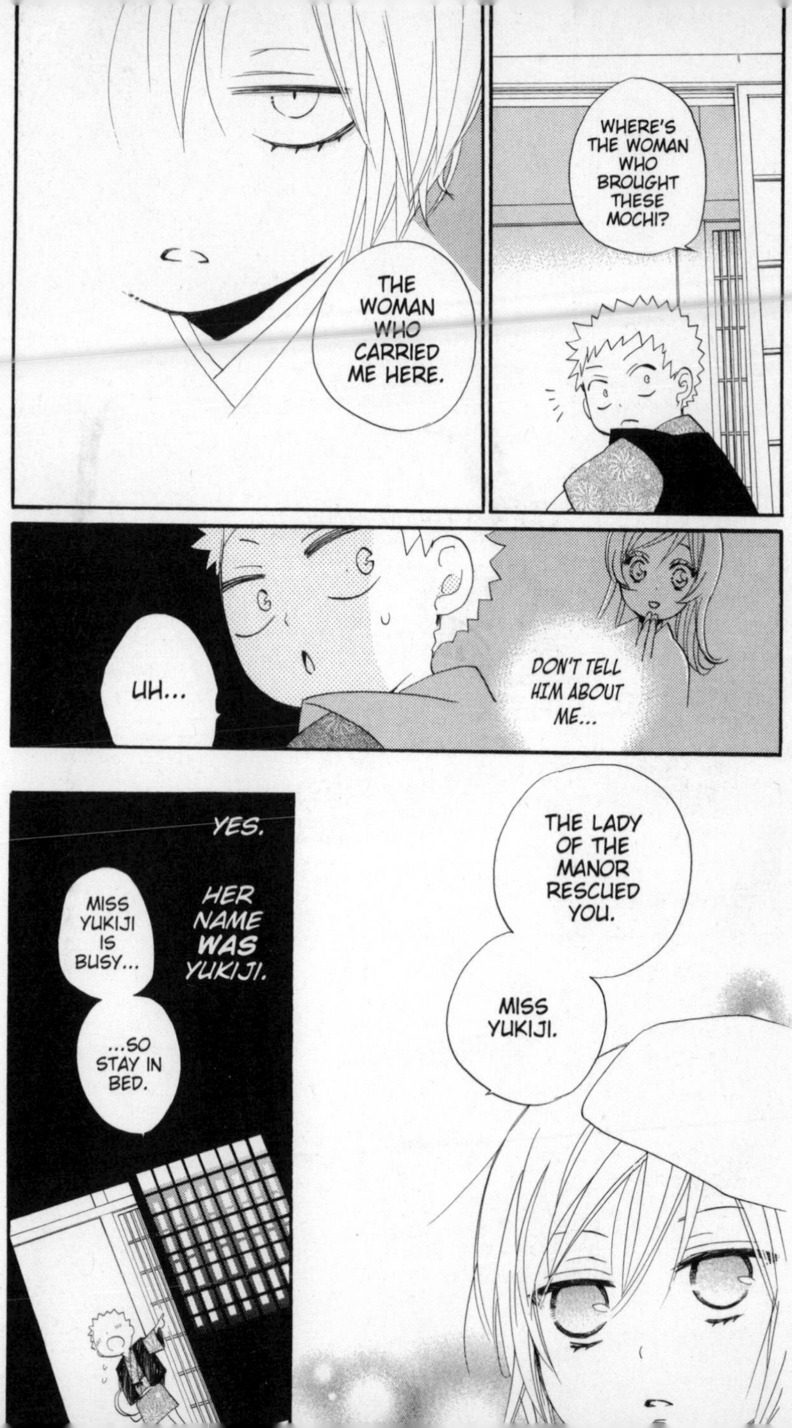
WHERE'S THE WOMAN WHO BROUGHT THESE MOCHI?
THE WOMAN WHO CARRIED ME HERE.
DON'T TELL HIM ABOUT ME...
UH...
THE LADY OF THE MANOR RESCUED YOU.
MISS YUKIJI.
YES.
HER NAME WAS YUKIJI.
MISS YUKIJI IS BUSY...
...SO STAY IN BED.

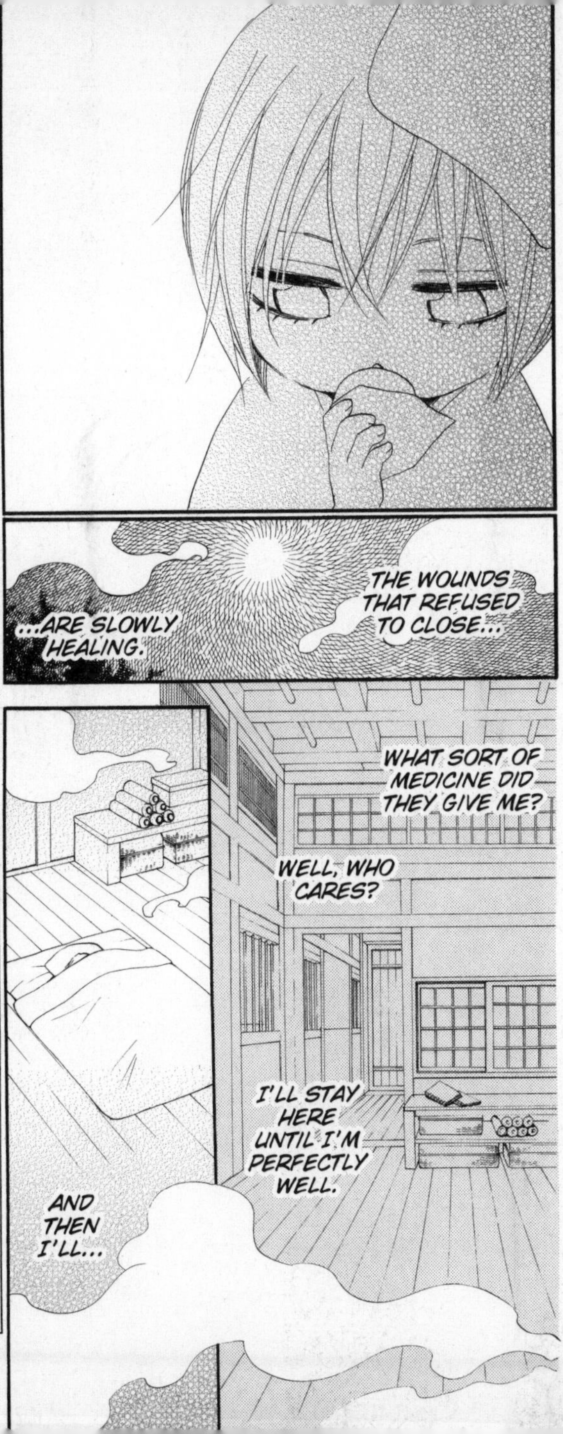
THE WOUNDS THAT REFUSED TO CLOSE...
...ARE SLOWLY HEALING.
WHAT SORT OF MEDICINE DID THEY GIVE ME?
WELL, WHO CARES?
I'LL STAY HERE UNTIL I'M PERFECTLY WELL.
AND THEN I'LL...

Nowadays I feel like doing handicrafts.

I want to make something cute by stitching with a needle.

Cuteness is justice!

My mother makes artificial flowers.

She made me some artificial roses as a housewarming gift.

I always wished I could make cute things like her.

Especially when the afternoons are peaceful and quiet.

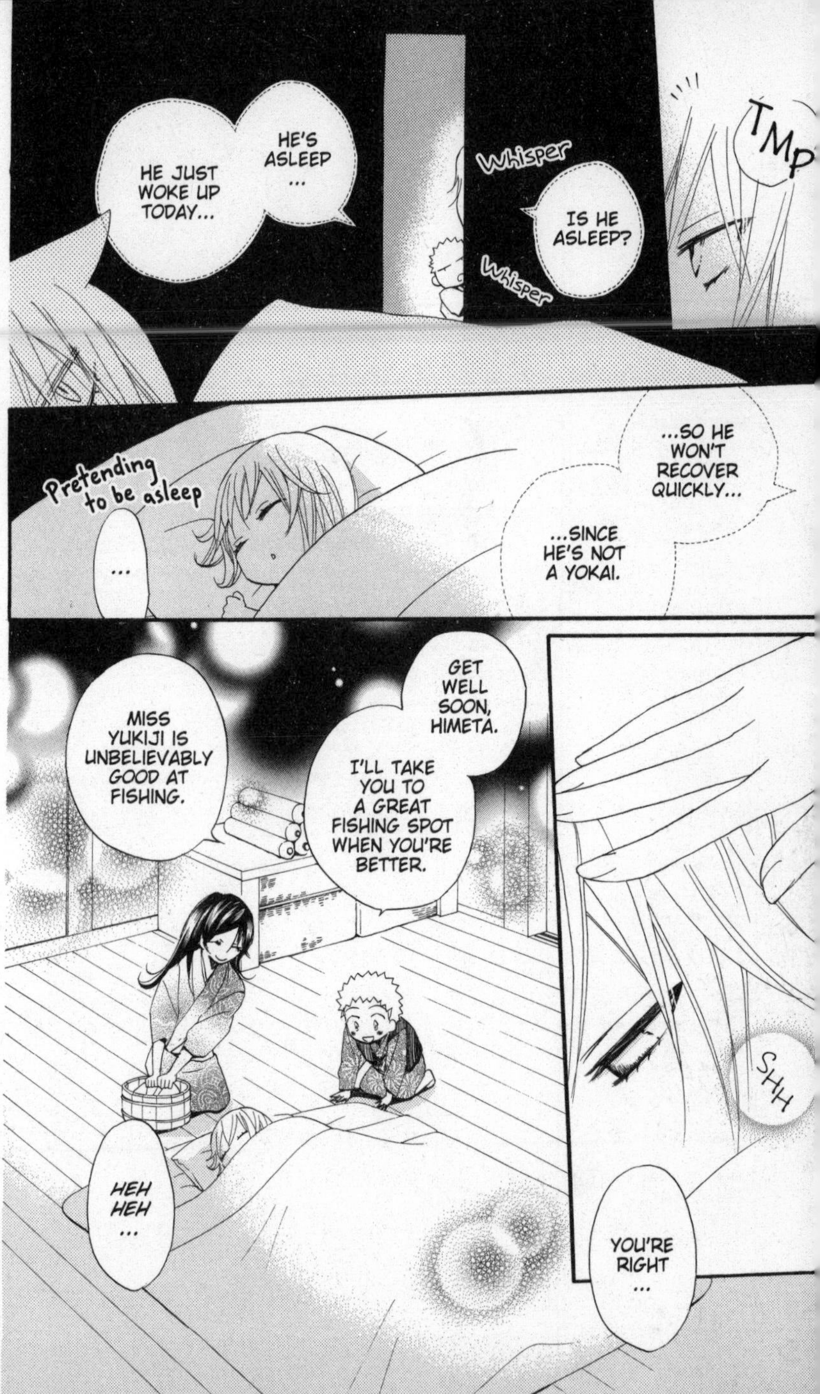
TMP
Whisper
IS HE ASLEEP?
Whisper
HE'S ASLEEP ...
HE JUST WOKE UP TODAY...
...SO HE WON'T RECOVER QUICKLY...
...SINCE HE'S NOT A YOKAI.
Pretending to be asleep
...
SHH
YOU'RE RIGHT ...
GET WELL SOON, HIMETA.
I'LL TAKE YOU TO A GREAT FISHING SPOT WHEN YOU'RE BETTER.
MISS YUKIJI IS UNBELIEVABLY GOOD AT FISHING.
HEH HEH ...

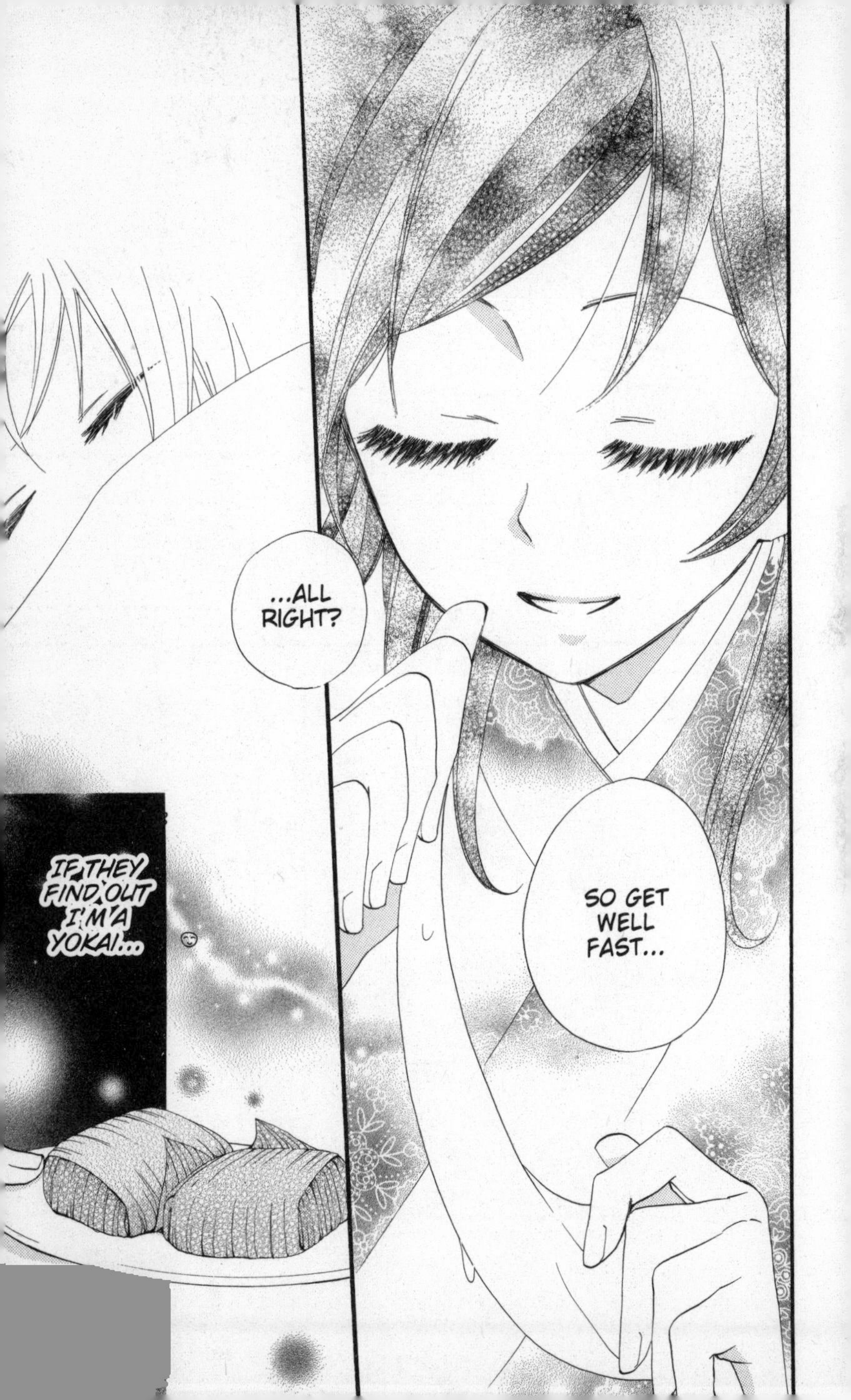
...ALL RIGHT?
SO GET WELL FAST...
IF THEY FIND OUT I'M A YOKAI...

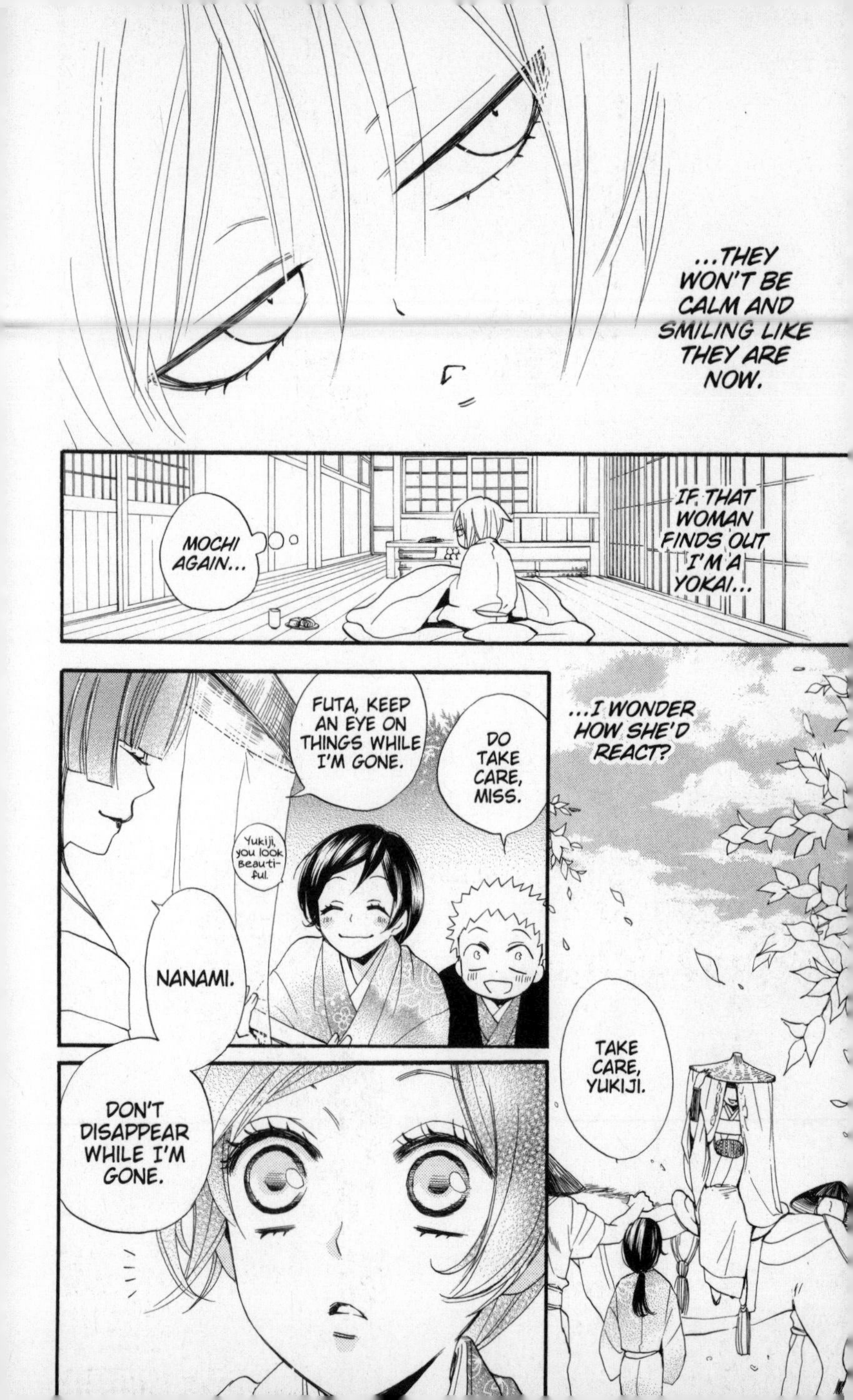

...THEY WON'T BE CALM AND SMILING LIKE THEY ARE NOW.
IF THAT WOMAN FINDS OUT I'M A YOKAI...
MOCHI AGAIN...
...I WONDER HOW SHE'D REACT?
TAKE CARE, YUKIJI.
FUTA, KEEP AN EYE ON THINGS WHILE I'M GONE.
DO TAKE CARE, MISS.
Yukiji, you look beauti-ful.
NANAMI.
DON'T DISAPPEAR WHILE I'M GONE.

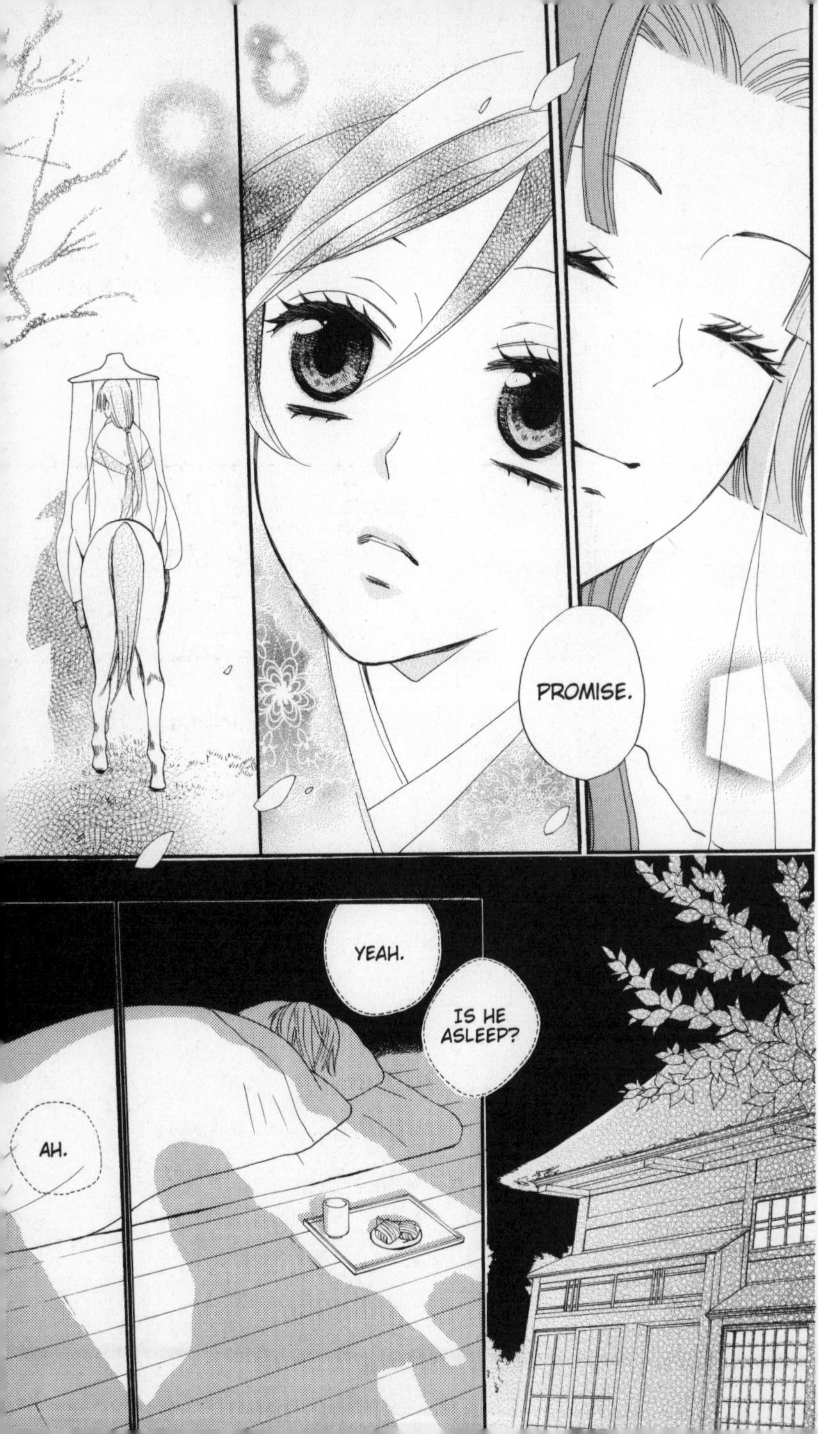
PROMISE.
IS HE ASLEEP?
YEAH.
AH.

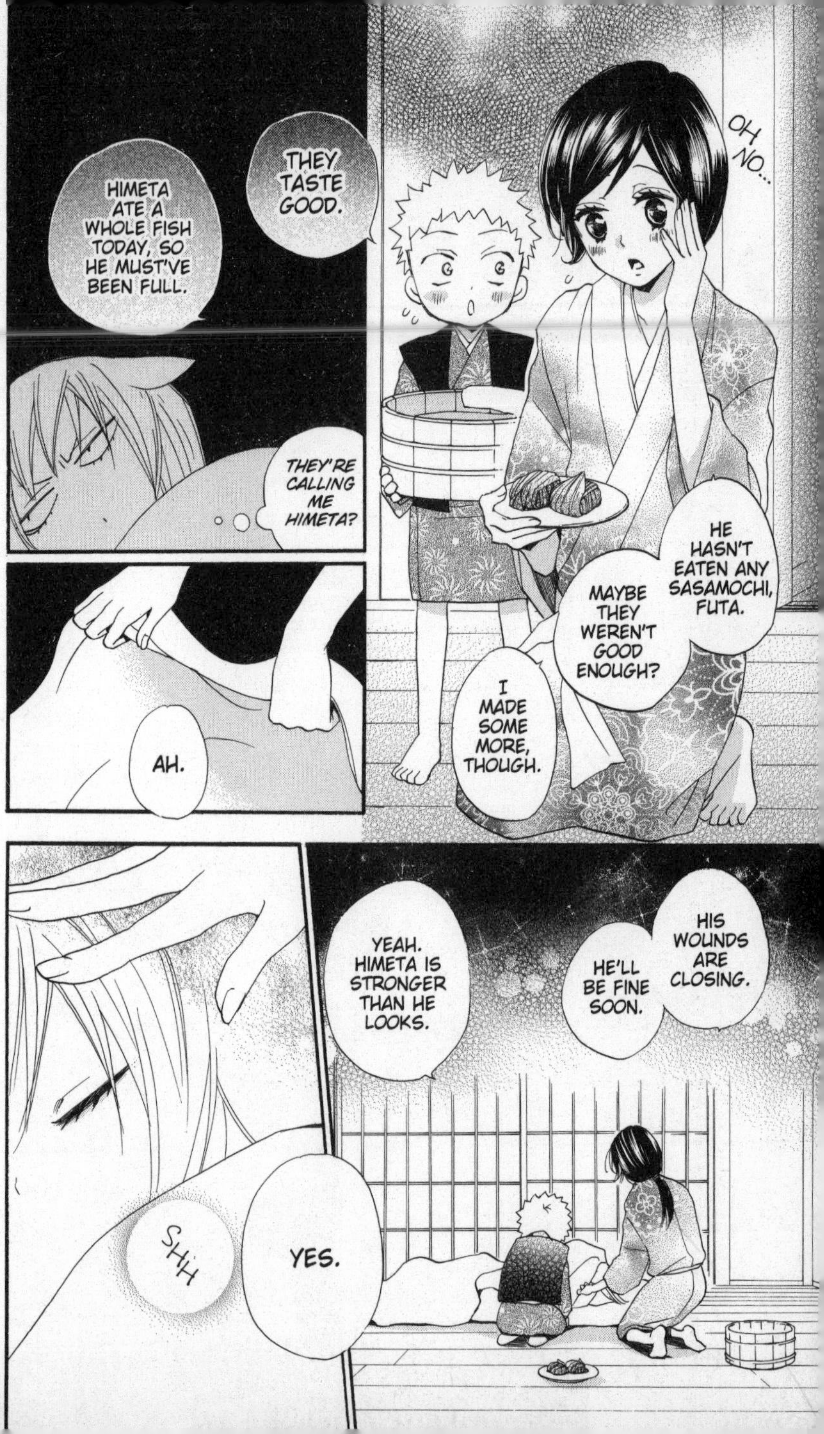
OH NO...
HE HASN'T EATEN ANY SASAMOCHI, FUTA.
MAYBE THEY WEREN'T GOOD ENOUGH?
I MADE SOME MORE, THOUGH.
THEY TASTE GOOD.
HIMETA ATE A WHOLE FISH TODAY, SO HE MUST'VE BEEN FULL.
THEY'RE CALLING ME HIMETA?
AH.
HIS WOUNDS ARE CLOSING.
HE'LL BE FINE SOON.
YEAH. HIMETA IS STRONGER THAN HE LOOKS.
YES.
SHH

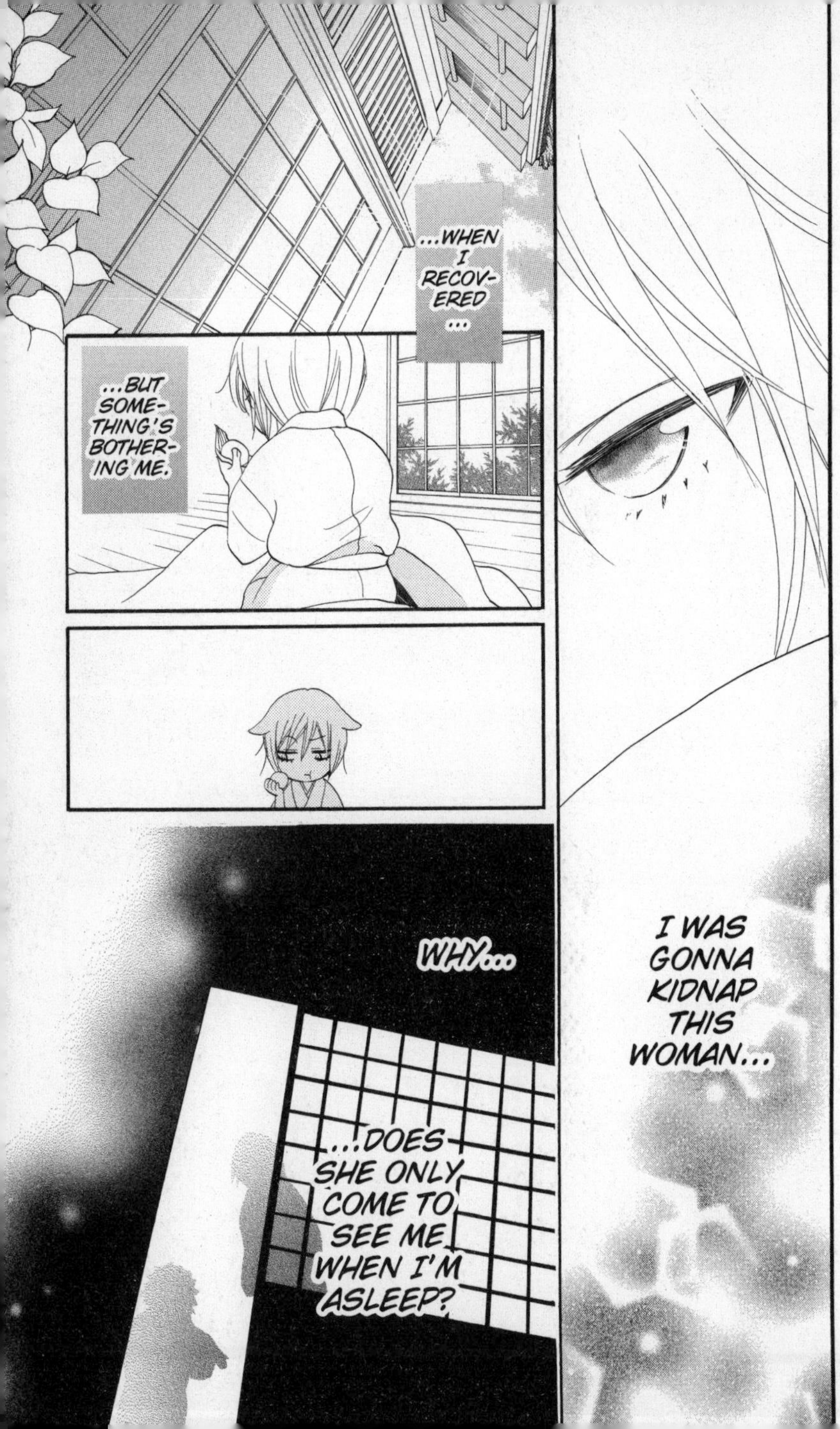
I WAS GONNA KIDNAP THIS WOMAN...
...WHEN I RECOVERED...
...BUT SOMETHING'S BOTHERING ME.
WHY...
...DOES SHE ONLY COME TO SEE ME WHEN I'M ASLEEP?

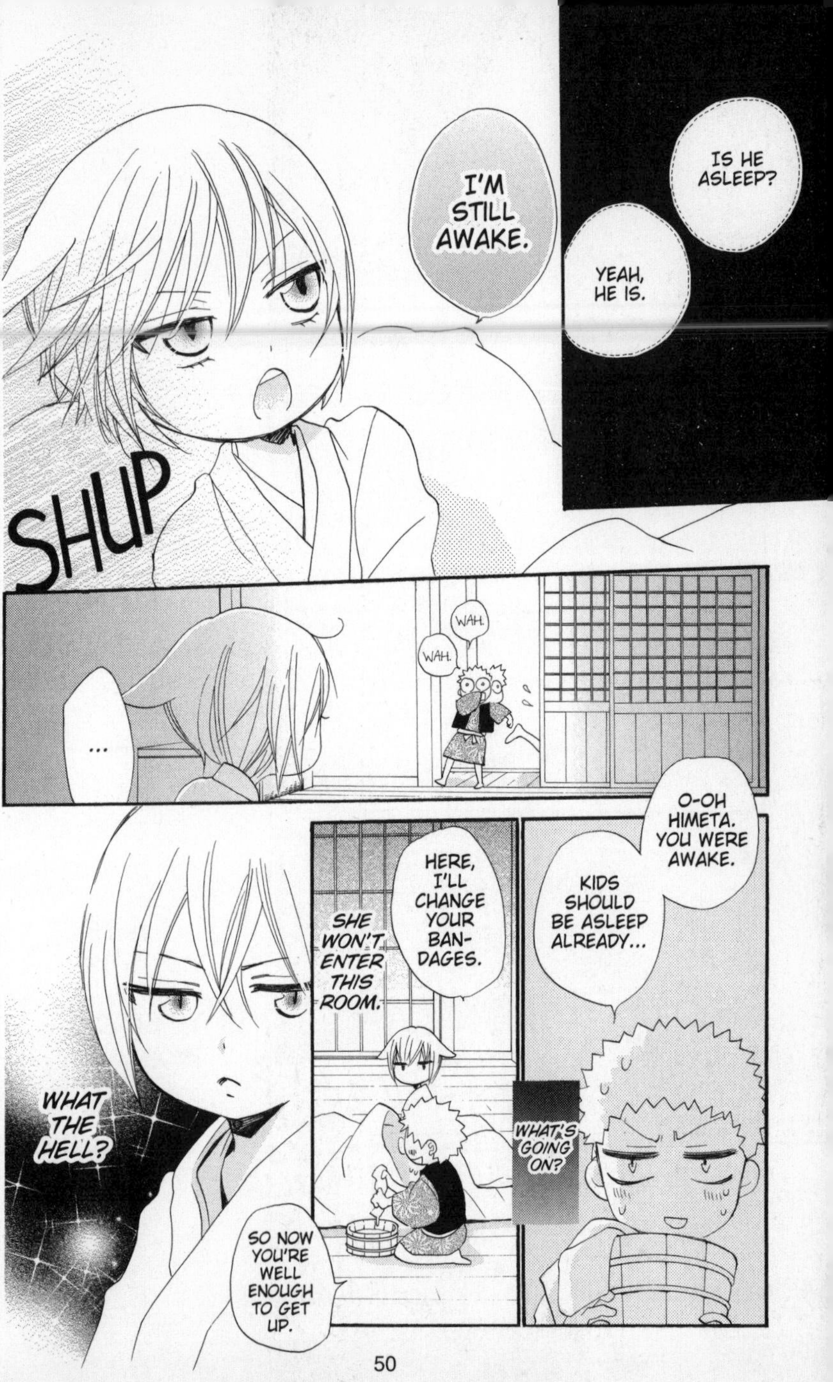
IS HE ASLEEP?
YEAH, HE IS.
I'M STILL AWAKE.
SHUP
WAH.
WAH.
...
O-OH HIMETA. YOU WERE AWAKE.
KIDS SHOULD BE ASLEEP ALREADY...
WHAT'S GOING ON?
HERE, I'LL CHANGE YOUR BAN-DAGES.
SHE WON'T ENTER THIS ROOM.
WHAT THE HELL?
SO NOW YOU'RE WELL ENOUGH TO GET UP.

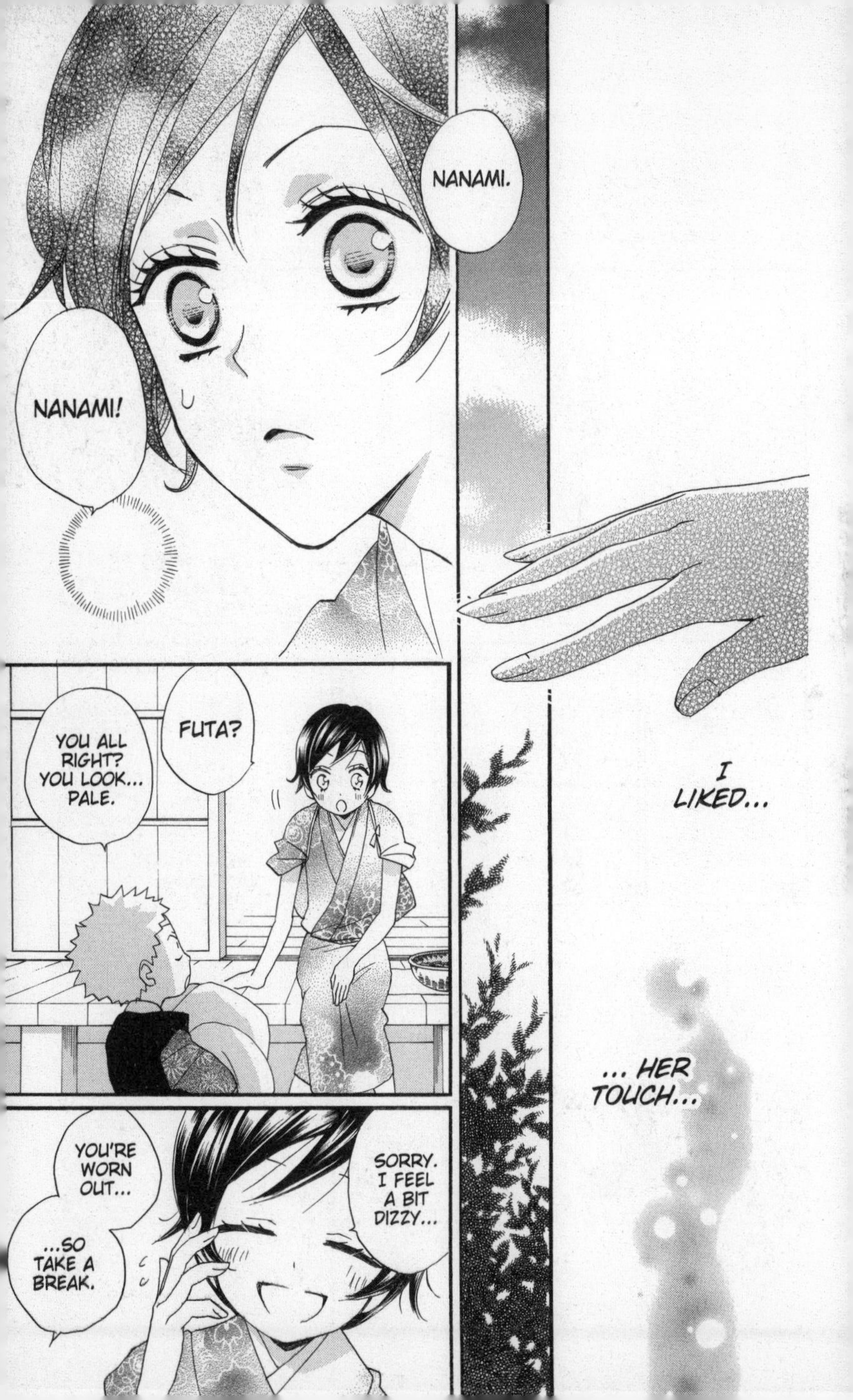
I LIKED...
... HER TOUCH...
NANAMI.
NANAMI!
FUTA?
YOU ALL RIGHT? YOU LOOK... PALE.
SORRY. I FEEL A BIT DIZZY...
YOU'RE WORN OUT...
...SO TAKE A BREAK.

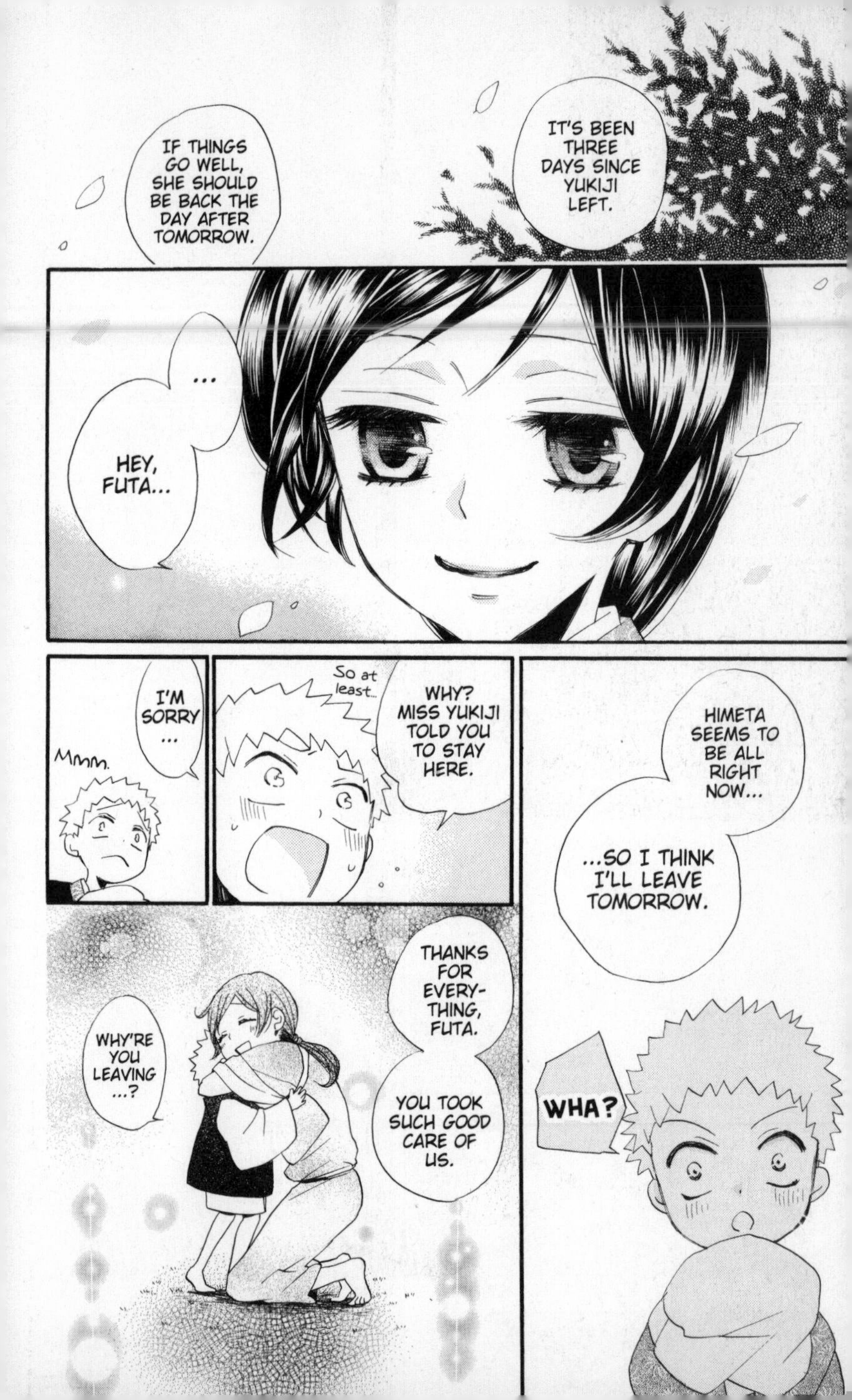
IT'S BEEN THREE DAYS SINCE YUKIJI LEFT.
IF THINGS GO WELL, SHE SHOULD BE BACK THE DAY AFTER TOMORROW.
...
HEY, FUTA...
HIMETA SEEMS TO BE ALL RIGHT NOW...
...SO I THINK I'LL LEAVE TOMORROW.
WHA?
WHY? MISS YUKIJI TOLD YOU TO STAY HERE.
So at least...
I'M SORRY...
Mmm.
THANKS FOR EVERY-THING, FUTA.
YOU TOOK SUCH GOOD CARE OF US.
WHY'RE YOU LEAVING...?

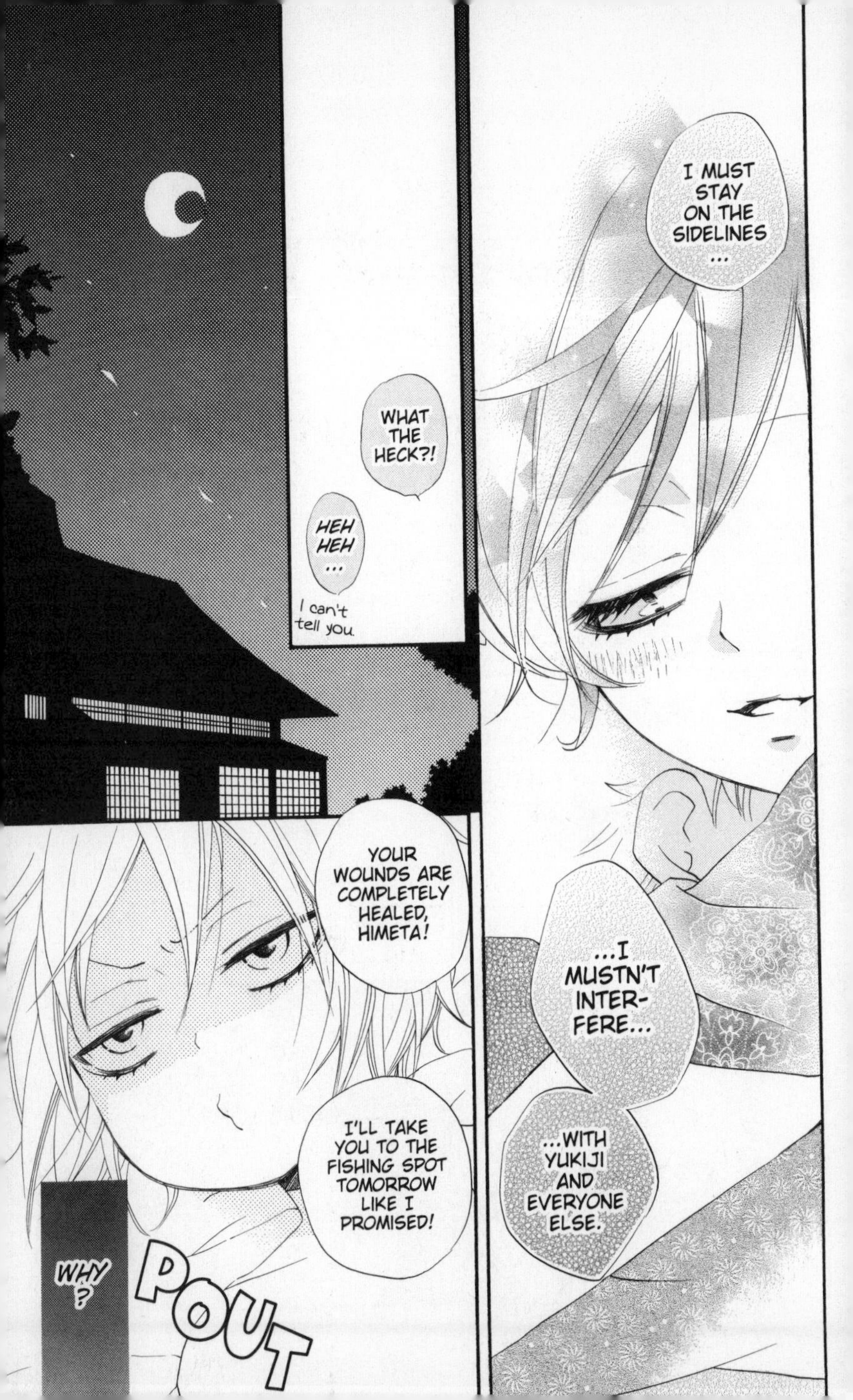
I MUST STAY ON THE SIDELINES...
...I MUSTN'T INTER-FERE...
...WITH YUKIJI AND EVERYONE ELSE.
WHAT THE HECK?!
HEH HEH...
I can't tell you.
YOUR WOUNDS ARE COMPLETELY HEALED, HIMETA!
I'LL TAKE YOU TO THE FISHING SPOT TOMORROW LIKE I PROMISED!
POUT
WHY?

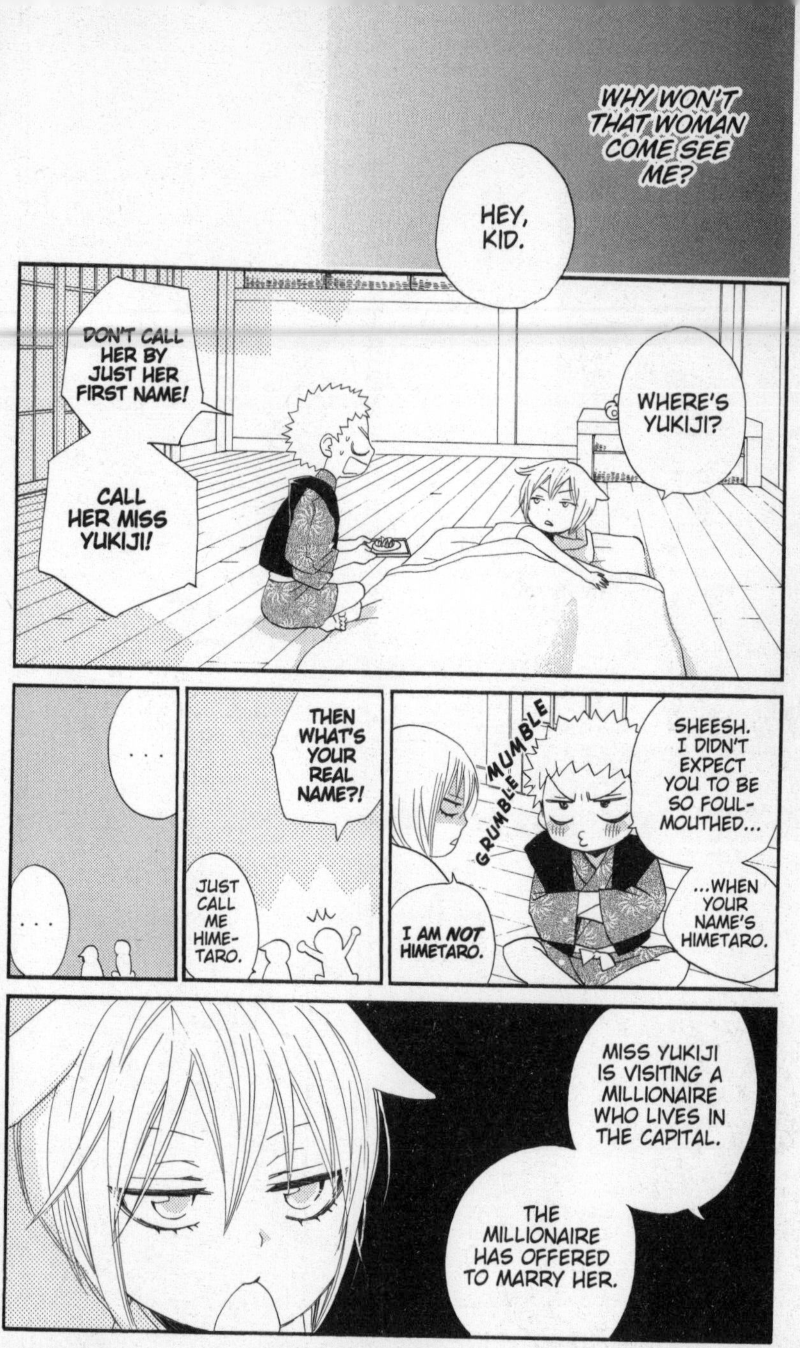

WHY WON'T THAT WOMAN COME SEE ME?
HEY, KID.
WHERE'S YUKIJI?
DON'T CALL HER BY JUST HER FIRST NAME!
CALL HER MISS YUKIJI!
SHEESH. I DIDN'T EXPECT YOU TO BE SO FOUL-MOUTHED...
...WHEN YOUR NAME'S HIMETARO.
MUMBLE GRUMBLE
I AM *NOT* HIMETARO.
THEN WHAT'S YOUR REAL NAME?!
JUST CALL ME HIME-TARO.
. . .
. . .
MISS YUKIJI IS VISITING A MILLIONAIRE WHO LIVES IN THE CAPITAL.
THE MILLIONAIRE HAS OFFERED TO MARRY HER.

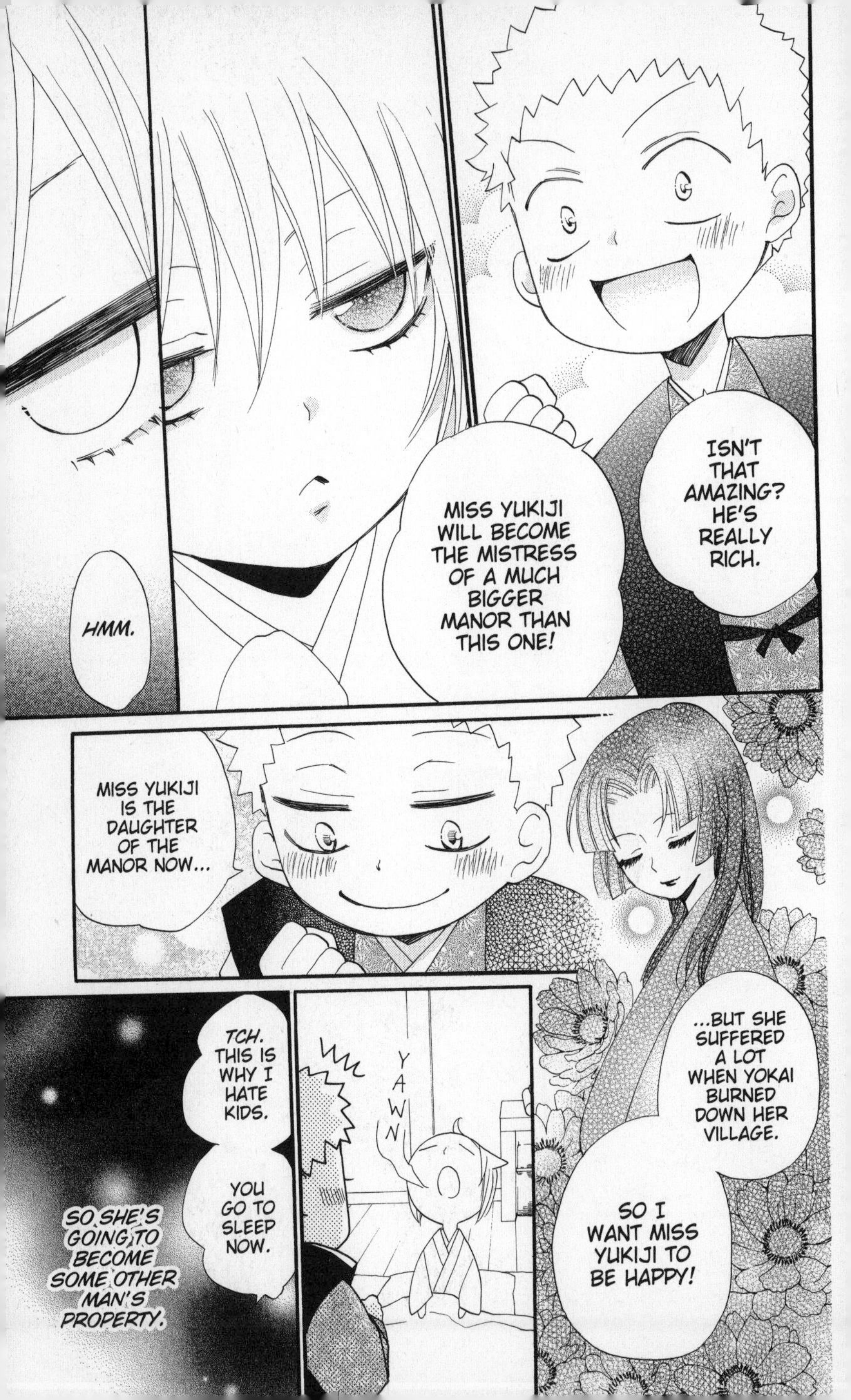
ISN'T THAT AMAZING? HE'S REALLY RICH.
MISS YUKIJI WILL BECOME THE MISTRESS OF A MUCH BIGGER MANOR THAN THIS ONE!
HMM.
MISS YUKIJI IS THE DAUGHTER OF THE MANOR NOW...
...BUT SHE SUFFERED A LOT WHEN YOKAI BURNED DOWN HER VILLAGE.
SO I WANT MISS YUKIJI TO BE HAPPY!
YAWN
TCH. THIS IS WHY I HATE KIDS.
YOU GO TO SLEEP NOW.
SO SHE'S GOING TO BECOME SOME OTHER MAN'S PROPERTY.

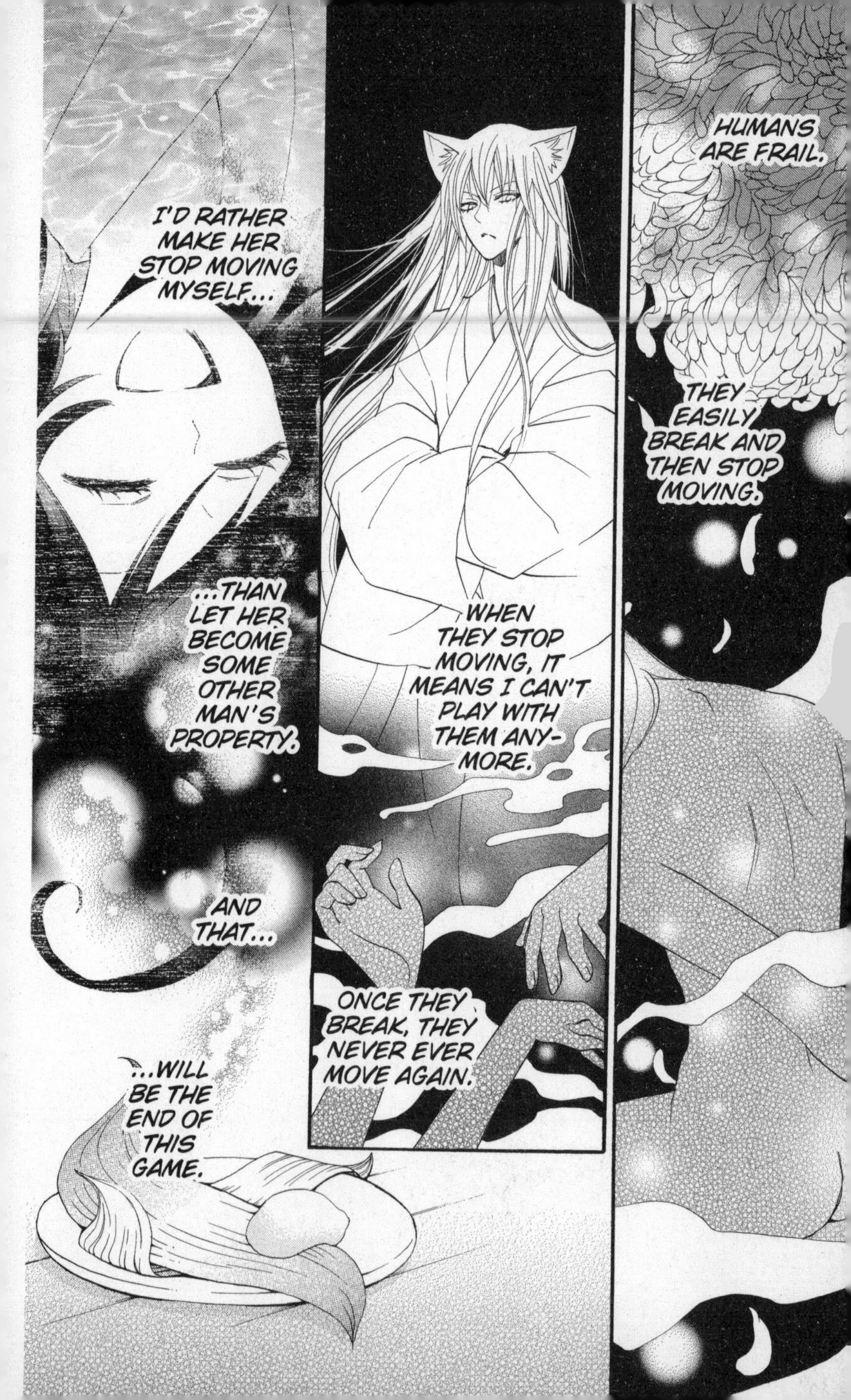
HUMANS ARE FRAIL.
THEY EASILY BREAK AND THEN STOP MOVING.
WHEN THEY STOP MOVING, IT MEANS I CAN'T PLAY WITH THEM ANY-MORE.
ONCE THEY BREAK, THEY NEVER EVER MOVE AGAIN.
I'D RATHER MAKE HER STOP MOVING MYSELF...
...THAN LET HER BECOME SOME OTHER MAN'S PROPERTY.
AND THAT...
...WILL BE THE END OF THIS GAME.

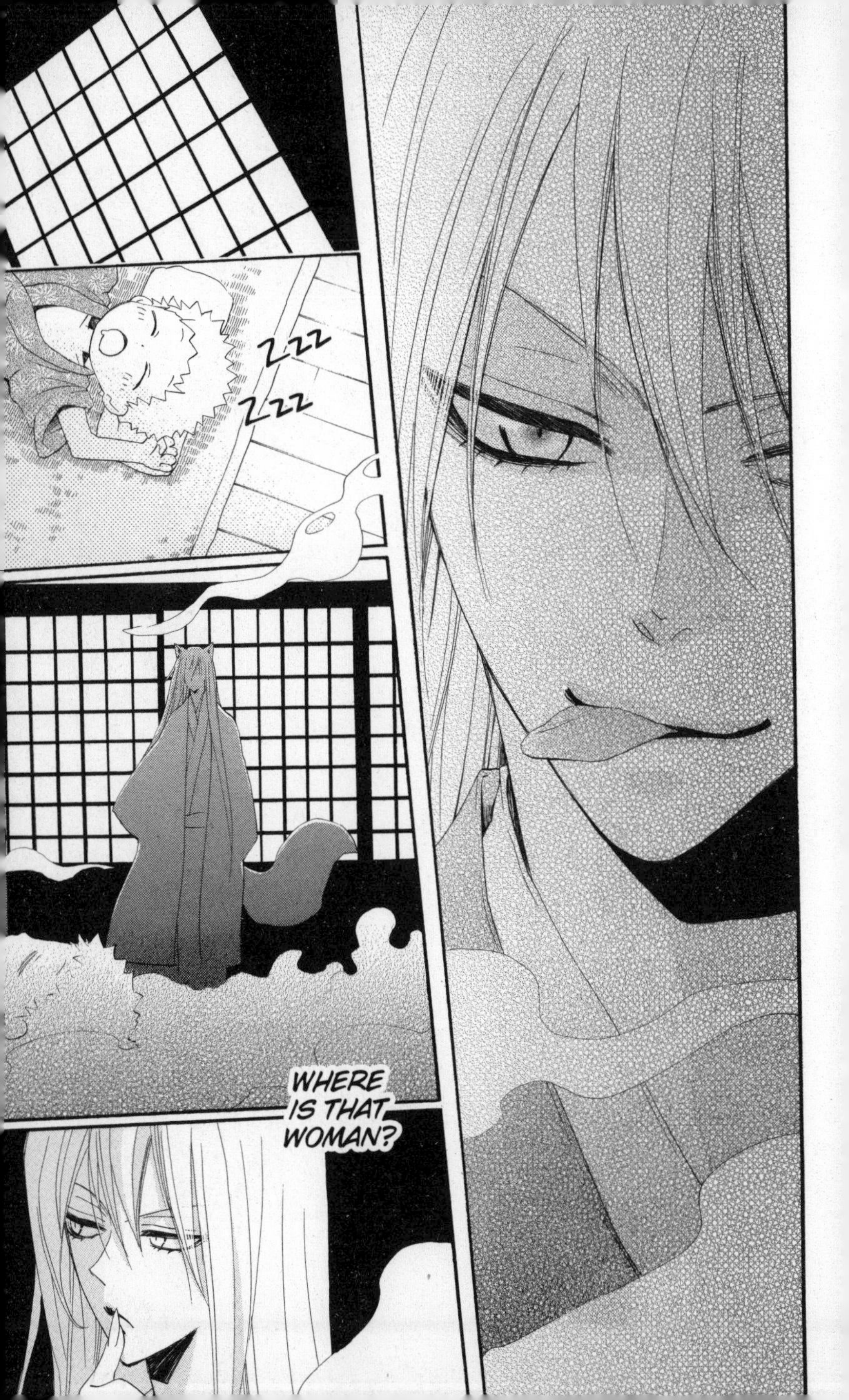
ZZZ
ZZZ
WHERE IS THAT WOMAN?

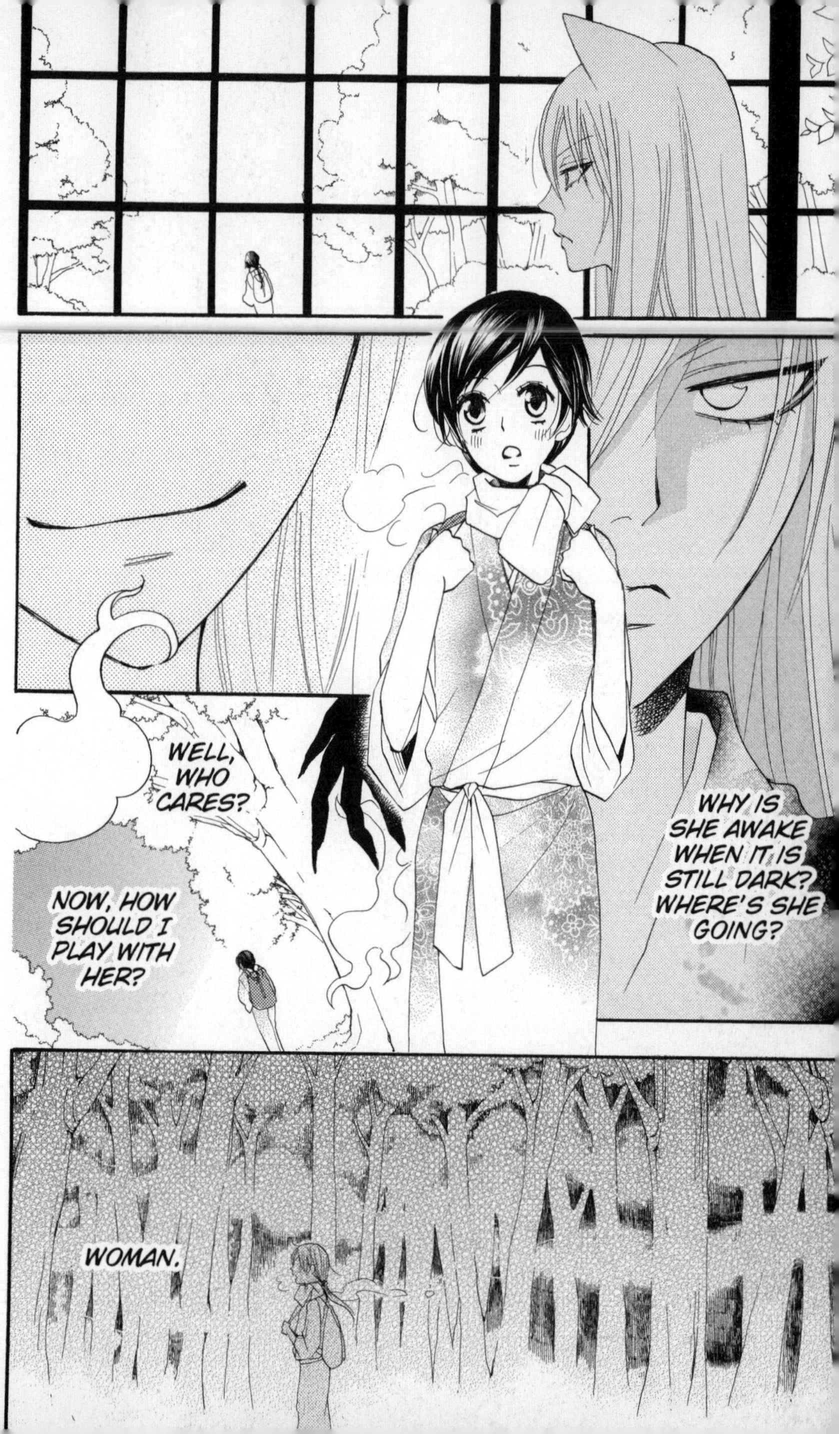
WHY IS SHE AWAKE WHEN IT IS STILL DARK? WHERE'S SHE GOING?
WELL, WHO CARES?
NOW, HOW SHOULD I PLAY WITH HER?
WOMAN.

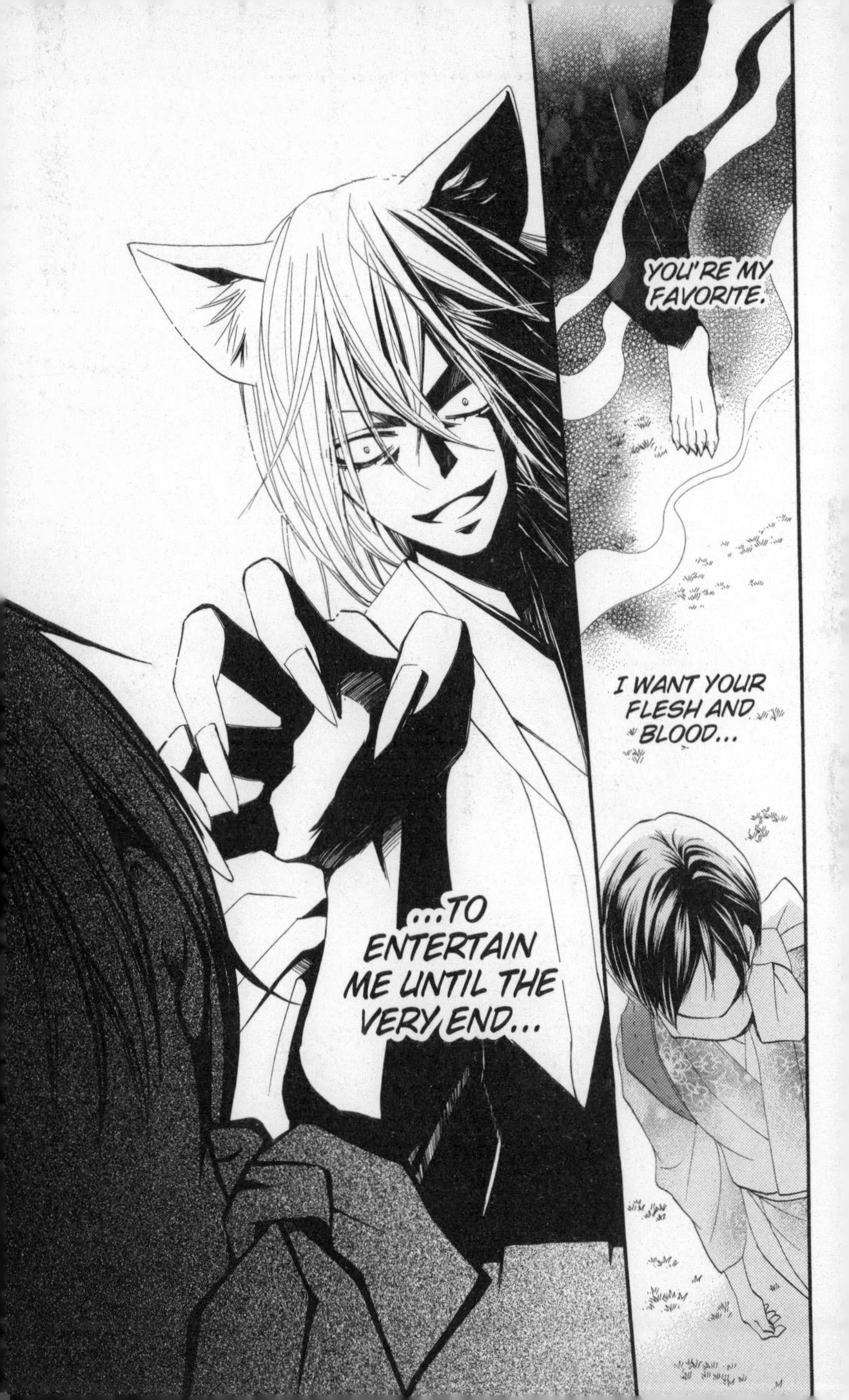
YOU'RE MY FAVORITE.
I WANT YOUR FLESH AND BLOOD...
...TO ENTERTAIN ME UNTIL THE VERY END...

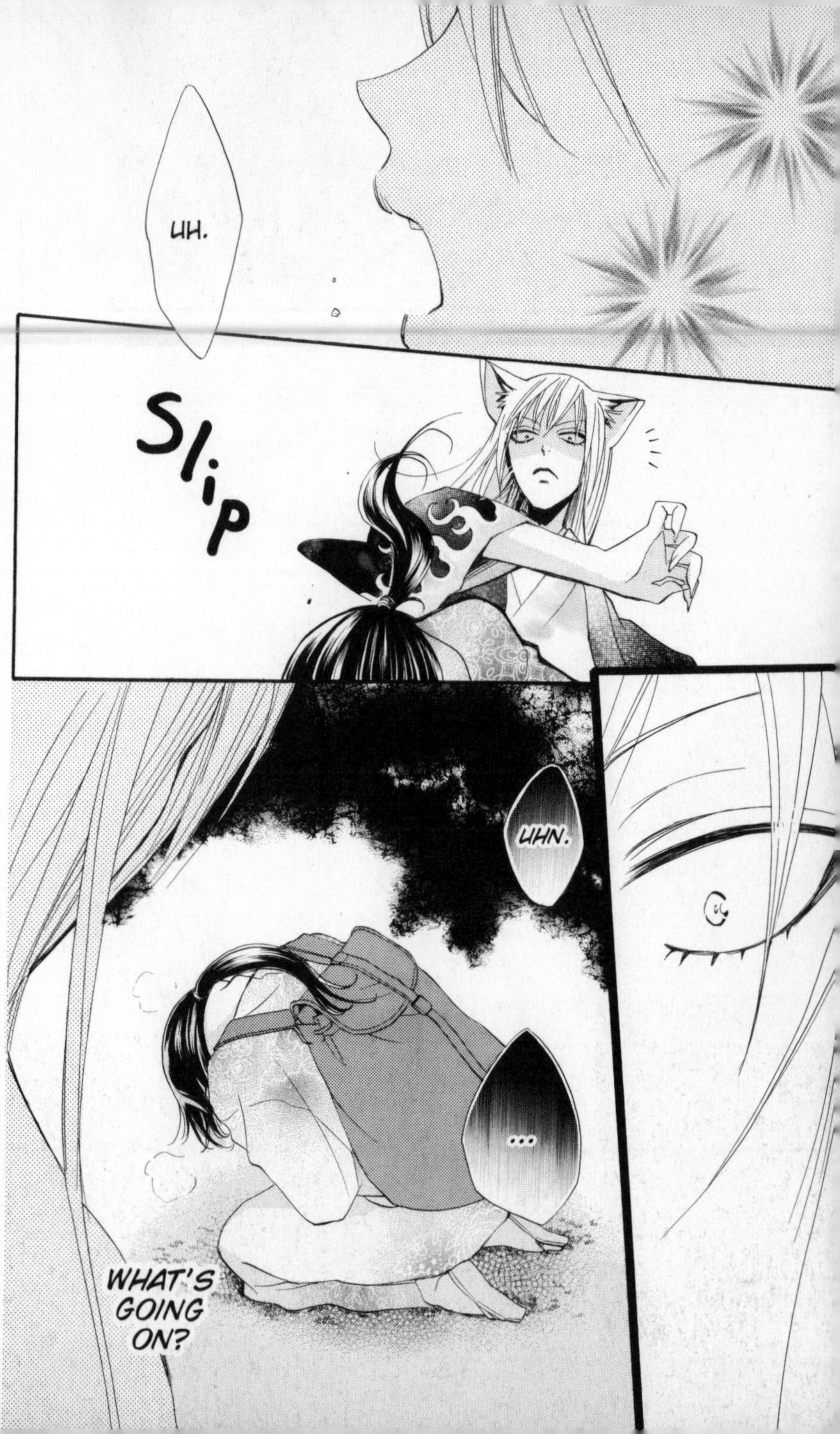
UH.
Slip
UHN.
...
WHAT'S GOING ON?

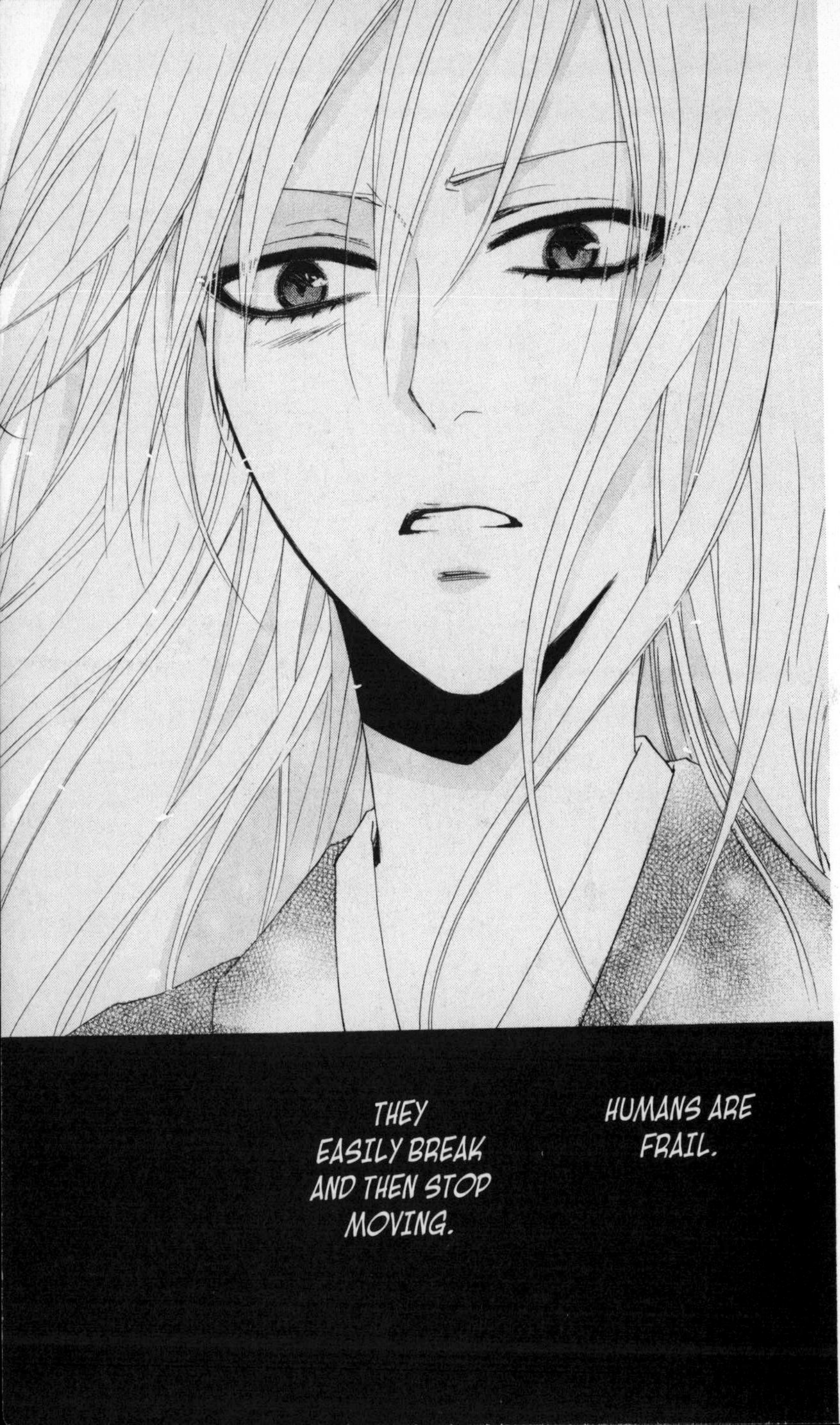
HUMANS ARE FRAIL.
THEY EASILY BREAK AND THEN STOP MOVING.

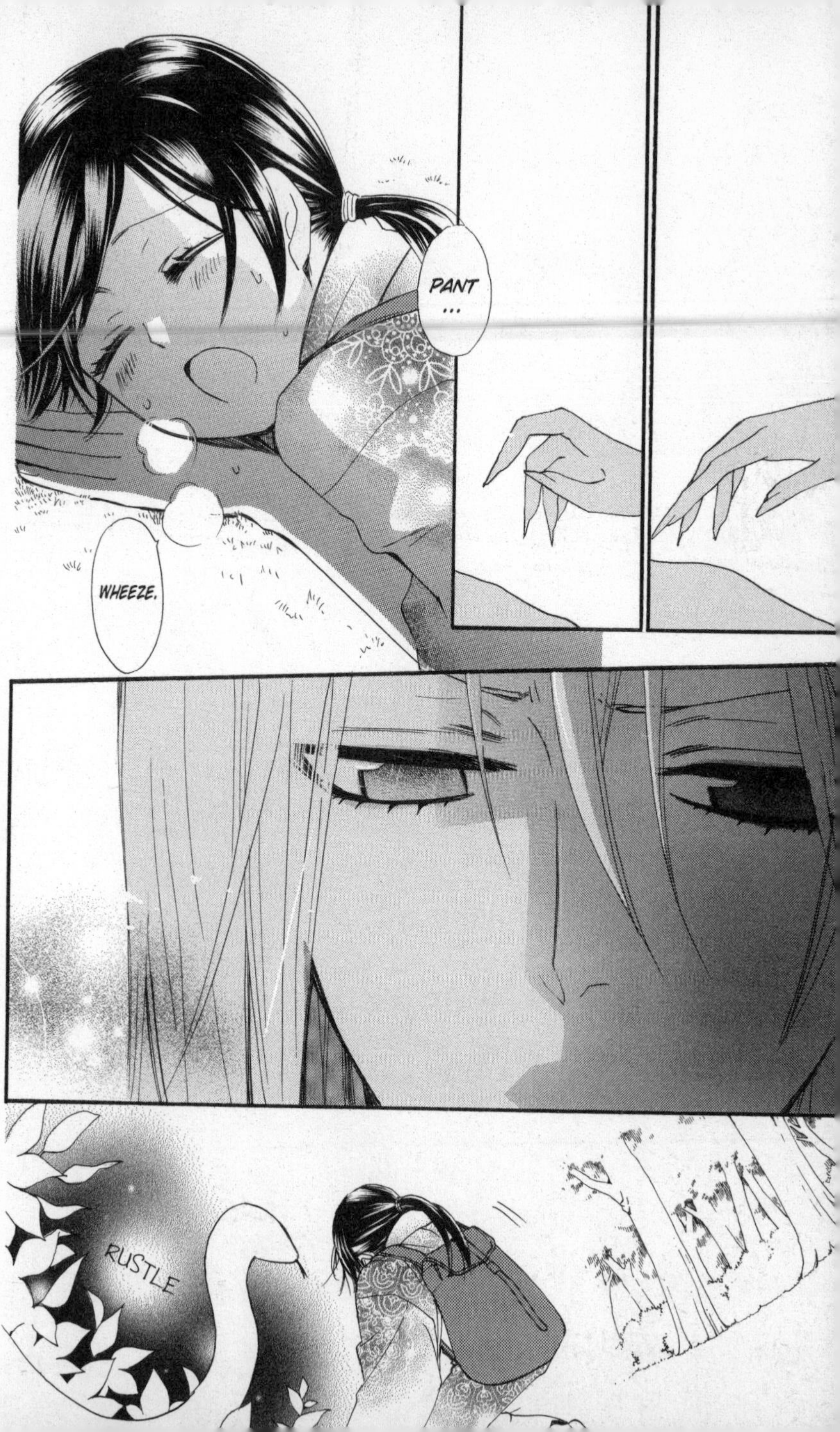
PANT ...
WHEEZE.
RUSTLE

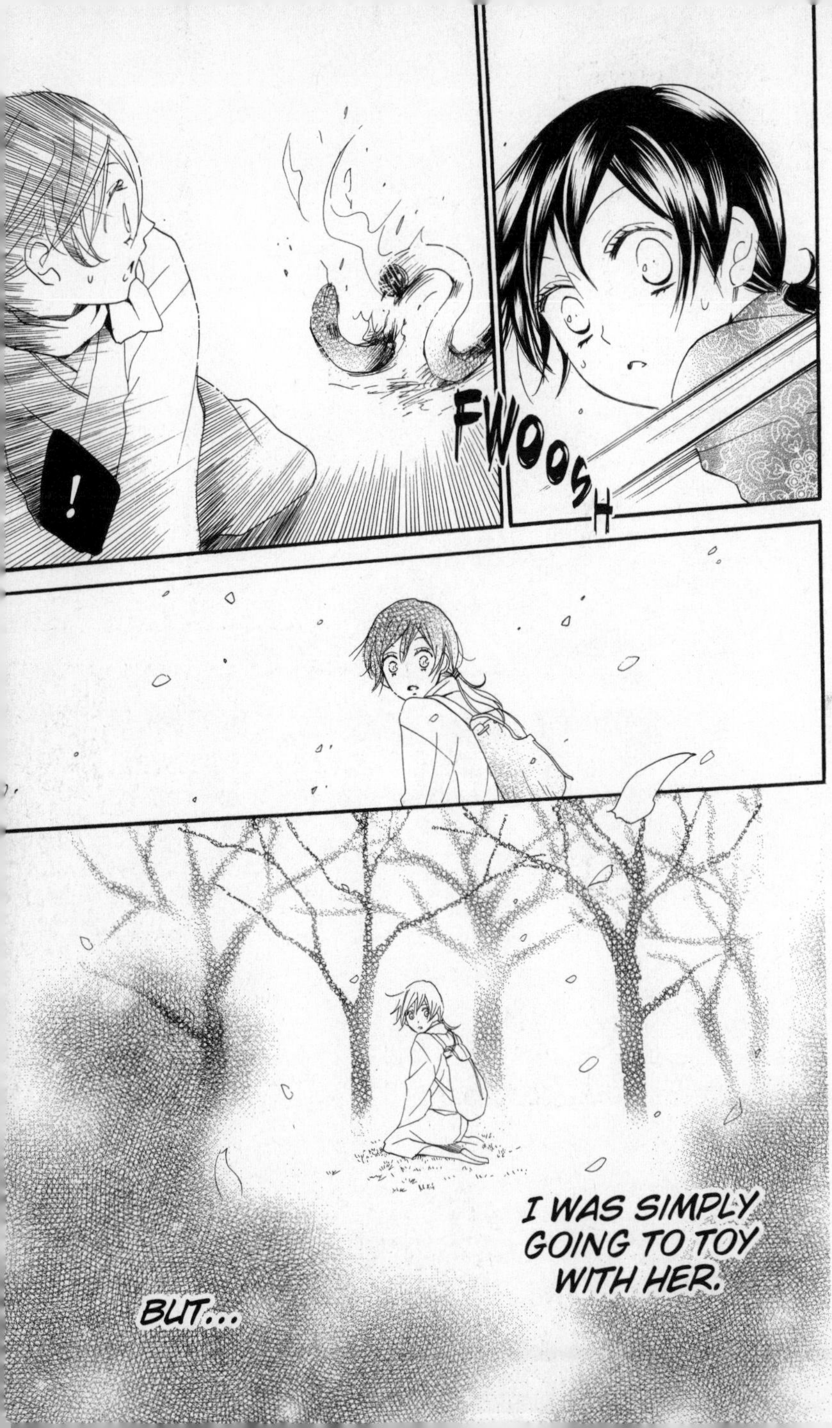
FWOOSH
!
I WAS SIMPLY GOING TO TOY WITH HER.
BUT...

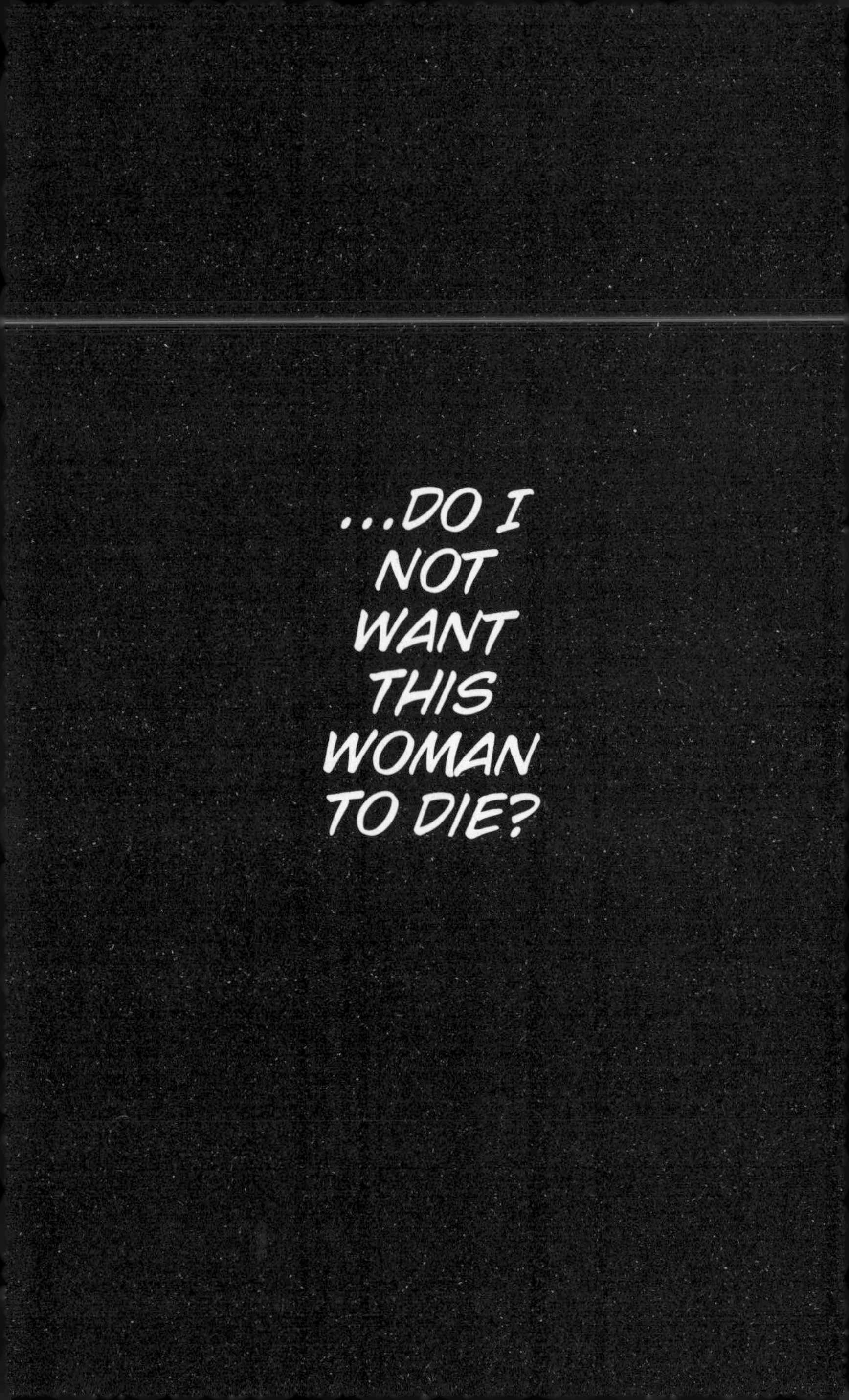
...DO I NOT WANT THIS WOMAN TO DIE?

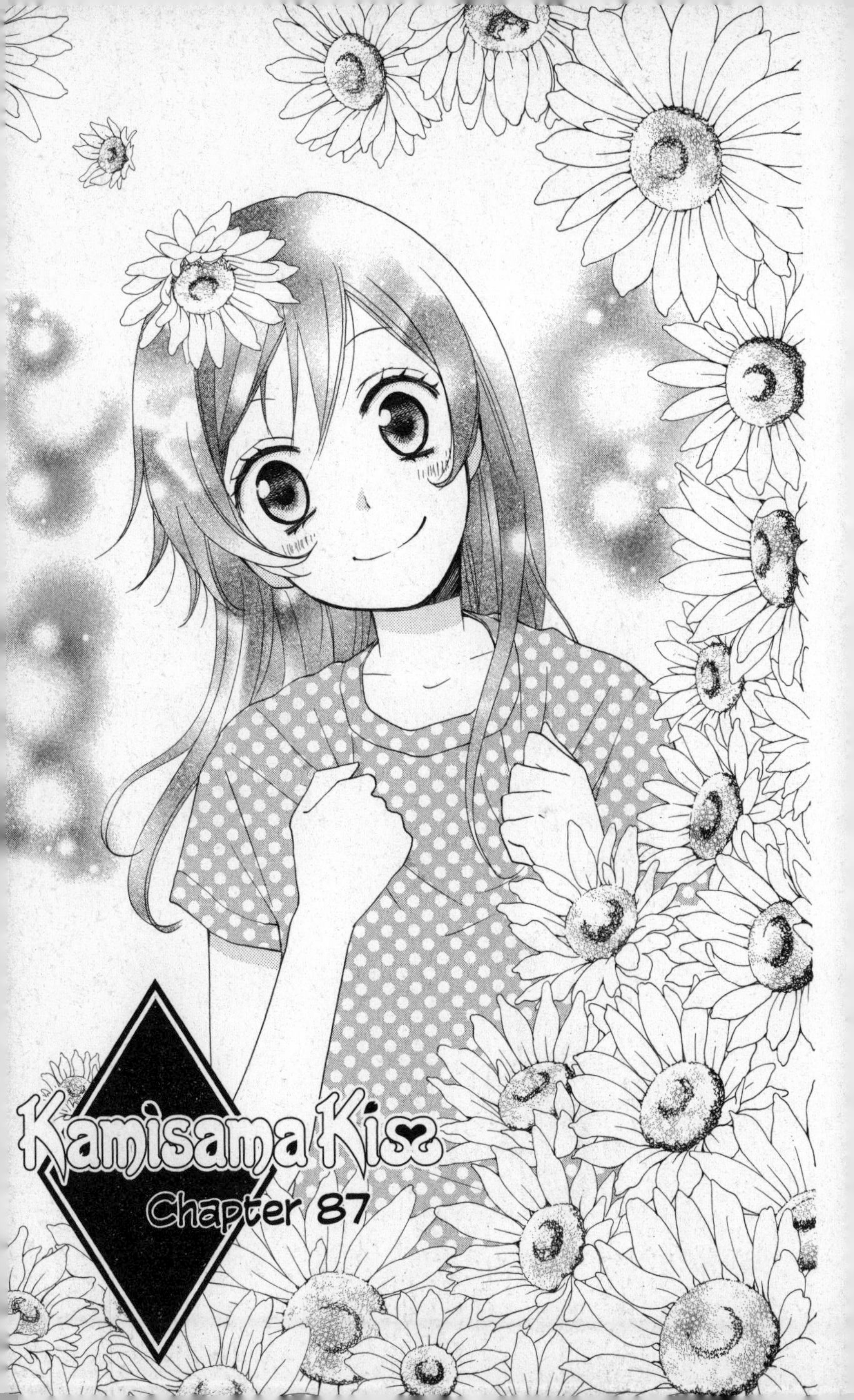
Kamisama Kiss
Chapter 87

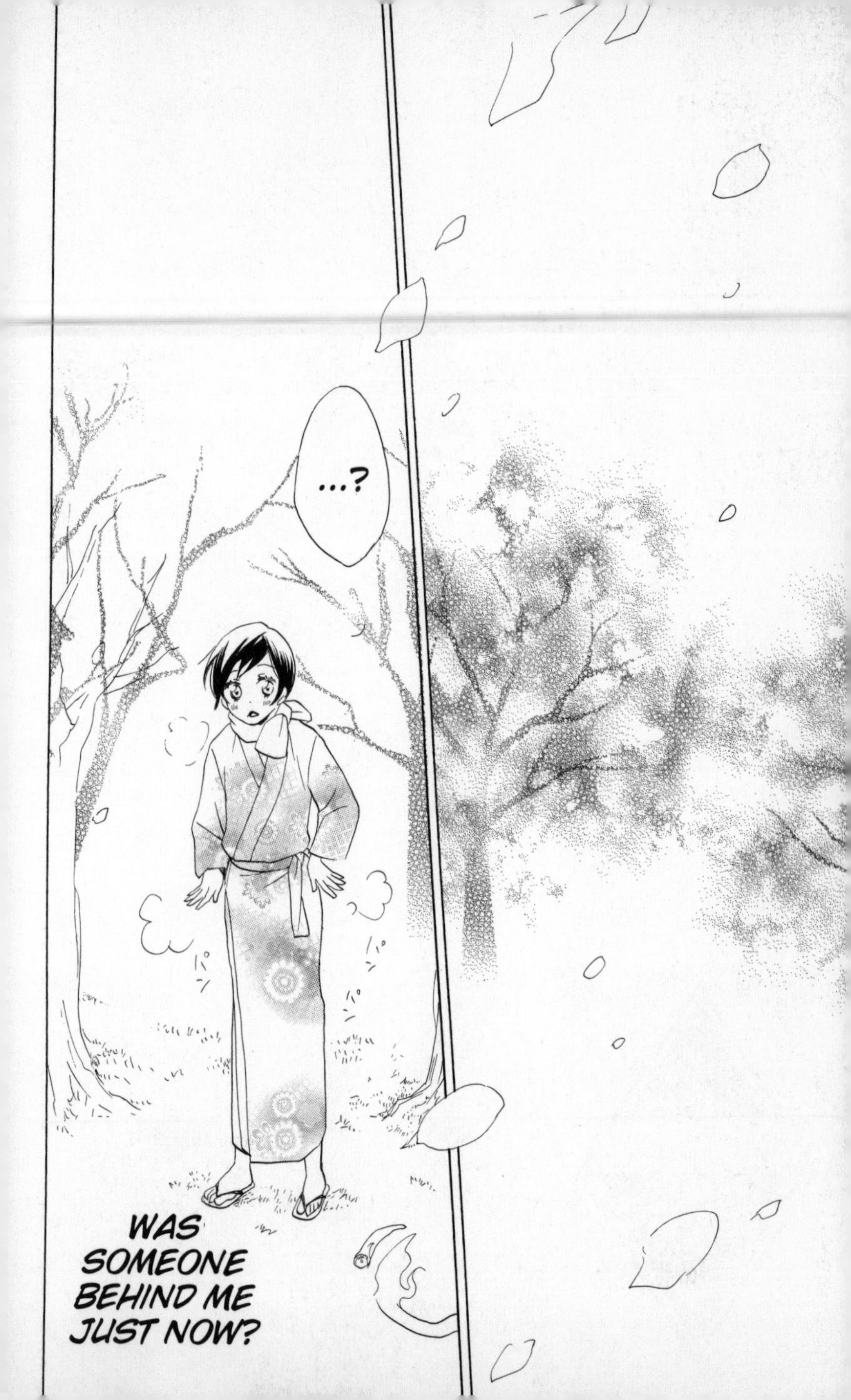
...?
WAS SOMEONE BEHIND ME JUST NOW?

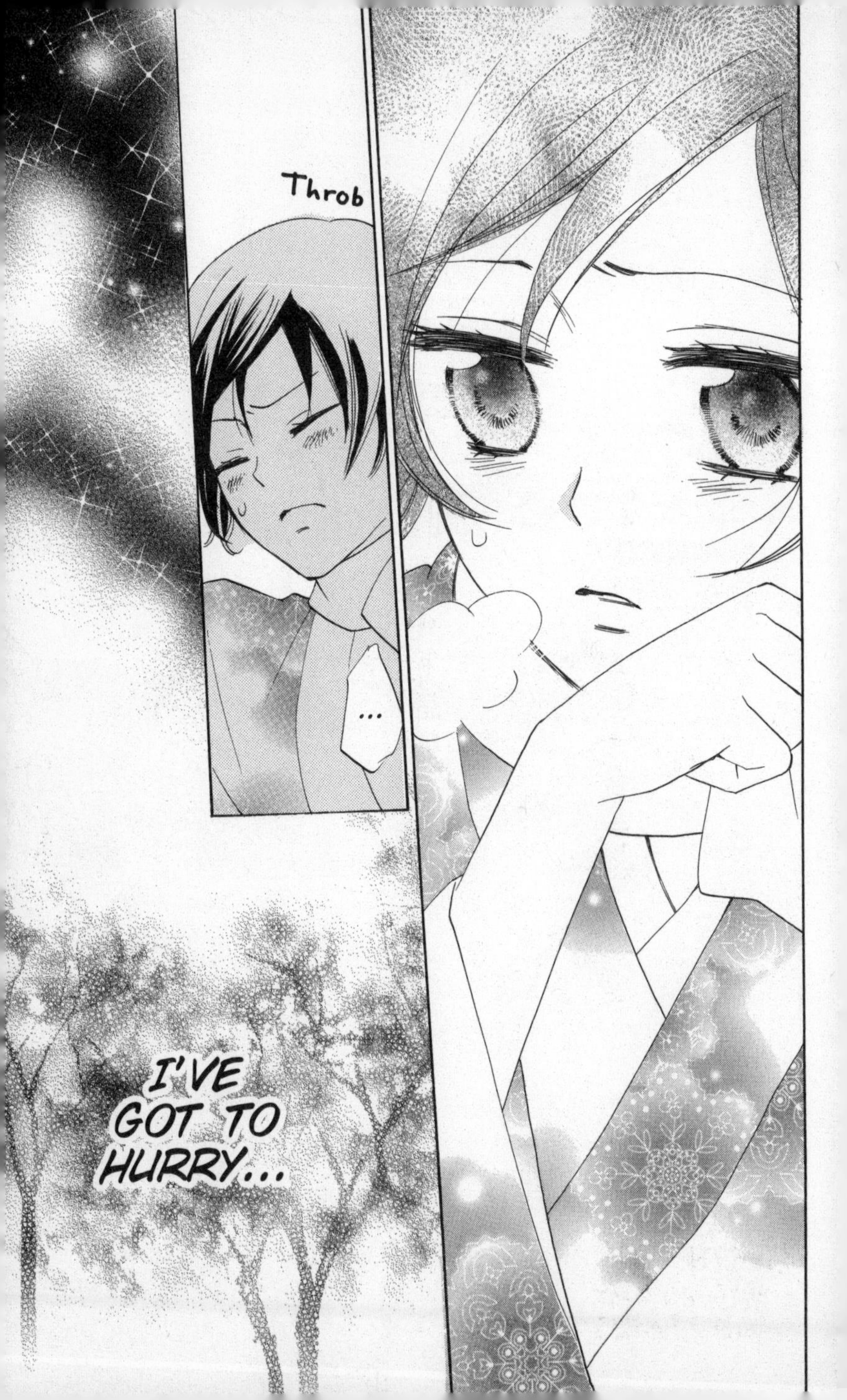
Throb
...
I'VE GOT TO HURRY...

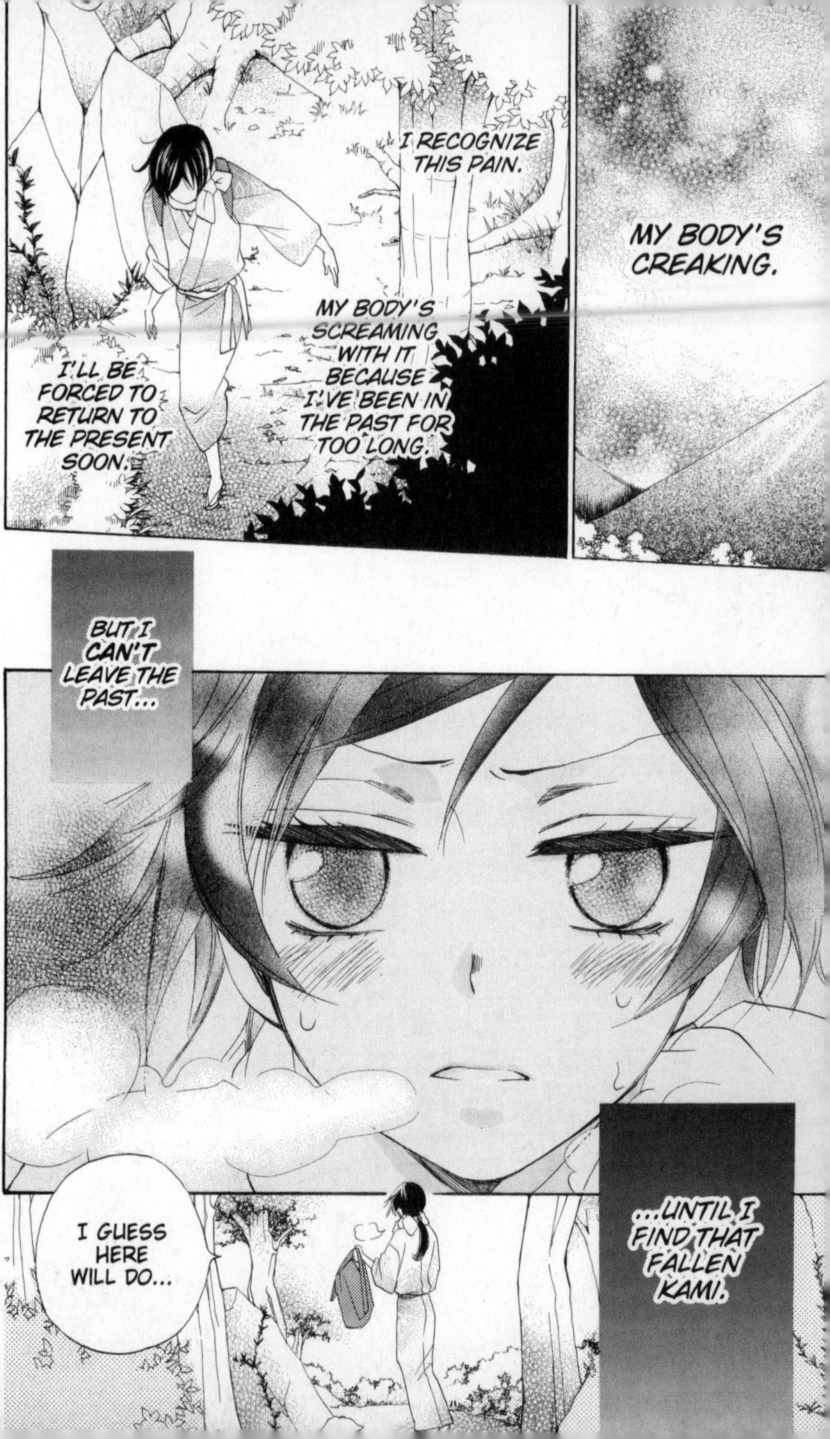
MY BODY'S CREAKING.
I RECOGNIZE THIS PAIN.
MY BODY'S SCREAMING WITH IT BECAUSE I'VE BEEN IN THE PAST FOR TOO LONG.
I'LL BE FORCED TO RETURN TO THE PRESENT SOON.
BUT I CAN'T LEAVE THE PAST...
...UNTIL I FIND THAT FALLEN KAMI.
I GUESS HERE WILL DO...

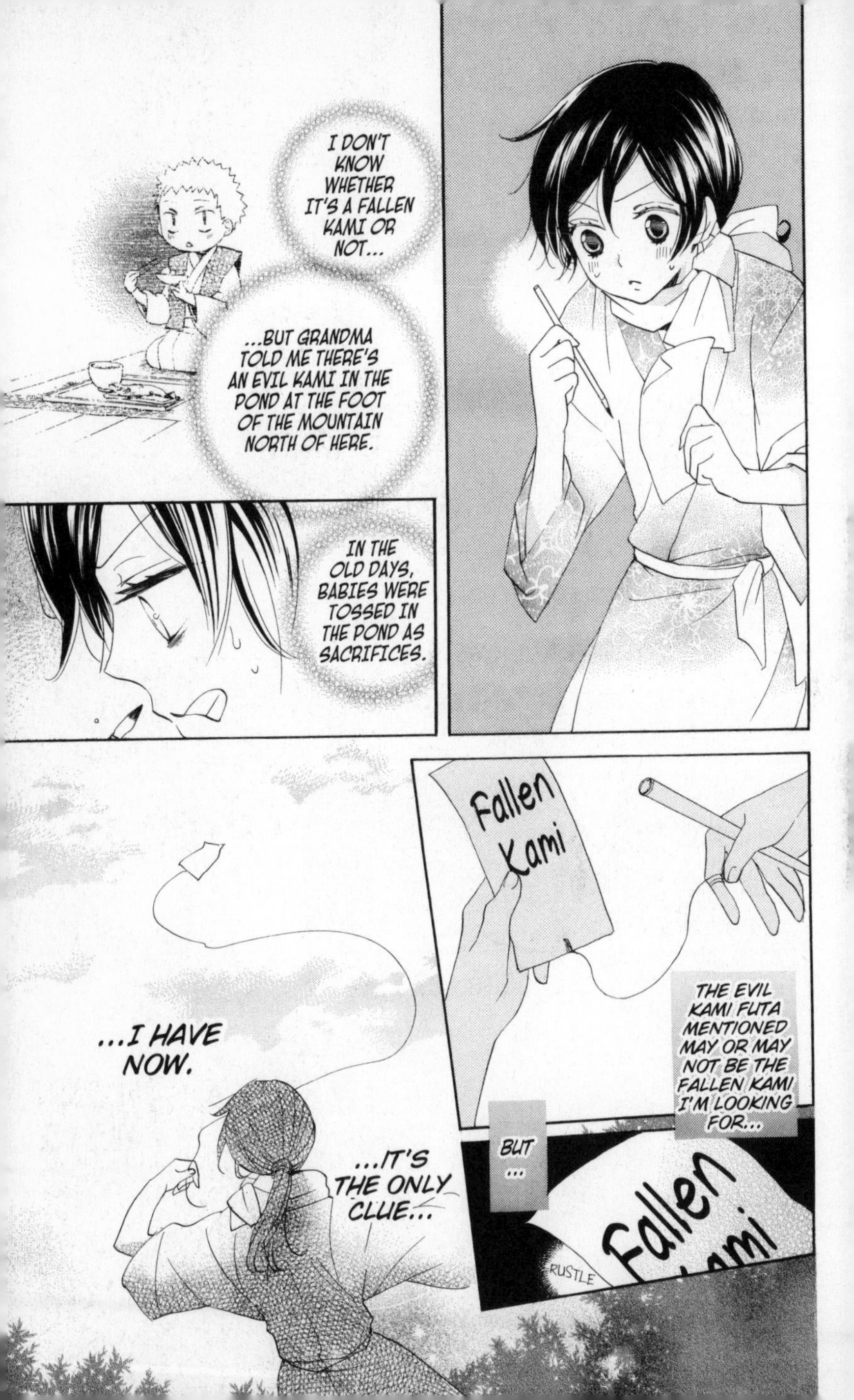
I DON'T KNOW WHETHER IT'S A FALLEN KAMI OR NOT...
...BUT GRANDMA TOLD ME THERE'S AN EVIL KAMI IN THE POND AT THE FOOT OF THE MOUNTAIN NORTH OF HERE.
IN THE OLD DAYS, BABIES WERE TOSSED IN THE POND AS SACRIFICES.
Fallen Kami
THE EVIL KAMI FUTA MENTIONED MAY OR MAY NOT BE THE FALLEN KAMI I'M LOOKING FOR...
BUT...
Fallen Kami
RUSTLE
...IT'S THE ONLY CLUE...
...I HAVE NOW.

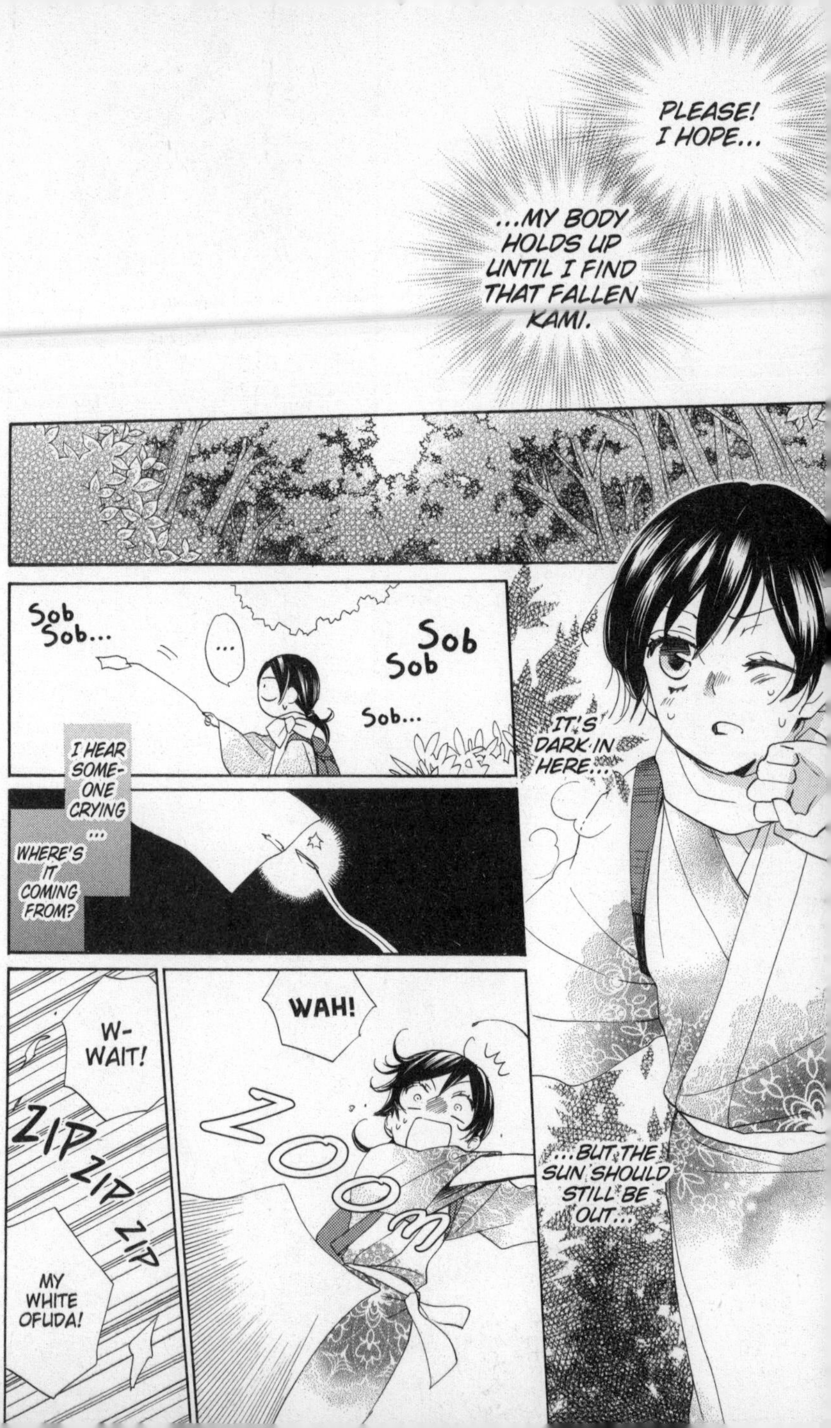
PLEASE! I HOPE...
...MY BODY HOLDS UP UNTIL I FIND THAT FALLEN KAMI.
IT'S DARK IN HERE...
...BUT THE SUN SHOULD STILL BE OUT...
Sob Sob
...
Sob Sob...
Sob...
I HEAR SOMEONE CRYING...
WHERE'S IT COMING FROM?
WAH!
ZOOM
W-WAIT!
ZIP ZIP ZIP
MY WHITE OFUDA!

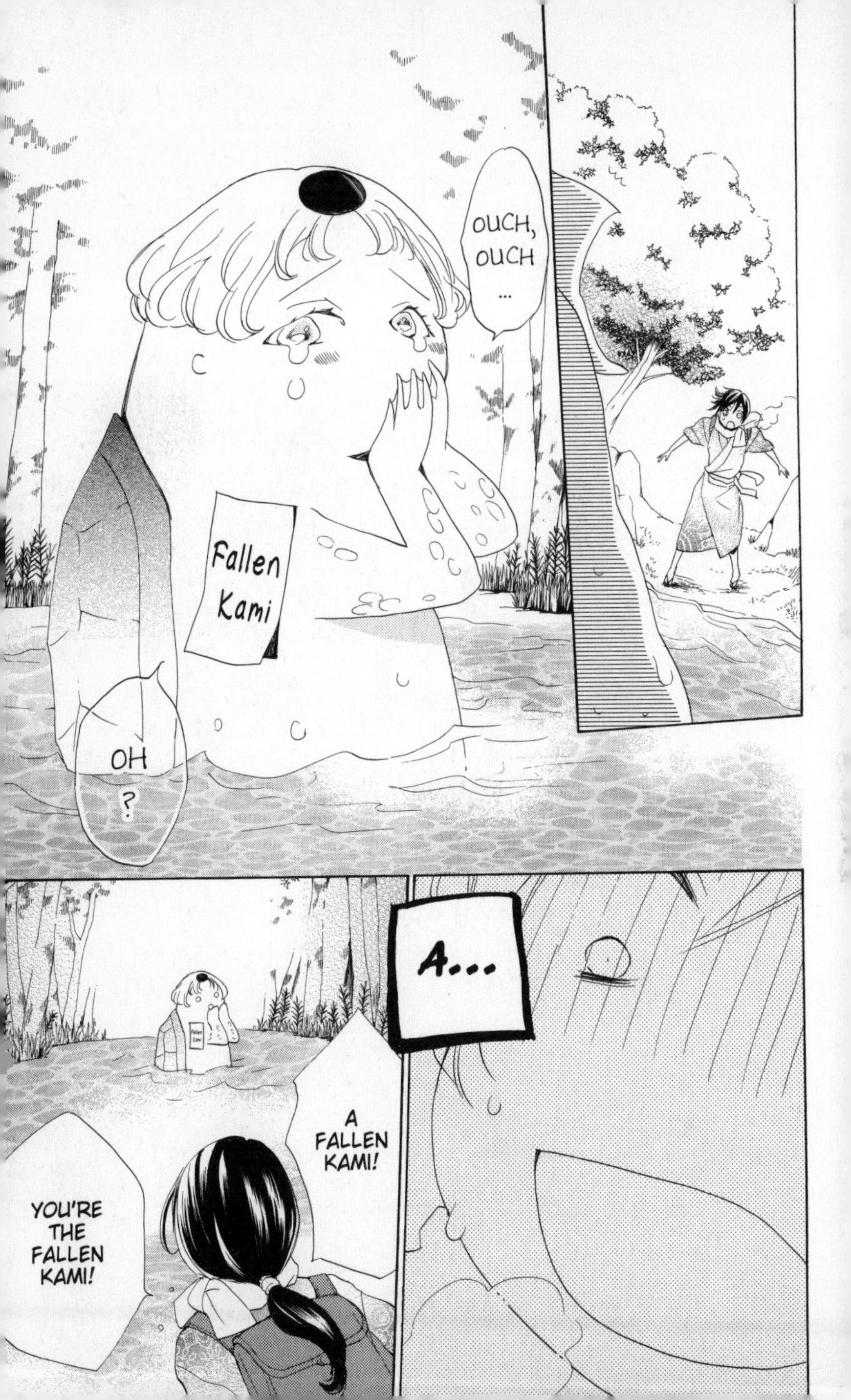
OUCH, OUCH ...
Fallen Kami
OH ?
A...
A FALLEN KAMI!
YOU'RE THE FALLEN KAMI!

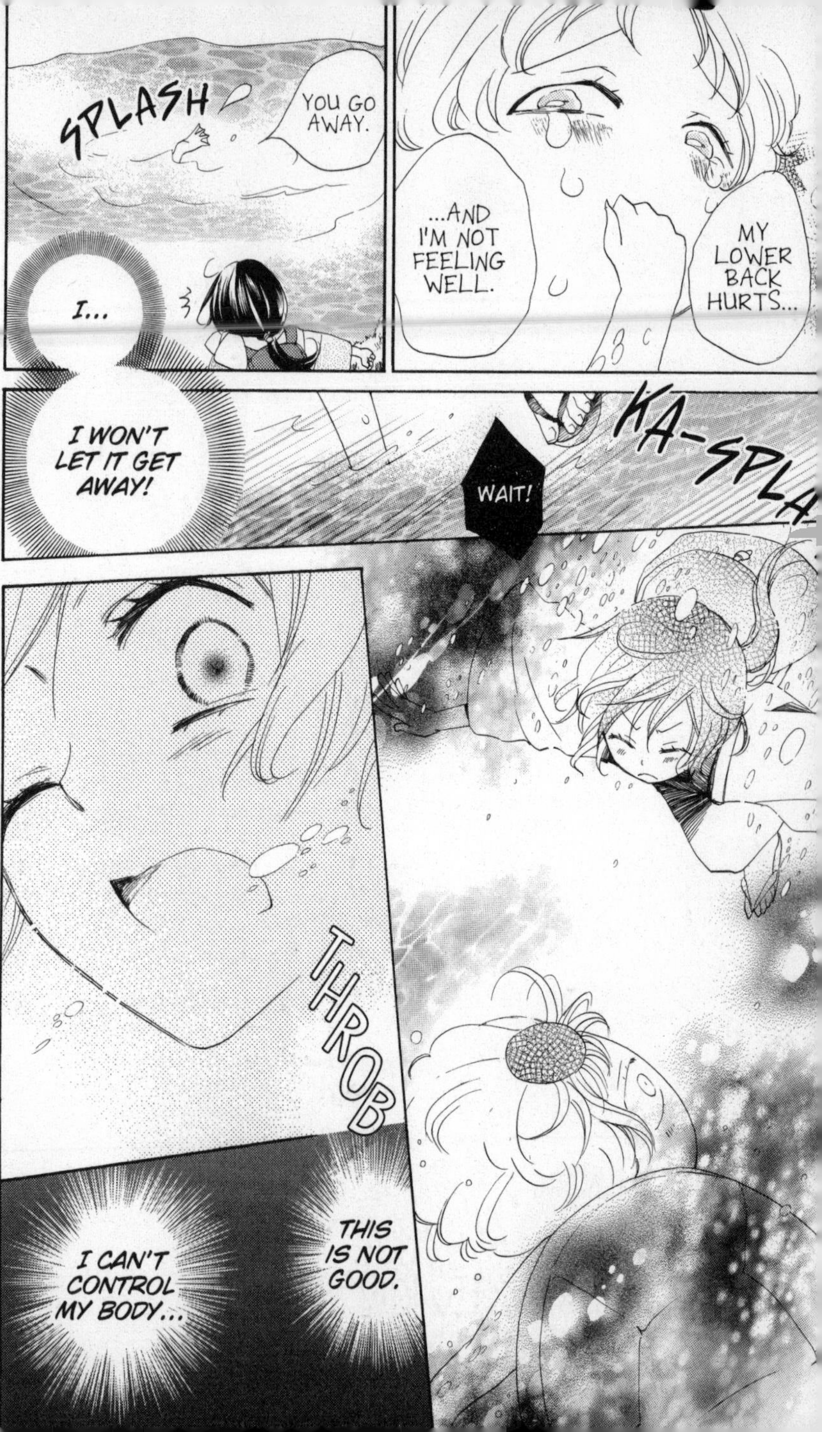
MY LOWER BACK HURTS...
...AND I'M NOT FEELING WELL.
YOU GO AWAY.
SPLASH
I...
KA-SPLA
WAIT!
I WON'T LET IT GET AWAY!
THROB
THIS IS NOT GOOD.
I CAN'T CONTROL MY BODY...

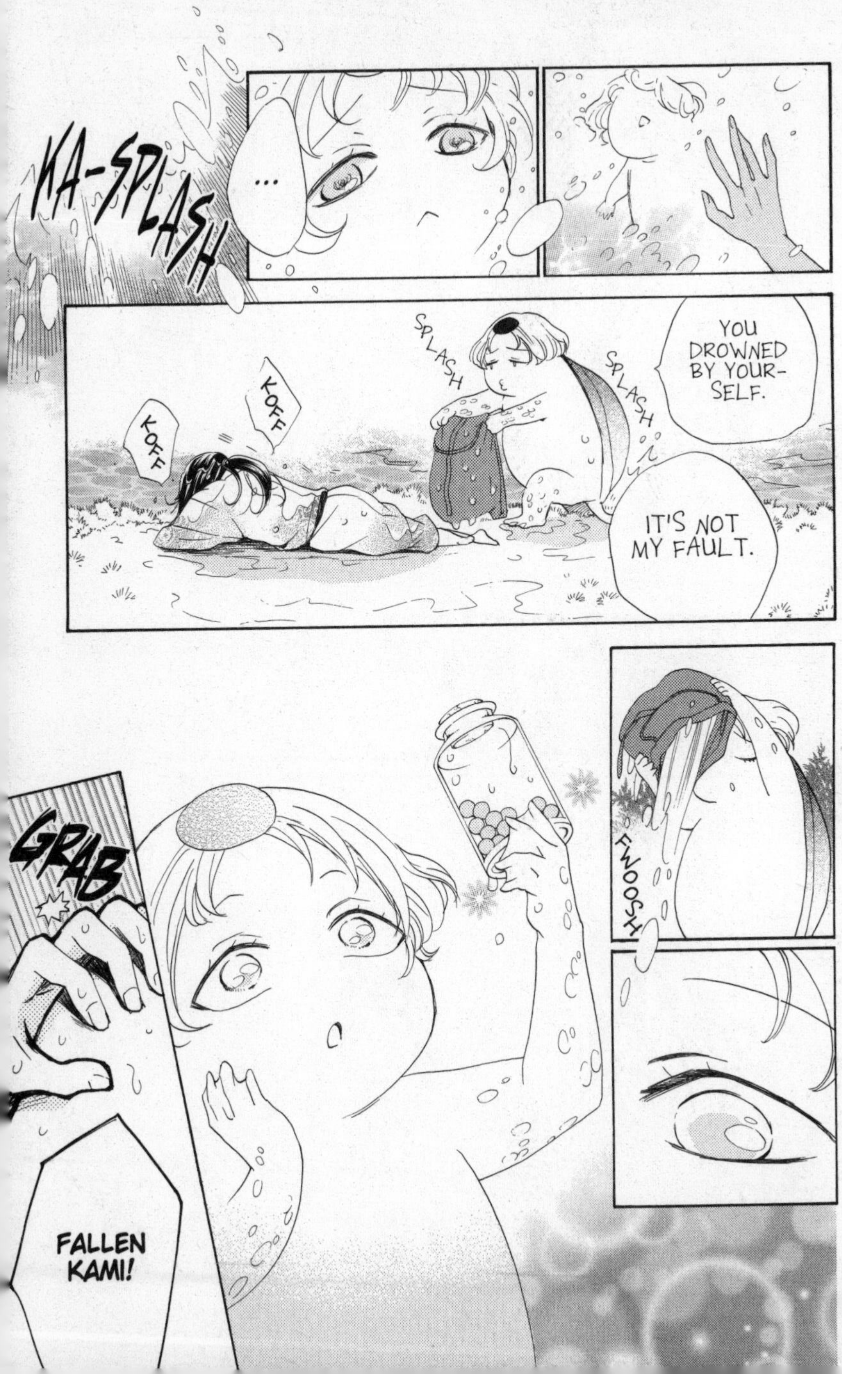
KA-SPLASH
...
YOU DROWNED BY YOUR-SELF.
IT'S NOT MY FAULT.
SPLASH
SPLASH
KOFF
KOFF
FWOOSH
GRAB
FALLEN KAMI!

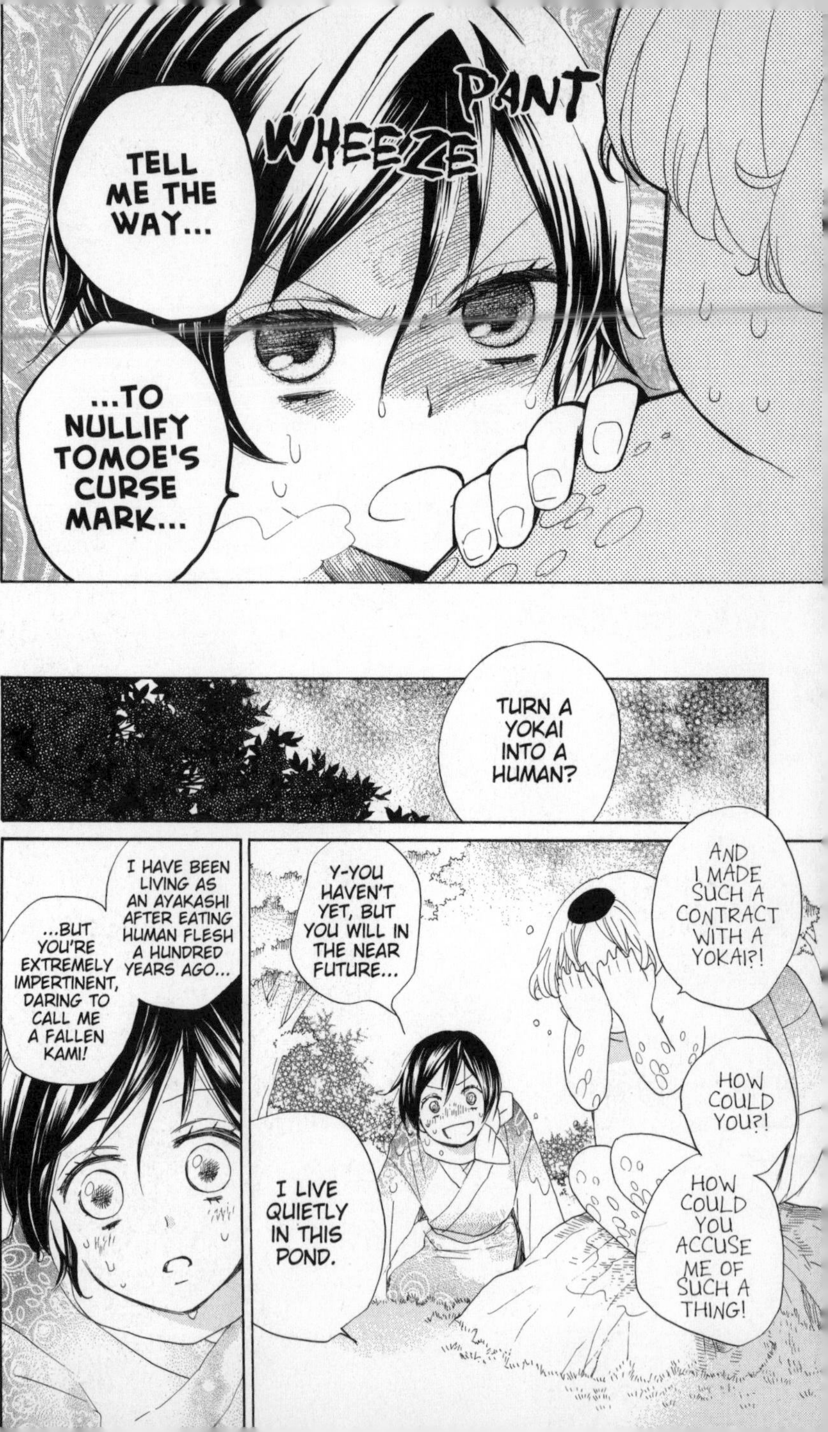
PANT
WHEEZE
TELL ME THE WAY...
...TO NULLIFY TOMOE'S CURSE MARK...
TURN A YOKAI INTO A HUMAN?
AND I MADE SUCH A CONTRACT WITH A YOKAI?!
Y-YOU HAVEN'T YET, BUT YOU WILL IN THE NEAR FUTURE...
HOW COULD YOU?!
HOW COULD YOU ACCUSE ME OF SUCH A THING!
I LIVE QUIETLY IN THIS POND.
I HAVE BEEN LIVING AS AN AYAKASHI AFTER EATING HUMAN FLESH A HUNDRED YEARS AGO...
...BUT YOU'RE EXTREMELY IMPERTINENT, DARING TO CALL ME A FALLEN KAMI!

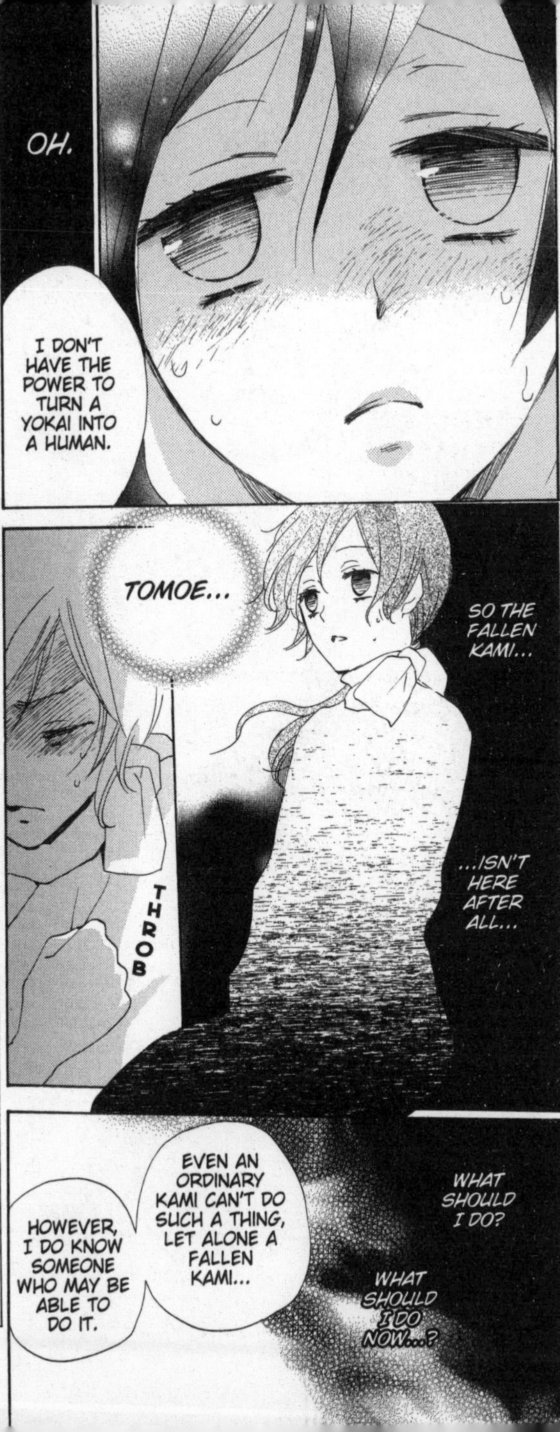
OH.
I DON'T HAVE THE POWER TO TURN A YOKAI INTO A HUMAN.
SO THE FALLEN KAMI...
...ISN'T HERE AFTER ALL...
TOMOE...
THROB
WHAT SHOULD I DO?
WHAT SHOULD I DO NOW...?
EVEN AN ORDINARY KAMI CAN'T DO SUCH A THING, LET ALONE A FALLEN KAMI...
HOWEVER, I DO KNOW SOMEONE WHO MAY BE ABLE TO DO IT.

Since last year, I've been saying that I'll go to Disneyland, but I haven't yet..

I can't fit a visit into my schedule.

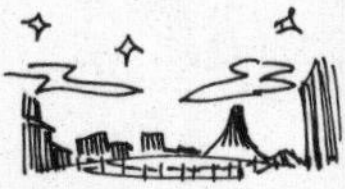

My editor went to some flea markets in London...

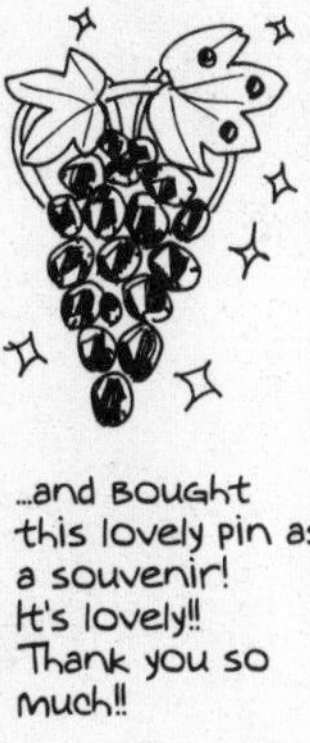

...and bought this lovely pin as a souvenir! It's lovely!! Thank you so much!!

Thank you for the chocolates too!

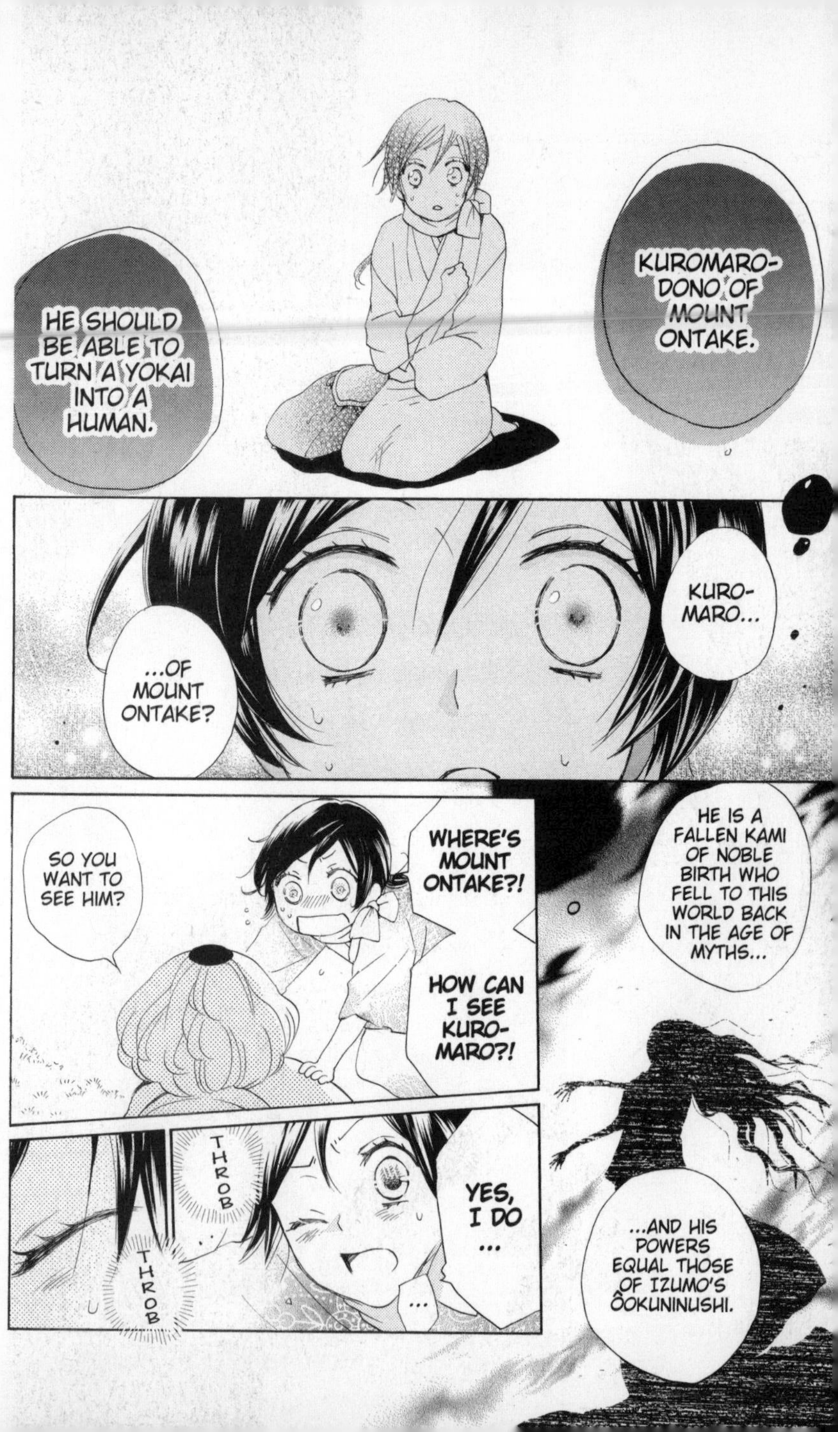
KUROMARO-DONO OF MOUNT ONTAKE.
HE SHOULD BE ABLE TO TURN A YOKAI INTO A HUMAN.
KURO-MARO...
...OF MOUNT ONTAKE?
HE IS A FALLEN KAMI OF NOBLE BIRTH WHO FELL TO THIS WORLD BACK IN THE AGE OF MYTHS...
...AND HIS POWERS EQUAL THOSE OF IZUMO'S ÔOKUNINUSHI.
WHERE'S MOUNT ONTAKE?!
HOW CAN I SEE KURO-MARO?!
SO YOU WANT TO SEE HIM?
YES, I DO ...
THROB
THROB
...

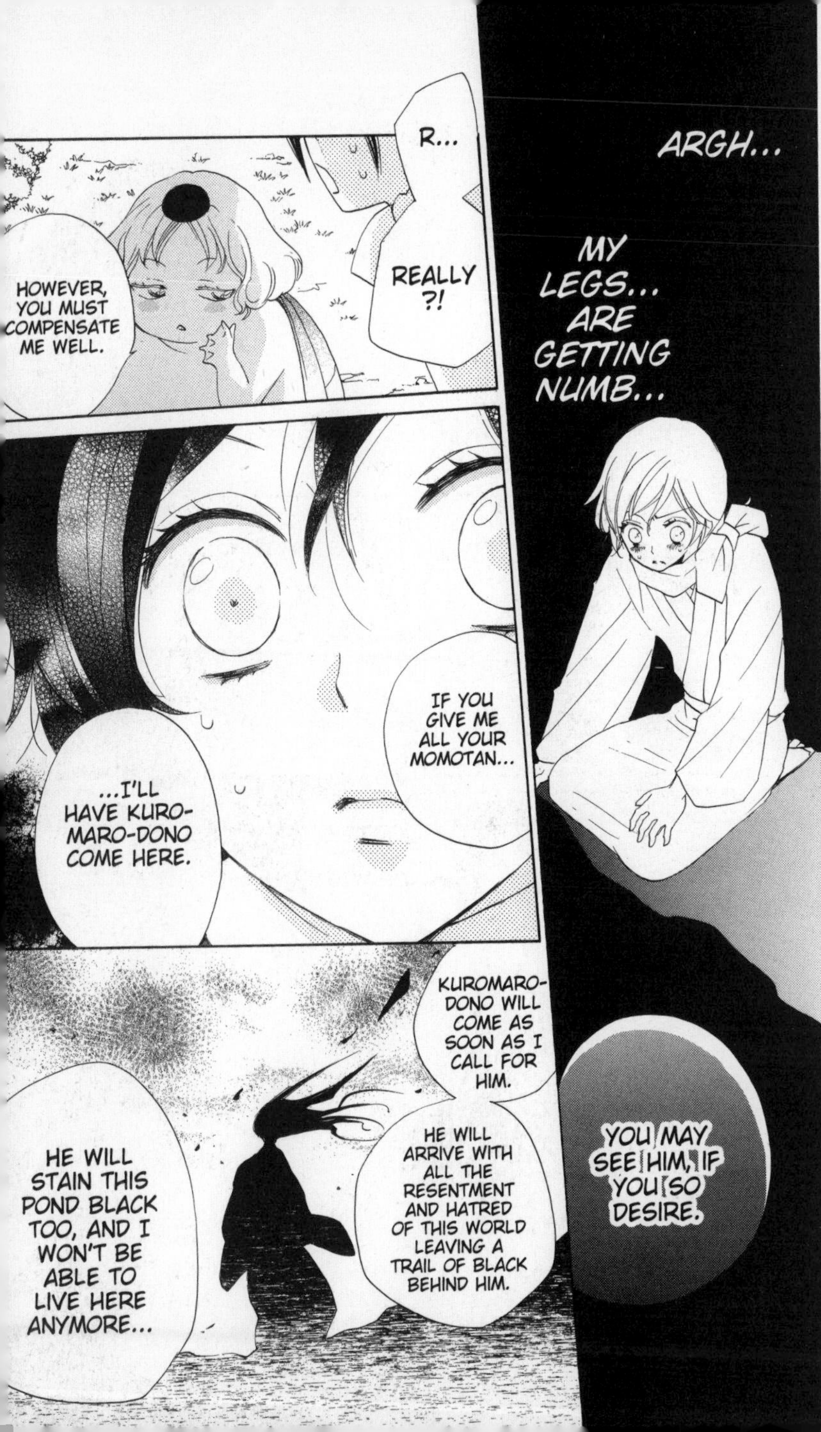
ARGH...
MY LEGS... ARE GETTING NUMB...
YOU MAY SEE HIM, IF YOU SO DESIRE.
HOWEVER, YOU MUST COMPENSATE ME WELL.
R...
REALLY ?!
IF YOU GIVE ME ALL YOUR MOMOTAN...
...I'LL HAVE KURO-MARO-DONO COME HERE.
KUROMARO-DONO WILL COME AS SOON AS I CALL FOR HIM.
HE WILL ARRIVE WITH ALL THE RESENTMENT AND HATRED OF THIS WORLD LEAVING A TRAIL OF BLACK BEHIND HIM.
HE WILL STAIN THIS POND BLACK TOO, AND I WON'T BE ABLE TO LIVE HERE ANYMORE...

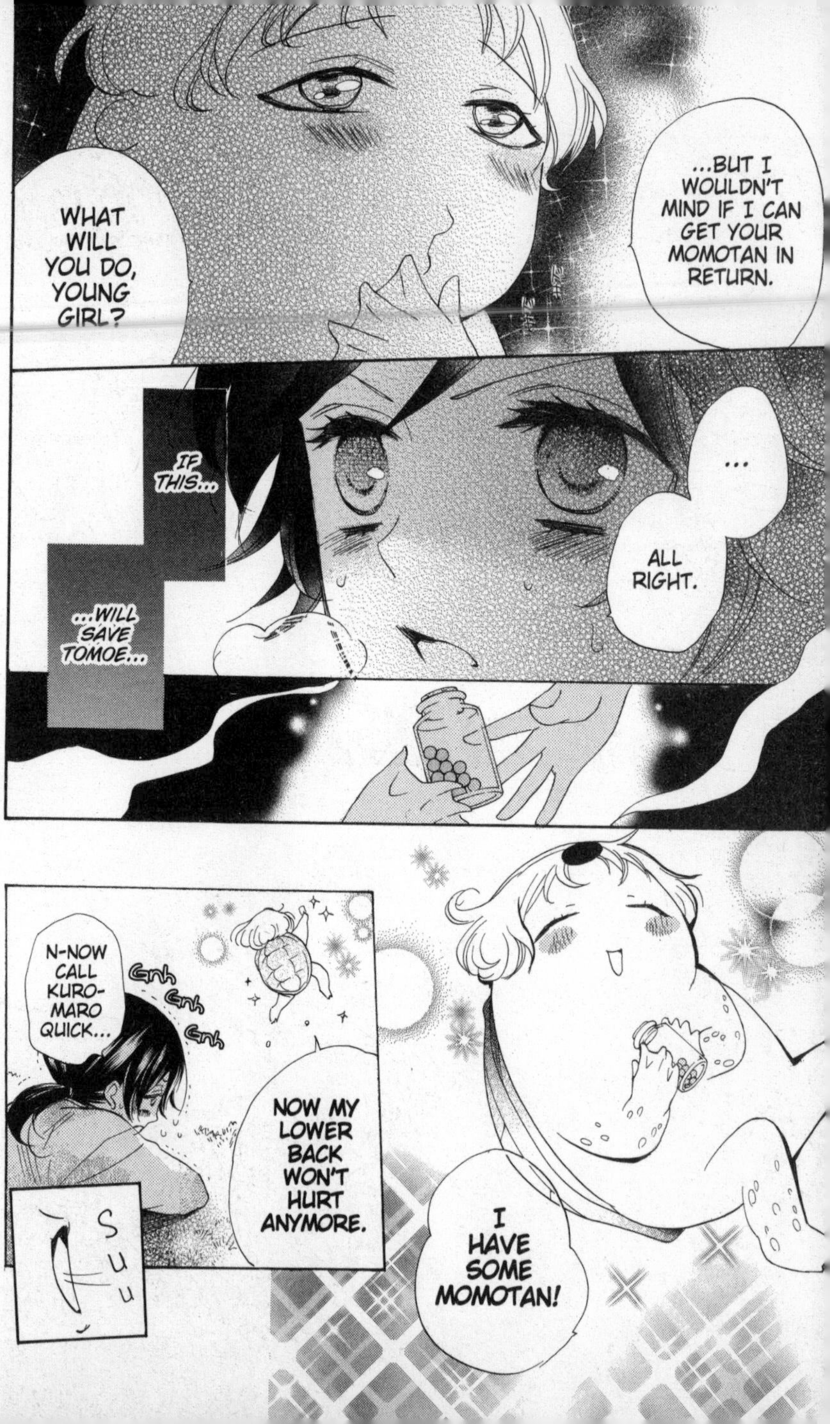
...BUT I WOULDN'T MIND IF I CAN GET YOUR MOMOTAN IN RETURN.
WHAT WILL YOU DO, YOUNG GIRL?
...
ALL RIGHT.
IF THIS...
...WILL SAVE TOMOE...
I HAVE SOME MOMOTAN!
NOW MY LOWER BACK WON'T HURT ANYMORE.
N-NOW CALL KURO-MARO QUICK...
Gnh
Gnh
Gnh
Suu

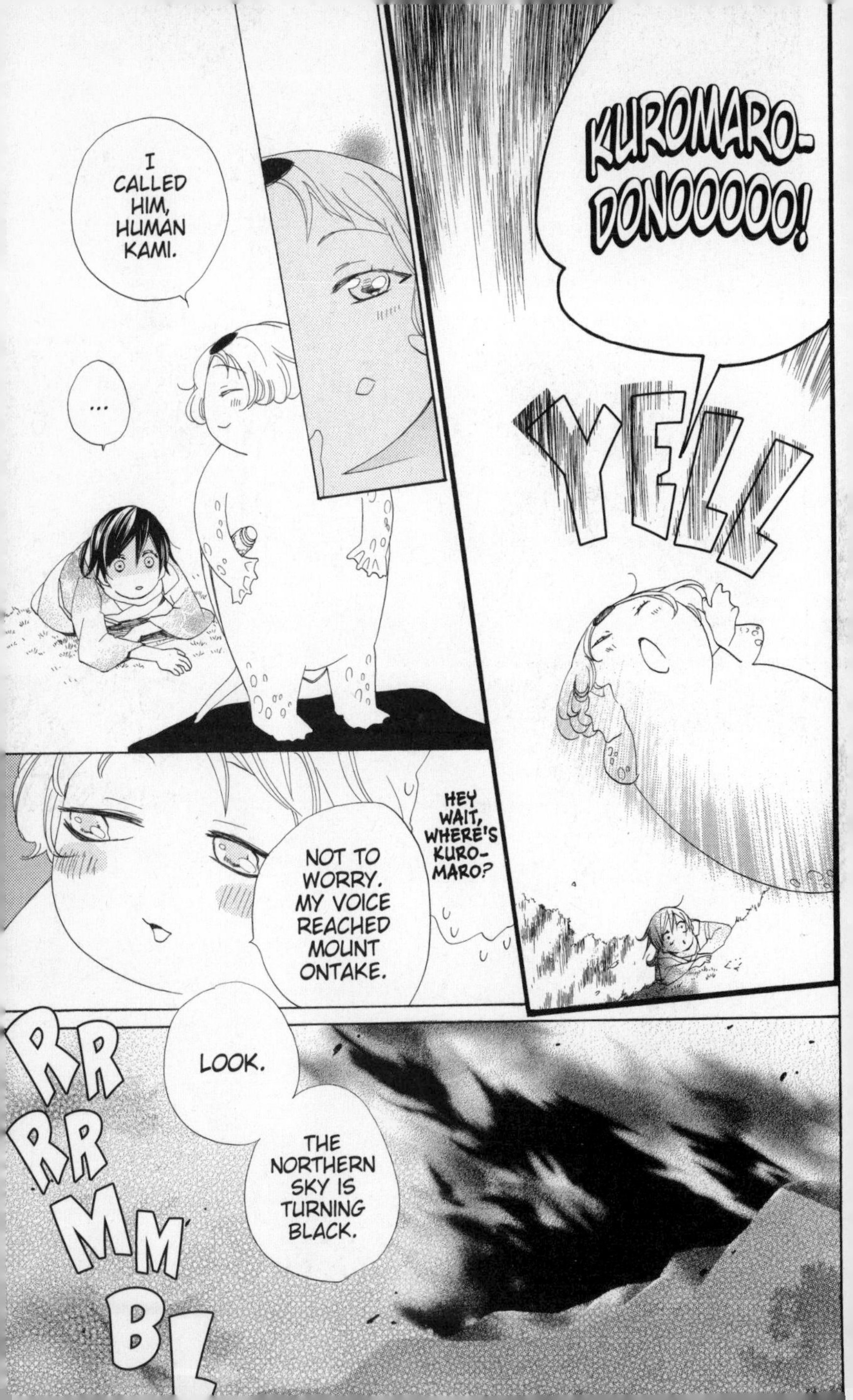
KUROMARO-DONOOOOOO!
YELL
HEY WAIT, WHERE'S KURO-MARO?
I CALLED HIM, HUMAN KAMI.
...
NOT TO WORRY. MY VOICE REACHED MOUNT ONTAKE.
RRRRMMM'BL
LOOK.
THE NORTHERN SKY IS TURNING BLACK.

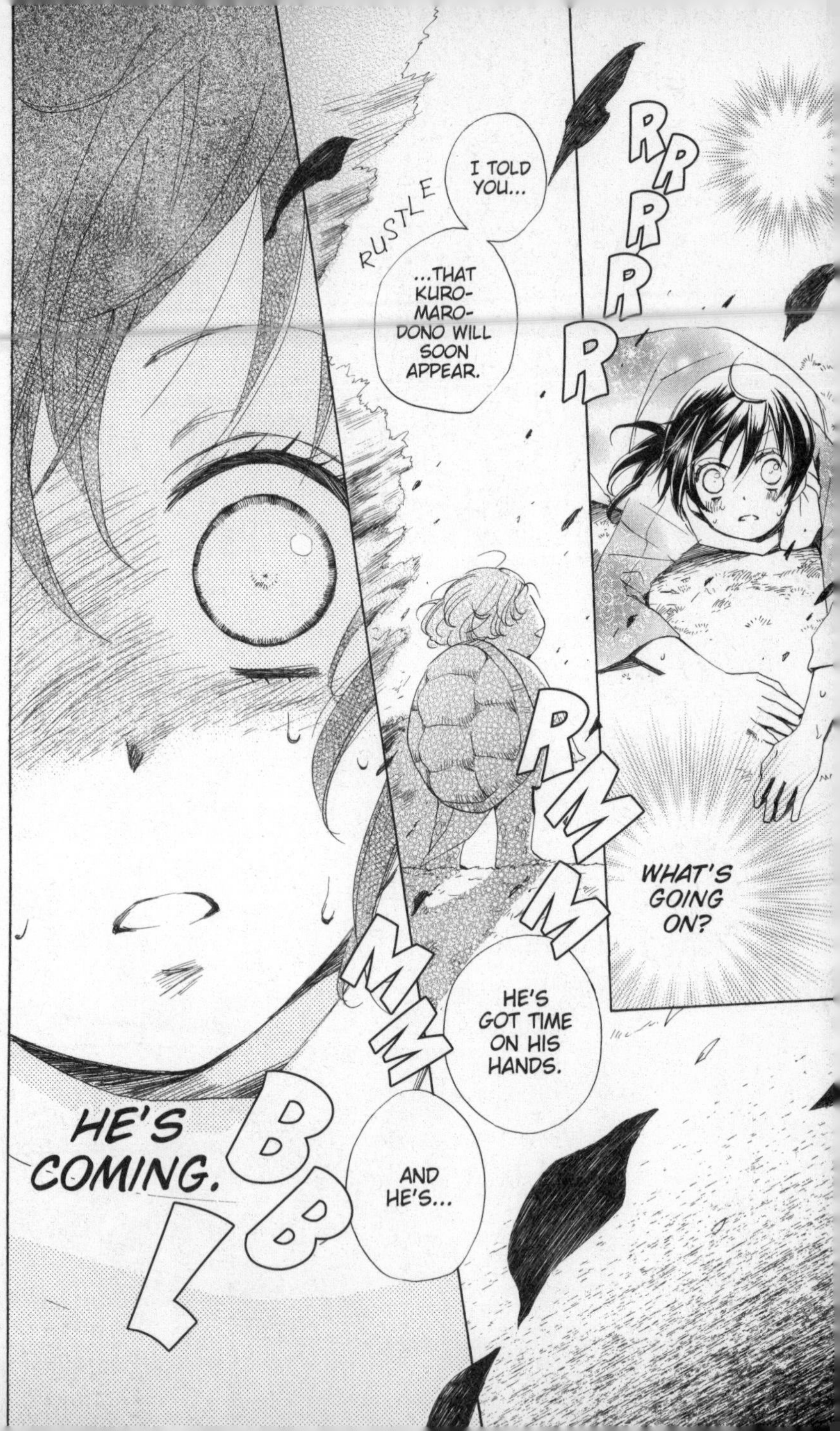
RRRRR
WHAT'S GOING ON?
RUSTLE
I TOLD YOU...
...THAT KURO-MARO-DONO WILL SOON APPEAR.
RMMMMMBBL
HE'S GOT TIME ON HIS HANDS.
AND HE'S...
HE'S COMING.

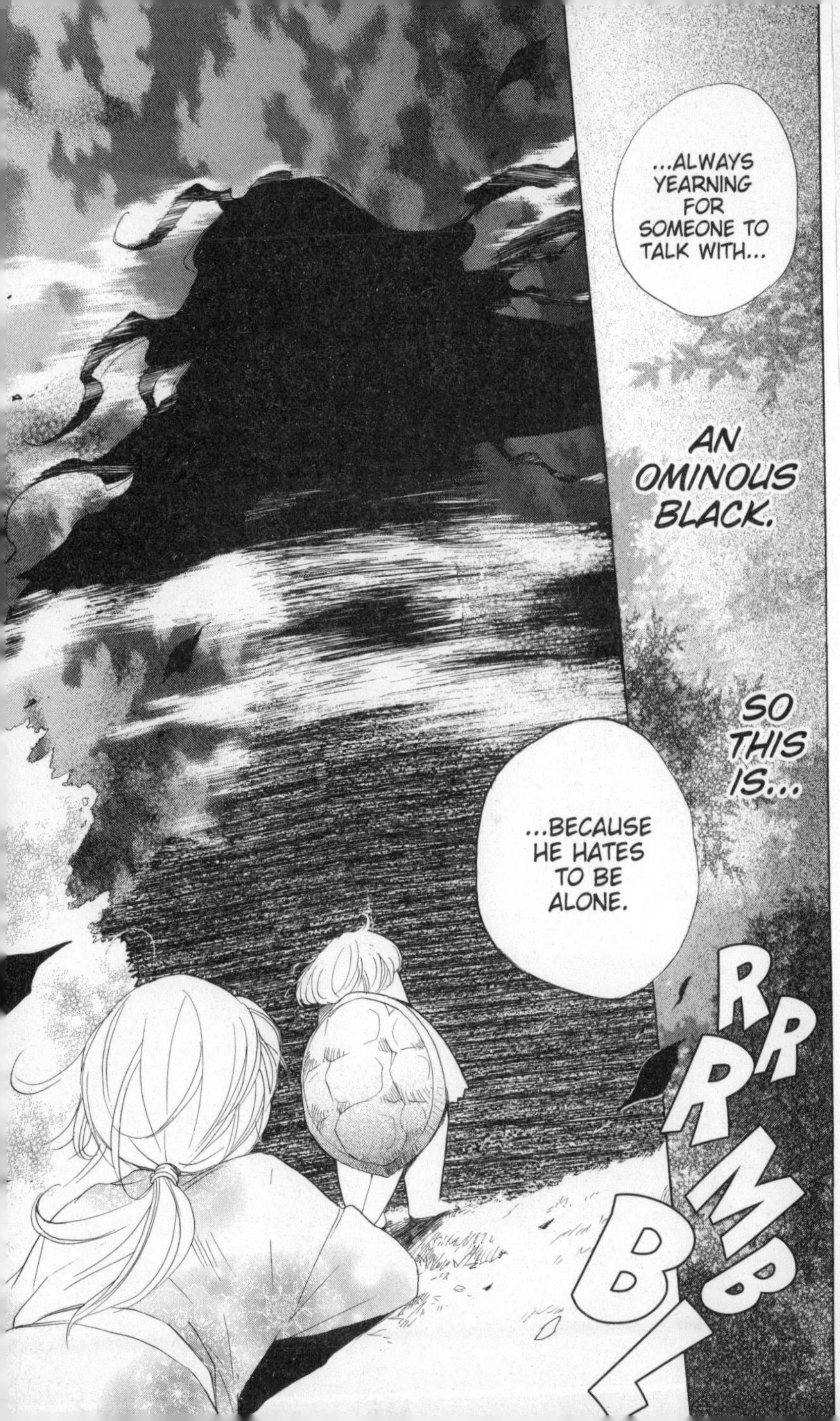
...ALWAYS YEARNING FOR SOMEONE TO TALK WITH...
AN OMINOUS BLACK.
SO THIS IS...
...BECAUSE HE HATES TO BE ALONE.
RRRMBL

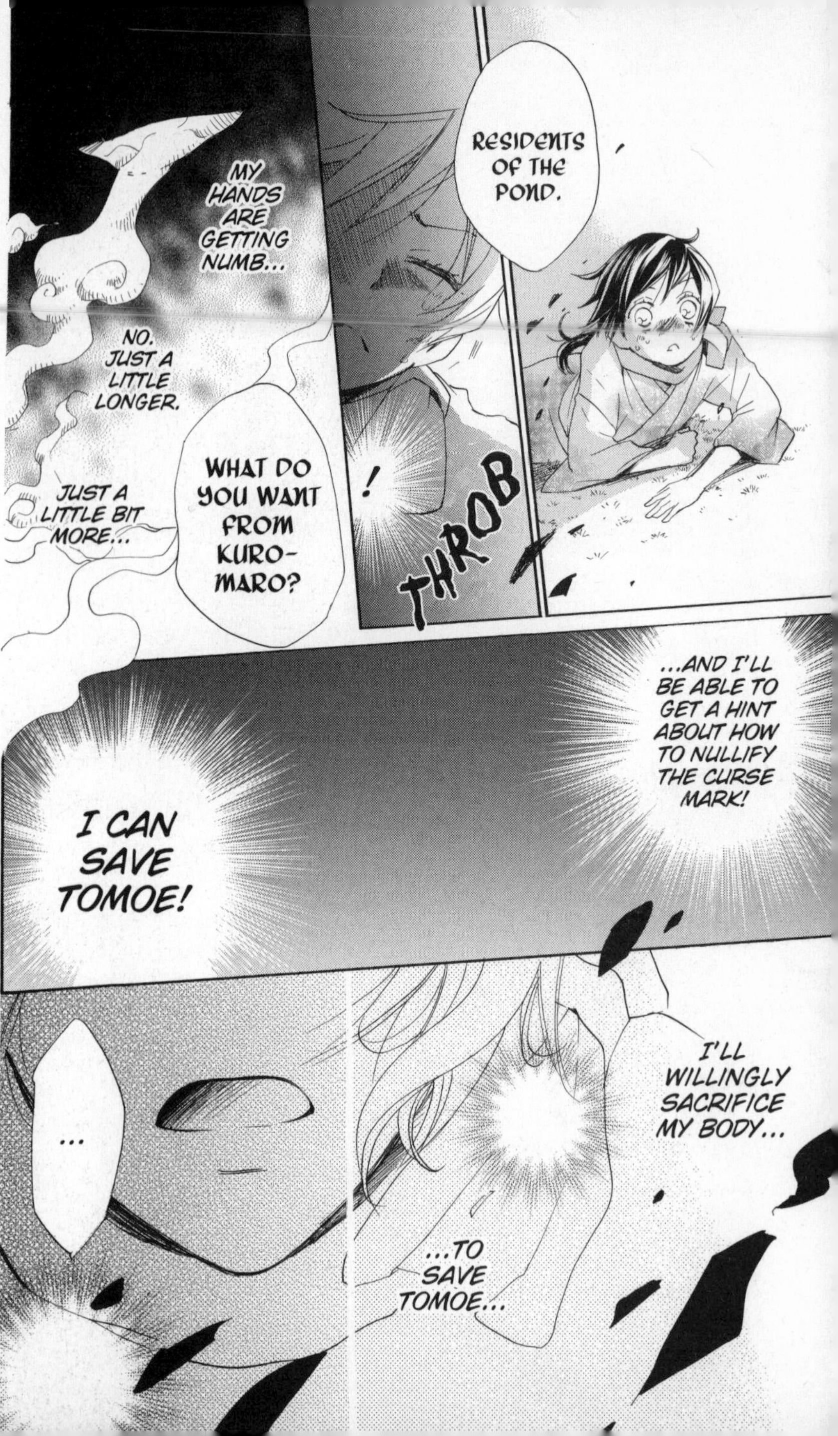
RESIDENTS OF THE POND.
!
THROB
MY HANDS ARE GETTING NUMB...
WHAT DO YOU WANT FROM KURO-MARO?
NO. JUST A LITTLE LONGER.
JUST A LITTLE BIT MORE...
...AND I'LL BE ABLE TO GET A HINT ABOUT HOW TO NULLIFY THE CURSE MARK!
I CAN SAVE TOMOE!
I'LL WILLINGLY SACRIFICE MY BODY...
...TO SAVE TOMOE...
...

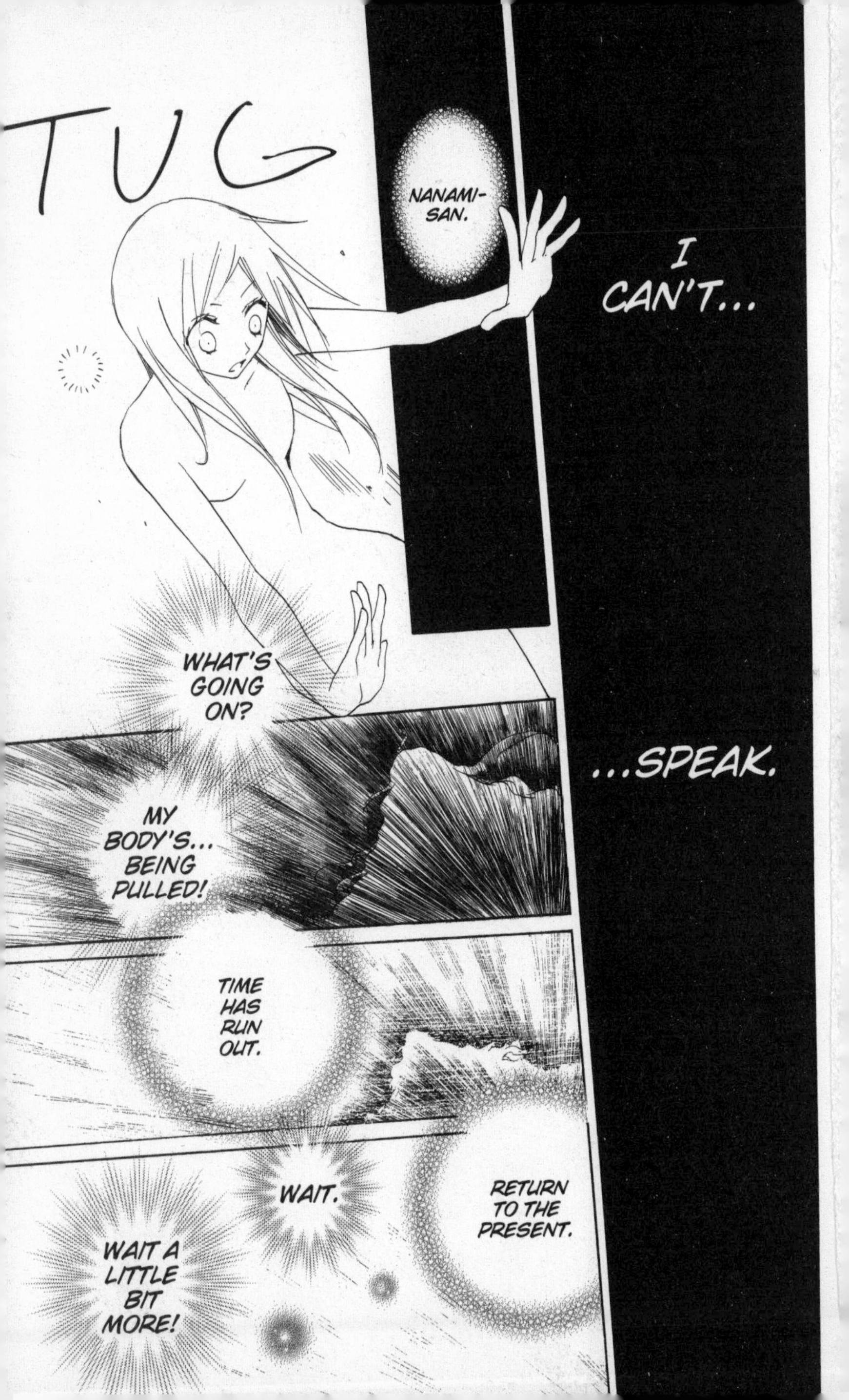
NANAMI-SAN.
I CAN'T...
TUG
...SPEAK.
WHAT'S GOING ON?
MY BODY'S... BEING PULLED!
TIME HAS RUN OUT.
RETURN TO THE PRESENT.
WAIT.
WAIT A LITTLE BIT MORE!

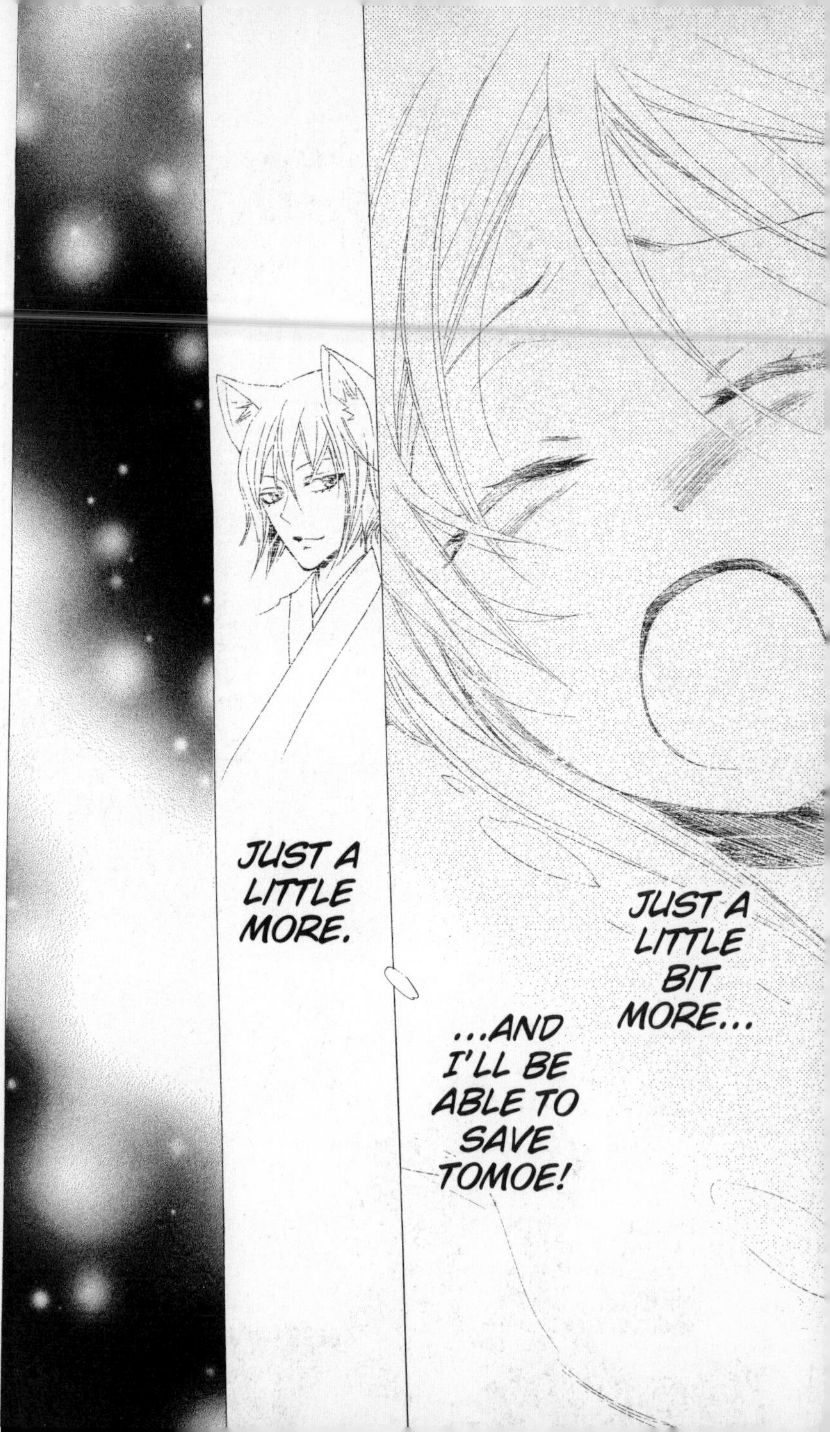
JUST A LITTLE BIT MORE...
...AND I'LL BE ABLE TO SAVE TOMOE!
JUST A LITTLE MORE.

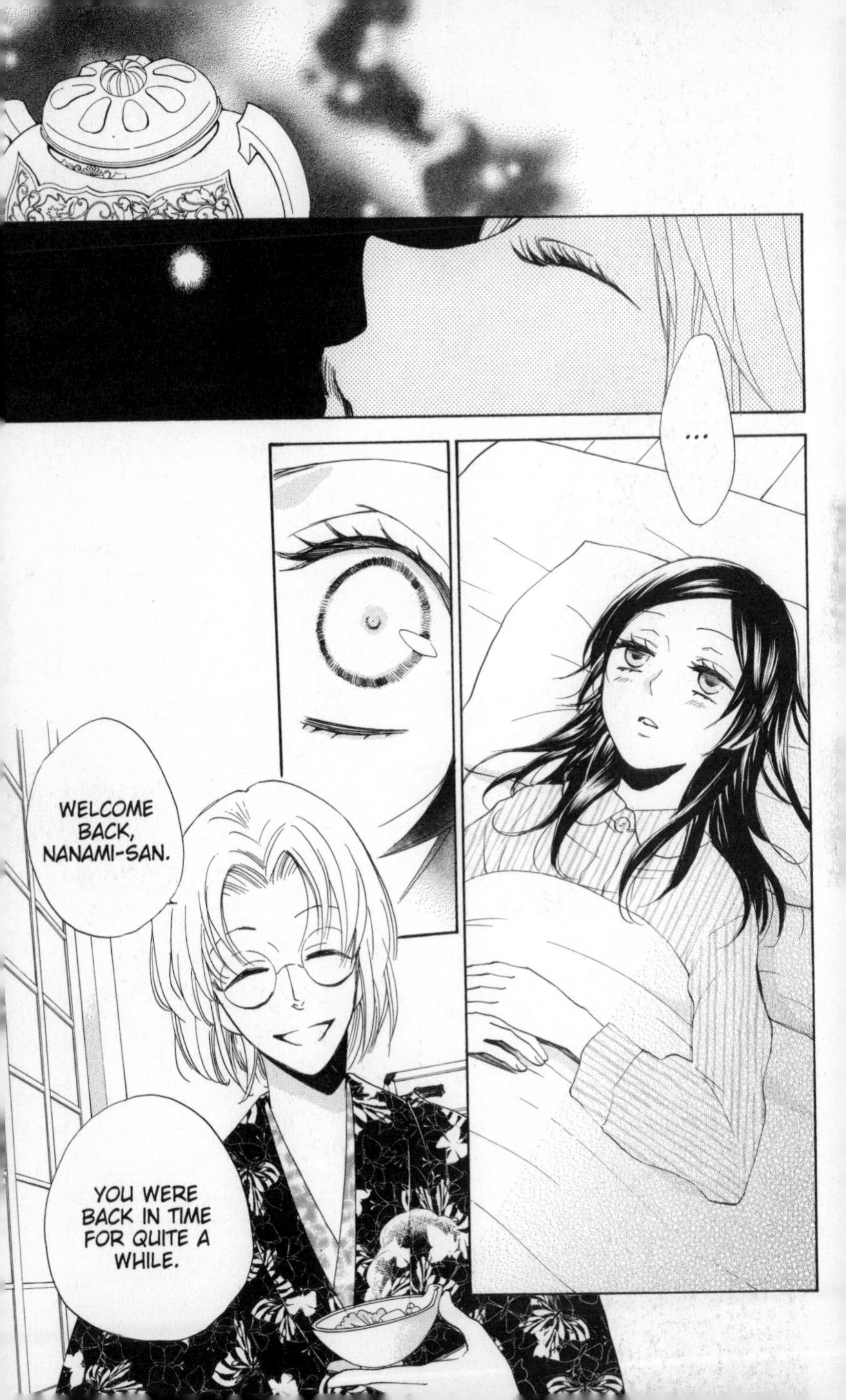
...
WELCOME BACK, NANAMI-SAN.
YOU WERE BACK IN TIME FOR QUITE A WHILE.

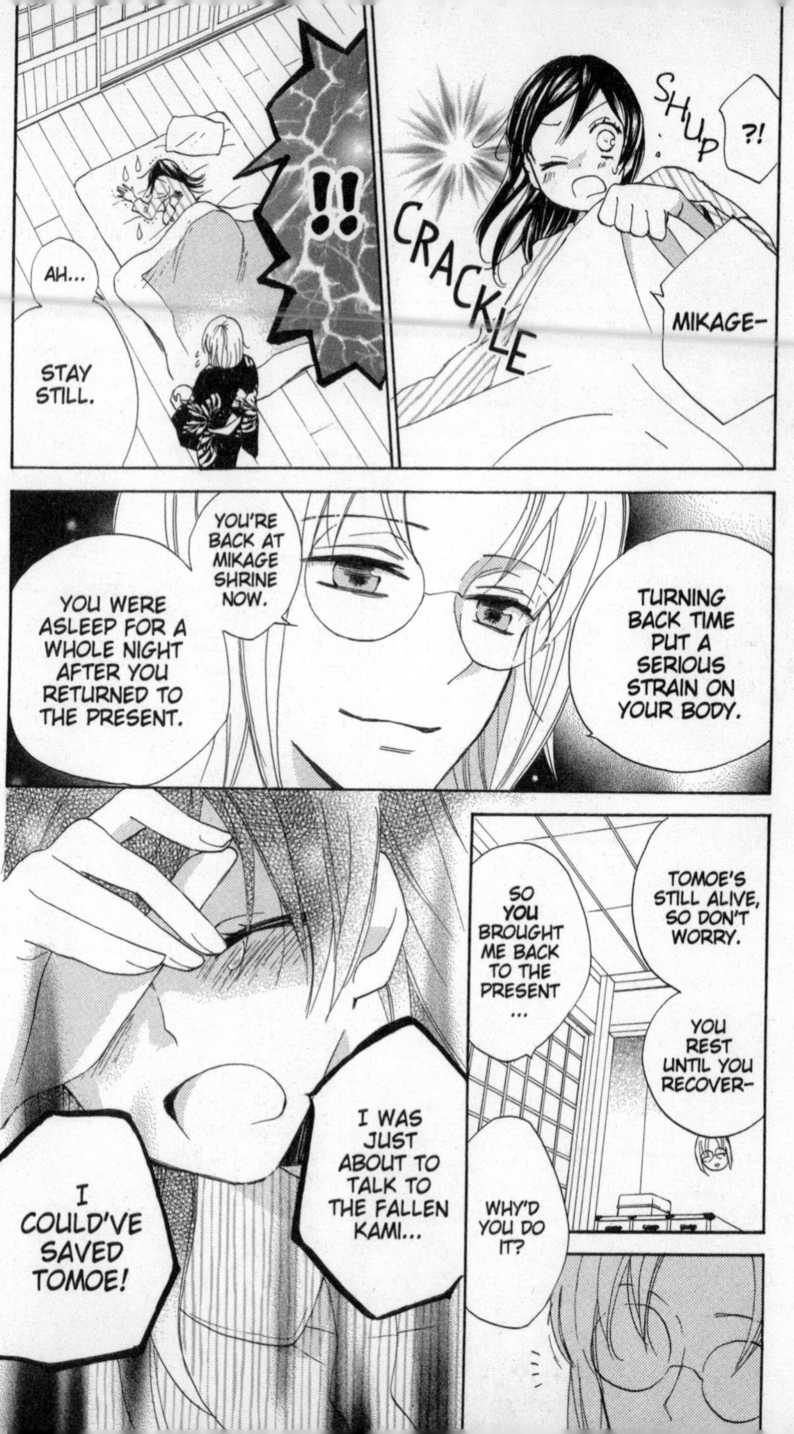

?!
SHUP
CRACKLE
MIKAGE-
!!
AH...
STAY STILL.
TURNING BACK TIME PUT A SERIOUS STRAIN ON YOUR BODY.
YOU'RE BACK AT MIKAGE SHRINE NOW.
YOU WERE ASLEEP FOR A WHOLE NIGHT AFTER YOU RETURNED TO THE PRESENT.
TOMOE'S STILL ALIVE, SO DON'T WORRY.
YOU REST UNTIL YOU RECOVER-
SO YOU BROUGHT ME BACK TO THE PRESENT...
WHY'D YOU DO IT?
I WAS JUST ABOUT TO TALK TO THE FALLEN KAMI...
I COULD'VE SAVED TOMOE!

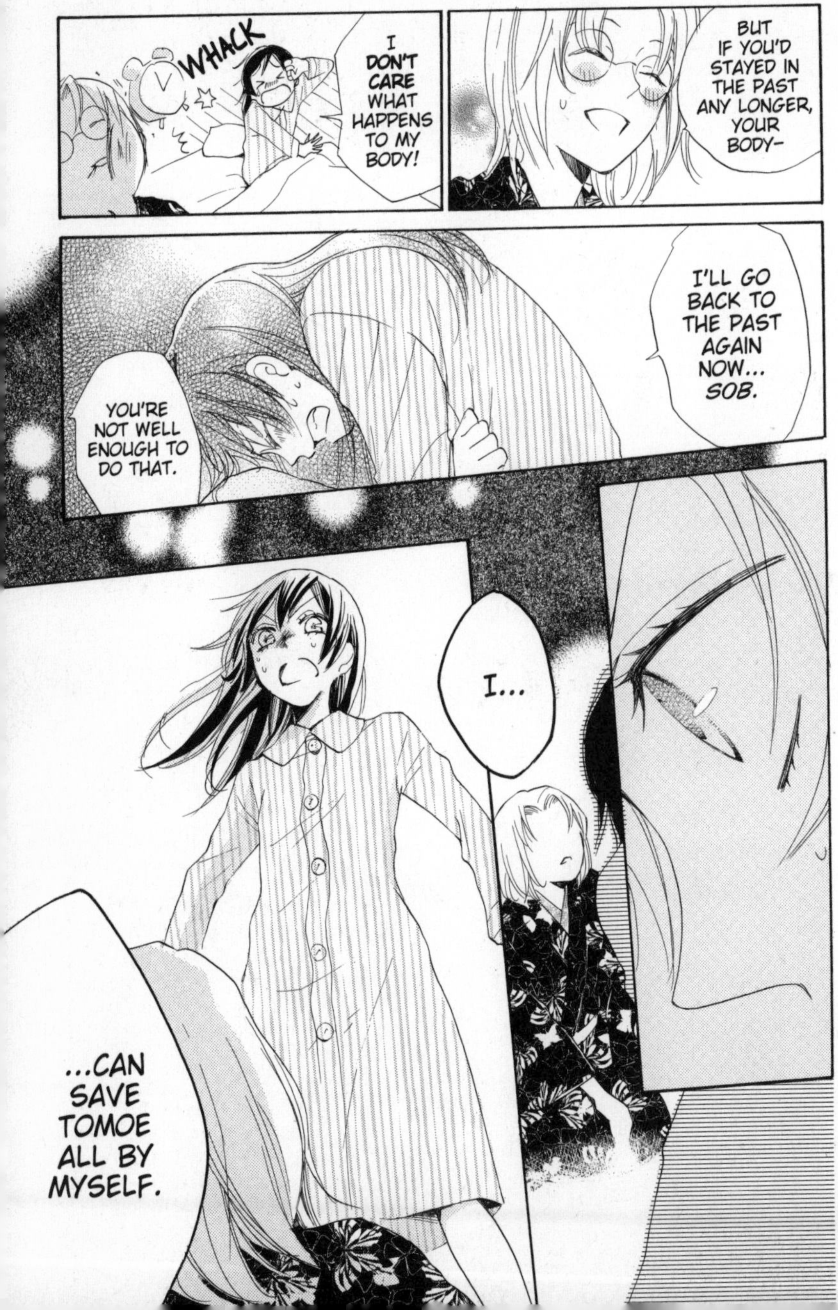
BUT IF YOU'D STAYED IN THE PAST ANY LONGER, YOUR BODY-
WHACK
I DON'T CARE WHAT HAPPENS TO MY BODY!
I'LL GO BACK TO THE PAST AGAIN NOW... SOB.
YOU'RE NOT WELL ENOUGH TO DO THAT.
I...
...CAN SAVE TOMOE ALL BY MYSELF.

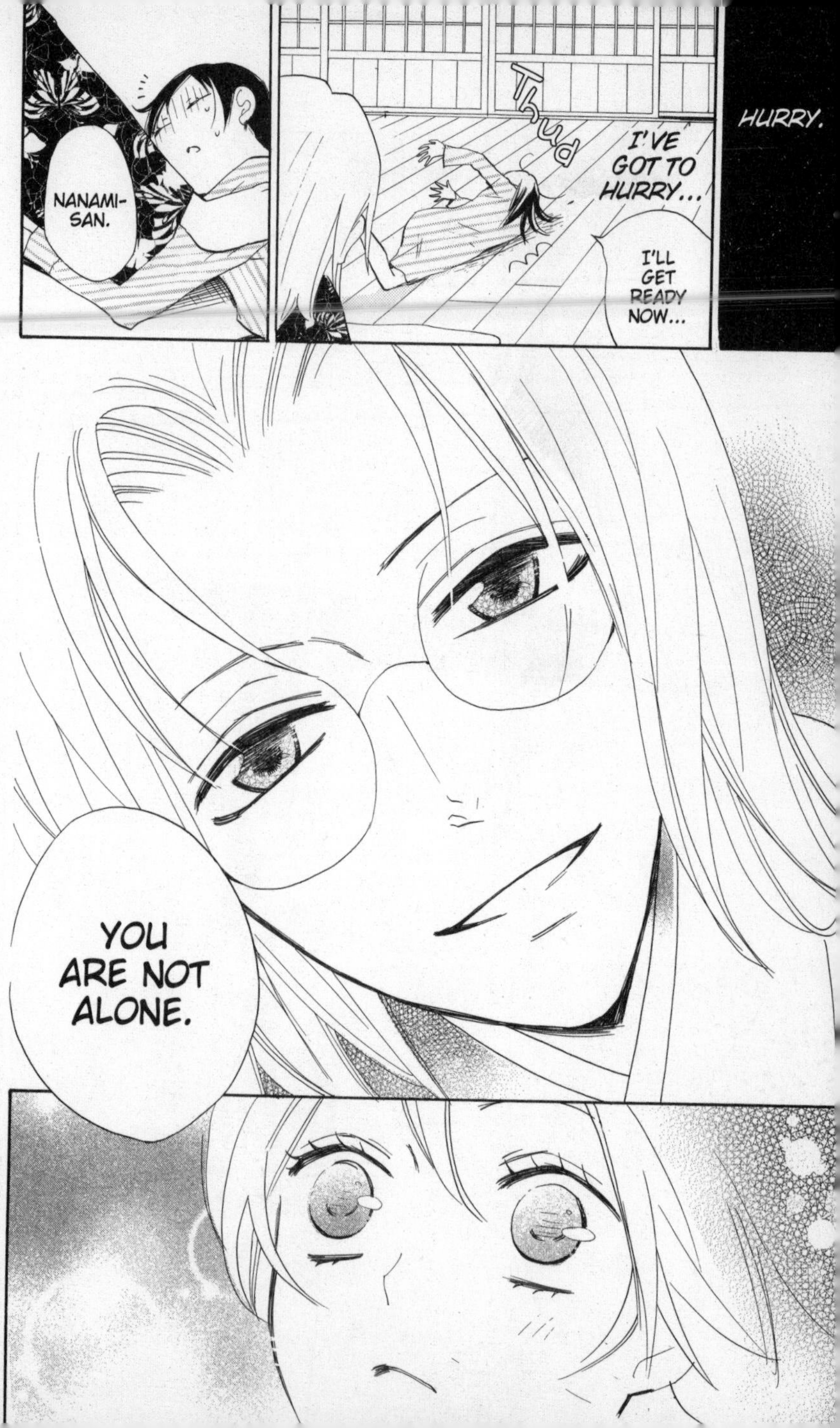
HURRY.
I'VE GOT TO HURRY...
Thud
I'LL GET READY NOW...
NANAMI-SAN.
YOU ARE NOT ALONE.

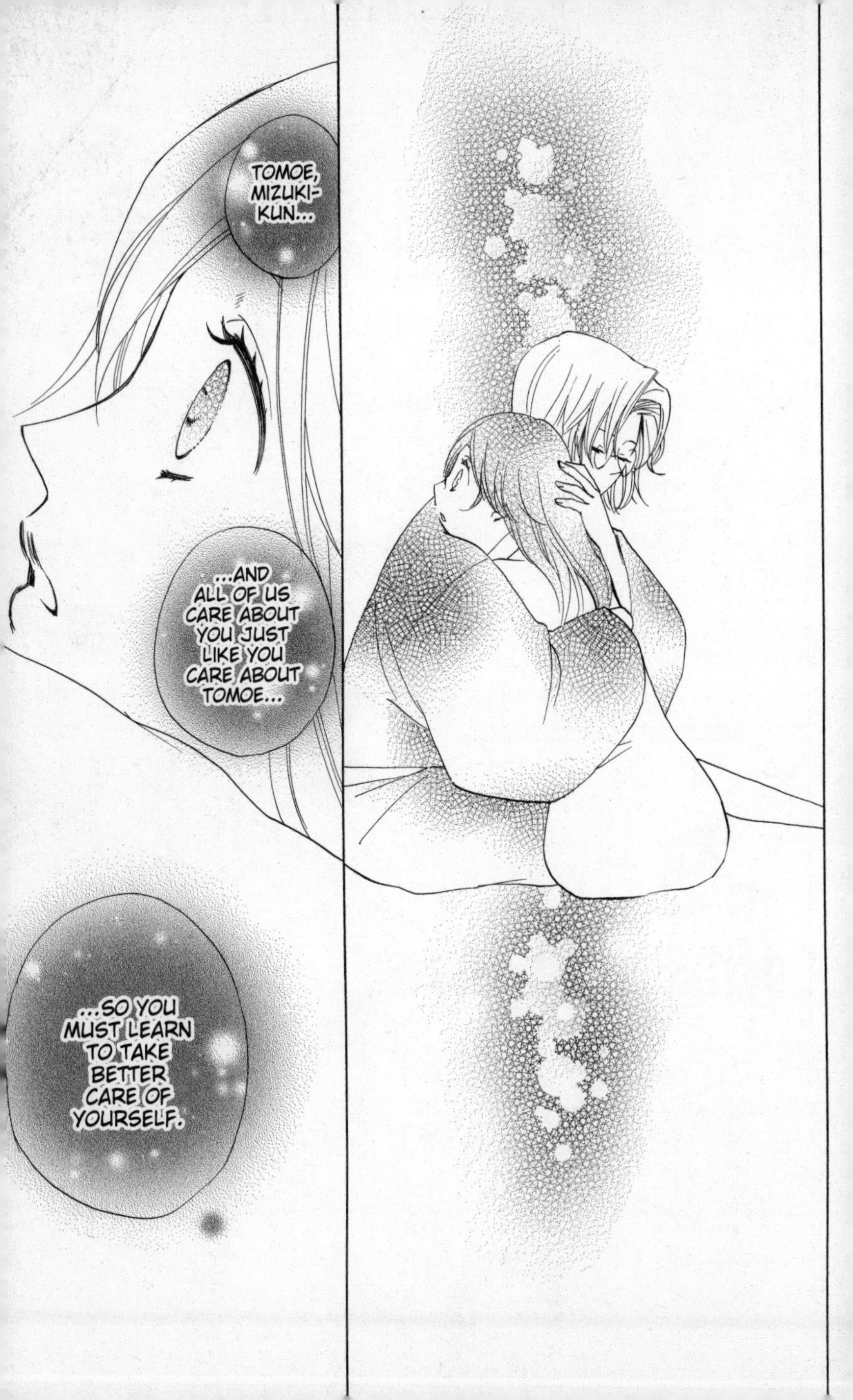
TOMOE, MIZUKI-KUN...
...AND ALL OF US CARE ABOUT YOU JUST LIKE YOU CARE ABOUT TOMOE...
...SO YOU MUST LEARN TO TAKE BETTER CARE OF YOURSELF.

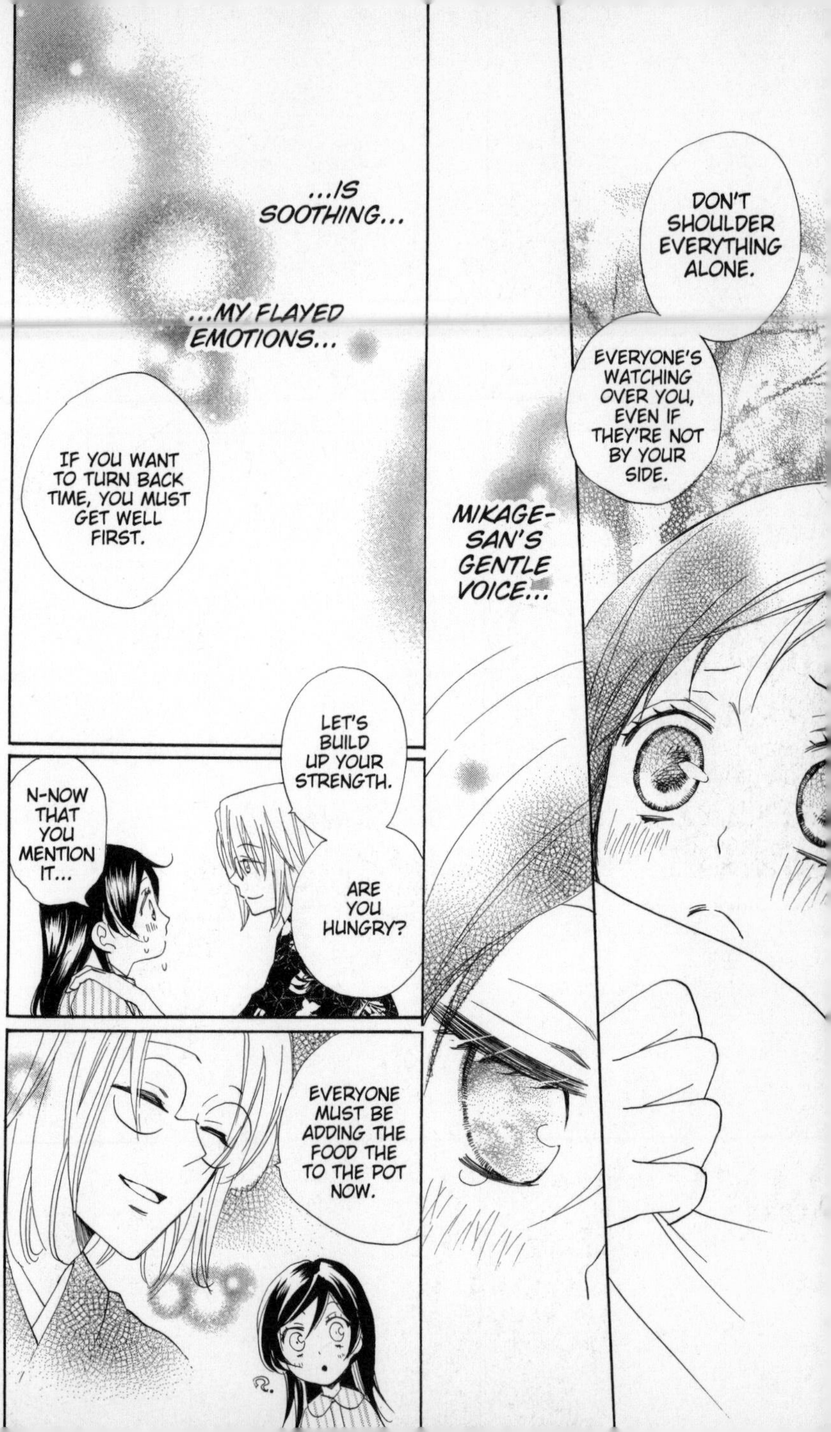
DON'T SHOULDER EVERYTHING ALONE.
EVERYONE'S WATCHING OVER YOU, EVEN IF THEY'RE NOT BY YOUR SIDE.
MIKAGE-SAN'S GENTLE VOICE...
...IS SOOTHING...
...MY FLAYED EMOTIONS...
IF YOU WANT TO TURN BACK TIME, YOU MUST GET WELL FIRST.
LET'S BUILD UP YOUR STRENGTH.
ARE YOU HUNGRY?
N-NOW THAT YOU MENTION IT...
EVERYONE MUST BE ADDING THE FOOD THE TO THE POT NOW.

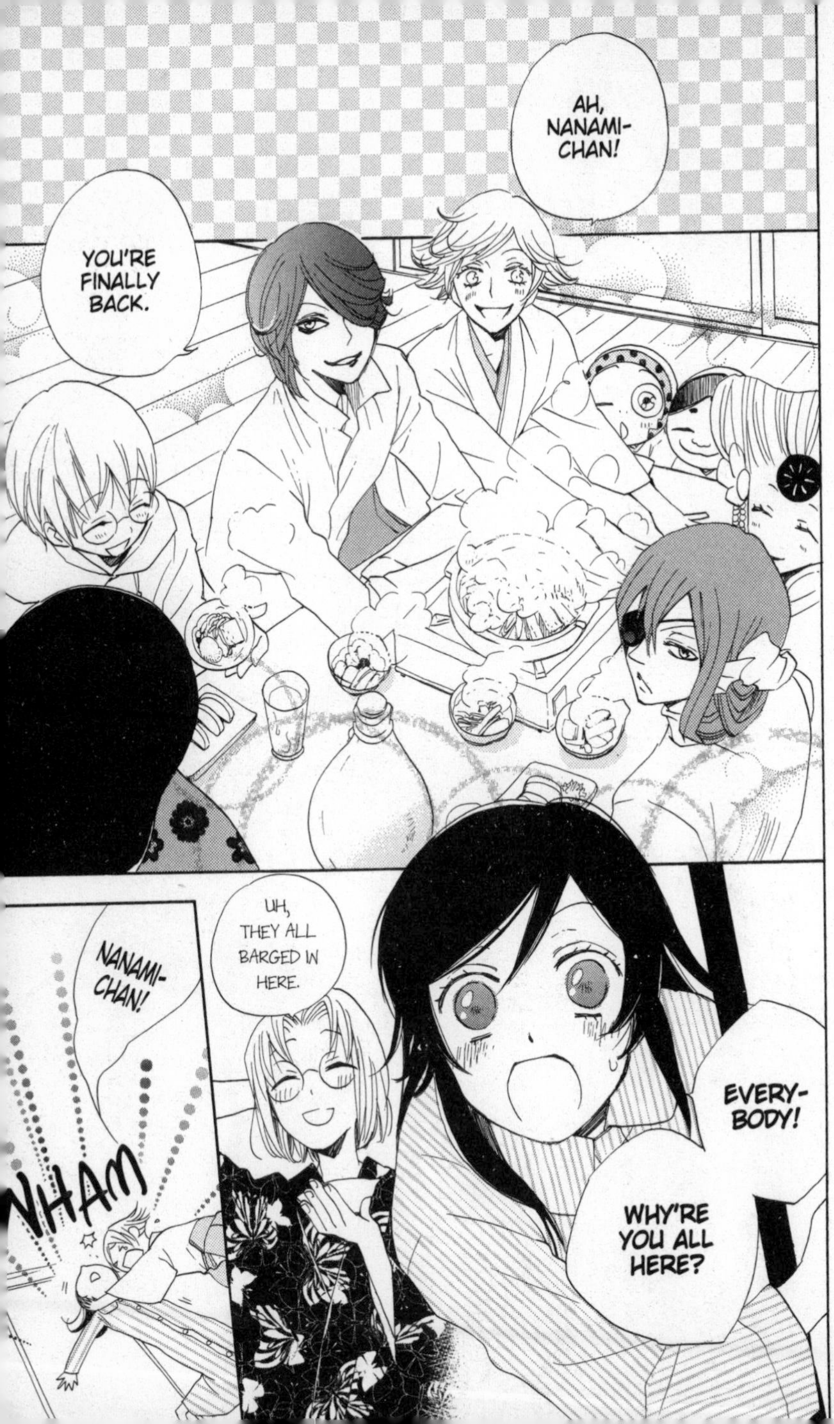
AH, NANAMI-CHAN!
YOU'RE FINALLY BACK.
EVERY-BODY!
WHY'RE YOU ALL HERE?
UH, THEY ALL BARGED IN HERE.
NANAMI-CHAN!
WHAM

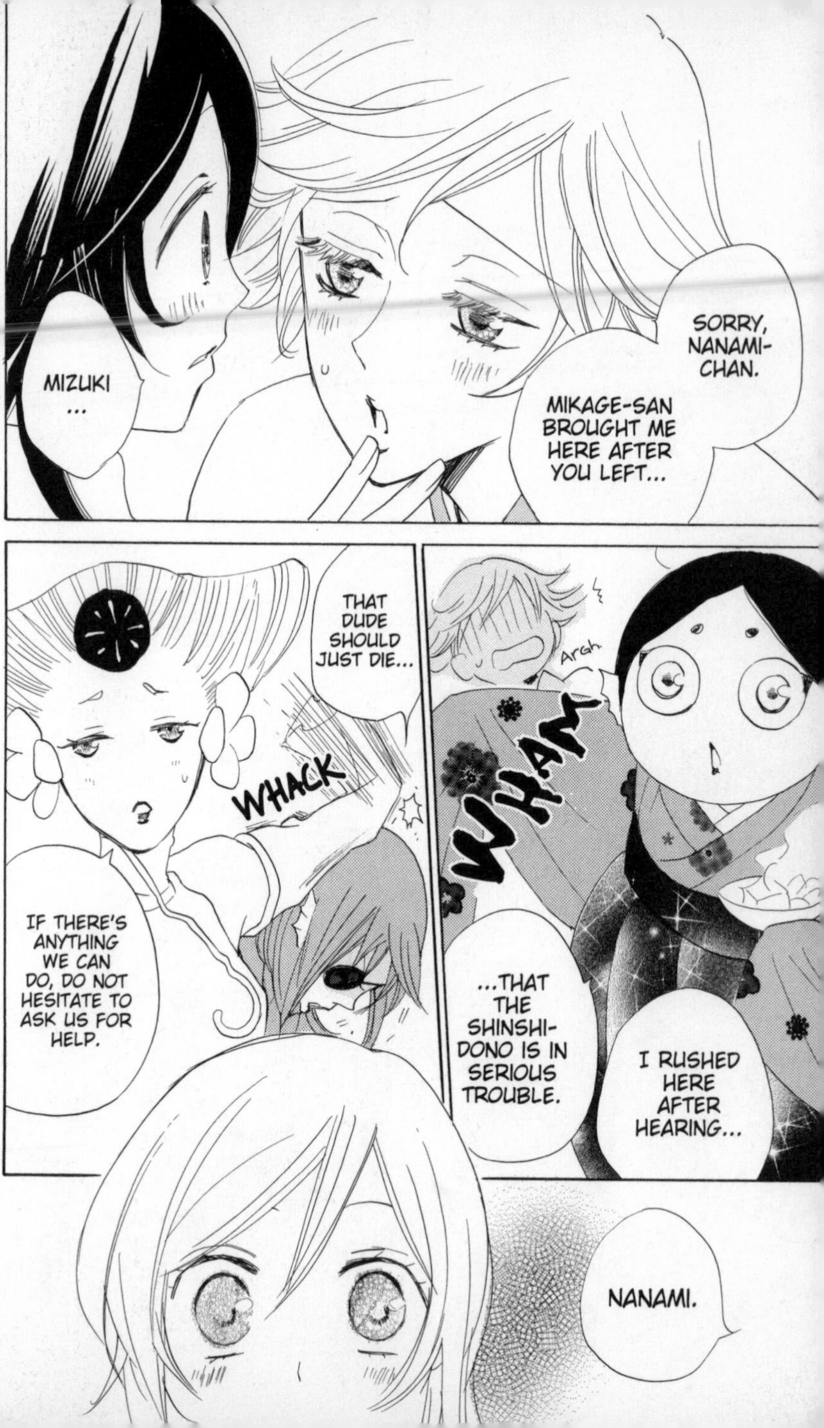
SORRY, NANAMI-CHAN.
MIKAGE-SAN BROUGHT ME HERE AFTER YOU LEFT...
MIZUKI ...
Argh.
WHAM
I RUSHED HERE AFTER HEARING...
...THAT THE SHINSHI-DONO IS IN SERIOUS TROUBLE.
THAT DUDE SHOULD JUST DIE...
WHACK
IF THERE'S ANYTHING WE CAN DO, DO NOT HESITATE TO ASK US FOR HELP.
NANAMI.

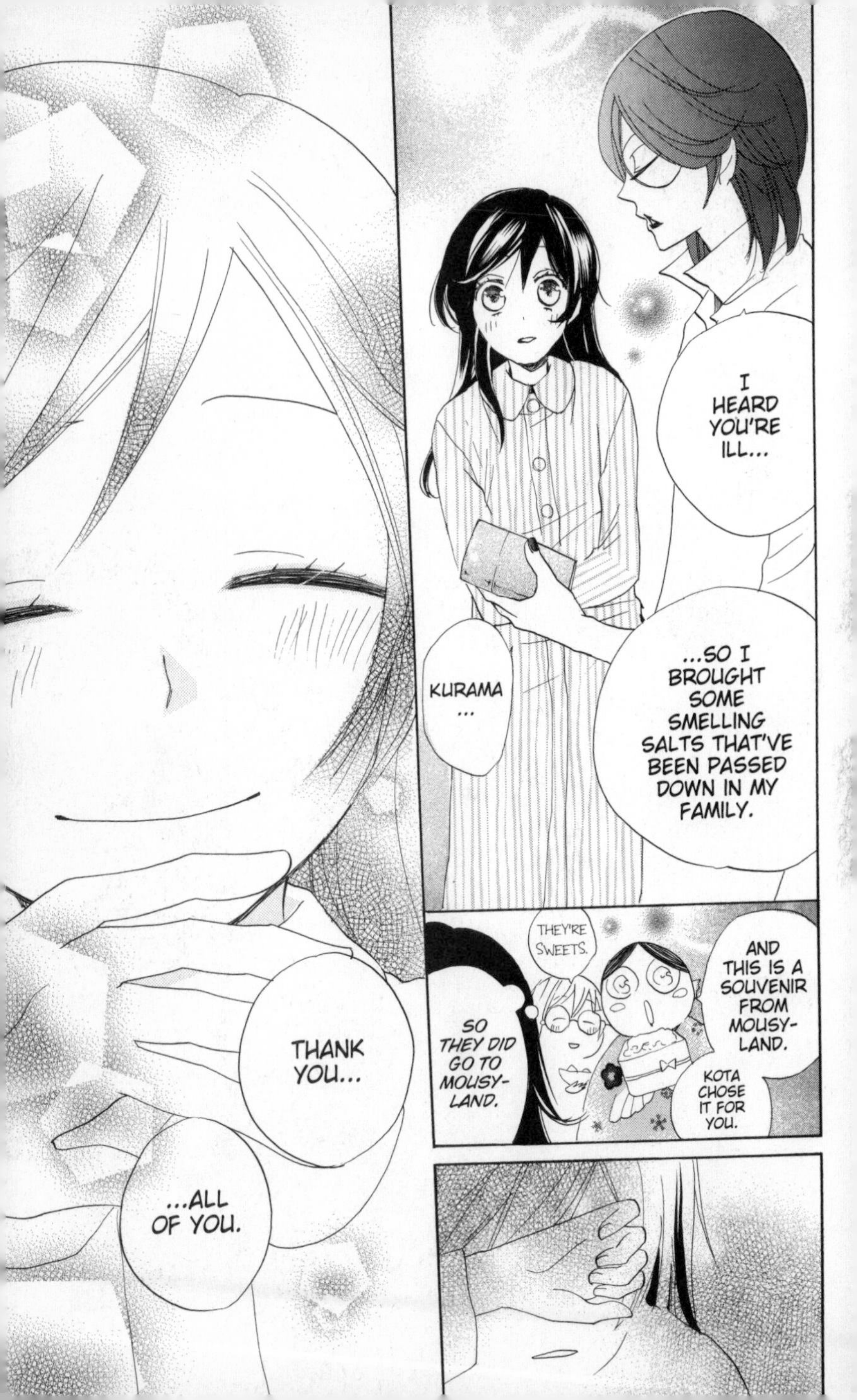
I HEARD YOU'RE ILL...
...SO I BROUGHT SOME SMELLING SALTS THAT'VE BEEN PASSED DOWN IN MY FAMILY.
KURAMA...
AND THIS IS A SOUVENIR FROM MOUSY-LAND.
KOTA CHOSE IT FOR YOU.
THEY'RE SWEETS.
SO THEY DID GO TO MOUSY-LAND.
THANK YOU...
...ALL OF YOU.

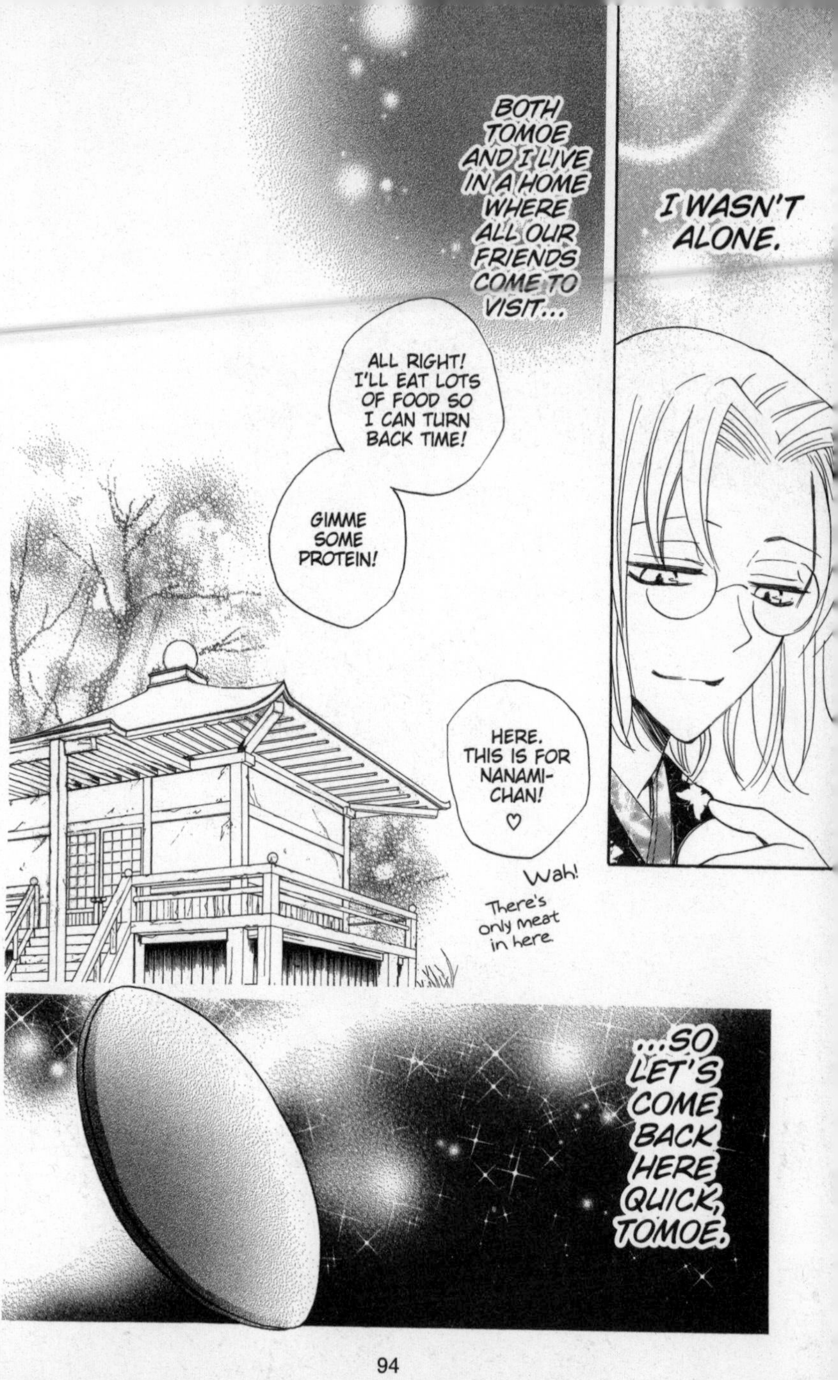
I WASN'T ALONE.
BOTH TOMOE AND I LIVE IN A HOME WHERE ALL OUR FRIENDS COME TO VISIT...
ALL RIGHT! I'LL EAT LOTS OF FOOD SO I CAN TURN BACK TIME!
GIMME SOME PROTEIN!
HERE. THIS IS FOR NANAMI-CHAN! ♡
Wah!
There's only meat in here
...SO LET'S COME BACK HERE QUICK, TOMOE.

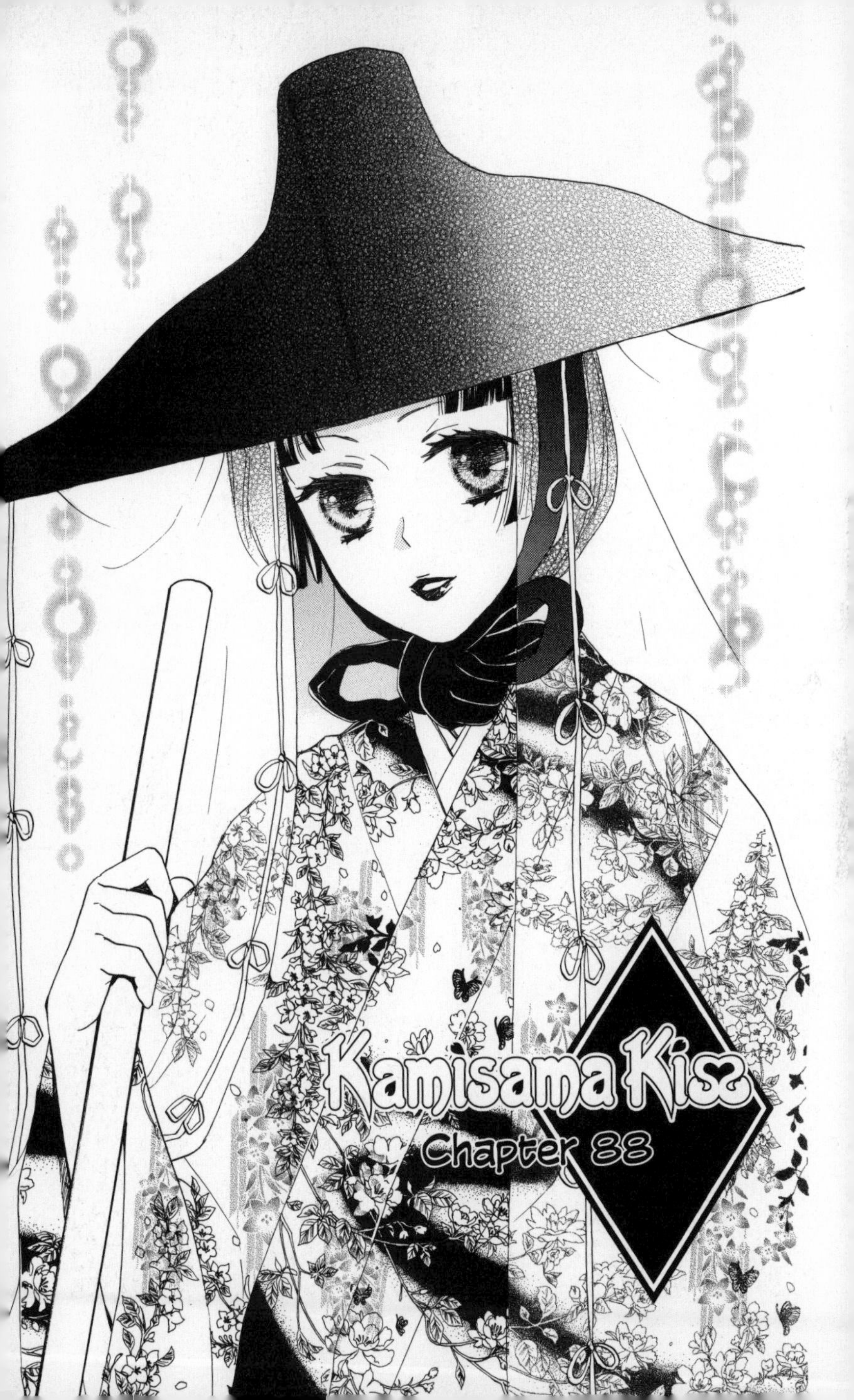
Kamisama Kiss
Chapter 88

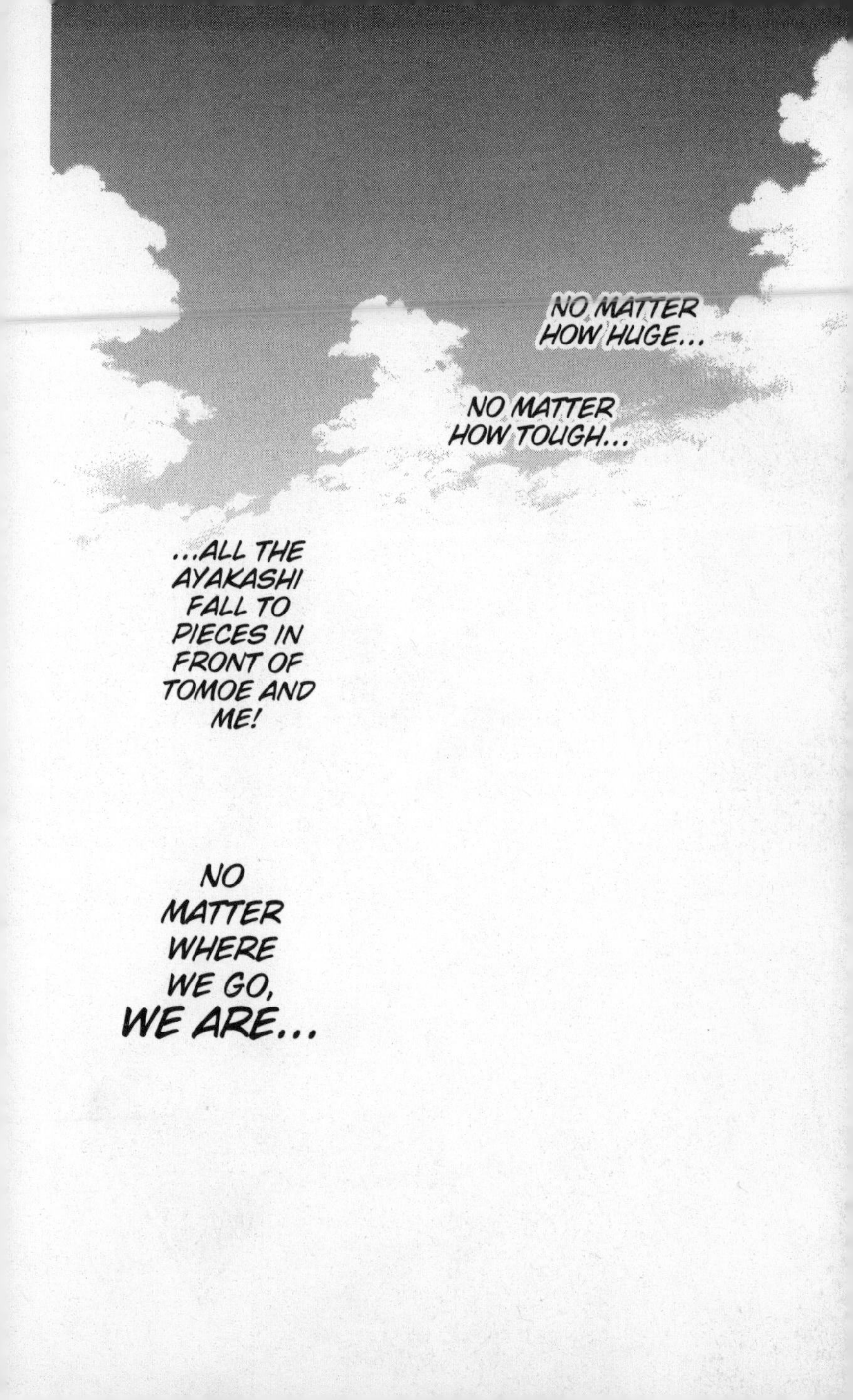
NO MATTER HOW HUGE...
NO MATTER HOW TOUGH...
...ALL THE AYAKASHI FALL TO PIECES IN FRONT OF TOMOE AND ME!
NO MATTER WHERE WE GO, WE ARE...

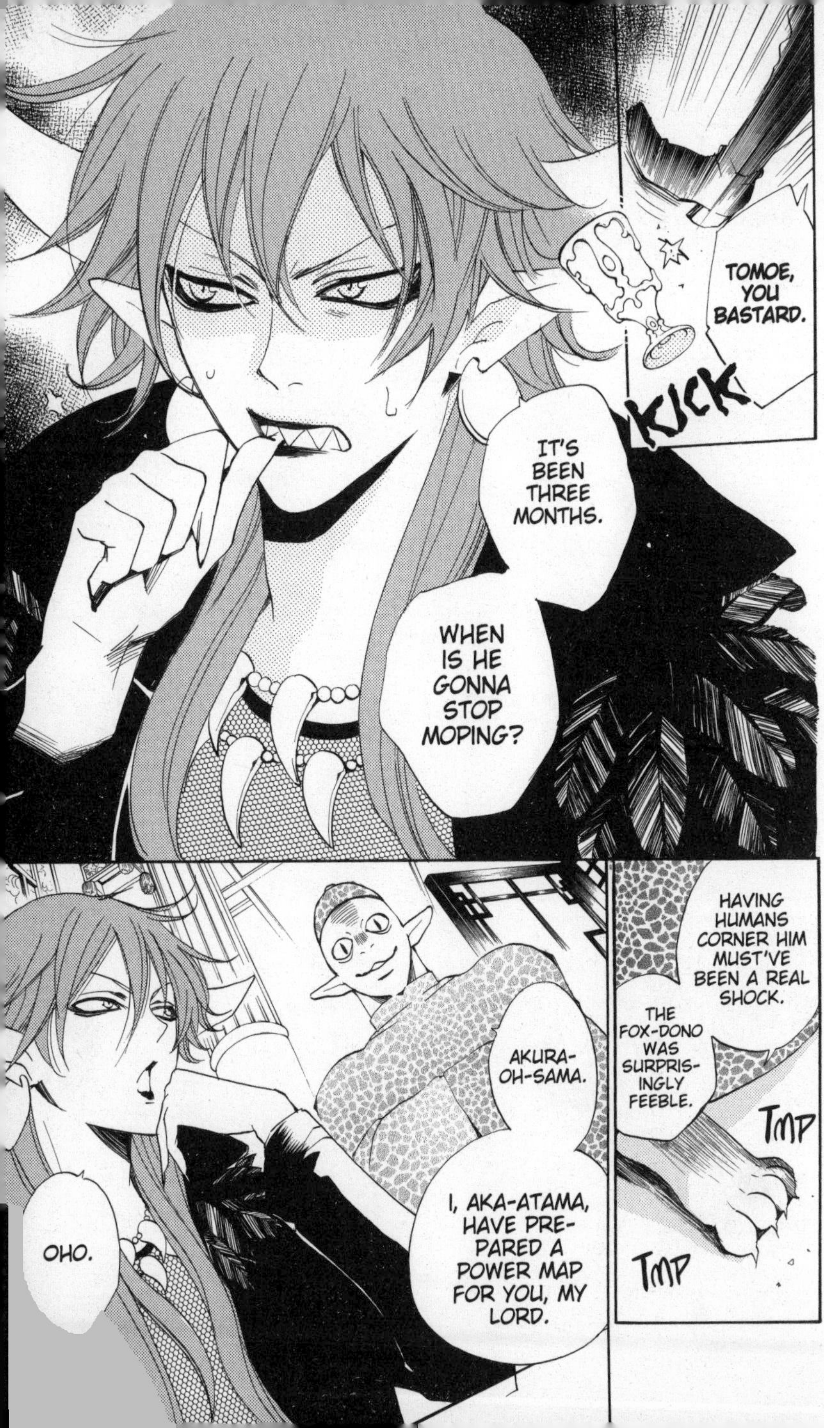
TOMOE, YOU BASTARD.
KICK
IT'S BEEN THREE MONTHS.
WHEN IS HE GONNA STOP MOPING?
HAVING HUMANS CORNER HIM MUST'VE BEEN A REAL SHOCK.
THE FOX-DONO WAS SURPRIS-INGLY FEEBLE.
TMP
TMP
AKURA-OH-SAMA.
I, AKA-ATAMA, HAVE PRE-PARED A POWER MAP FOR YOU, MY LORD.
OHO.

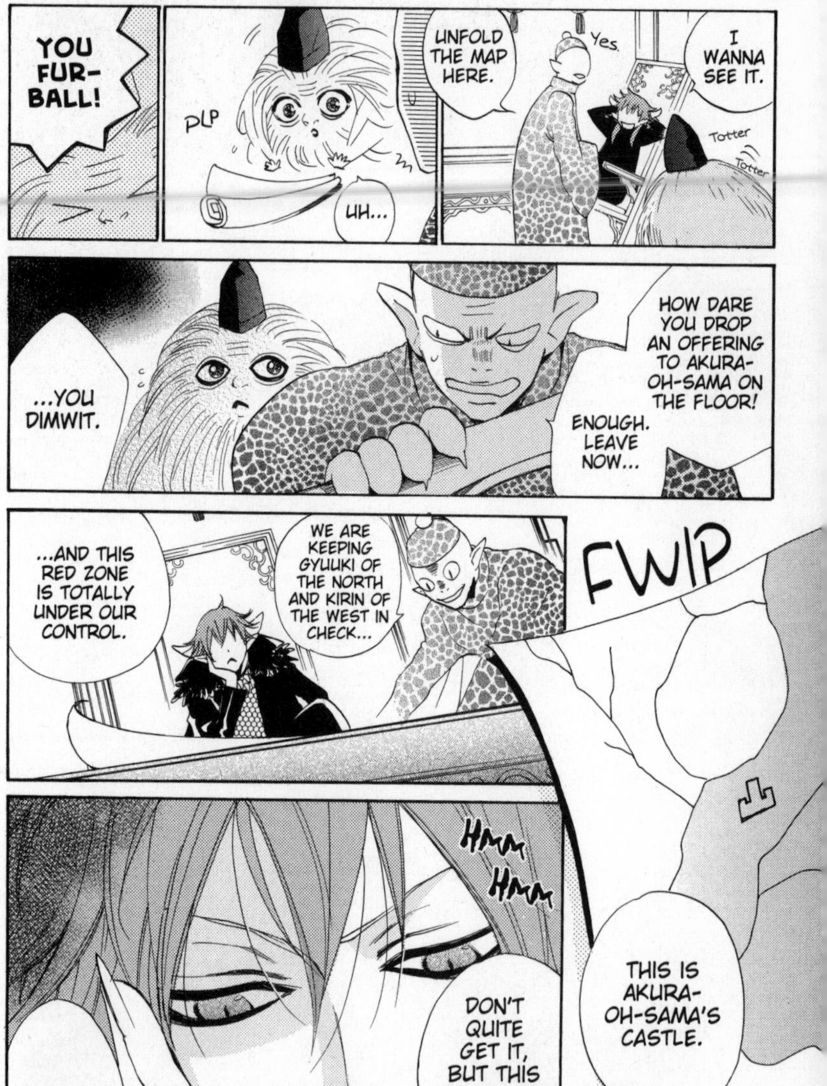
I WANNA SEE IT.
Yes.
Totter
Totter
UNFOLD THE MAP HERE.
PLP
UH...
YOU FUR-BALL!
HOW DARE YOU DROP AN OFFERING TO AKURA-OH-SAMA ON THE FLOOR!
ENOUGH. LEAVE NOW...
...YOU DIMWIT.
FWIP
THIS IS AKURA-OH-SAMA'S CASTLE.
WE ARE KEEPING GYUUKI OF THE NORTH AND KIRIN OF THE WEST IN CHECK...
...AND THIS RED ZONE IS TOTALLY UNDER OUR CONTROL.
HMM
HMM
DON'T QUITE GET IT, BUT THIS RED IS MY COLOR...
INTEREST-ING.

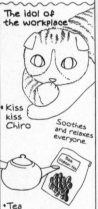

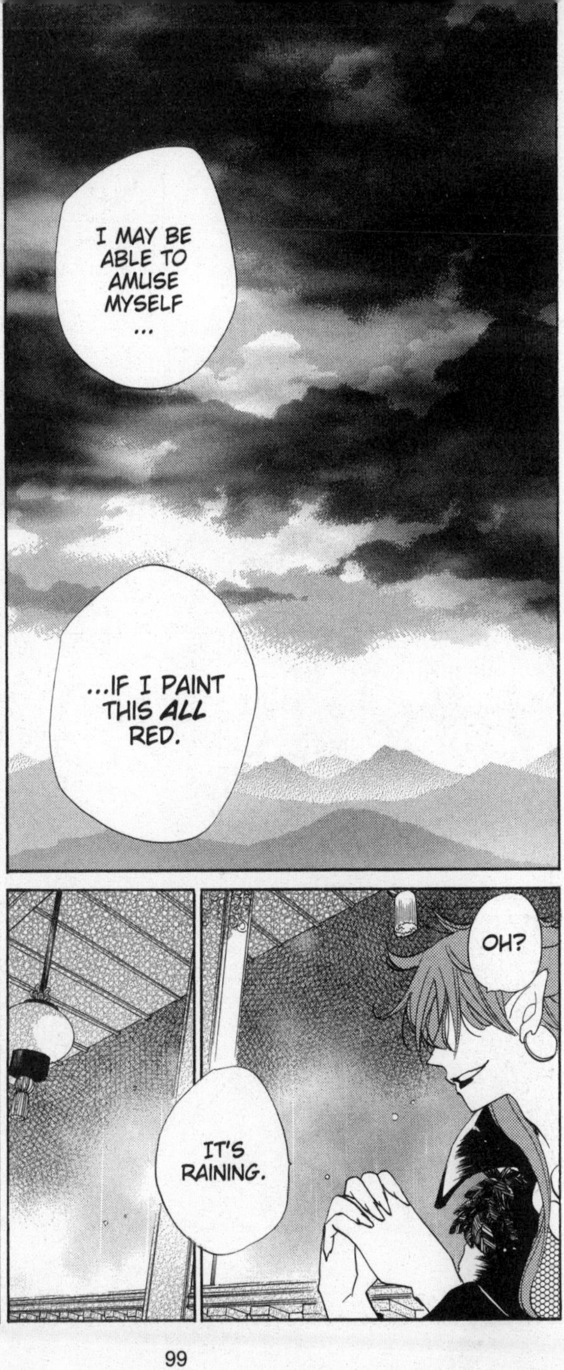
I MAY BE ABLE TO AMUSE MYSELF ...
...IF I PAINT THIS ALL RED.
OH?
IT'S RAINING.

Congratulations Volume 15 ☆

In this sidebar, I'll introduce some items that are a must-have at Juli Sensei's workplace.

The idol of the workplace

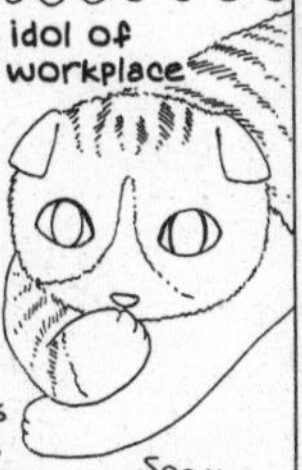

* Kiss kiss Chiro

Soothes and relaxes everyone.

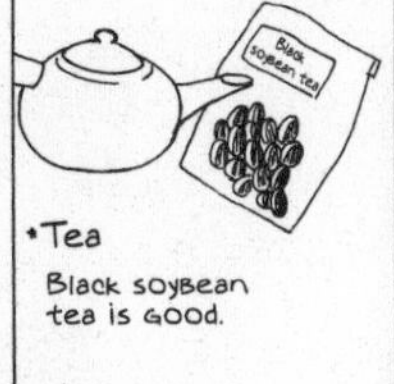
Black soybean tea

* Tea

Black soybean tea is good.

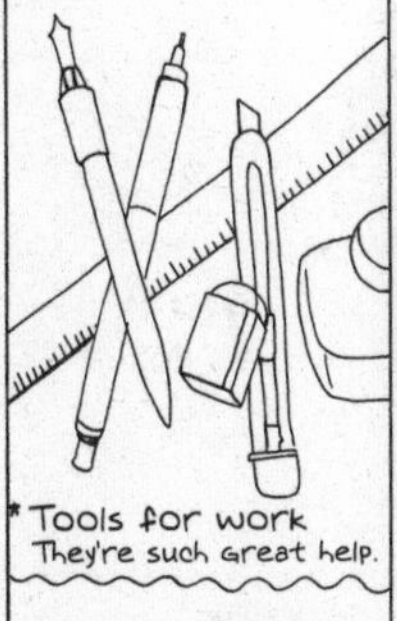

* Tools for work

They're such great help.

We're always able to work happily thanks to various items.

~Okazaki

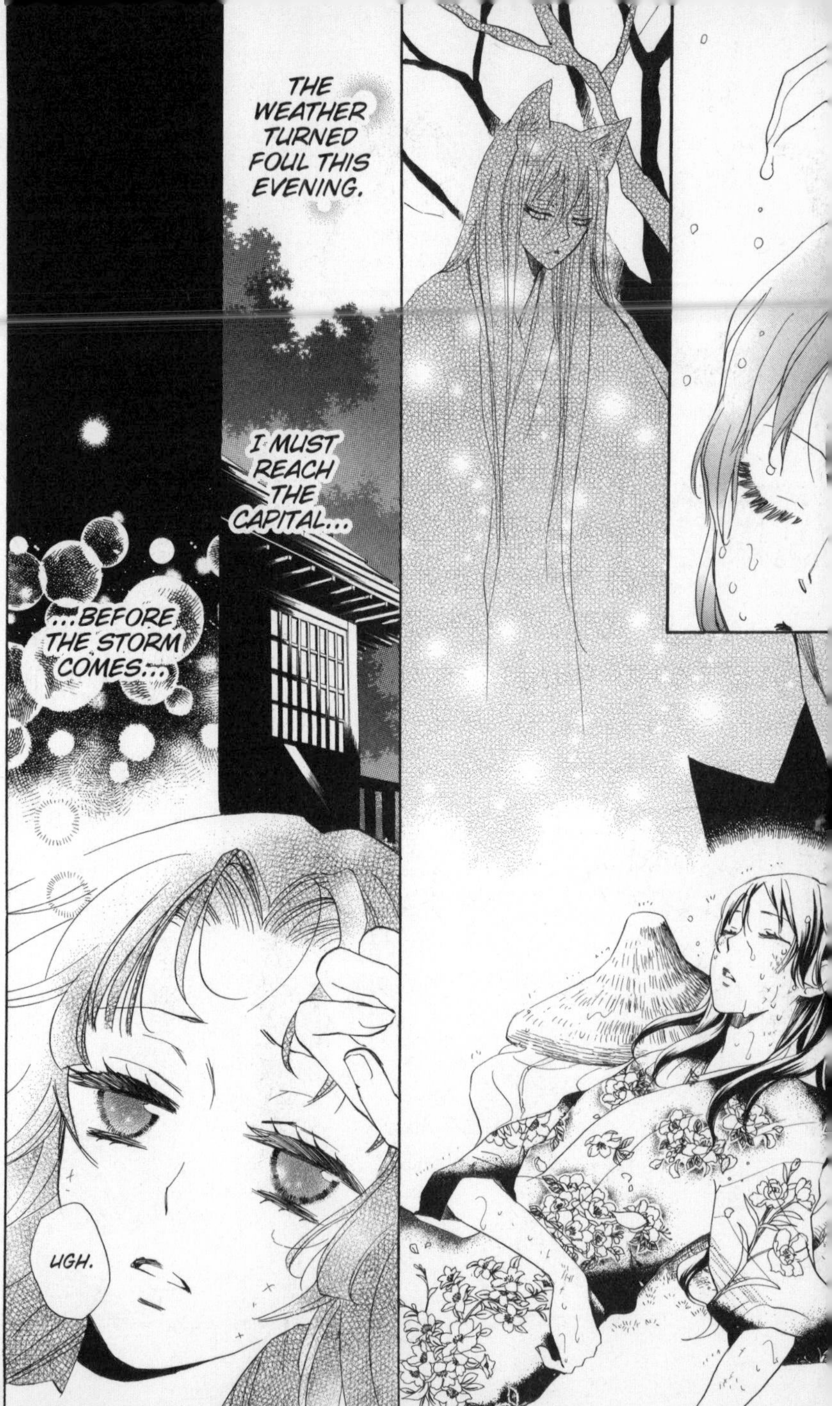
THE WEATHER TURNED FOUL THIS EVENING.
I MUST REACH THE CAPITAL...
...BEFORE THE STORM COMES...
UGH.

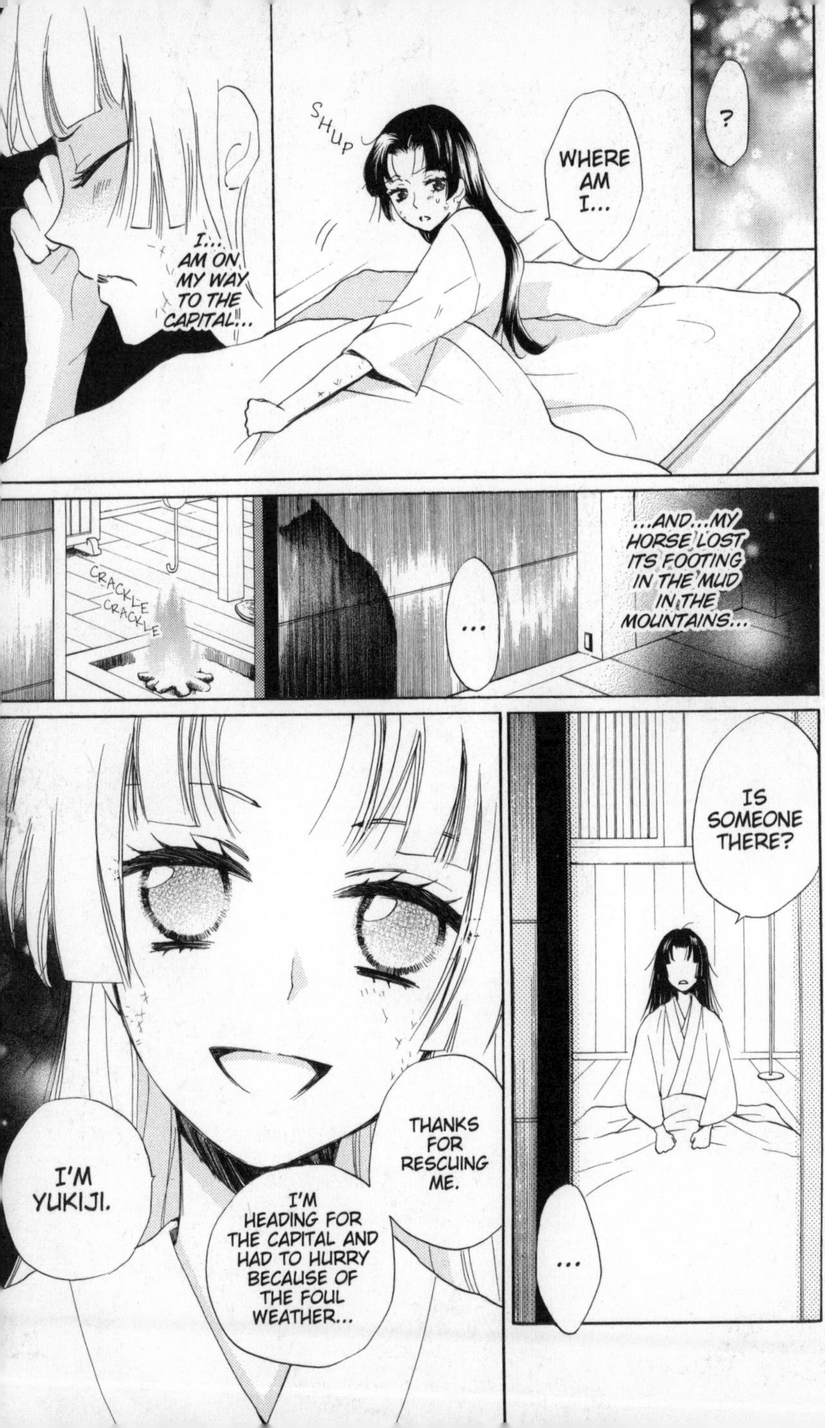
?
WHERE AM I...
SHUP
I... AM ON MY WAY TO THE CAPITAL...
...AND...MY HORSE LOST ITS FOOTING IN THE MUD IN THE MOUNTAINS...
...
CRACKLE CRACKLE
IS SOMEONE THERE?
...
THANKS FOR RESCUING ME.
I'M HEADING FOR THE CAPITAL AND HAD TO HURRY BECAUSE OF THE FOUL WEATHER...
I'M YUKIJI.

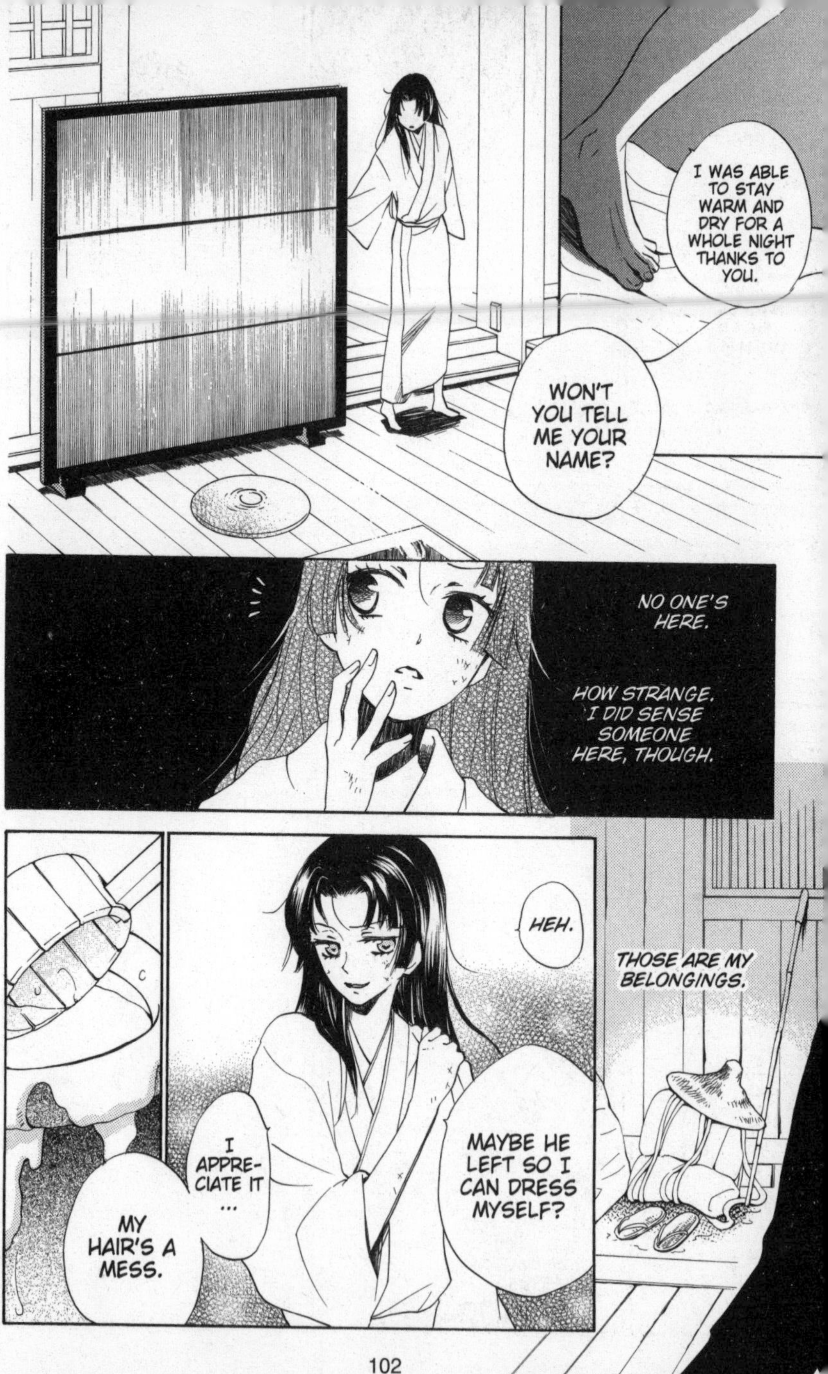
I WAS ABLE TO STAY WARM AND DRY FOR A WHOLE NIGHT THANKS TO YOU.
WON'T YOU TELL ME YOUR NAME?
NO ONE'S HERE.
HOW STRANGE. I DID SENSE SOMEONE HERE, THOUGH.
THOSE ARE MY BELONGINGS.
HEH.
MAYBE HE LEFT SO I CAN DRESS MYSELF?
I APPRE-CIATE IT ...
MY HAIR'S A MESS.

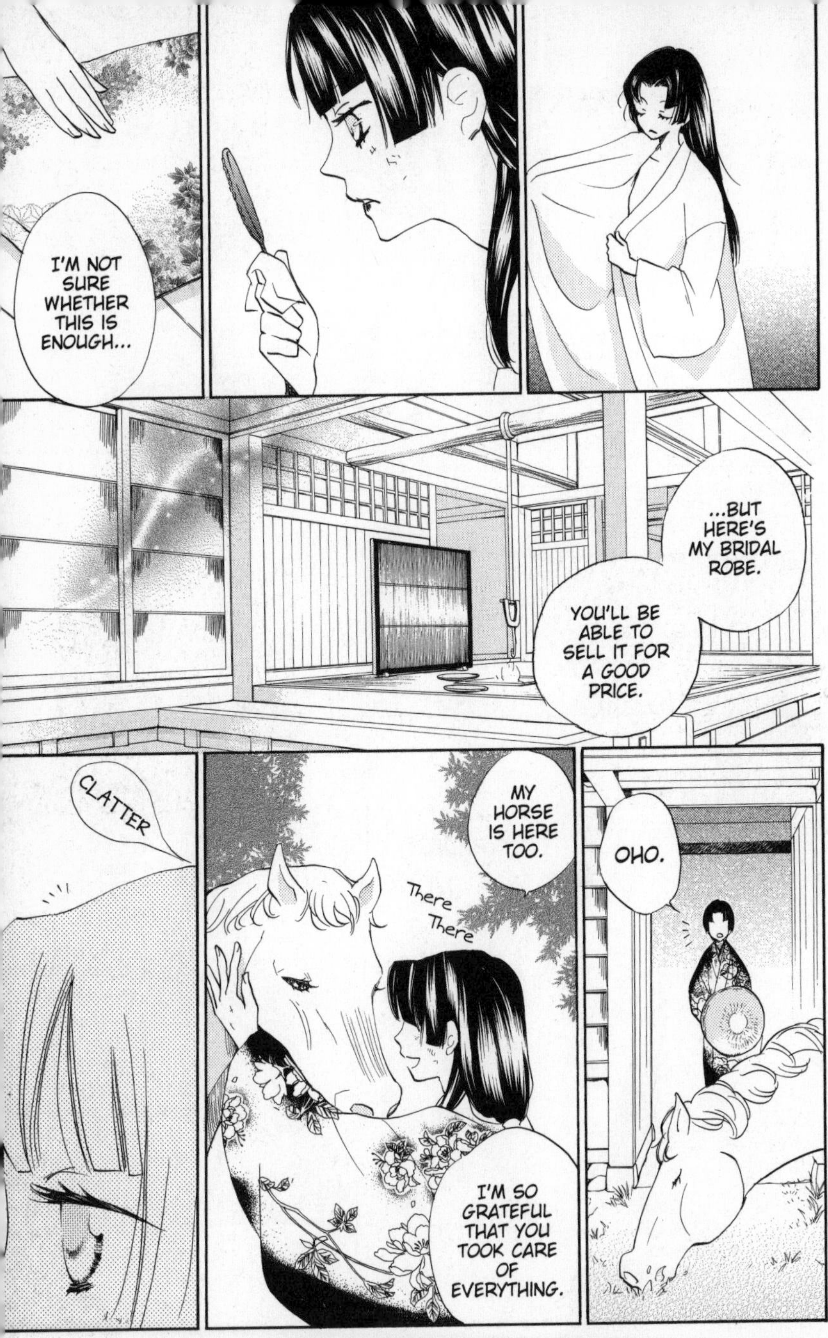
I'M NOT SURE WHETHER THIS IS ENOUGH...
...BUT HERE'S MY BRIDAL ROBE.
YOU'LL BE ABLE TO SELL IT FOR A GOOD PRICE.
OHO.
MY HORSE IS HERE TOO.
There There
I'M SO GRATEFUL THAT YOU TOOK CARE OF EVERYTHING.
CLATTER

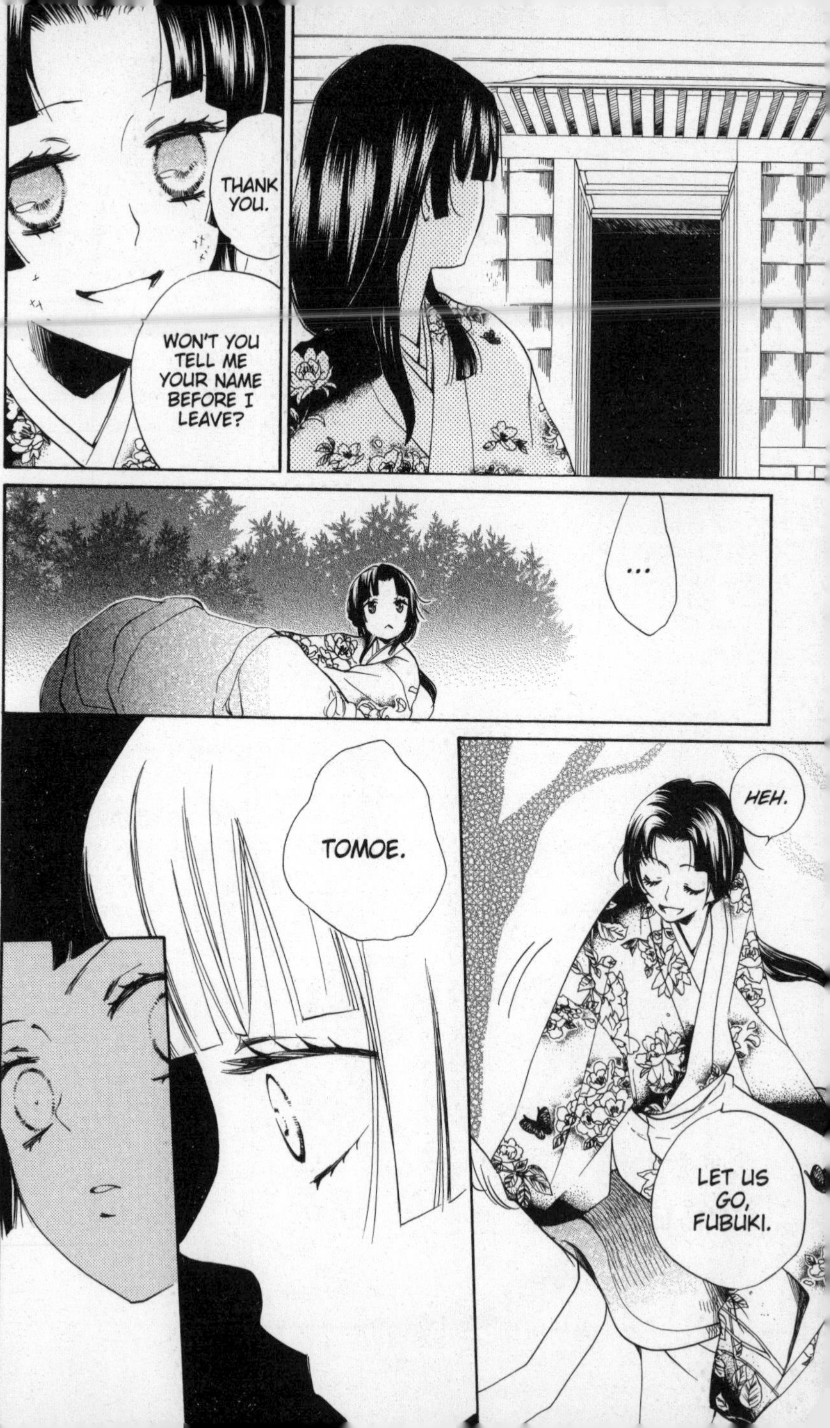
THANK YOU.
WON'T YOU TELL ME YOUR NAME BEFORE I LEAVE?
...
TOMOE.
HEH.
LET US GO, FUBUKI.

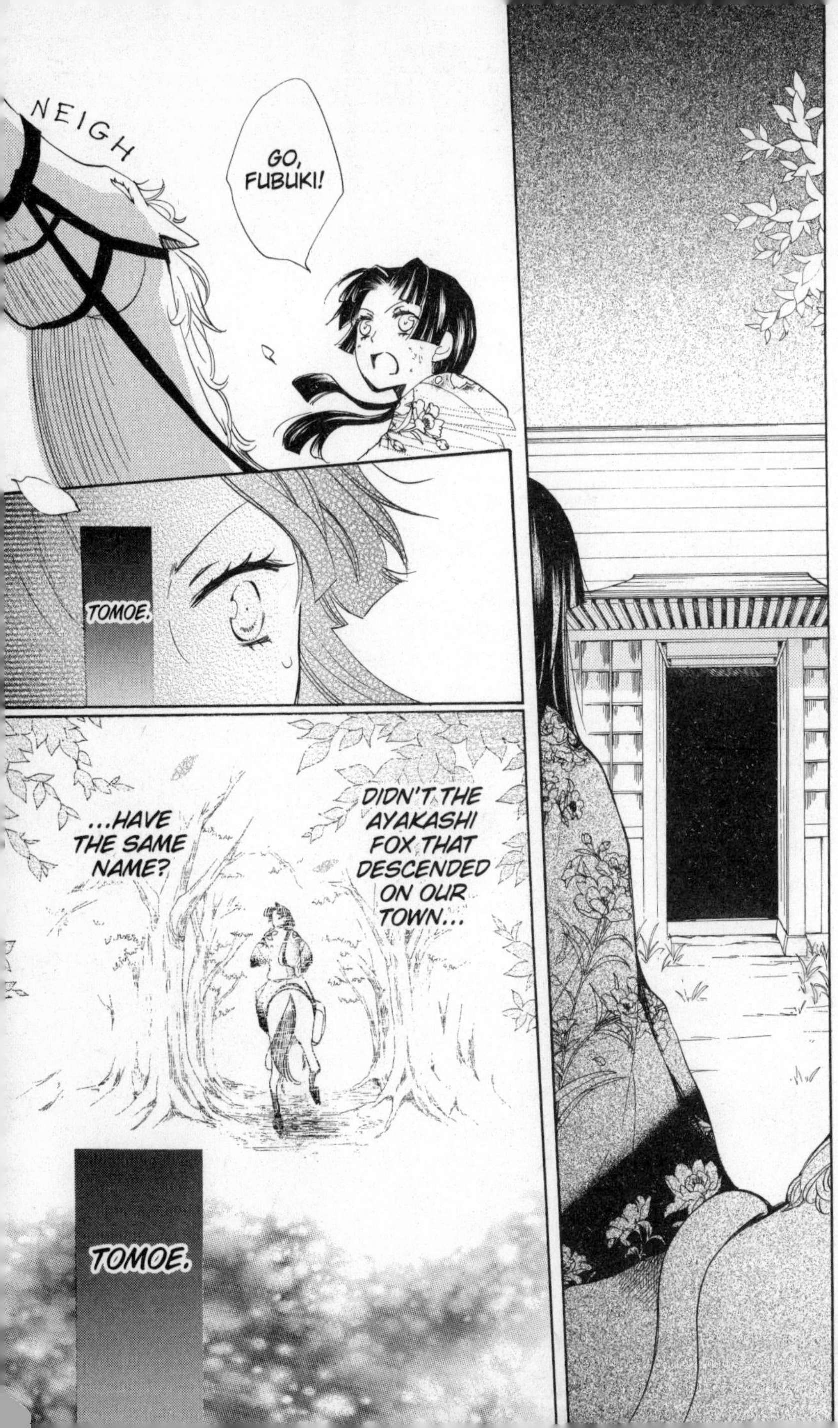
NEIGH
GO, FUBUKI!
TOMOE.
DIDN'T THE AYAKASHI FOX THAT DESCENDED ON OUR TOWN...
...HAVE THE SAME NAME?
TOMOE.

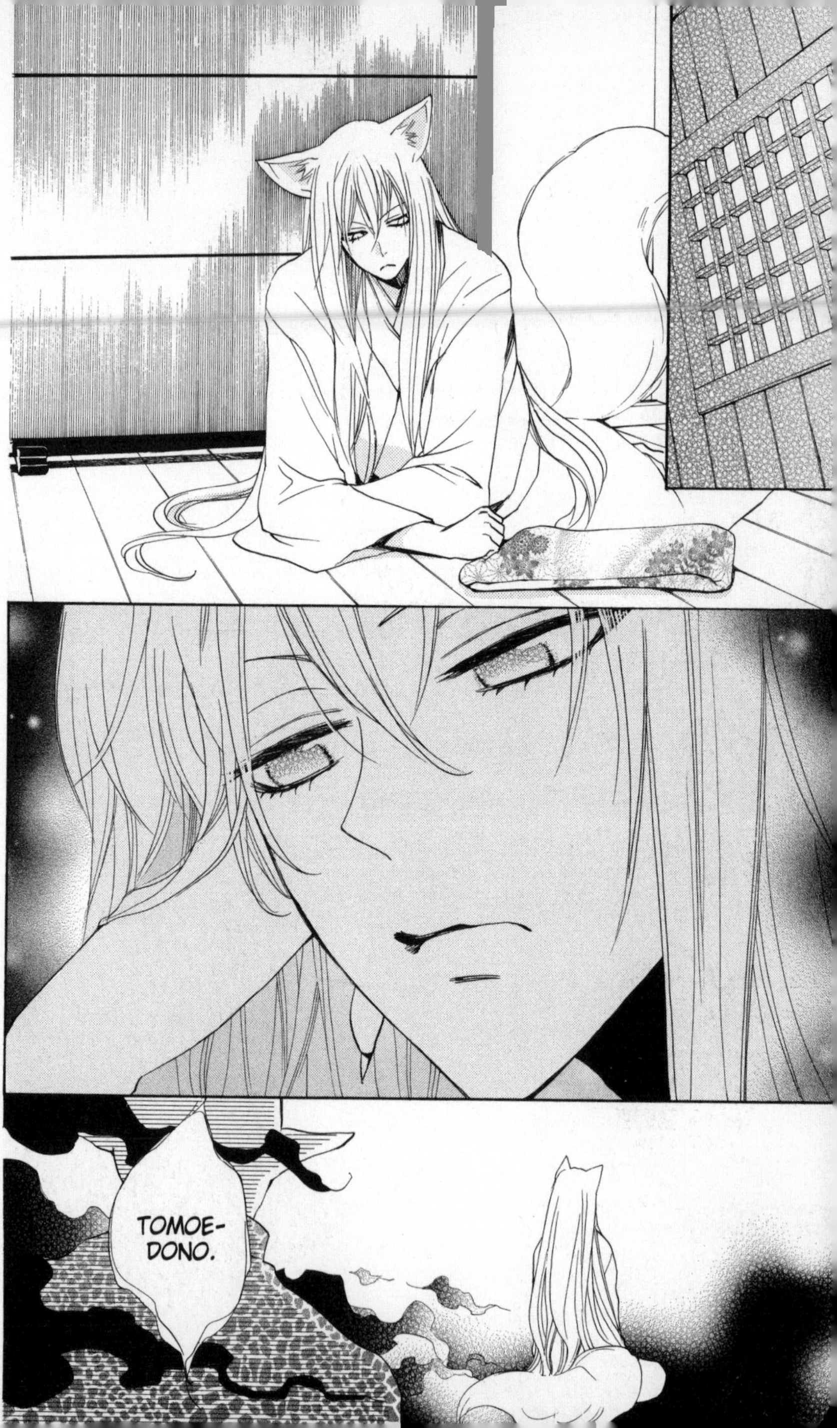
TOMOE-DONO.

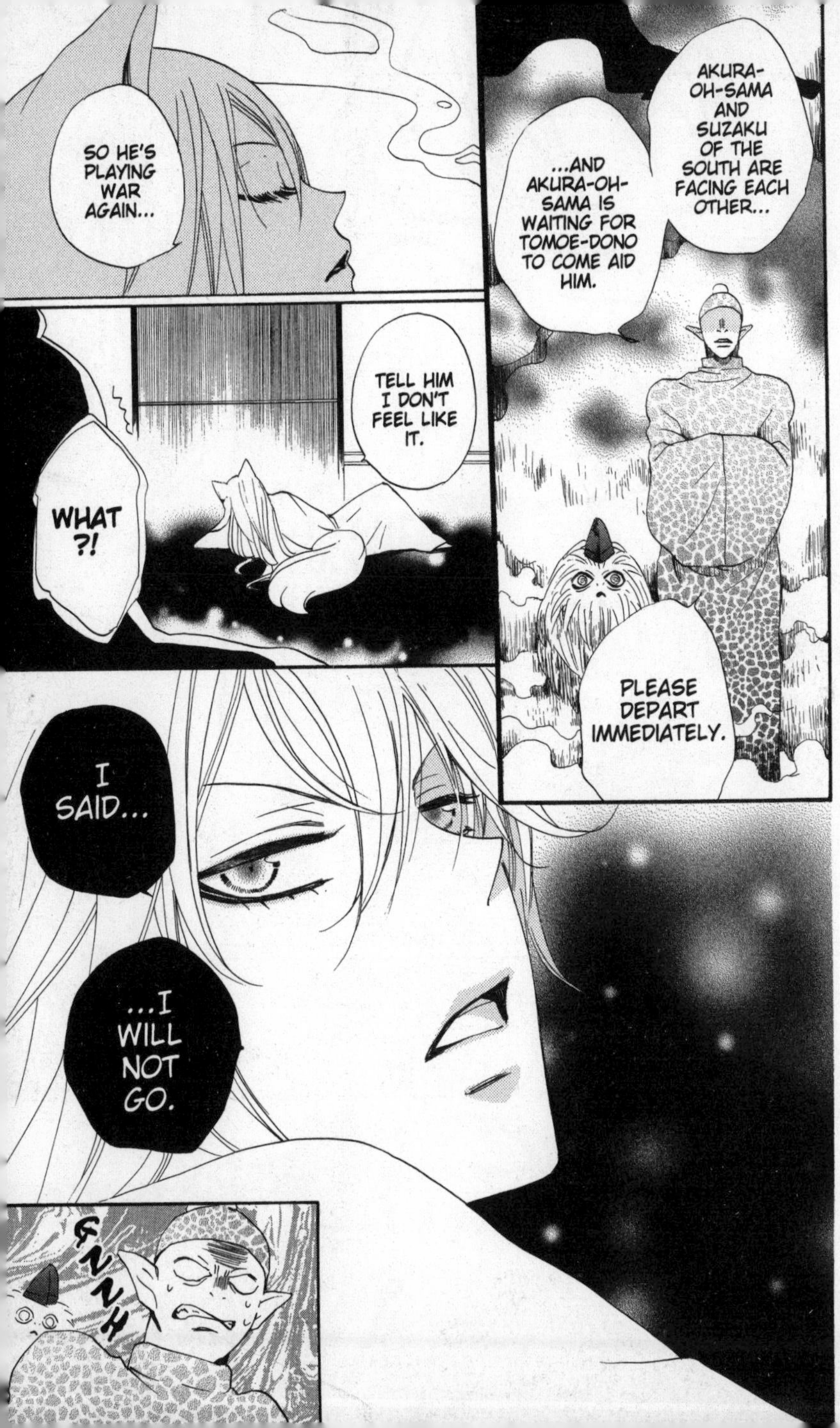
AKURA-OH-SAMA AND SUZAKU OF THE SOUTH ARE FACING EACH OTHER...
...AND AKURA-OH-SAMA IS WAITING FOR TOMOE-DONO TO COME AID HIM.
PLEASE DEPART IMMEDIATELY.
SO HE'S PLAYING WAR AGAIN...
TELL HIM I DON'T FEEL LIKE IT.
WHAT?!
I SAID...
...I WILL NOT GO.
GNNH

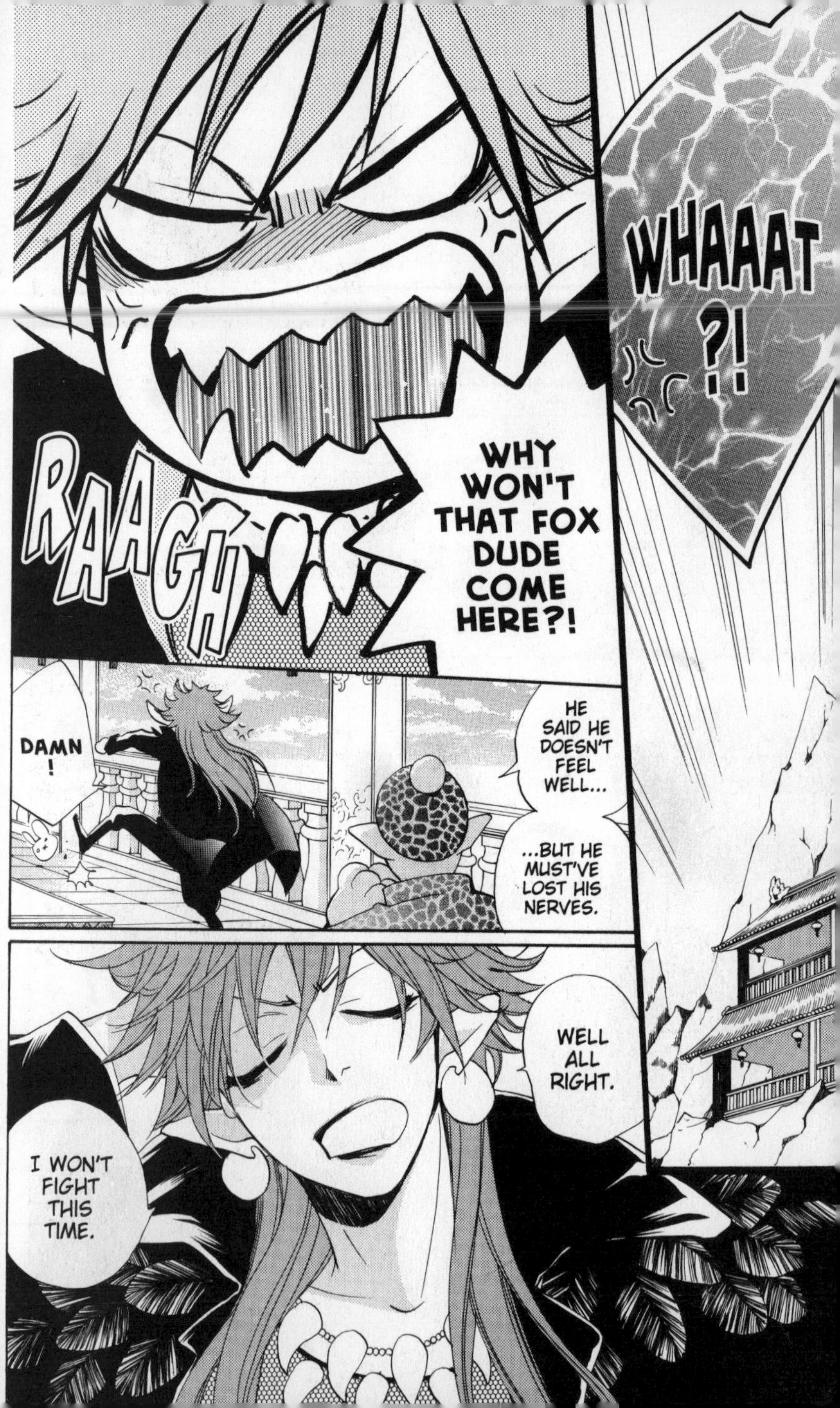
WHAAAT ?!
RAAGH
WHY WON'T THAT FOX DUDE COME HERE?!
HE SAID HE DOESN'T FEEL WELL...
...BUT HE MUST'VE LOST HIS NERVES.
DAMN!
WELL ALL RIGHT.
I WON'T FIGHT THIS TIME.

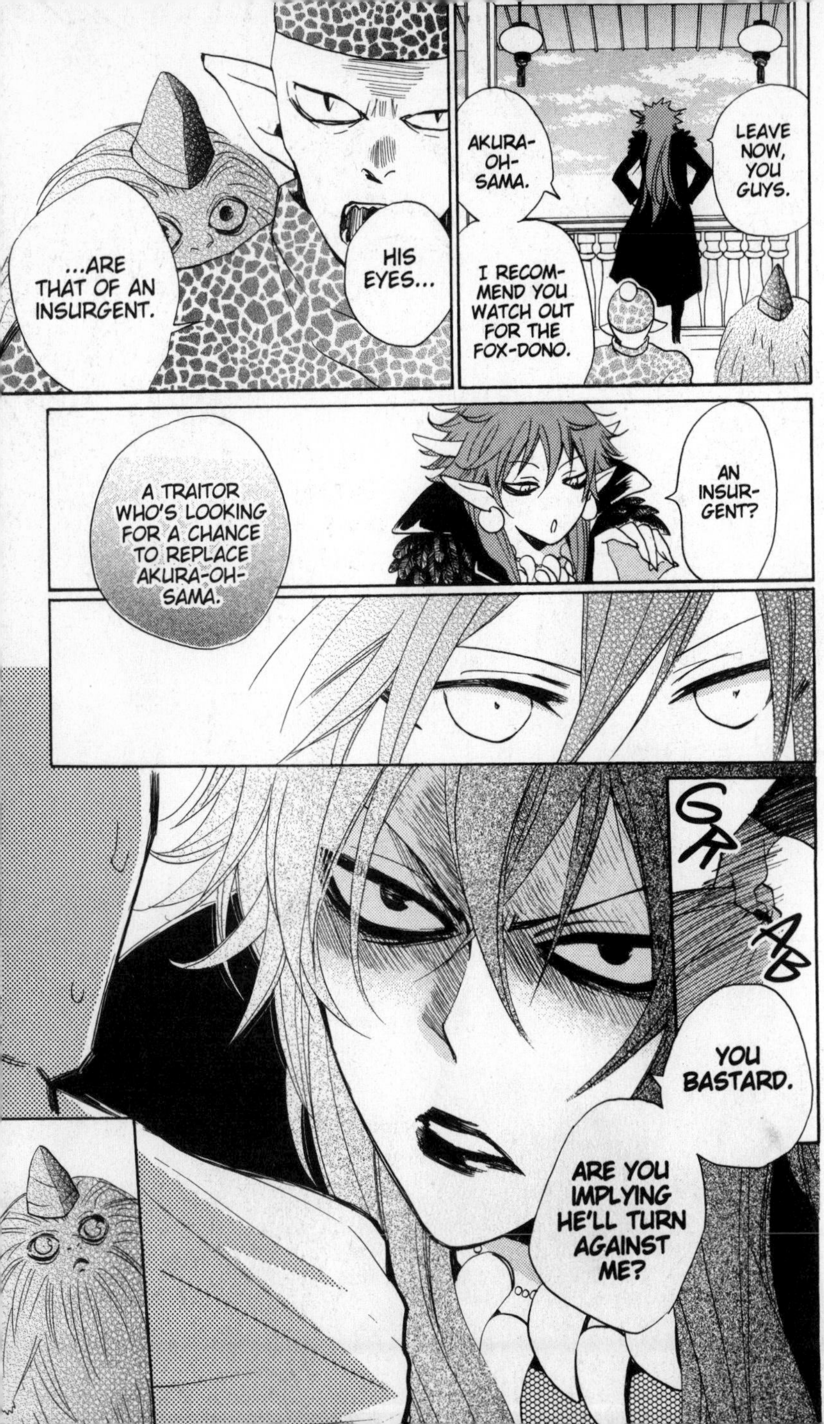
LEAVE NOW, YOU GUYS.
AKURA-OH-SAMA.
I RECOMMEND YOU WATCH OUT FOR THE FOX-DONO.
HIS EYES...
...ARE THAT OF AN INSURGENT.
AN INSURGENT?
A TRAITOR WHO'S LOOKING FOR A CHANCE TO REPLACE AKURA-OH-SAMA.
GRAB
YOU BASTARD.
ARE YOU IMPLYING HE'LL TURN AGAINST ME?

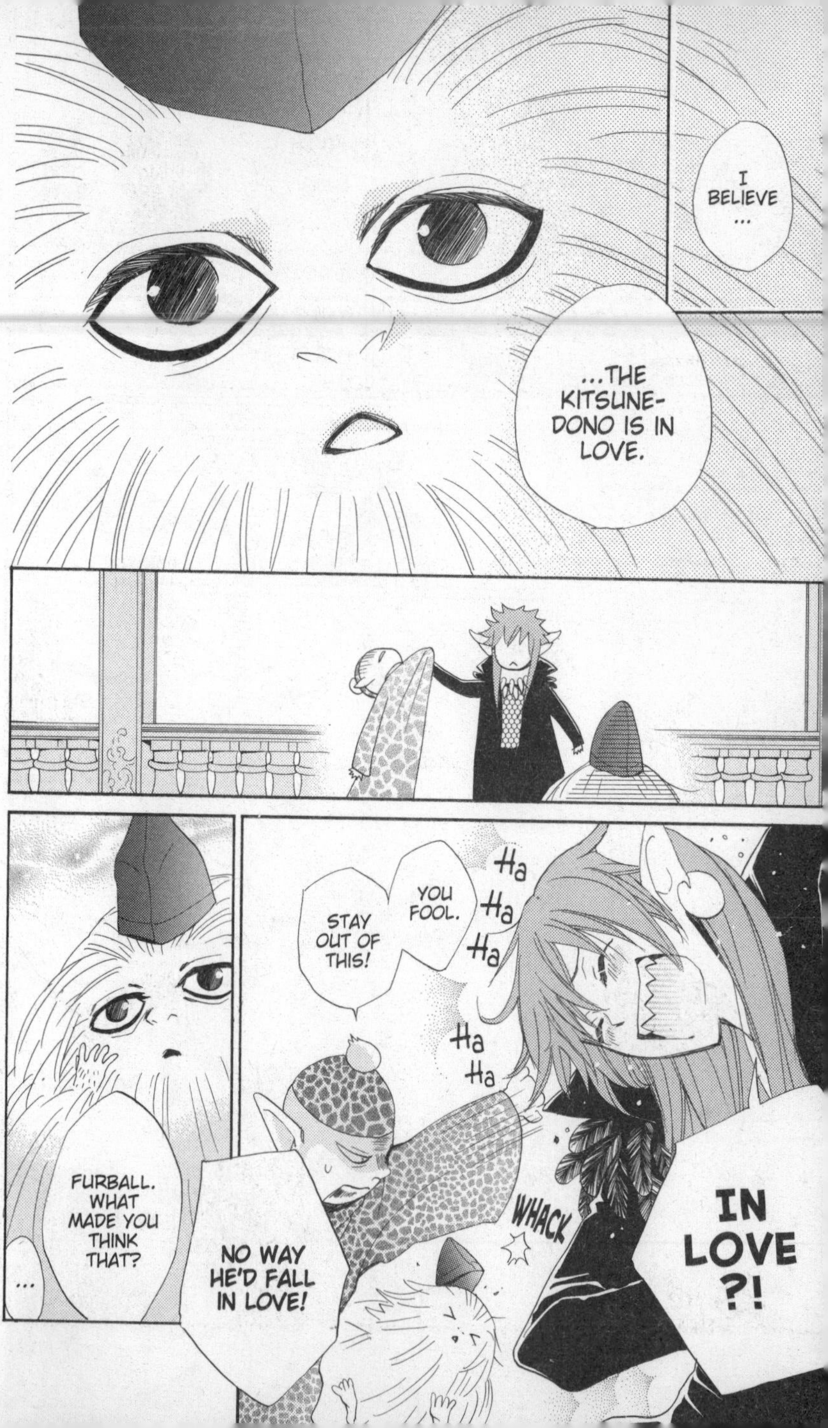
I BELIEVE ...
...THE KITSUNE-DONO IS IN LOVE.
IN LOVE ?!
NO WAY HE'D FALL IN LOVE!
Ha Ha Ha
YOU FOOL.
STAY OUT OF THIS!
Ha Ha
WHACK
FURBALL. WHAT MADE YOU THINK THAT?
...

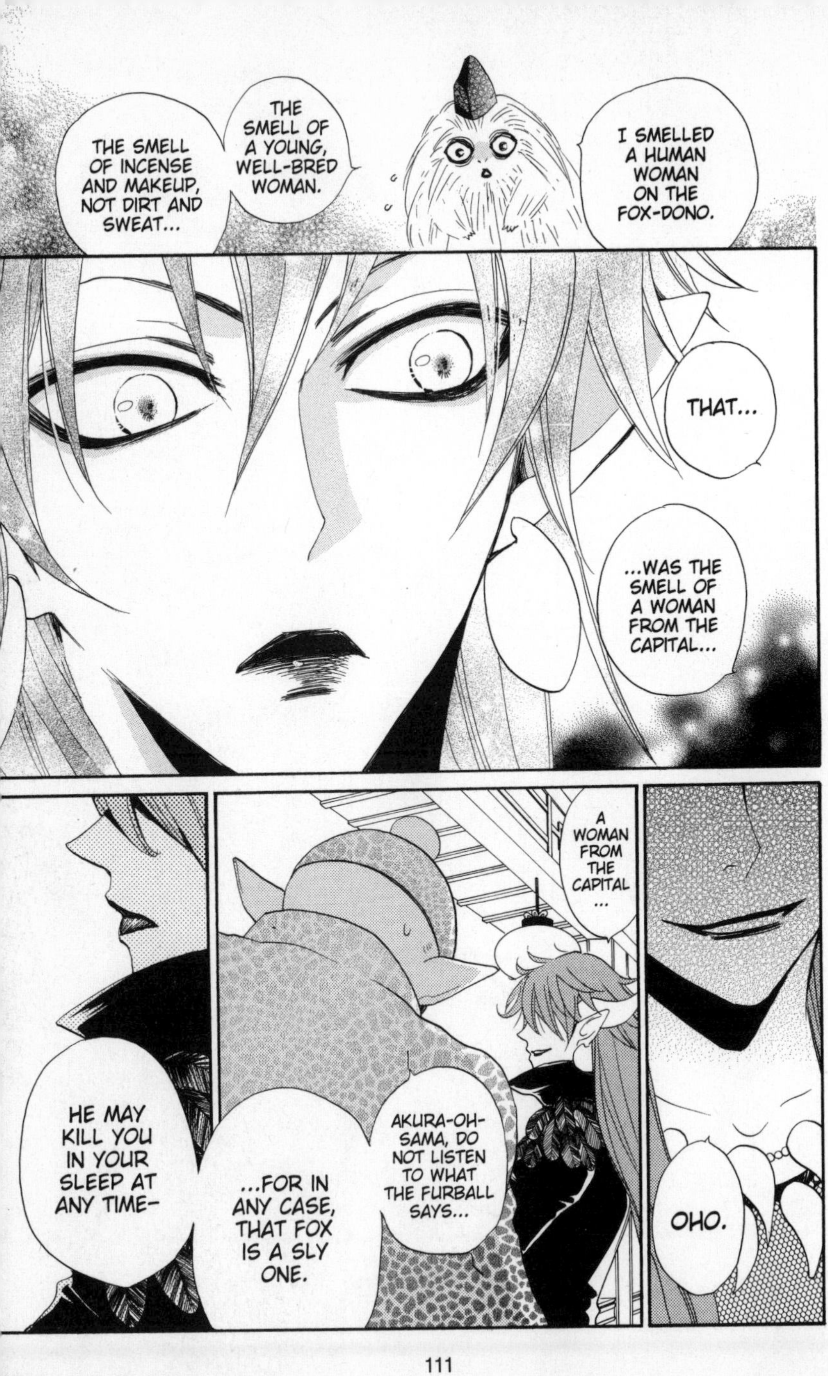
I SMELLED A HUMAN WOMAN ON THE FOX-DONO.
THE SMELL OF A YOUNG, WELL-BRED WOMAN.
THE SMELL OF INCENSE AND MAKEUP, NOT DIRT AND SWEAT...
THAT...
...WAS THE SMELL OF A WOMAN FROM THE CAPITAL...
OHO.
A WOMAN FROM THE CAPITAL...
AKURA-OH-SAMA, DO NOT LISTEN TO WHAT THE FURBALL SAYS...
...FOR IN ANY CASE, THAT FOX IS A SLY ONE.
HE MAY KILL YOU IN YOUR SLEEP AT ANY TIME-

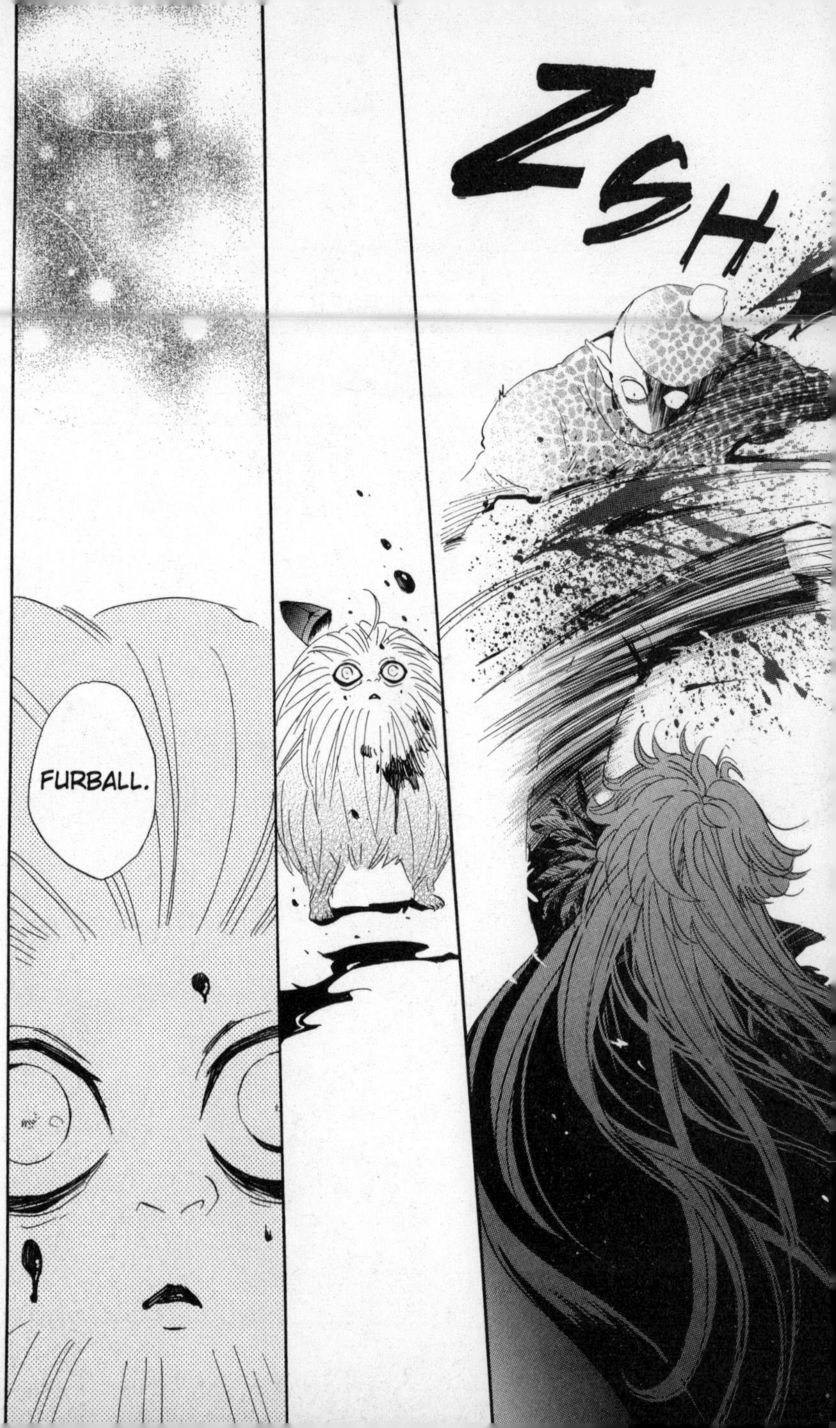
ZSH
FURBALL.

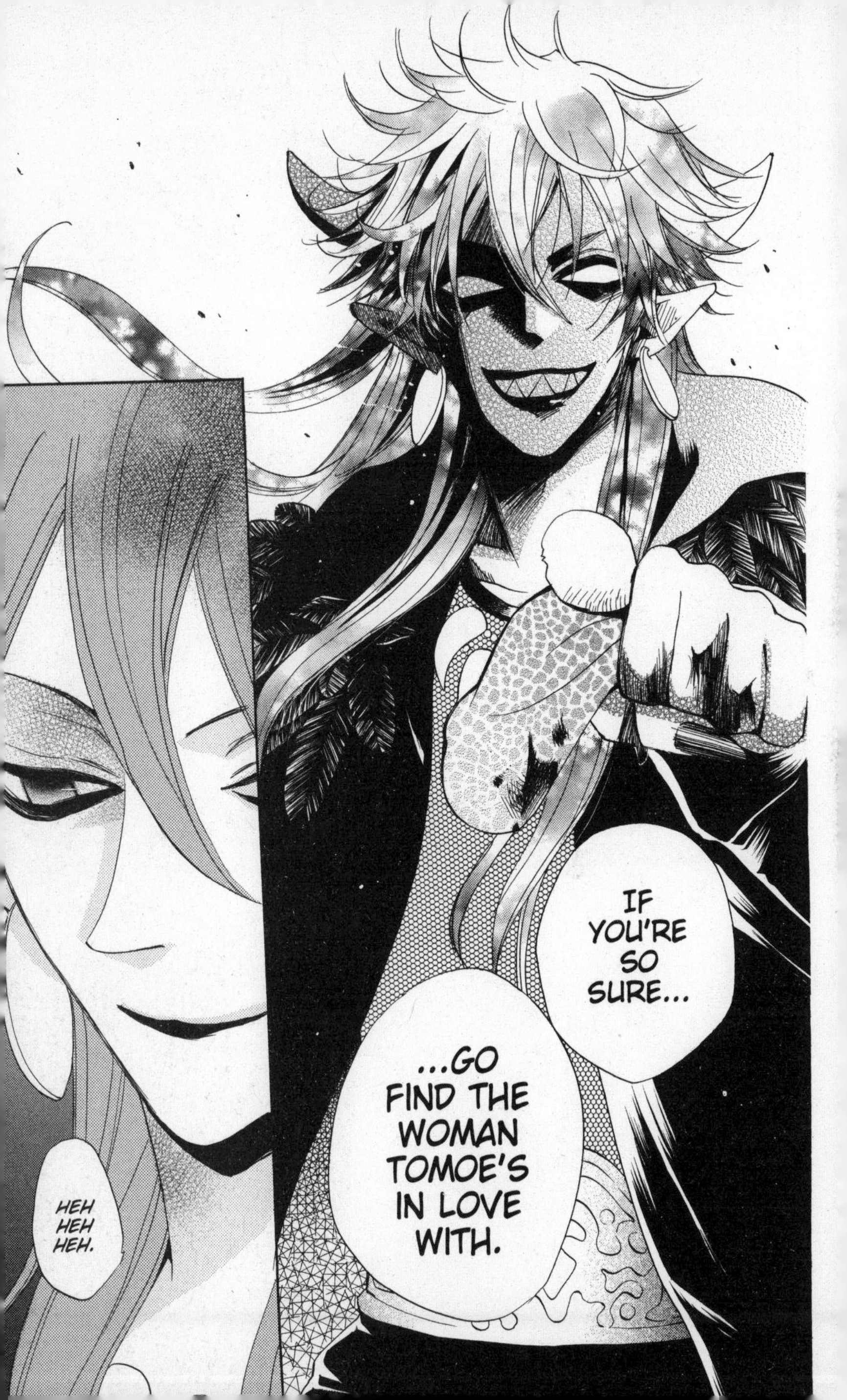
IF YOU'RE SO SURE...
...GO FIND THE WOMAN TOMOE'S IN LOVE WITH.
HEH HEH HEH.

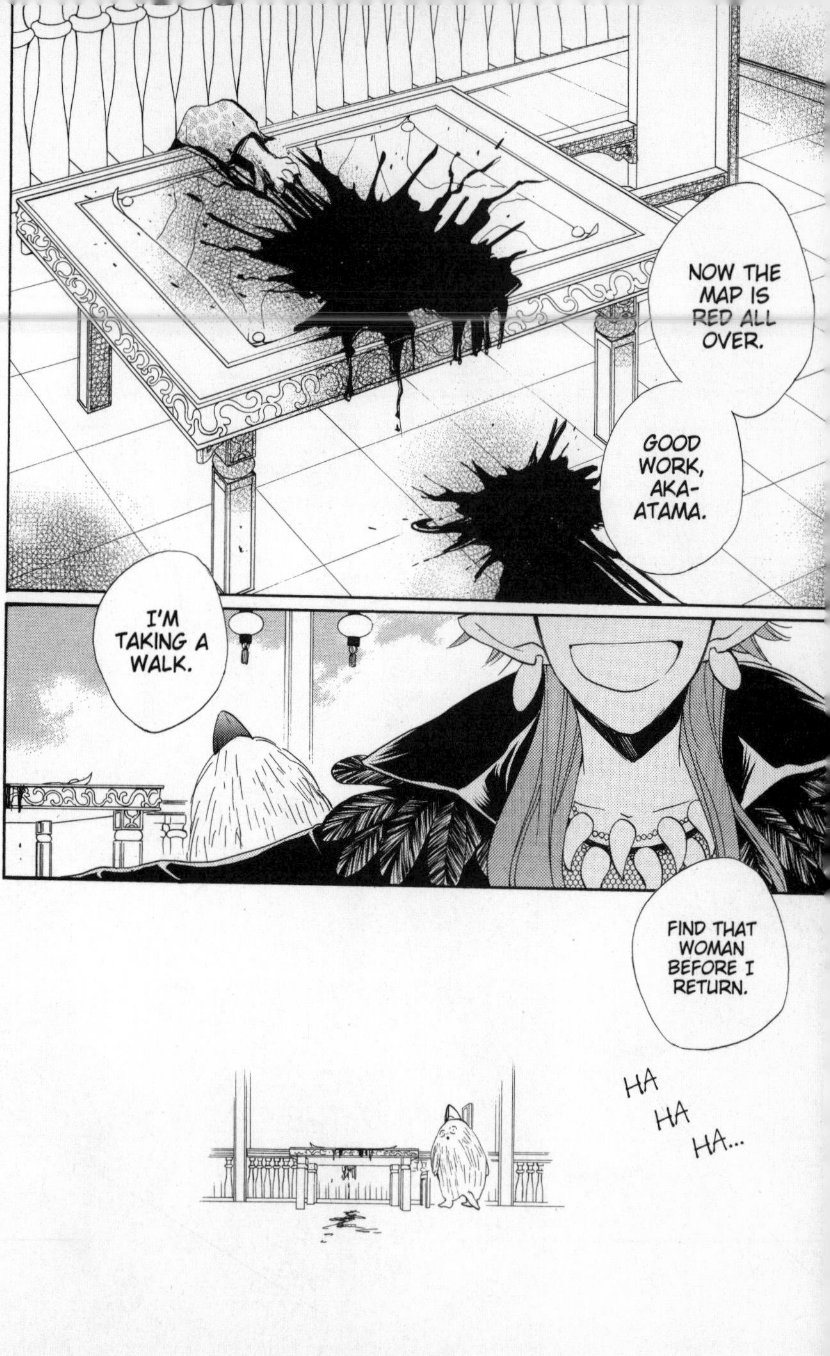
NOW THE MAP IS RED ALL OVER.
GOOD WORK, AKA-ATAMA.
I'M TAKING A WALK.
FIND THAT WOMAN BEFORE I RETURN.
HA HA HA...

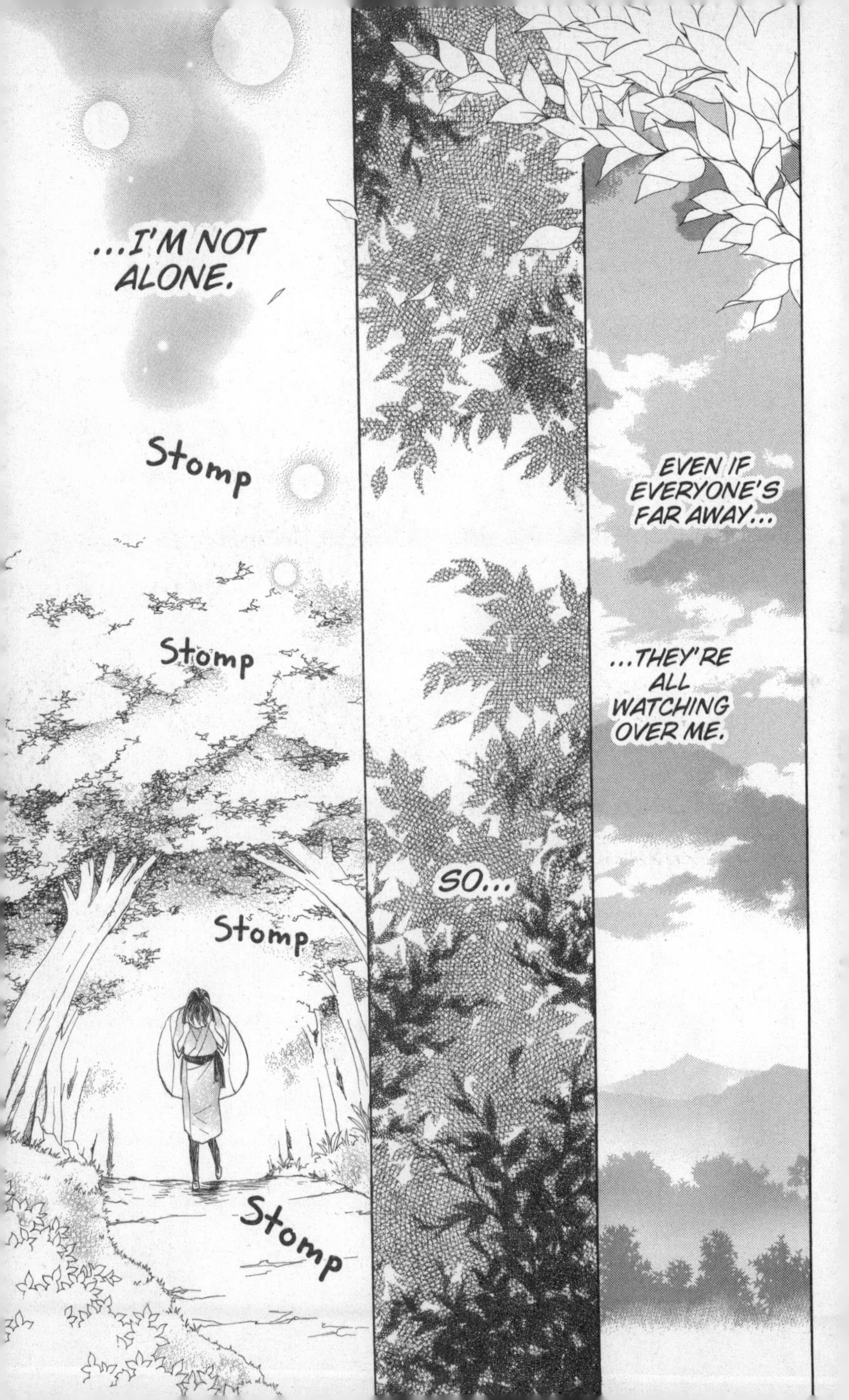
EVEN IF EVERYONE'S FAR AWAY...
...THEY'RE ALL WATCHING OVER ME.
SO...
...I'M NOT ALONE.
Stomp
Stomp
Stomp
Stomp

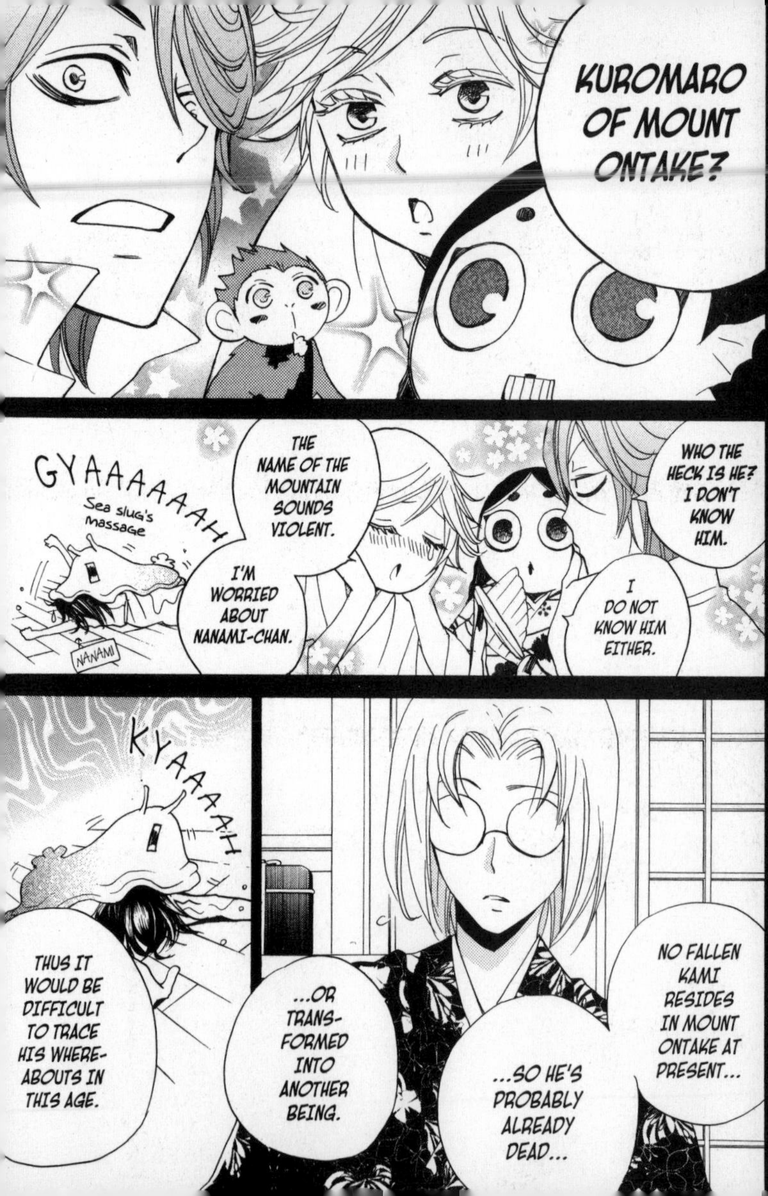
KUROMARO OF MOUNT ONTAKE?
WHO THE HECK IS HE? I DON'T KNOW HIM.
I DO NOT KNOW HIM EITHER.
THE NAME OF THE MOUNTAIN SOUNDS VIOLENT.
I'M WORRIED ABOUT NANAMI-CHAN.
GYAAAAAAAAH
Sea slug's massage
NANAMI
NO FALLEN KAMI RESIDES IN MOUNT ONTAKE AT PRESENT...
...SO HE'S PROBABLY ALREADY DEAD...
...OR TRANS-FORMED INTO ANOTHER BEING.
THUS IT WOULD BE DIFFICULT TO TRACE HIS WHERE-ABOUTS IN THIS AGE.
KYAAAAAH

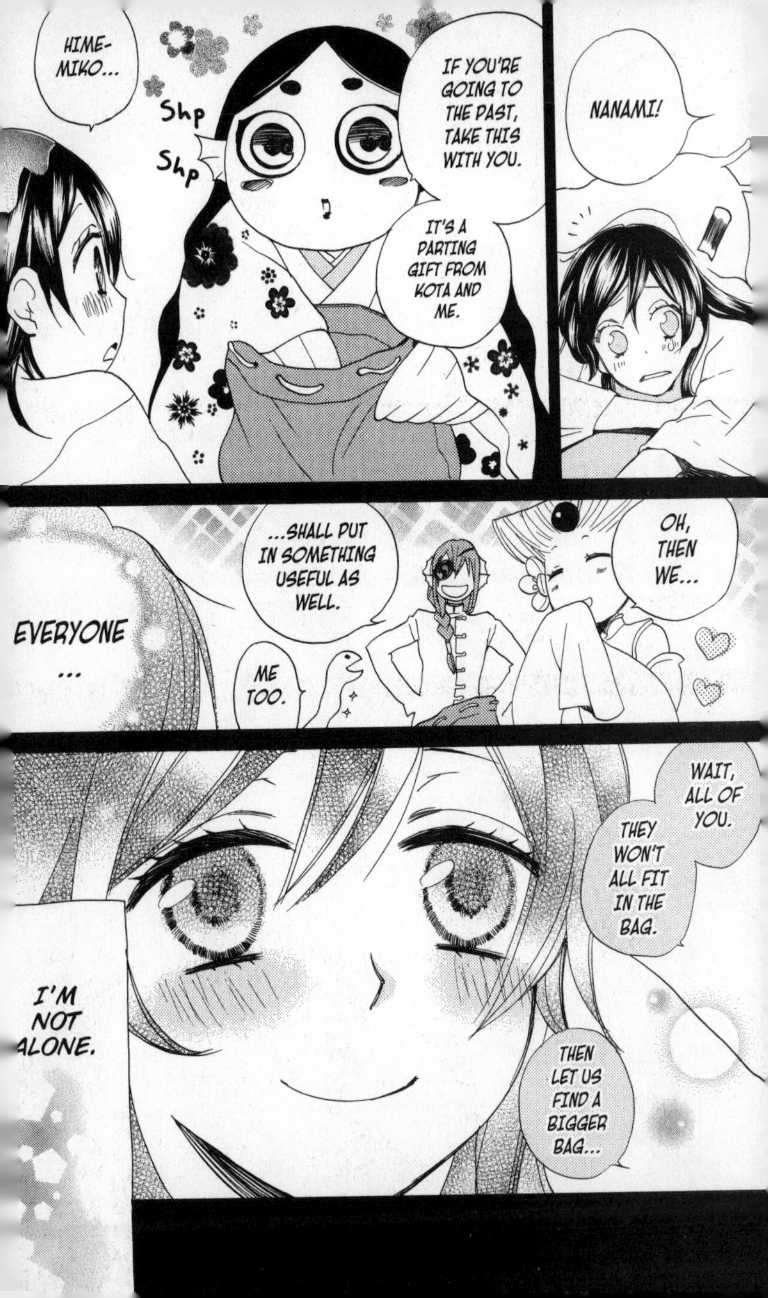
NANAMI!
IF YOU'RE GOING TO THE PAST, TAKE THIS WITH YOU.
HIME-MIKO...
Shp
Shp
IT'S A PARTING GIFT FROM KOTA AND ME.
OH, THEN WE...
...SHALL PUT IN SOMETHING USEFUL AS WELL.
ME TOO.
EVERYONE ...
WAIT, ALL OF YOU.
THEY WON'T ALL FIT IN THE BAG.
THEN LET US FIND A BIGGER BAG...
I'M NOT ALONE.

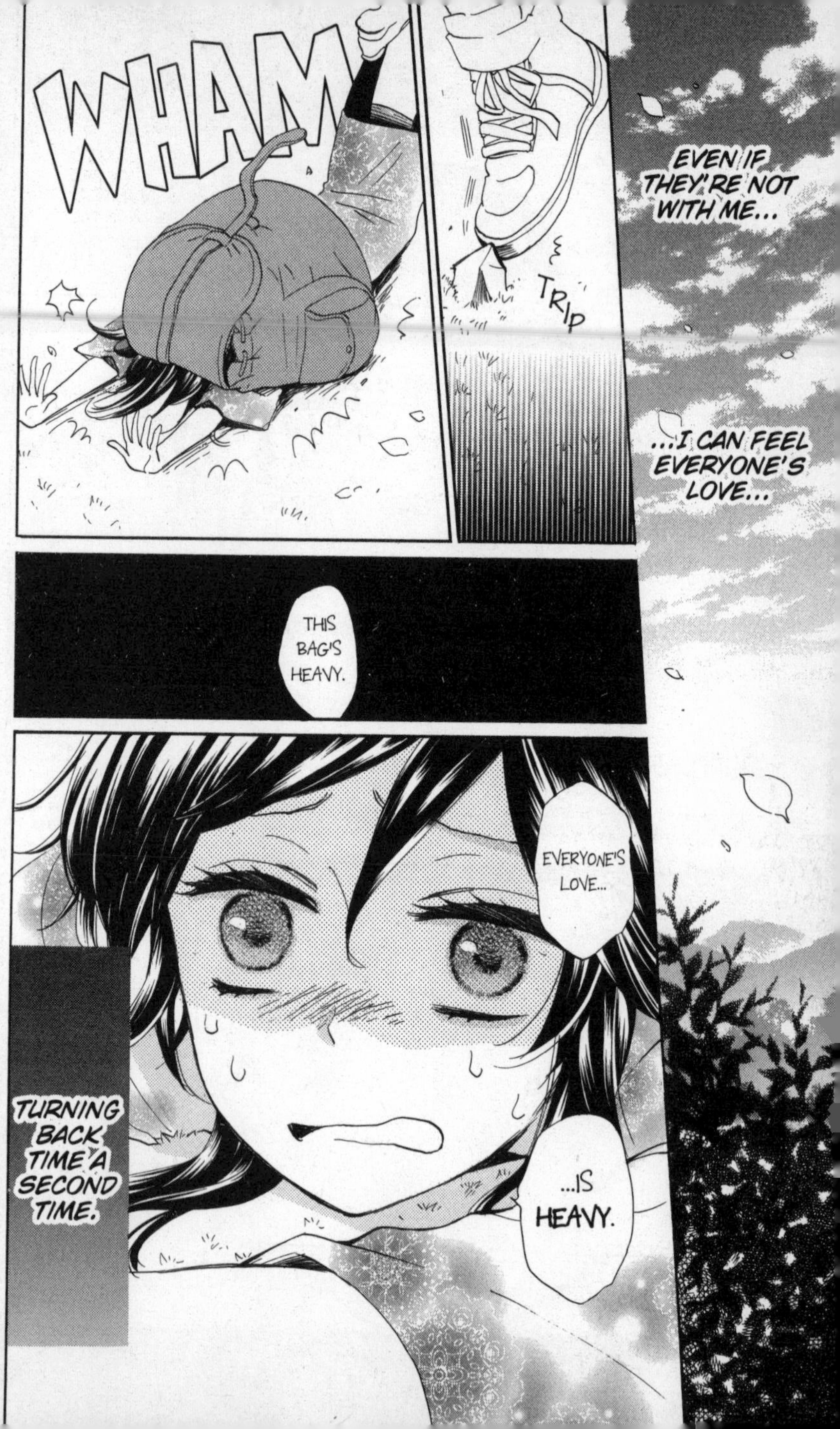
EVEN IF THEY'RE NOT WITH ME...
...I CAN FEEL EVERYONE'S LOVE...
TRIP
WHAM
THIS BAG'S HEAVY.
EVERYONE'S LOVE...
...IS HEAVY.
TURNING BACK TIME A SECOND TIME.

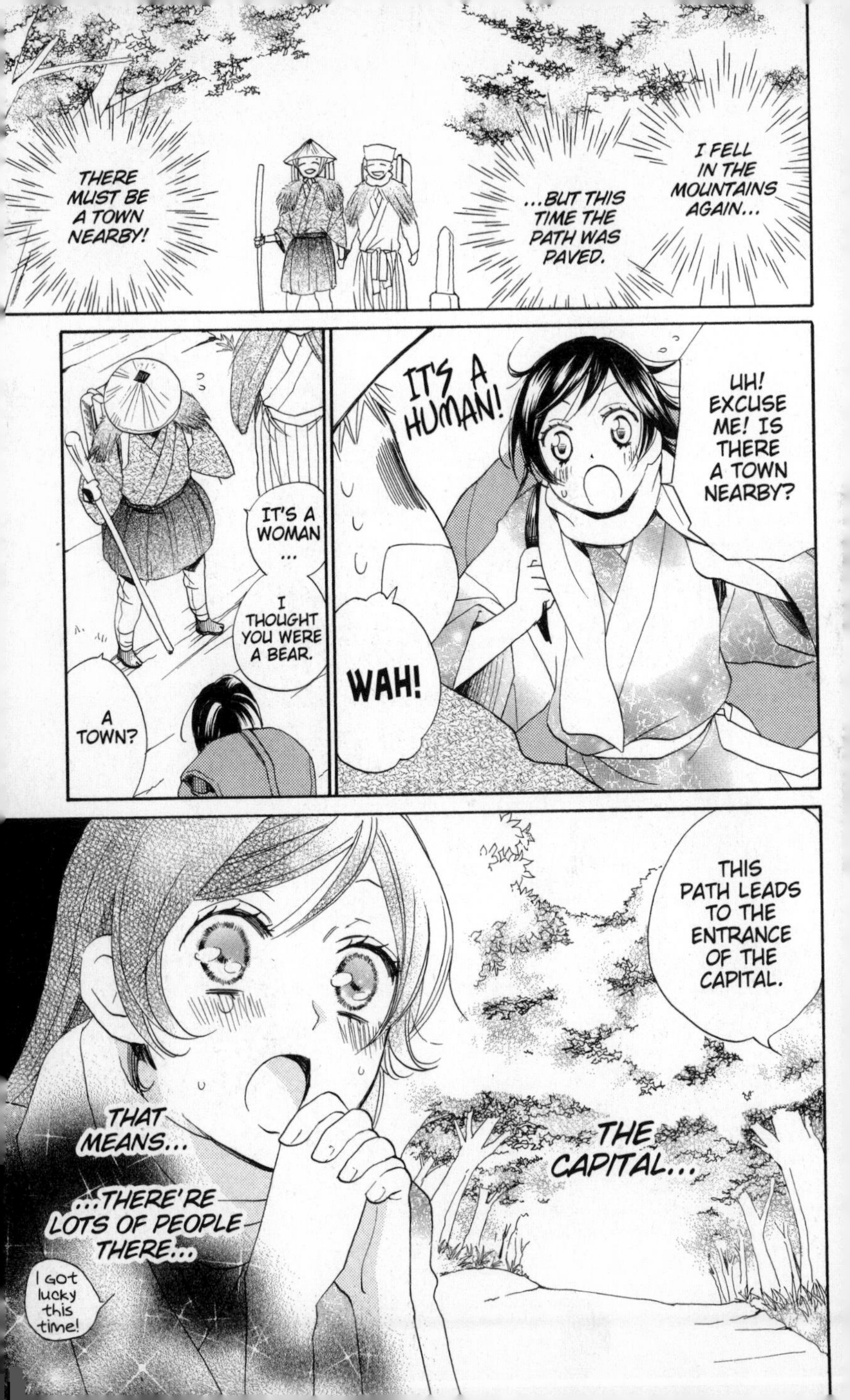
I FELL IN THE MOUNTAINS AGAIN...
...BUT THIS TIME THE PATH WAS PAVED.
THERE MUST BE A TOWN NEARBY!
UH! EXCUSE ME! IS THERE A TOWN NEARBY?
IT'S A HUMAN!
WAH!
IT'S A WOMAN...
I THOUGHT YOU WERE A BEAR.
A TOWN?
THIS PATH LEADS TO THE ENTRANCE OF THE CAPITAL.
THE CAPITAL...
THAT MEANS...
...THERE'RE LOTS OF PEOPLE THERE...
I got lucky this time!

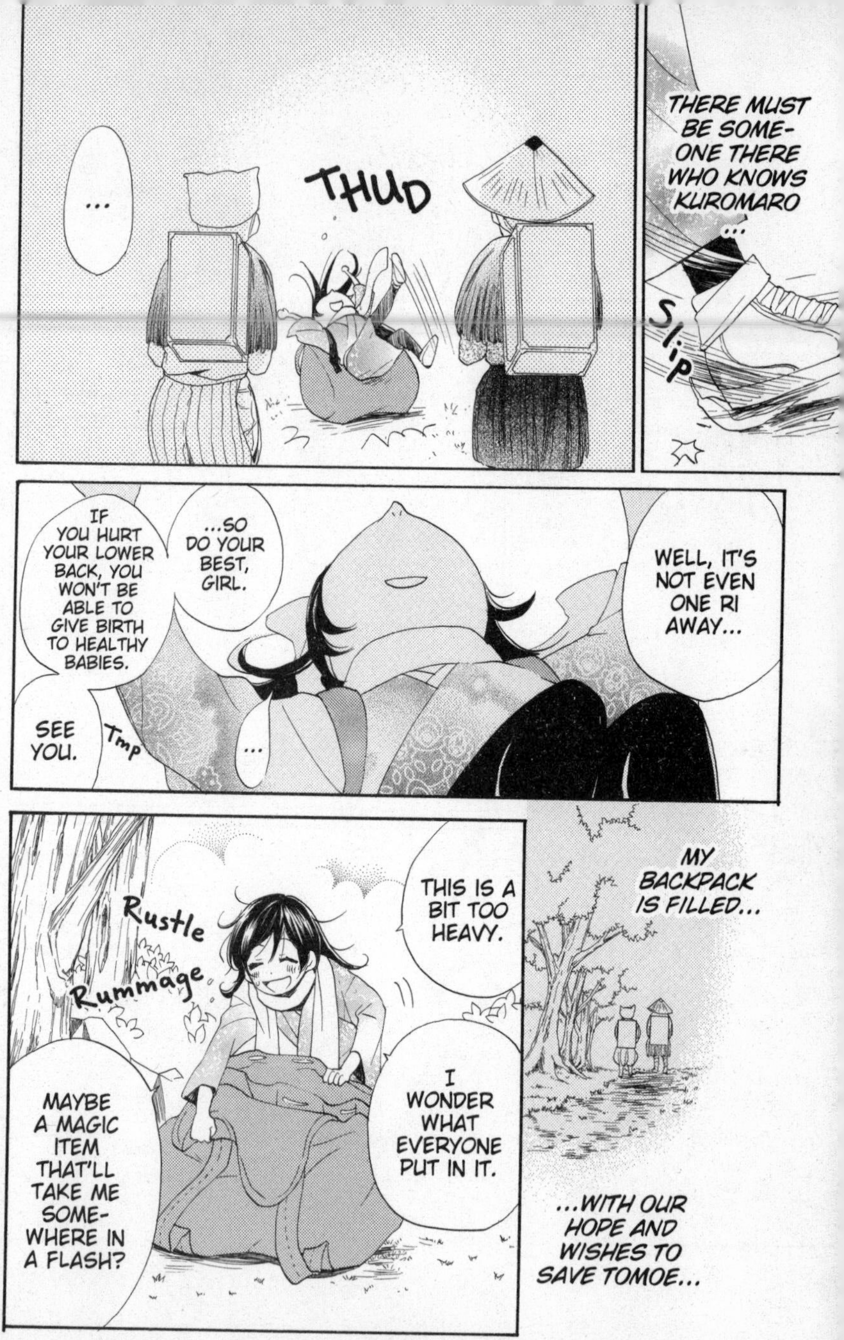
THERE MUST BE SOME-ONE THERE WHO KNOWS KUROMARO...
Slip
THUD
...
WELL, IT'S NOT EVEN ONE RI AWAY...
...SO DO YOUR BEST, GIRL.
IF YOU HURT YOUR LOWER BACK, YOU WON'T BE ABLE TO GIVE BIRTH TO HEALTHY BABIES.
...
Tmp
SEE YOU.
MY BACKPACK IS FILLED...
...WITH OUR HOPE AND WISHES TO SAVE TOMOE...
THIS IS A BIT TOO HEAVY.
Rustle
Rummage
I WONDER WHAT EVERYONE PUT IN IT.
MAYBE A MAGIC ITEM THAT'LL TAKE ME SOME-WHERE IN A FLASH?

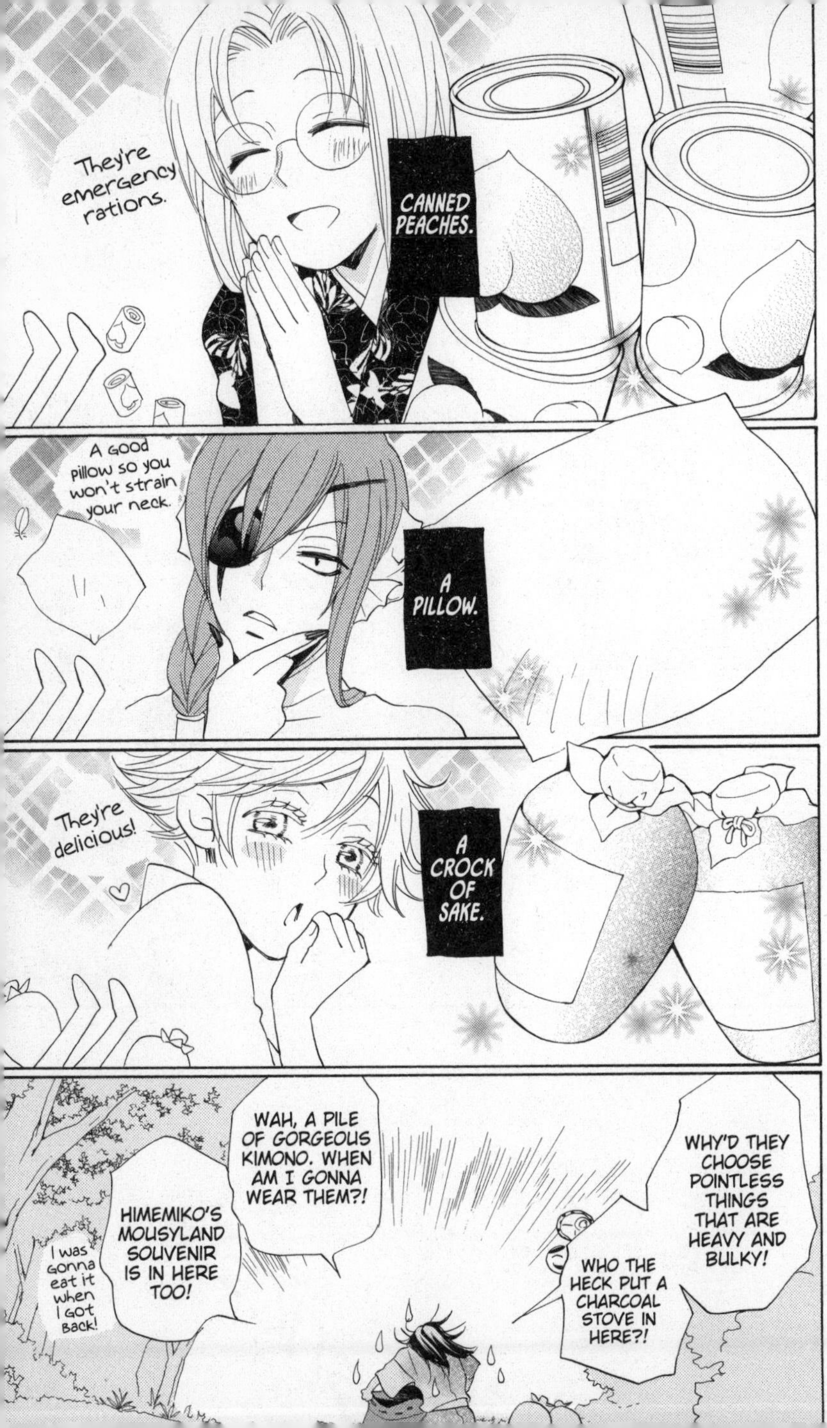
CANNED PEACHES.
They're emergency rations.
A PILLOW.
A good pillow so you won't strain your neck.
A CROCK OF SAKE.
They're delicious!
WHY'D THEY CHOOSE POINTLESS THINGS THAT ARE HEAVY AND BULKY!
WAH, A PILE OF GORGEOUS KIMONO. WHEN AM I GONNA WEAR THEM?!
WHO THE HECK PUT A CHARCOAL STOVE IN HERE?!
HIMEMIKO'S MOUSYLAND SOUVENIR IS IN HERE TOO!
I was gonna eat it when I got back!

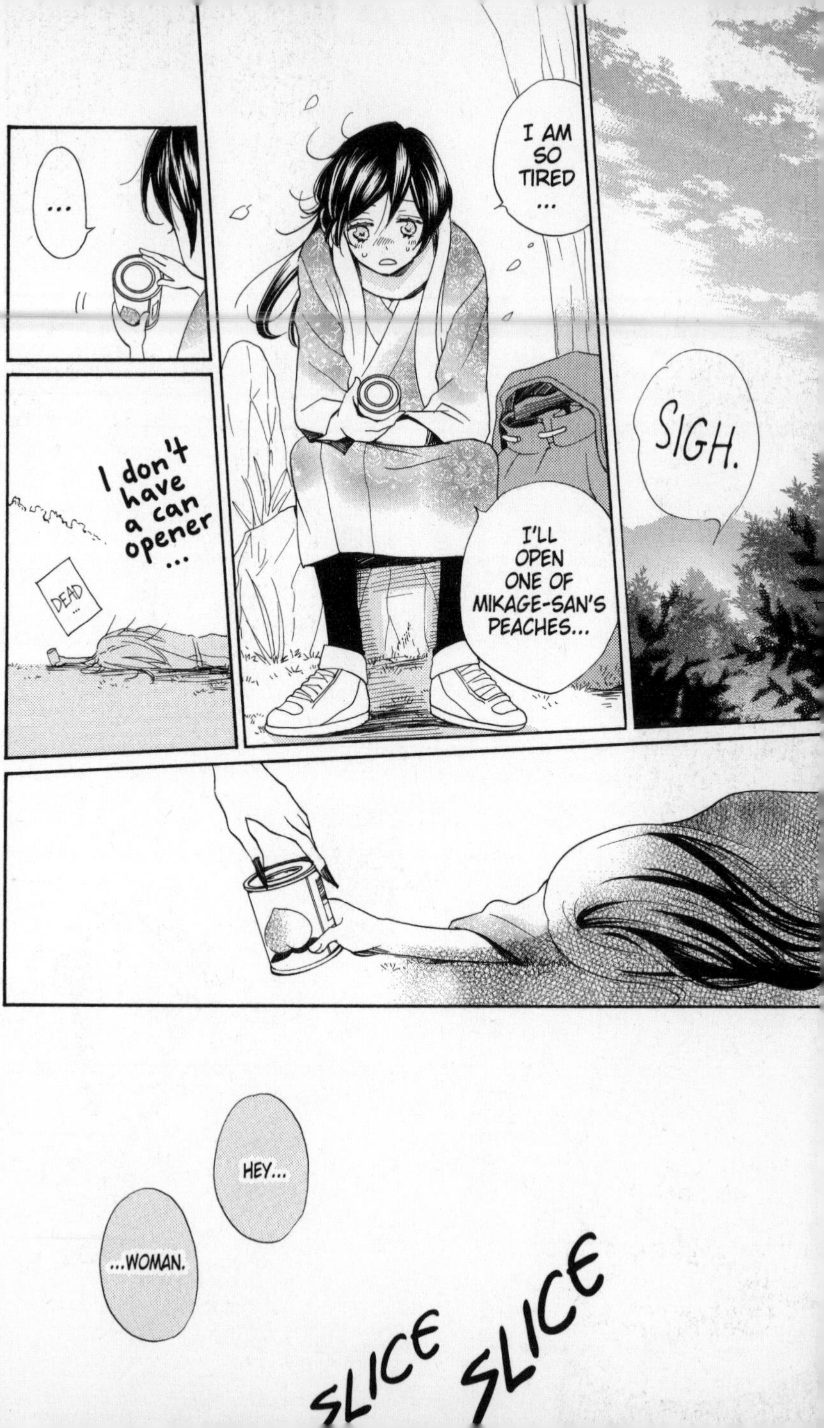
SIGH.
I AM SO TIRED...
I'LL OPEN ONE OF MIKAGE-SAN'S PEACHES...
...
I don't have a can opener...
DEAD...
HEY...
...WOMAN.
SLICE
SLICE

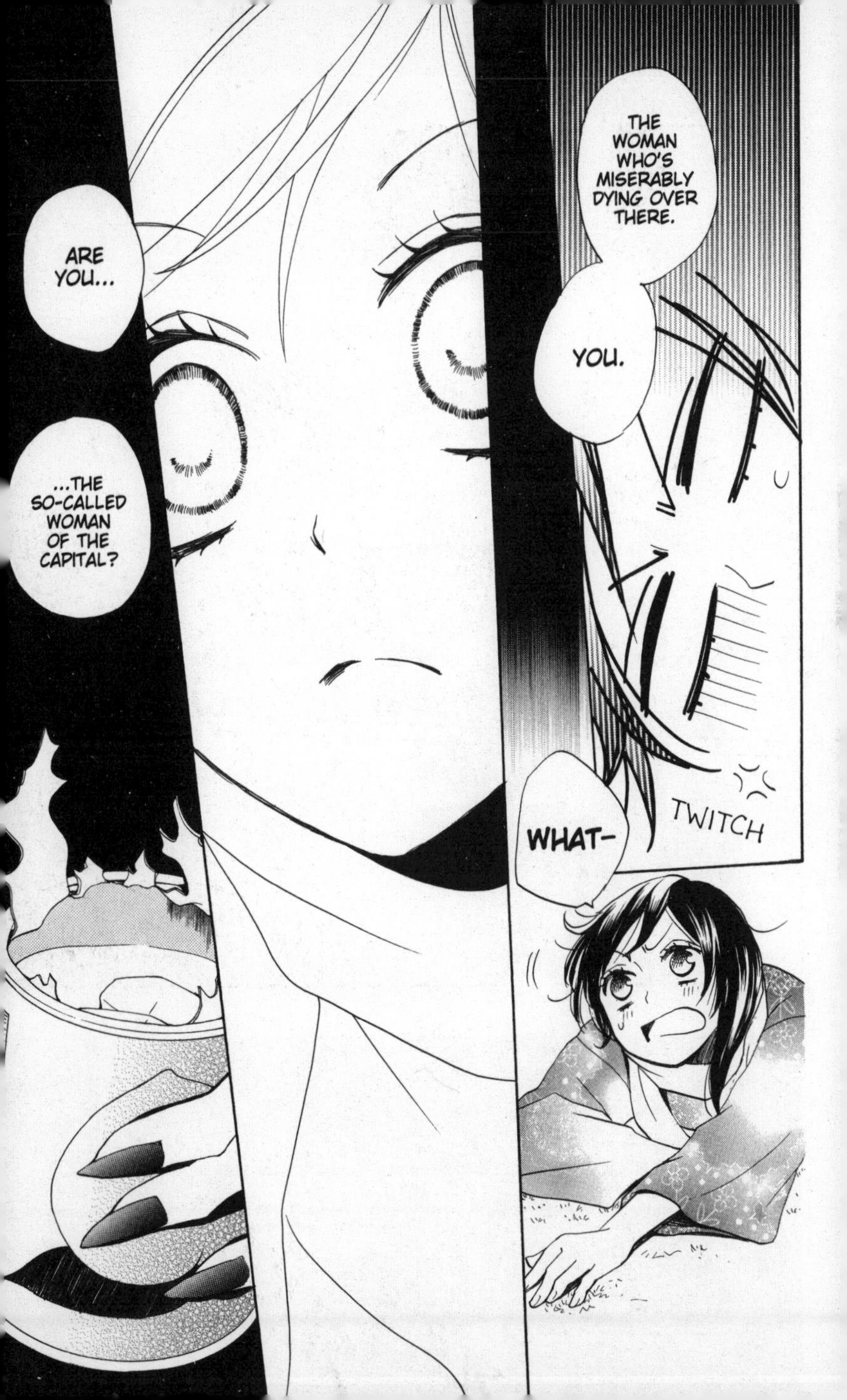
THE WOMAN WHO'S MISERABLY DYING OVER THERE.
YOU.
TWITCH
WHAT-
ARE YOU...
...THE SO-CALLED WOMAN OF THE CAPITAL?

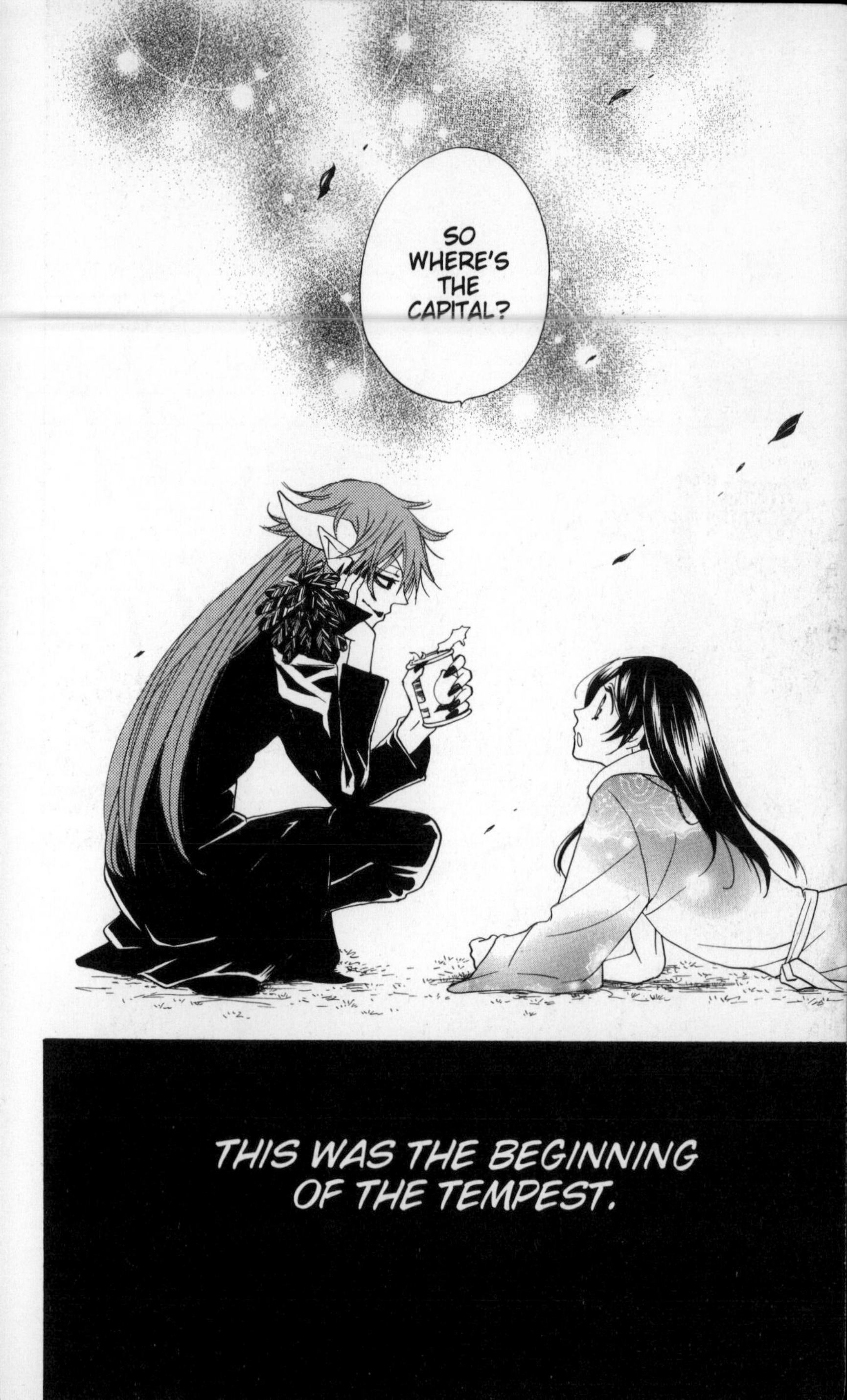
SO WHERE'S THE CAPITAL?
THIS WAS THE BEGINNING OF THE TEMPEST.

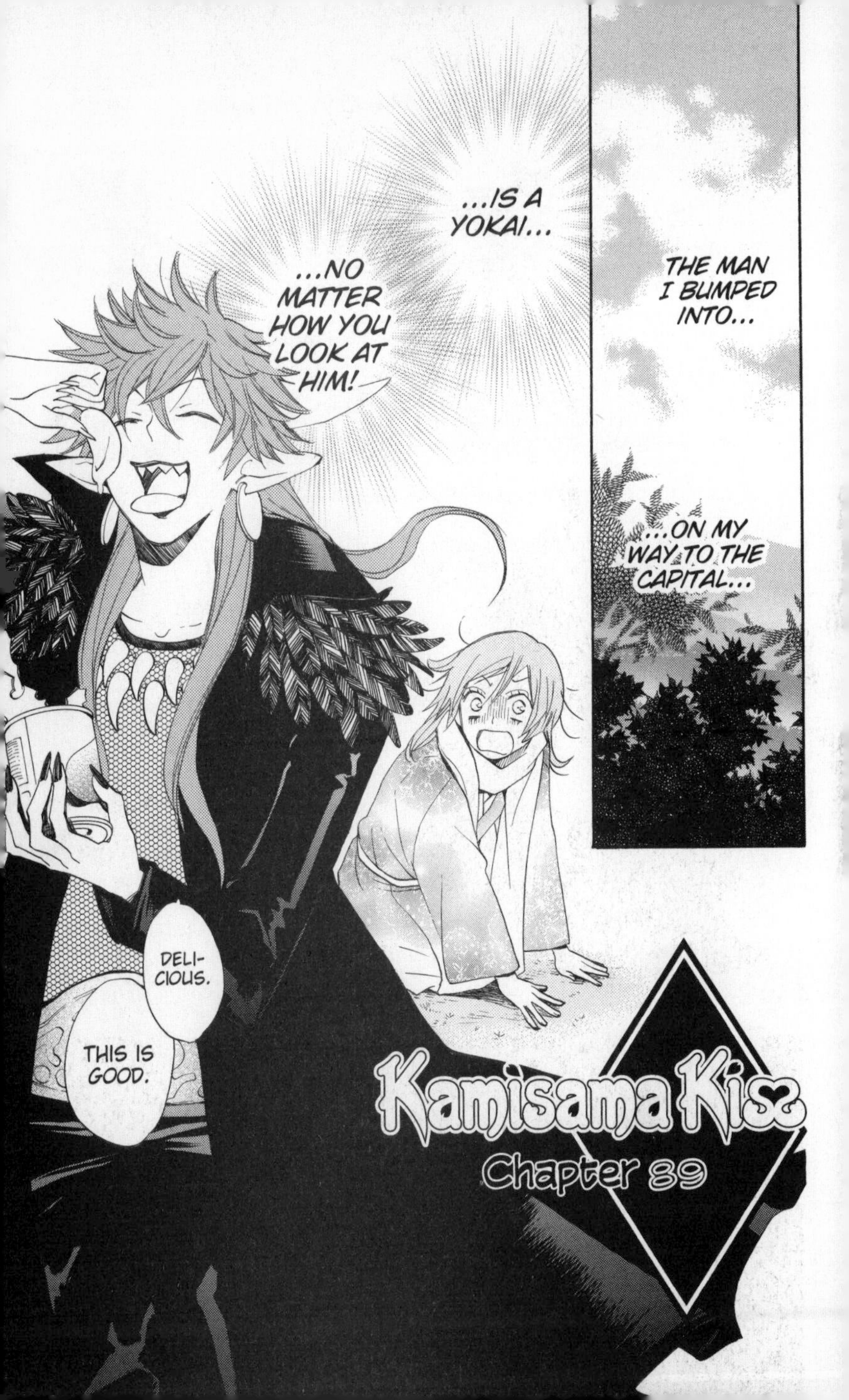
THE MAN I BUMPED INTO...
...ON MY WAY TO THE CAPITAL...
...IS A YOKAI...
...NO MATTER HOW YOU LOOK AT HIM!
DELICIOUS.
THIS IS GOOD.
Kamisama Kiss
Chapter 89

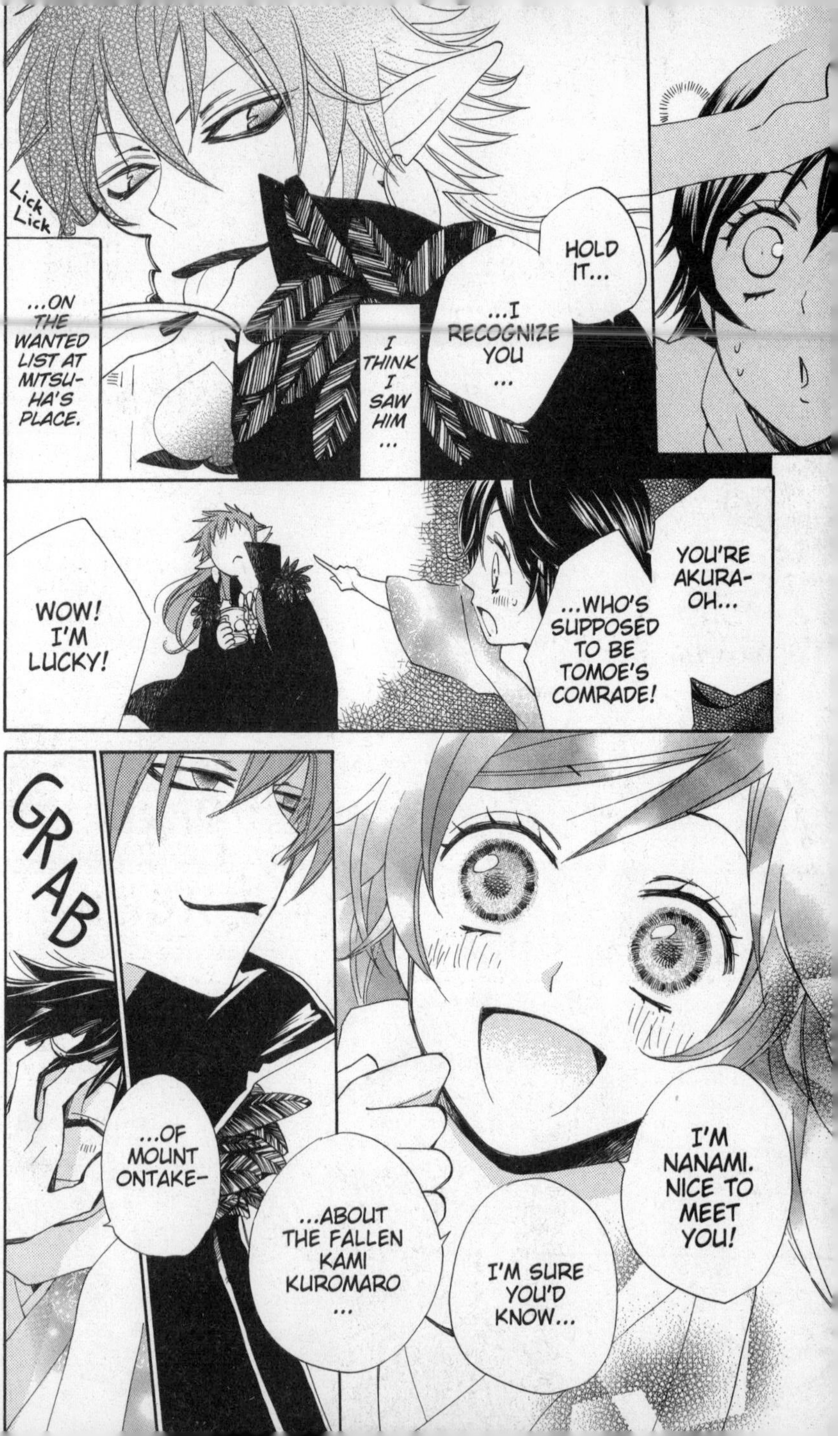
HOLD IT...
...I RECOGNIZE YOU ...
I THINK I SAW HIM ...
Lick Lick
...ON THE WANTED LIST AT MITSU-HA'S PLACE.
YOU'RE AKURA-OH...
...WHO'S SUPPOSED TO BE TOMOE'S COMRADE!
WOW! I'M LUCKY!
I'M NANAMI. NICE TO MEET YOU!
I'M SURE YOU'D KNOW...
...ABOUT THE FALLEN KAMI KUROMARO ...
...OF MOUNT ONTAKE-
GRAB

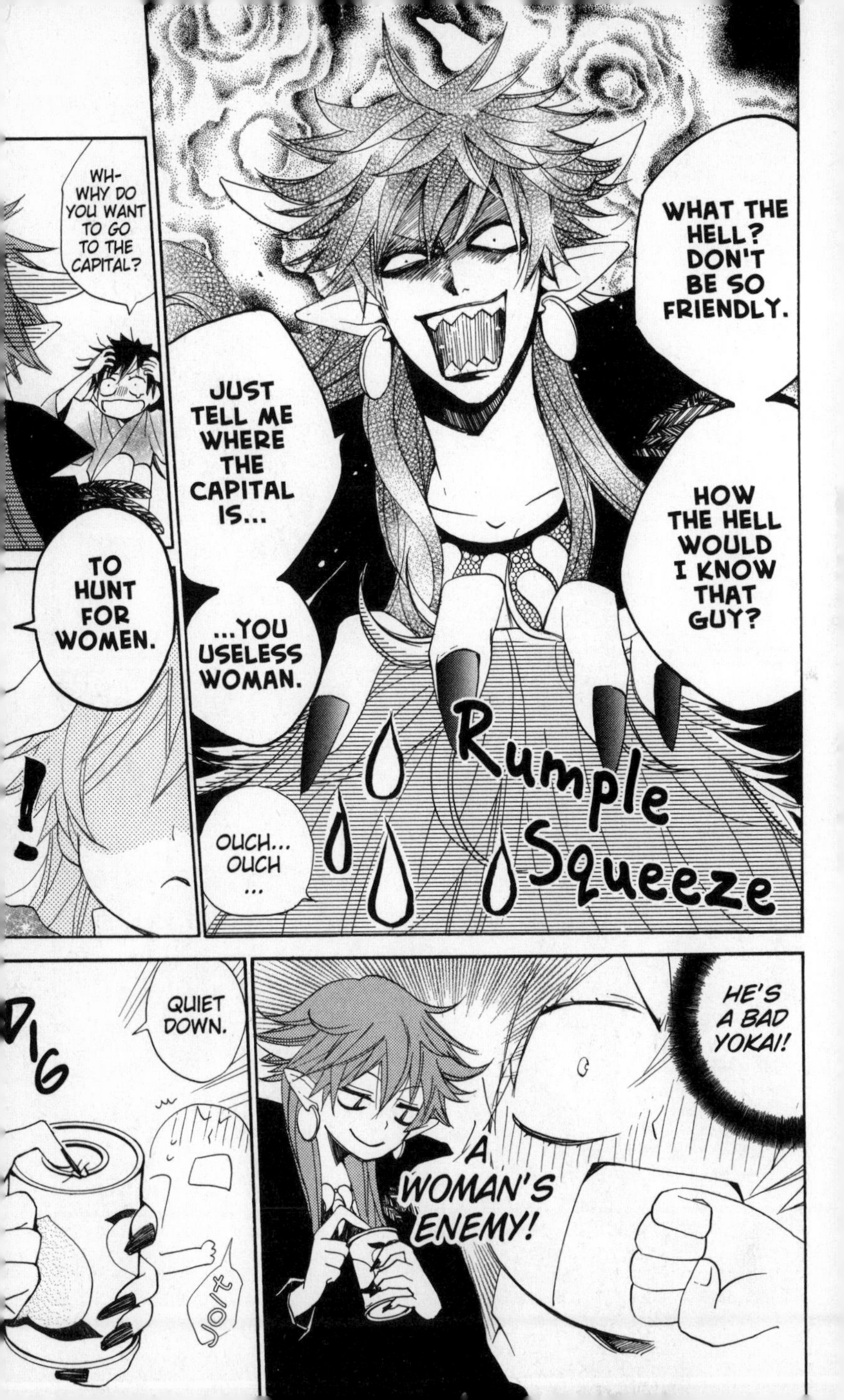
WHAT THE HELL? DON'T BE SO FRIENDLY.
HOW THE HELL WOULD I KNOW THAT GUY?
JUST TELL ME WHERE THE CAPITAL IS...
...YOU USELESS WOMAN.
Rumple Squeeze
OUCH... OUCH ...
WH- WHY DO YOU WANT TO GO TO THE CAPITAL?
TO HUNT FOR WOMEN.
!
HE'S A BAD YOKAI!
A WOMAN'S ENEMY!
QUIET DOWN.
DIG
Jolt

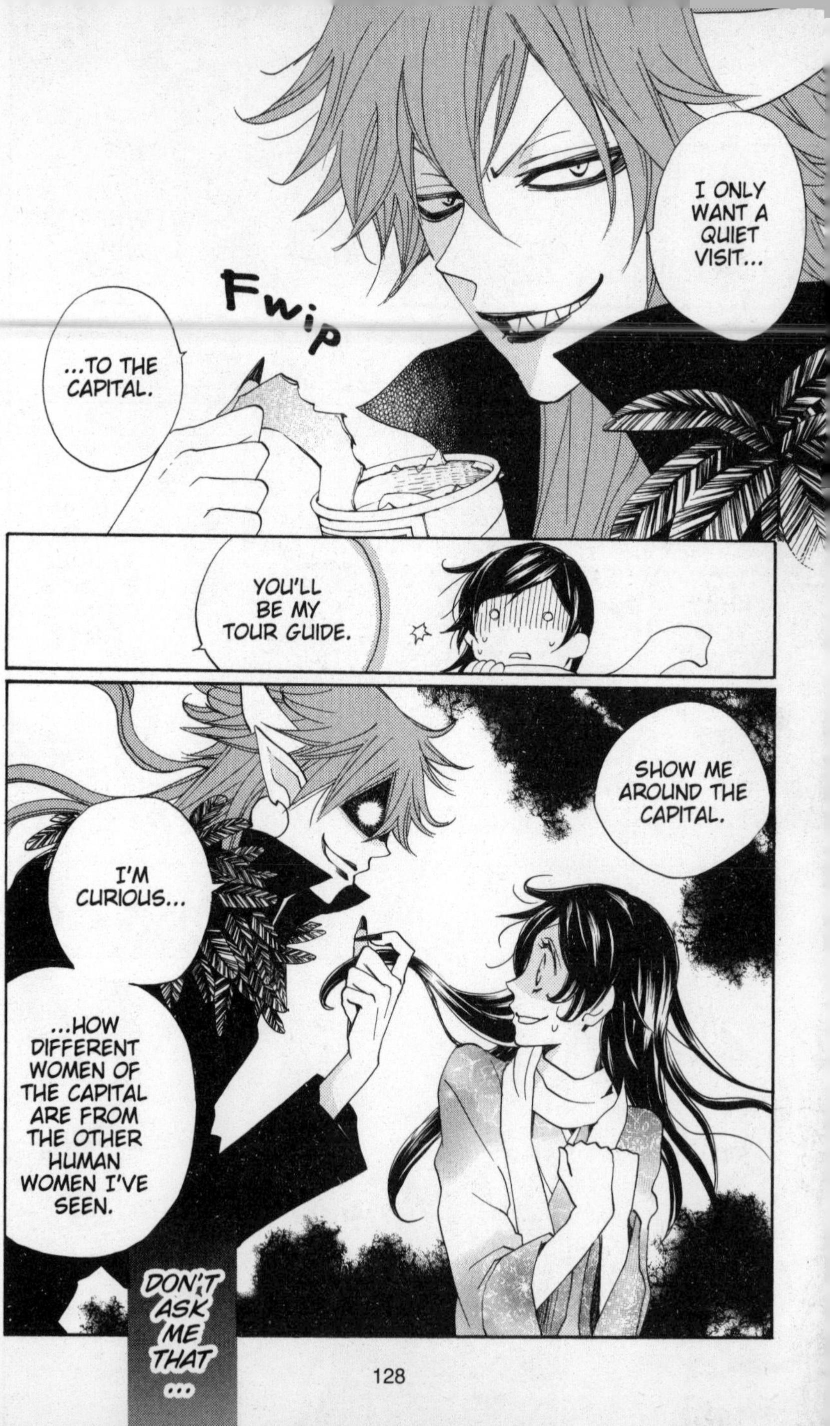
I ONLY WANT A QUIET VISIT...
Fwip
...TO THE CAPITAL.
YOU'LL BE MY TOUR GUIDE.
SHOW ME AROUND THE CAPITAL.
I'M CURIOUS...
...HOW DIFFERENT WOMEN OF THE CAPITAL ARE FROM THE OTHER HUMAN WOMEN I'VE SEEN.
DON'T ASK ME THAT...

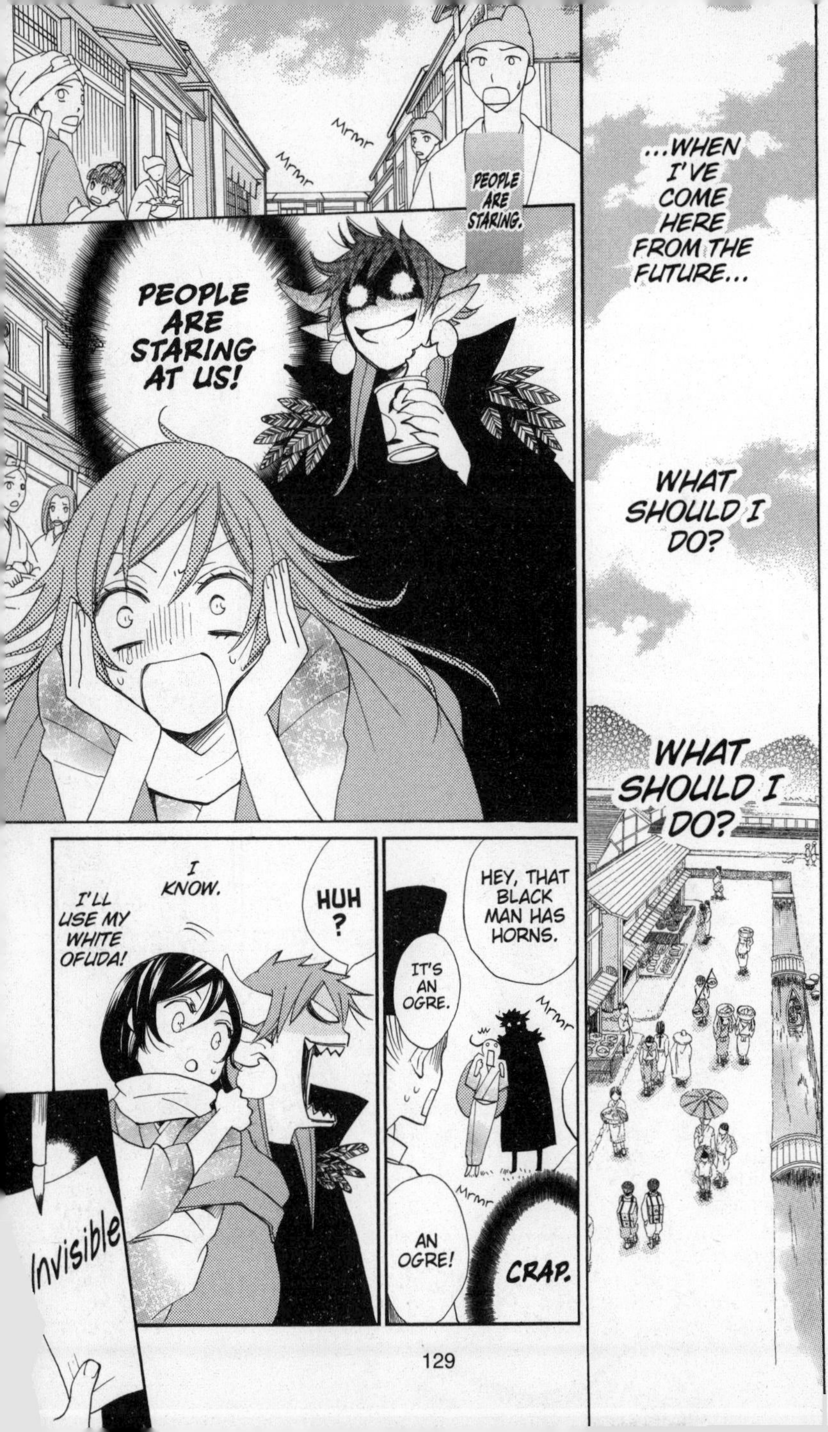
...WHEN I'VE COME HERE FROM THE FUTURE...
WHAT SHOULD I DO?
WHAT SHOULD I DO?
Mrmr
Mrmr
PEOPLE ARE STARING.
PEOPLE ARE STARING AT US!
HEY, THAT BLACK MAN HAS HORNS.
IT'S AN OGRE.
Mrmr
Mrmr
AN OGRE!
CRAP.
HUH?
I KNOW.
I'LL USE MY WHITE OFUDA!
Invisible

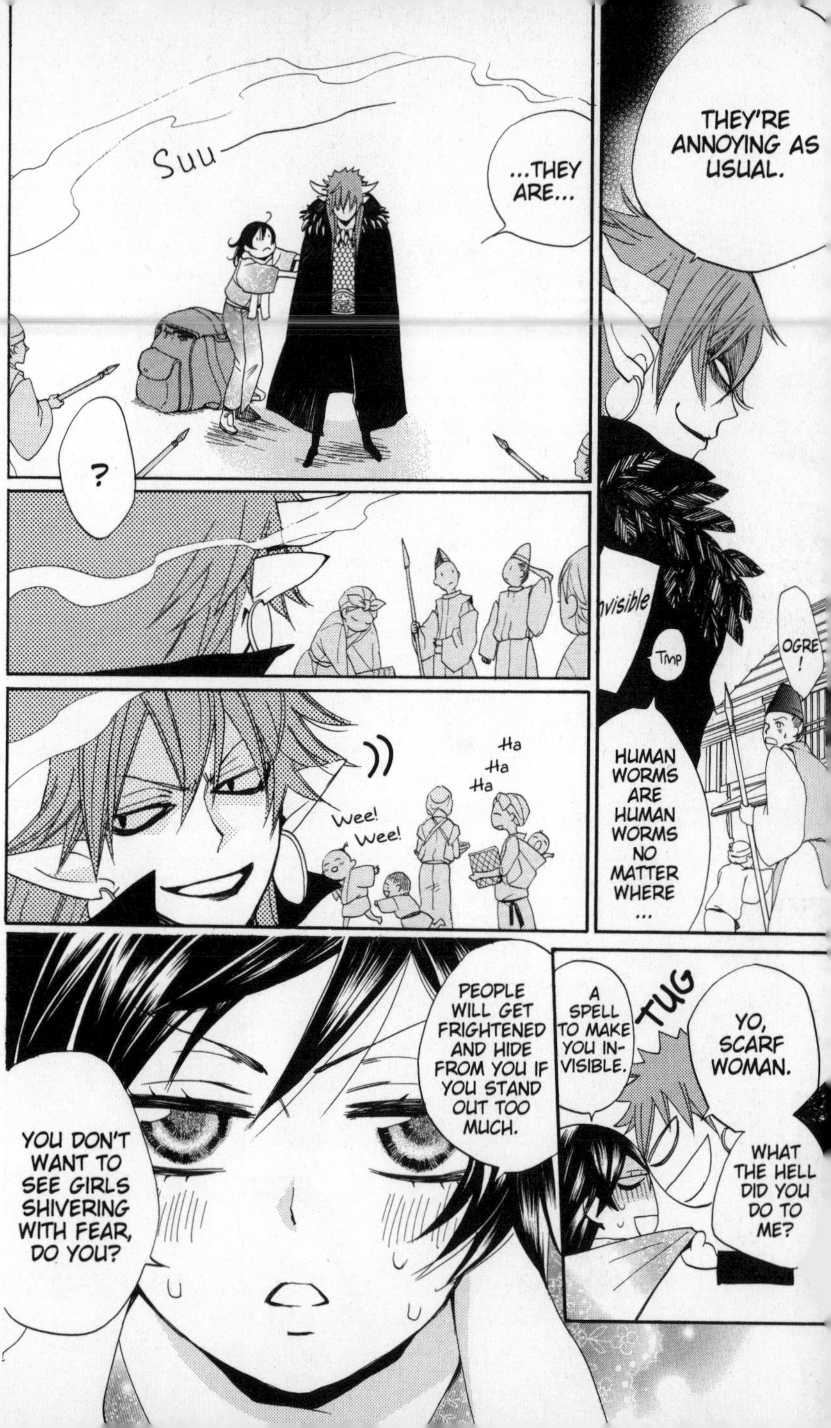

THEY'RE ANNOYING AS USUAL.
nvisible
Tmp
OGRE!
HUMAN WORMS ARE HUMAN WORMS NO MATTER WHERE...
Suu
...THEY ARE...
?
Wee! Wee!
Ha Ha Ha
TUG
YO, SCARF WOMAN.
WHAT THE HELL DID YOU DO TO ME?
A SPELL TO MAKE YOU IN-VISIBLE.
PEOPLE WILL GET FRIGHTENED AND HIDE FROM YOU IF YOU STAND OUT TOO MUCH.
YOU DON'T WANT TO SEE GIRLS SHIVERING WITH FEAR, DO YOU?

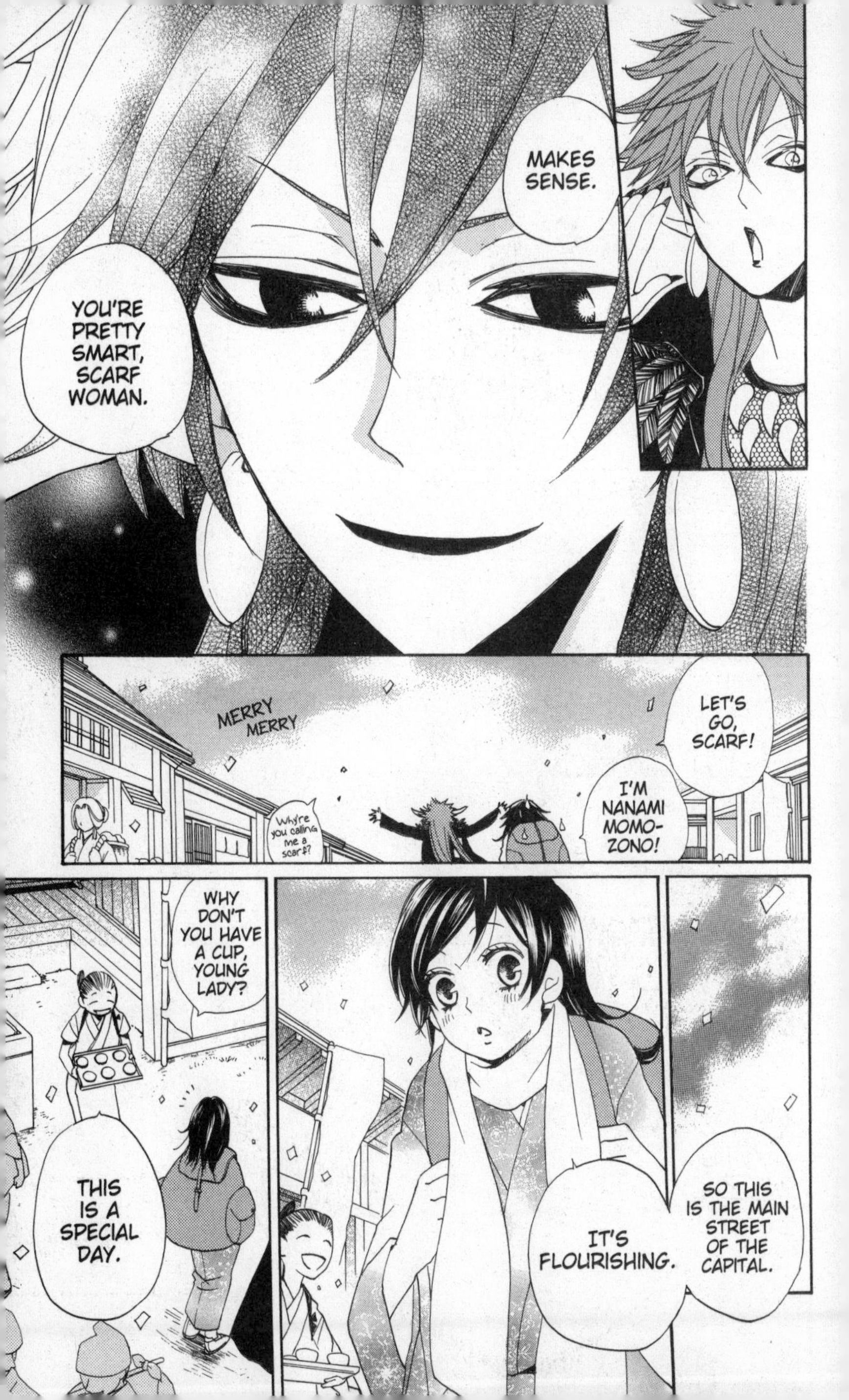
MAKES SENSE.
YOU'RE PRETTY SMART, SCARF WOMAN.
LET'S GO, SCARF!
I'M NANAMI MOMO-ZONO!
MERRY MERRY
Why're you calling me a scarf?
SO THIS IS THE MAIN STREET OF THE CAPITAL.
IT'S FLOURISHING.
WHY DON'T YOU HAVE A CUP, YOUNG LADY?
THIS IS A SPECIAL DAY.

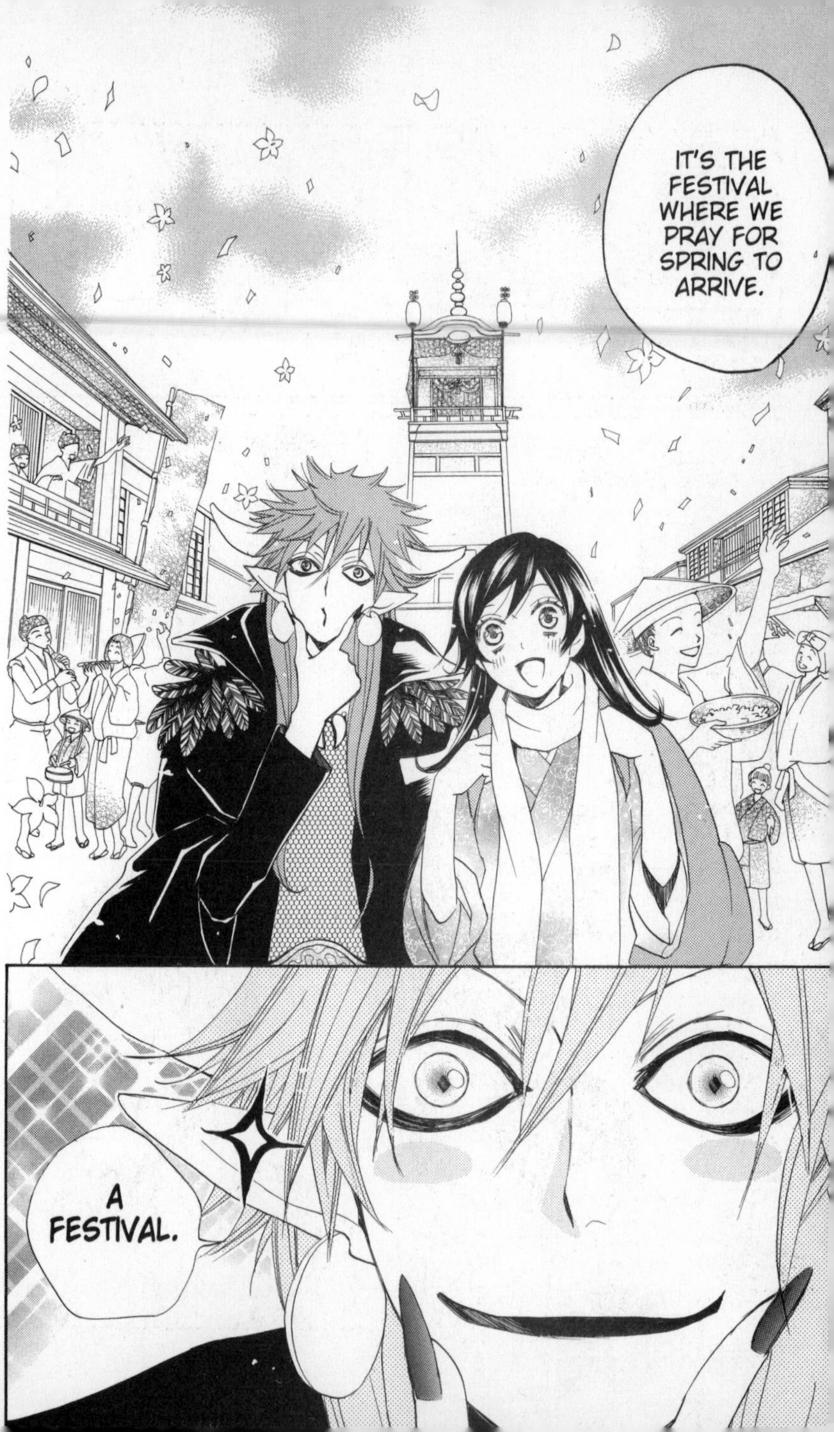
IT'S THE FESTIVAL WHERE WE PRAY FOR SPRING TO ARRIVE.
A FESTIVAL.

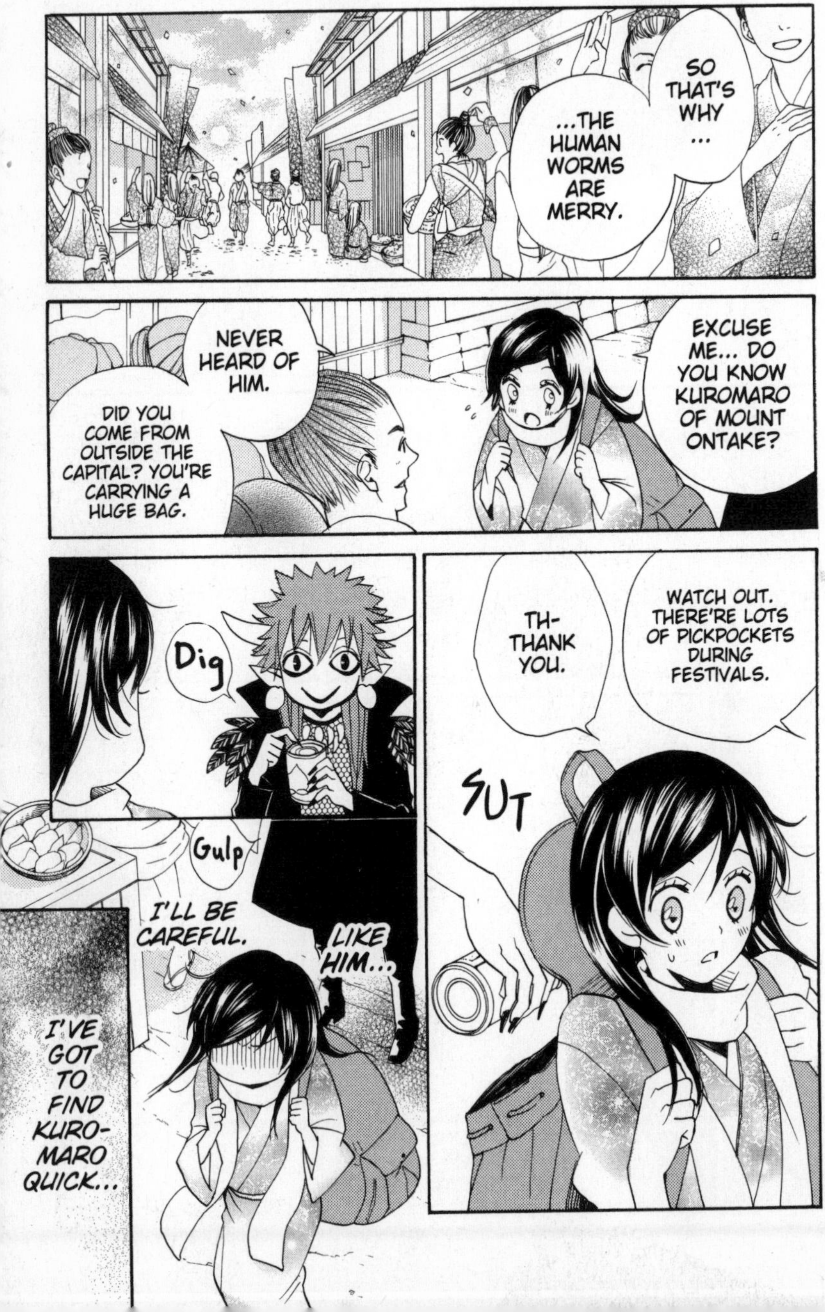
SO THAT'S WHY...
...THE HUMAN WORMS ARE MERRY.
EXCUSE ME... DO YOU KNOW KUROMARO OF MOUNT ONTAKE?
NEVER HEARD OF HIM.
DID YOU COME FROM OUTSIDE THE CAPITAL? YOU'RE CARRYING A HUGE BAG.
WATCH OUT. THERE'RE LOTS OF PICKPOCKETS DURING FESTIVALS.
TH-THANK YOU.
SUT
Dig
Gulp
I'LL BE CAREFUL.
LIKE HIM...
I'VE GOT TO FIND KURO-MARO QUICK...

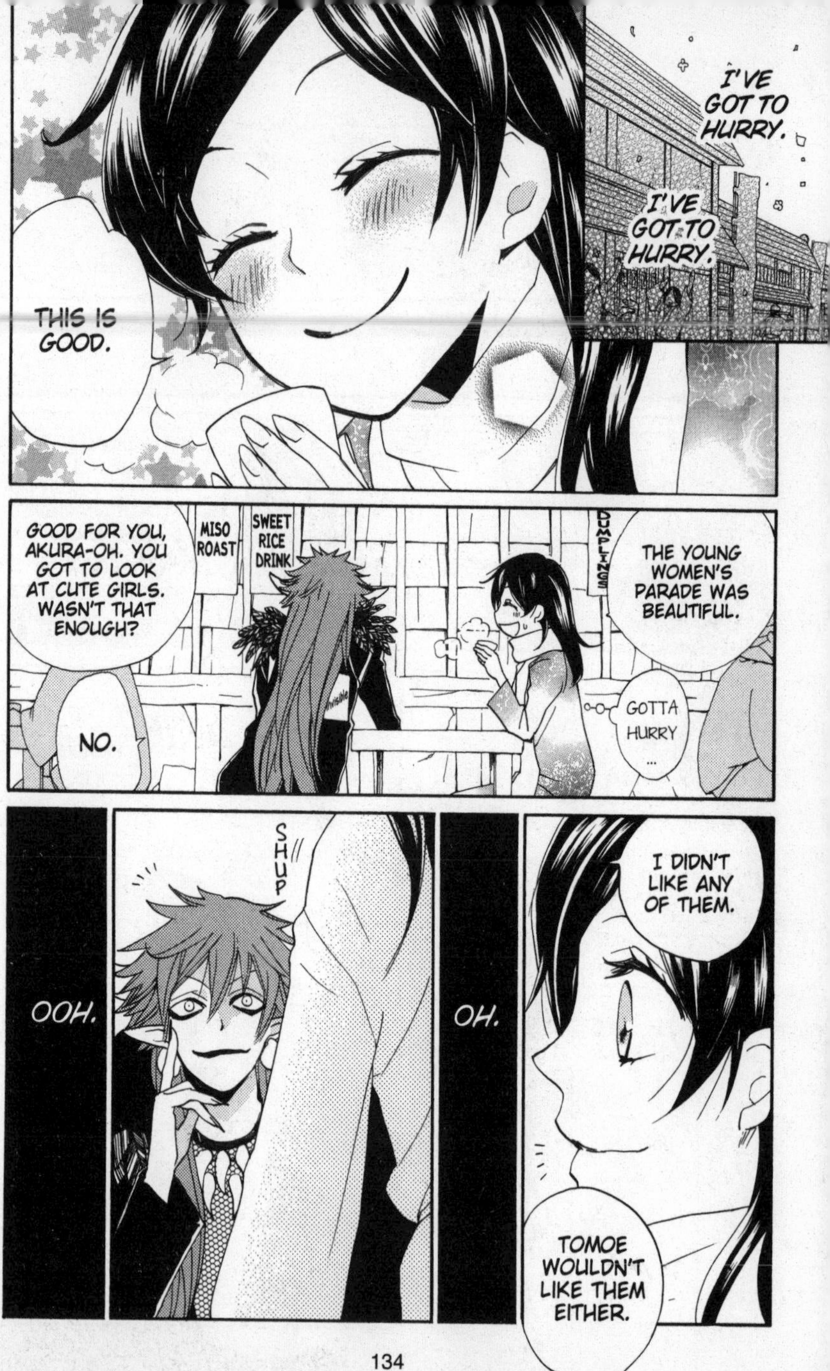
I'VE GOT TO HURRY.
I'VE GOT TO HURRY.
THIS IS GOOD.
DUMPLINGS
THE YOUNG WOMEN'S PARADE WAS BEAUTIFUL.
GOTTA HURRY ...
SWEET RICE DRINK
MISO ROAST
GOOD FOR YOU, AKURA-OH. YOU GOT TO LOOK AT CUTE GIRLS. WASN'T THAT ENOUGH?
Invisible
NO.
I DIDN'T LIKE ANY OF THEM.
OH.
TOMOE WOULDN'T LIKE THEM EITHER.
SHUP
OOH.

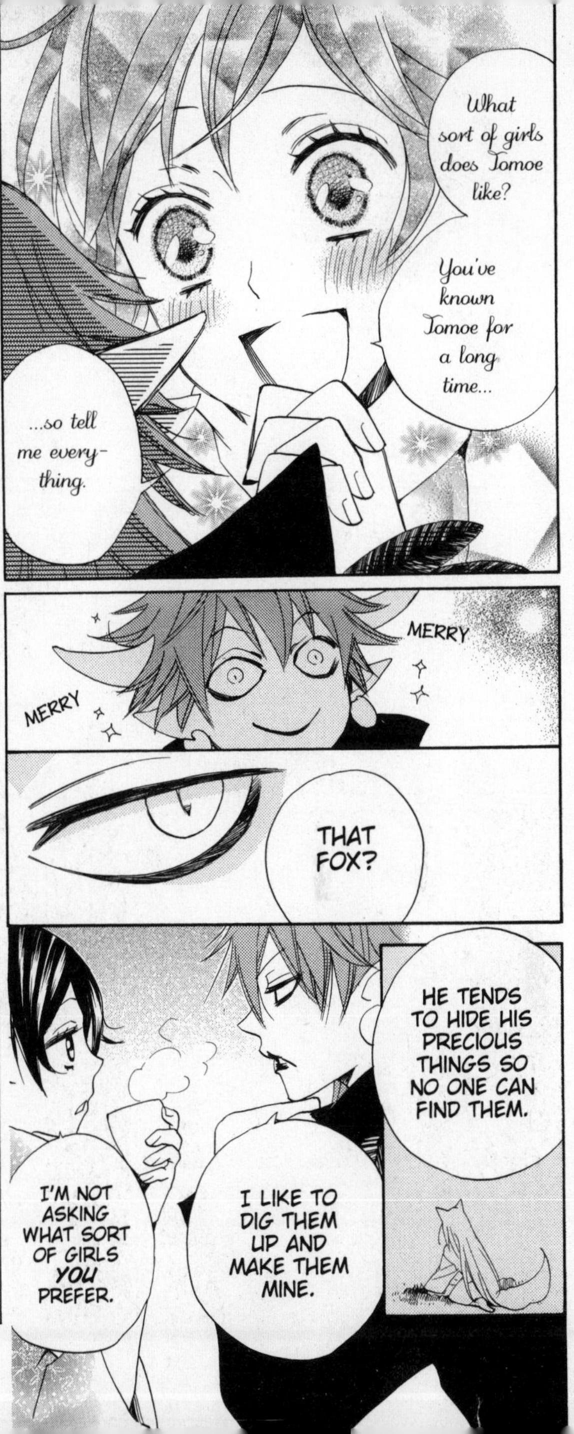
What sort of girls does Tomoe like?
You've known Tomoe for a long time...
...so tell me every-thing.
MERRY
MERRY
THAT FOX?
HE TENDS TO HIDE HIS PRECIOUS THINGS SO NO ONE CAN FIND THEM.
I LIKE TO DIG THEM UP AND MAKE THEM MINE.
I'M NOT ASKING WHAT SORT OF GIRLS *YOU* PREFER.

Thank you for reading this far! I hope you are enjoying it.

Because the series was running while the anime was being broadcast, this volume contains an extra story and a short side story that were published in "Hana to Yume."

I hope you enjoy reading them as a breather of sorts.

I hadn't drawn 16-page manga in a while, so I found it a new experience. ☺

Nanami will do her best in the past, so I hope you'll read it as well!

Well then!

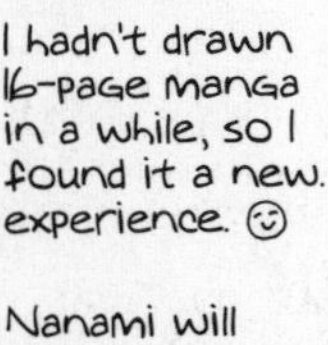
This is the year of the snake!

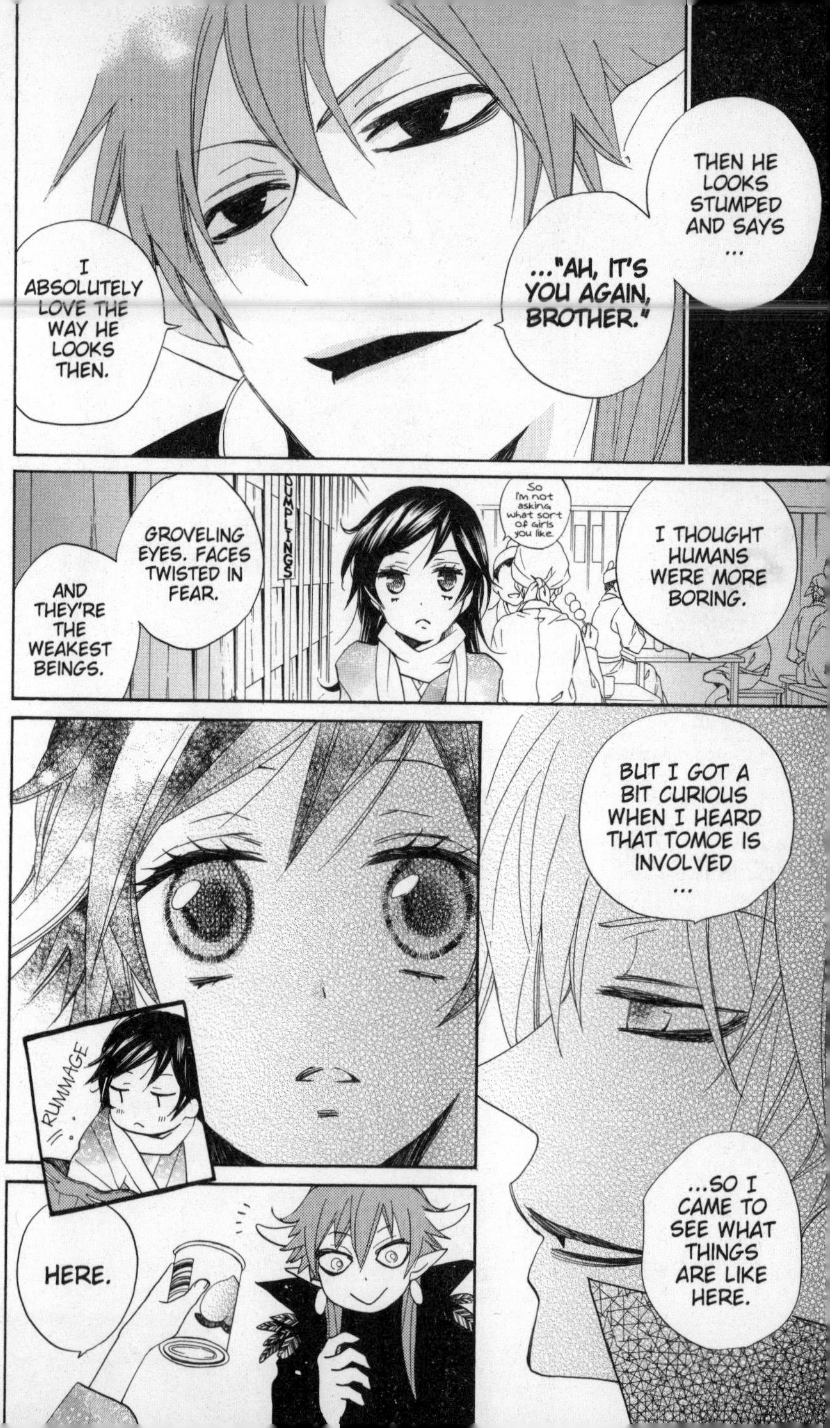
THEN HE LOOKS STUMPED AND SAYS ...
..."AH, IT'S YOU AGAIN, BROTHER."
I ABSOLUTELY LOVE THE WAY HE LOOKS THEN.
I THOUGHT HUMANS WERE MORE BORING.
So I'm not asking what sort of girls you like.
DUMPLINGS
GROVELING EYES. FACES TWISTED IN FEAR.
AND THEY'RE THE WEAKEST BEINGS.
BUT I GOT A BIT CURIOUS WHEN I HEARD THAT TOMOE IS INVOLVED ...
RUMMAGE
...SO I CAME TO SEE WHAT THINGS ARE LIKE HERE.
HERE.

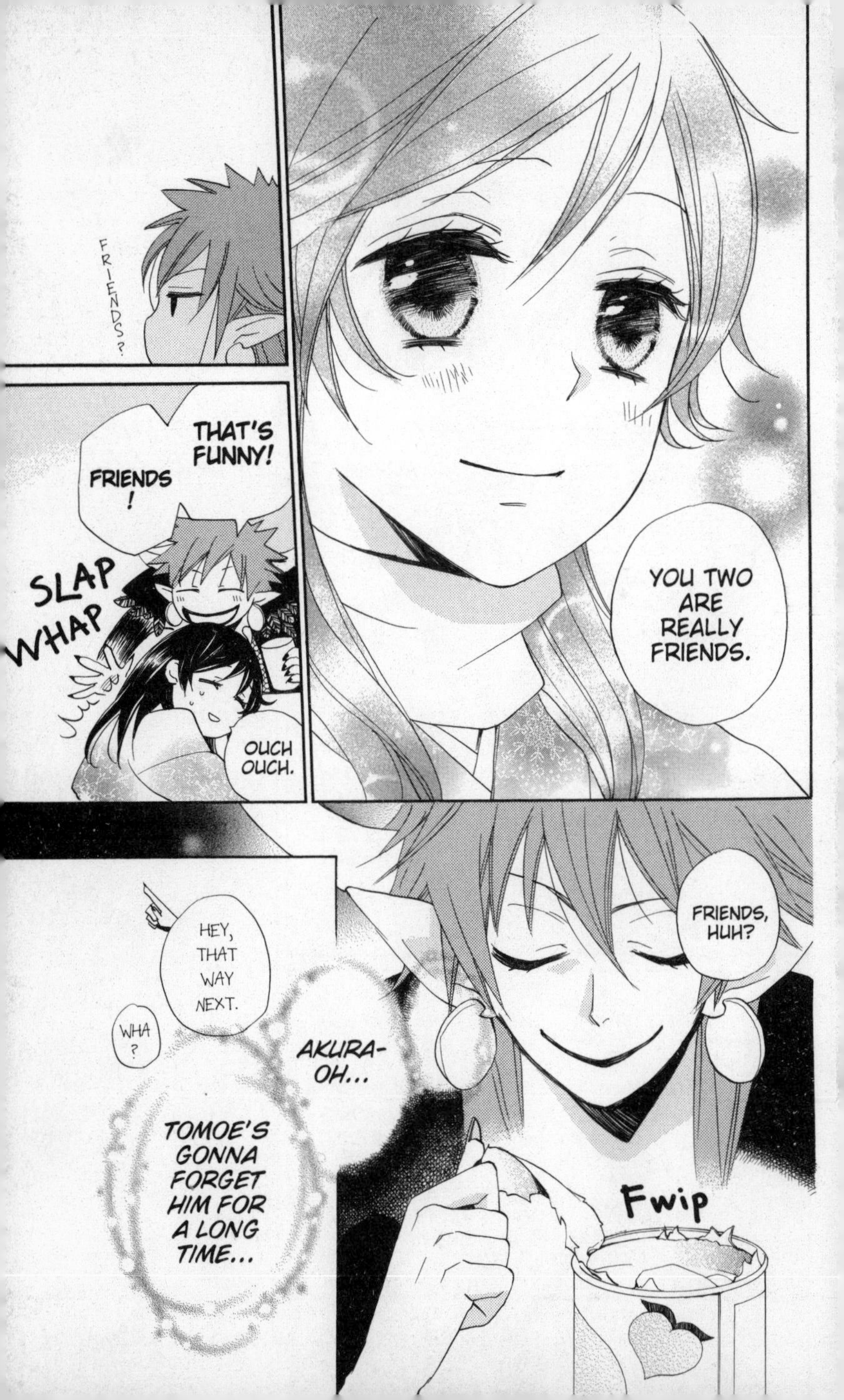
YOU TWO ARE REALLY FRIENDS.
FRIENDS?
THAT'S FUNNY!
FRIENDS!
SLAP WHAP
OUCH OUCH.
FRIENDS, HUH?
HEY, THAT WAY NEXT.
WHA?
AKURA-OH...
TOMOE'S GONNA FORGET HIM FOR A LONG TIME...
Fwip

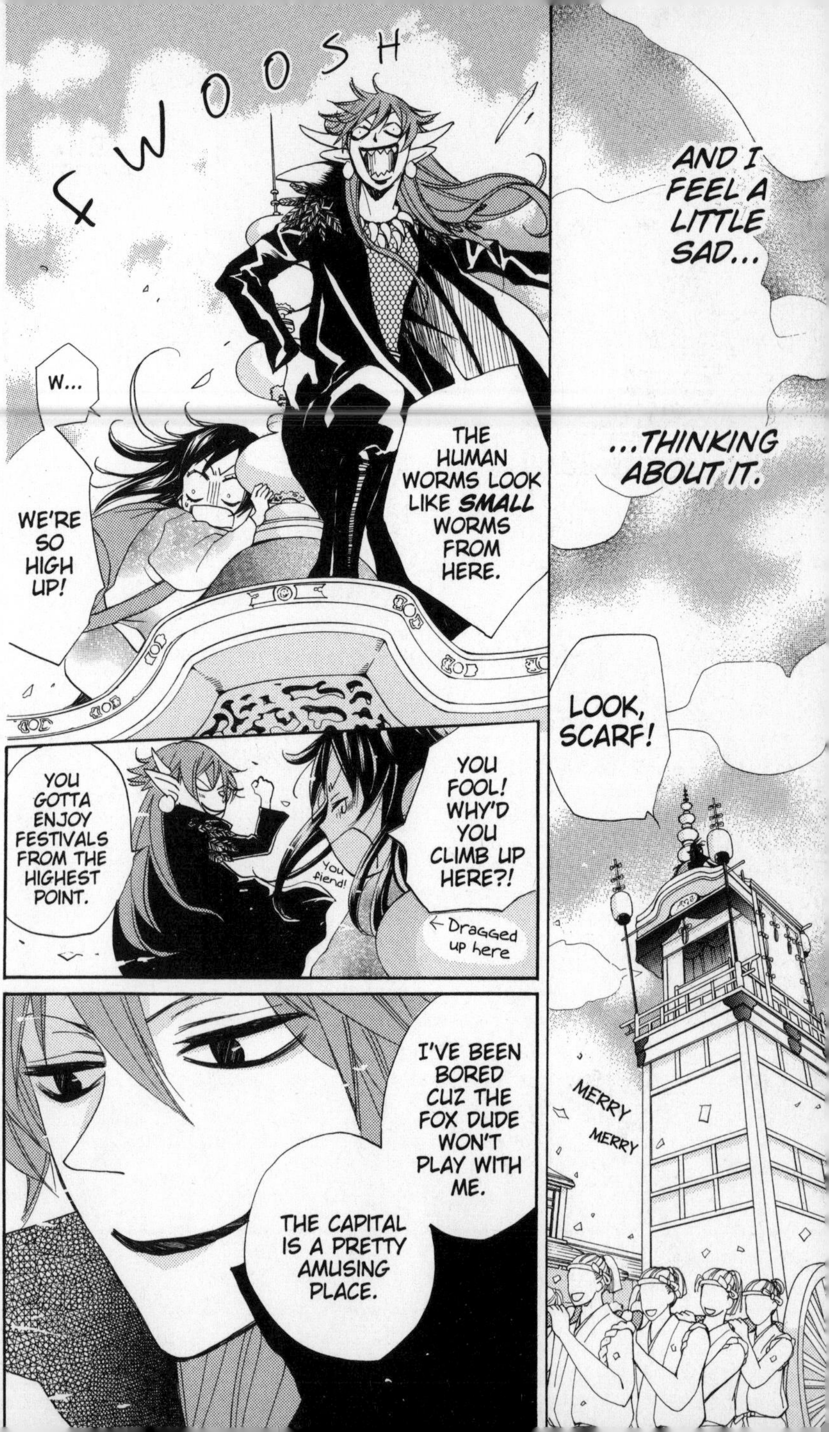
AND I FEEL A LITTLE SAD...
...THINKING ABOUT IT.
LOOK, SCARF!
MERRY
MERRY
FWOOSH
THE HUMAN WORMS LOOK LIKE SMALL WORMS FROM HERE.
W...
WE'RE SO HIGH UP!
YOU FOOL! WHY'D YOU CLIMB UP HERE?!
← Dragged up here
You fiend!
YOU GOTTA ENJOY FESTIVALS FROM THE HIGHEST POINT.
I'VE BEEN BORED CUZ THE FOX DUDE WON'T PLAY WITH ME.
THE CAPITAL IS A PRETTY AMUSING PLACE.

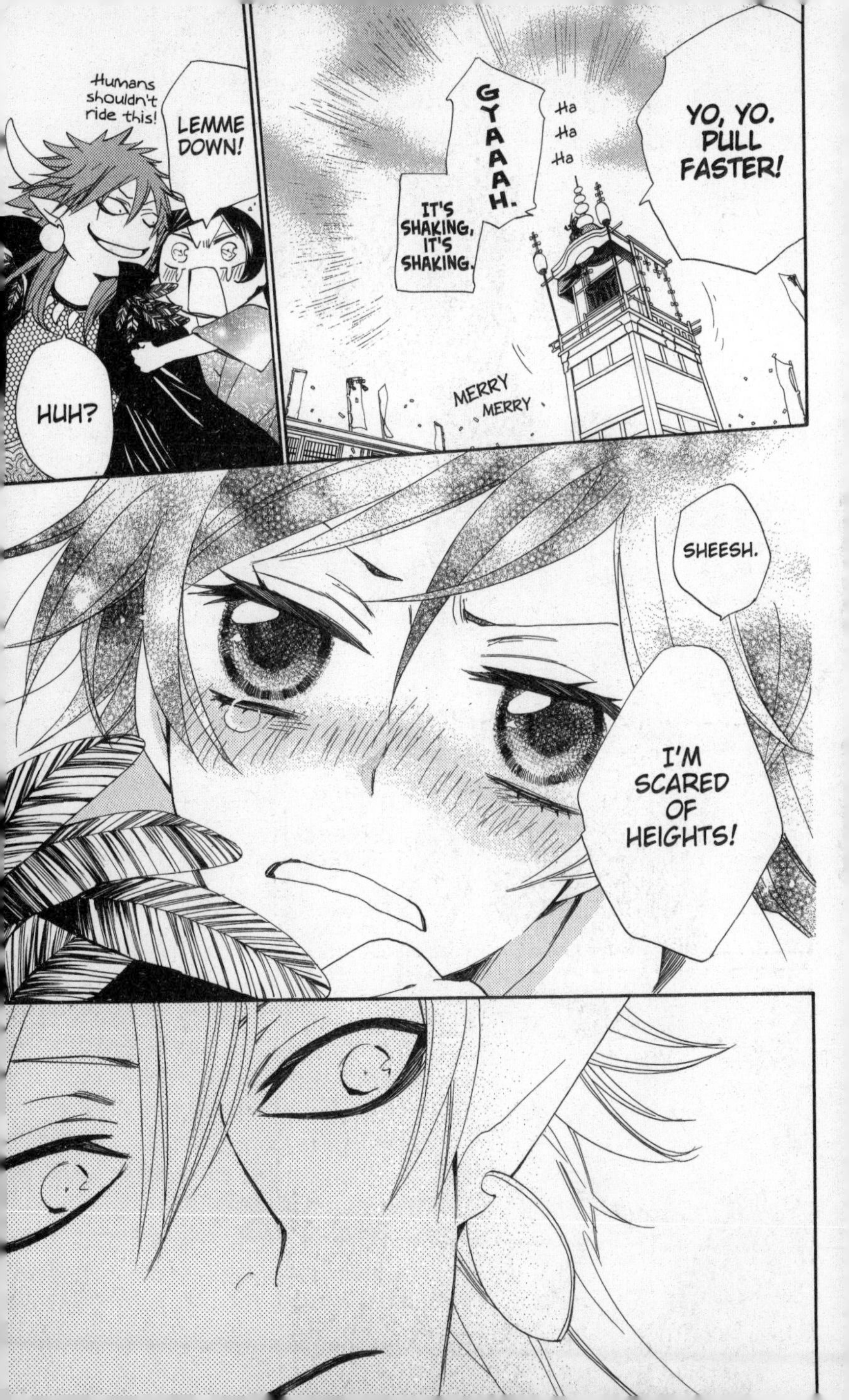
YO, YO. PULL FASTER!
Ha Ha Ha
GYAAAH.
IT'S SHAKING, IT'S SHAKING.
MERRY MERRY
LEMME DOWN!
Humans shouldn't ride this!
HUH?
SHEESH.
I'M SCARED OF HEIGHTS!

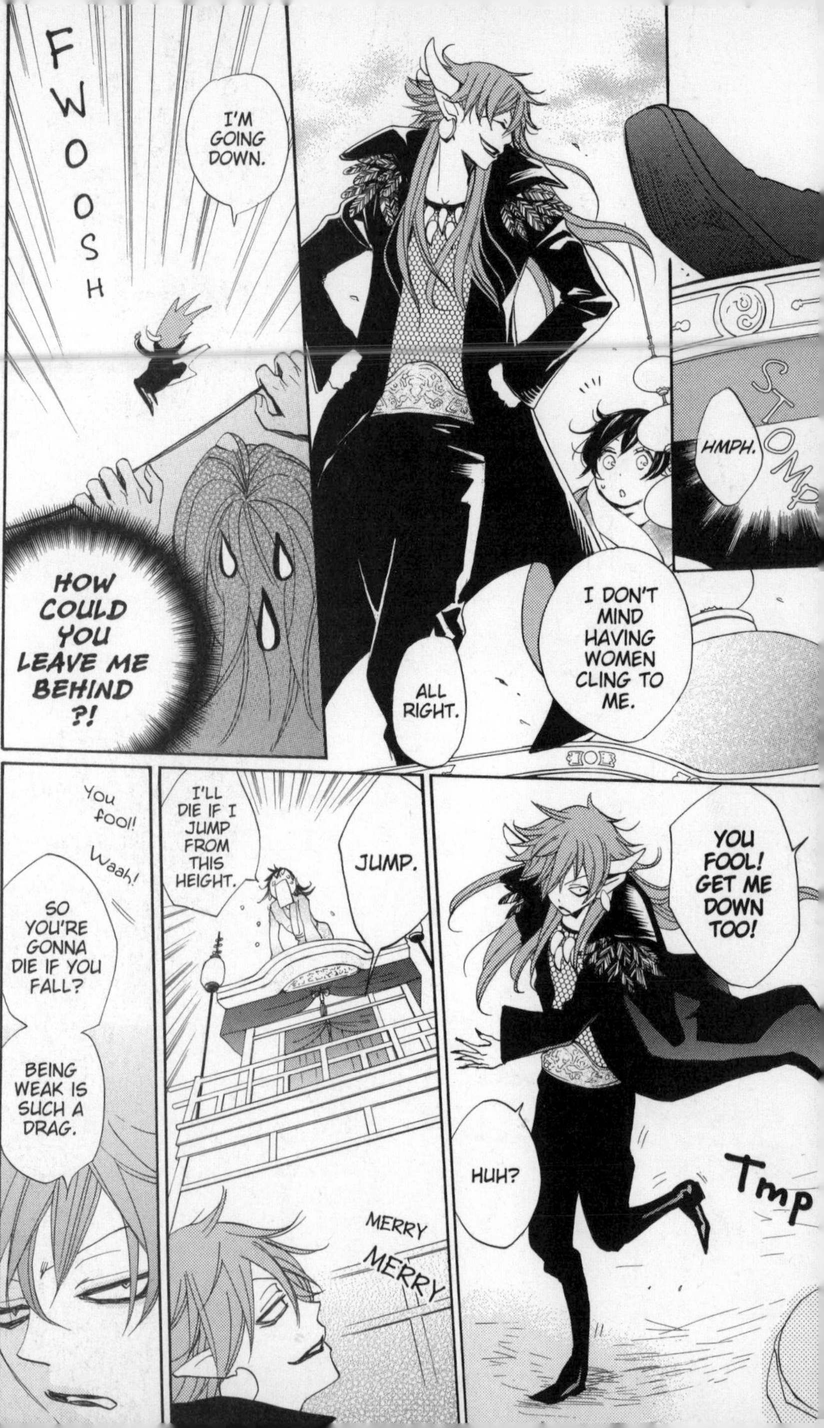
HMPH.
STOMP
I DON'T MIND HAVING WOMEN CLING TO ME.
ALL RIGHT.
I'M GOING DOWN.
FWOOSH
HOW COULD YOU LEAVE ME BEHIND ?!
YOU FOOL! GET ME DOWN TOO!
Tmp
HUH?
JUMP.
I'LL DIE IF I JUMP FROM THIS HEIGHT.
MERRY
MERRY
You fool!
Waah!
SO YOU'RE GONNA DIE IF YOU FALL?
BEING WEAK IS SUCH A DRAG.

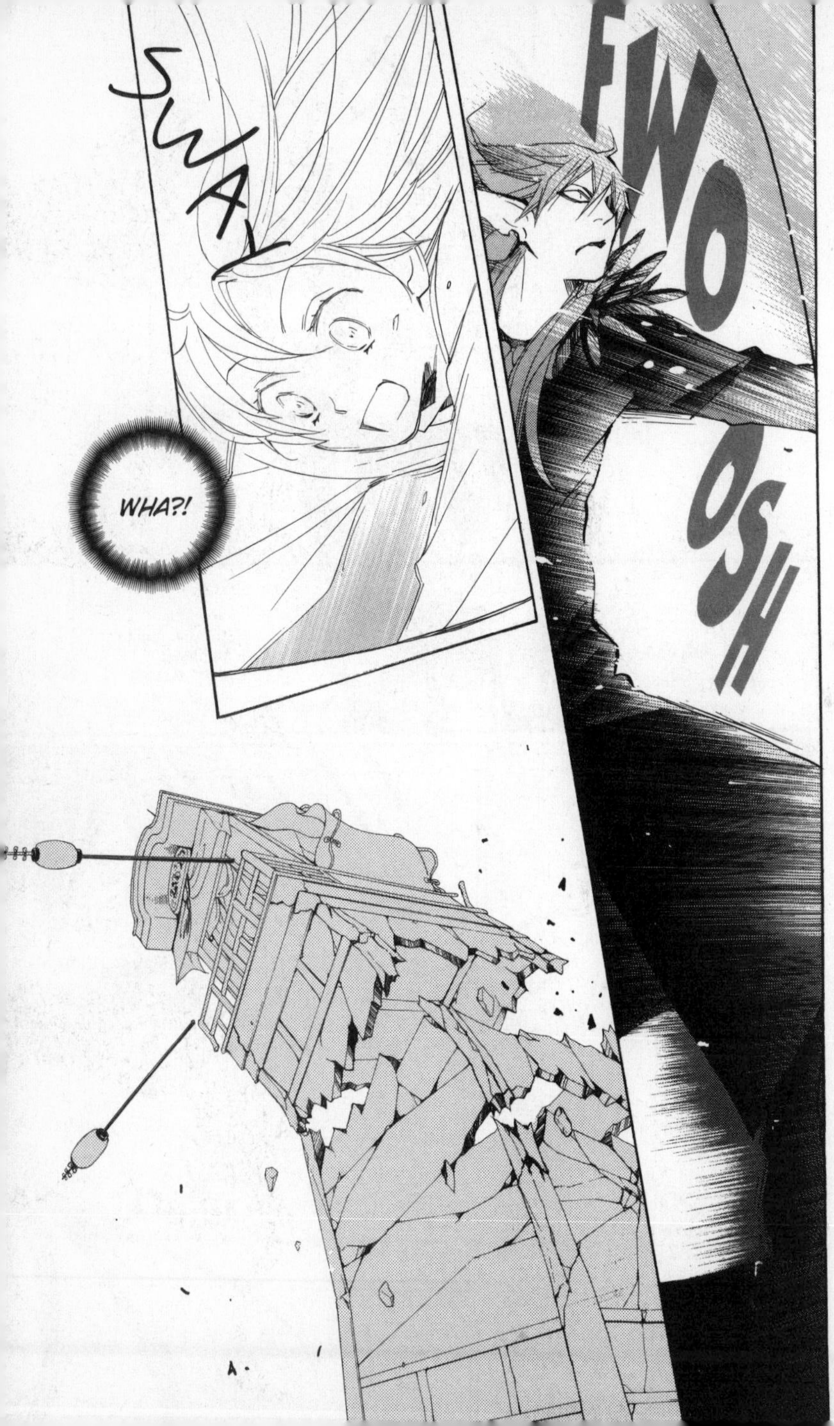
FWOOSH
SWAY
WHA?!

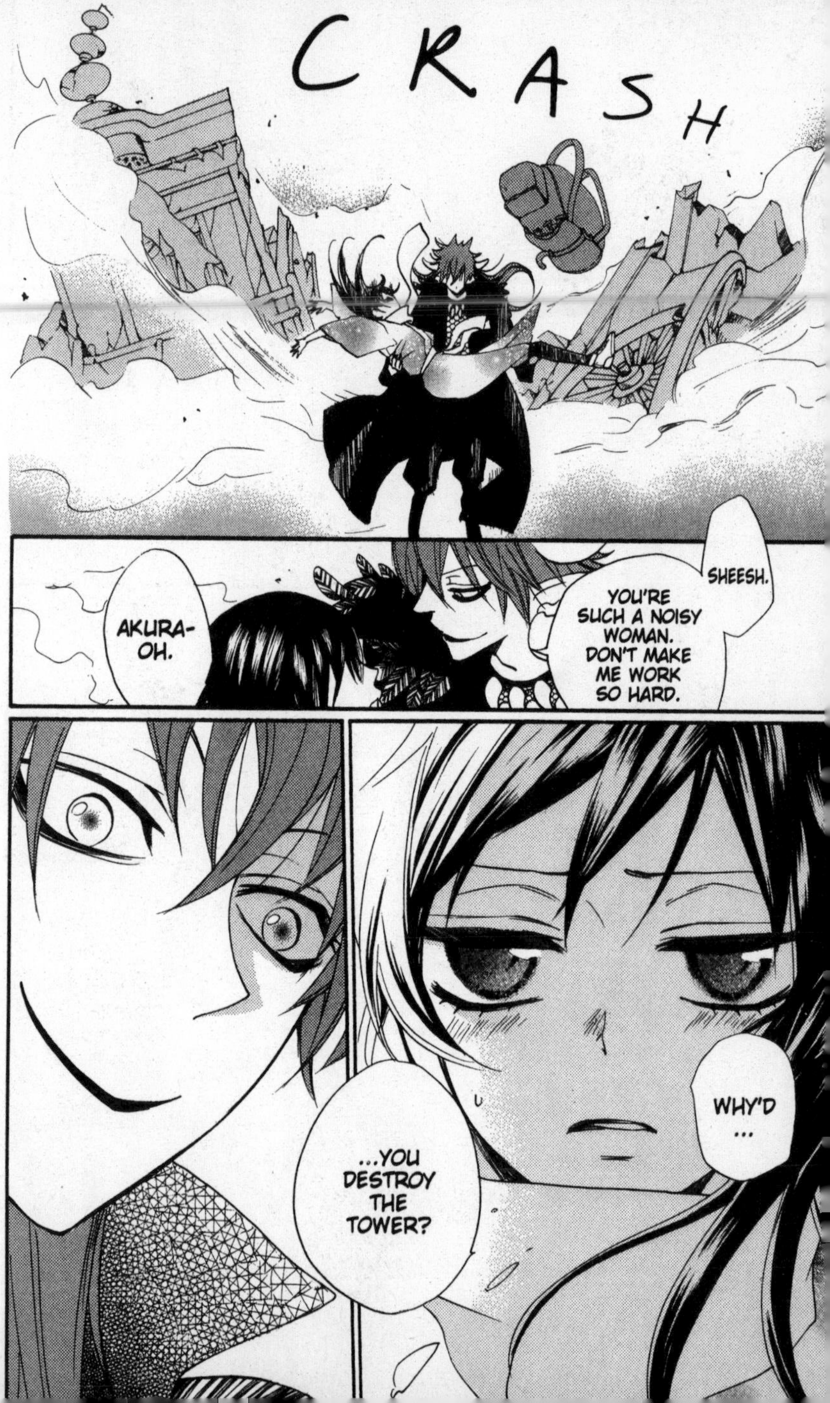
CRASH
SHEESH.
YOU'RE SUCH A NOISY WOMAN. DON'T MAKE ME WORK SO HARD.
AKURA-OH.
WHY'D ...
...YOU DESTROY THE TOWER?

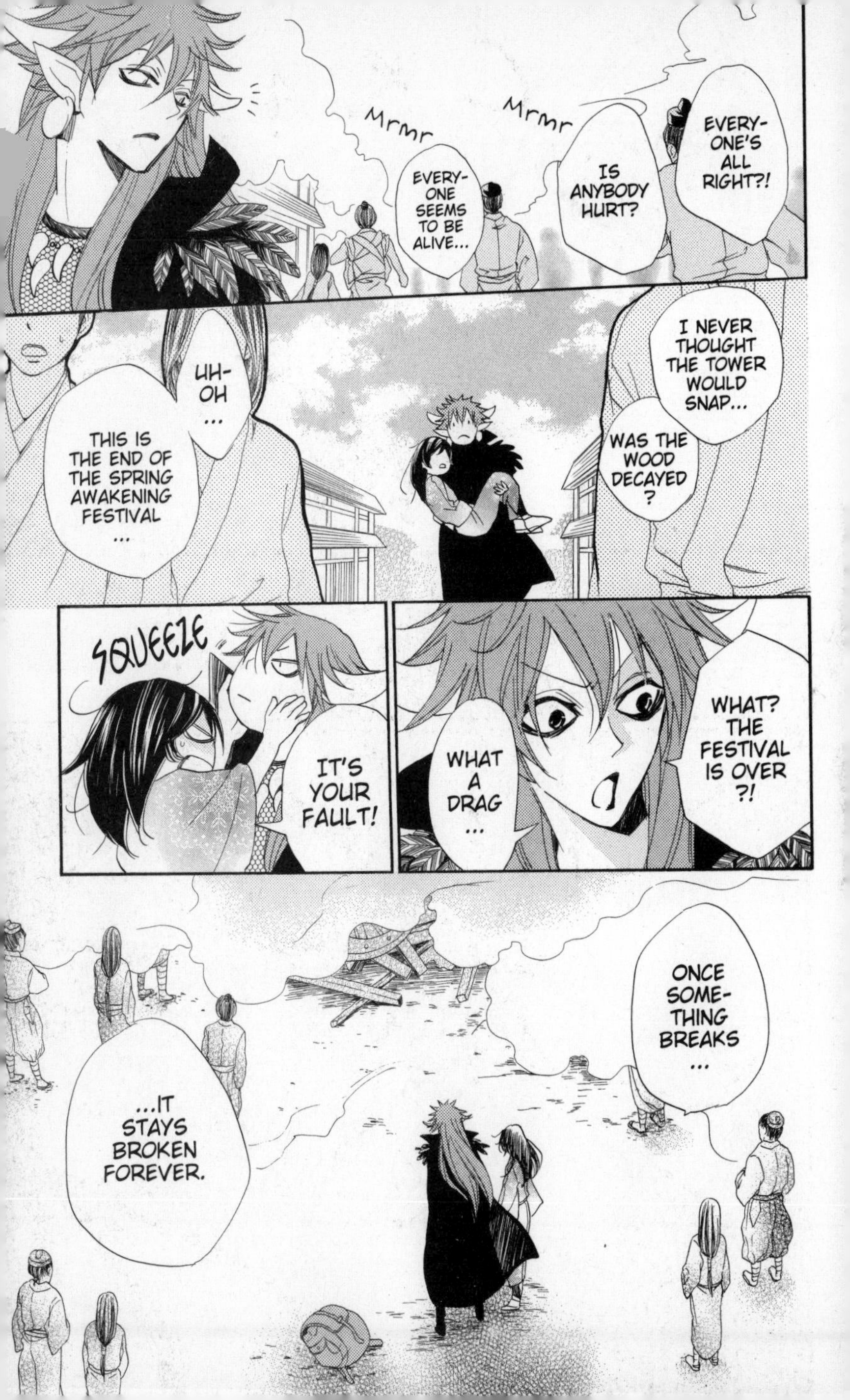
EVERY-ONE'S ALL RIGHT?!
IS ANYBODY HURT?
Mrmr
Mrmr
EVERY-ONE SEEMS TO BE ALIVE...
I NEVER THOUGHT THE TOWER WOULD SNAP...
WAS THE WOOD DECAYED?
UH-OH...
THIS IS THE END OF THE SPRING AWAKENING FESTIVAL...
WHAT? THE FESTIVAL IS OVER?!
WHAT A DRAG...
SQUEEZE
IT'S YOUR FAULT!
ONCE SOME-THING BREAKS...
...IT STAYS BROKEN FOREVER.

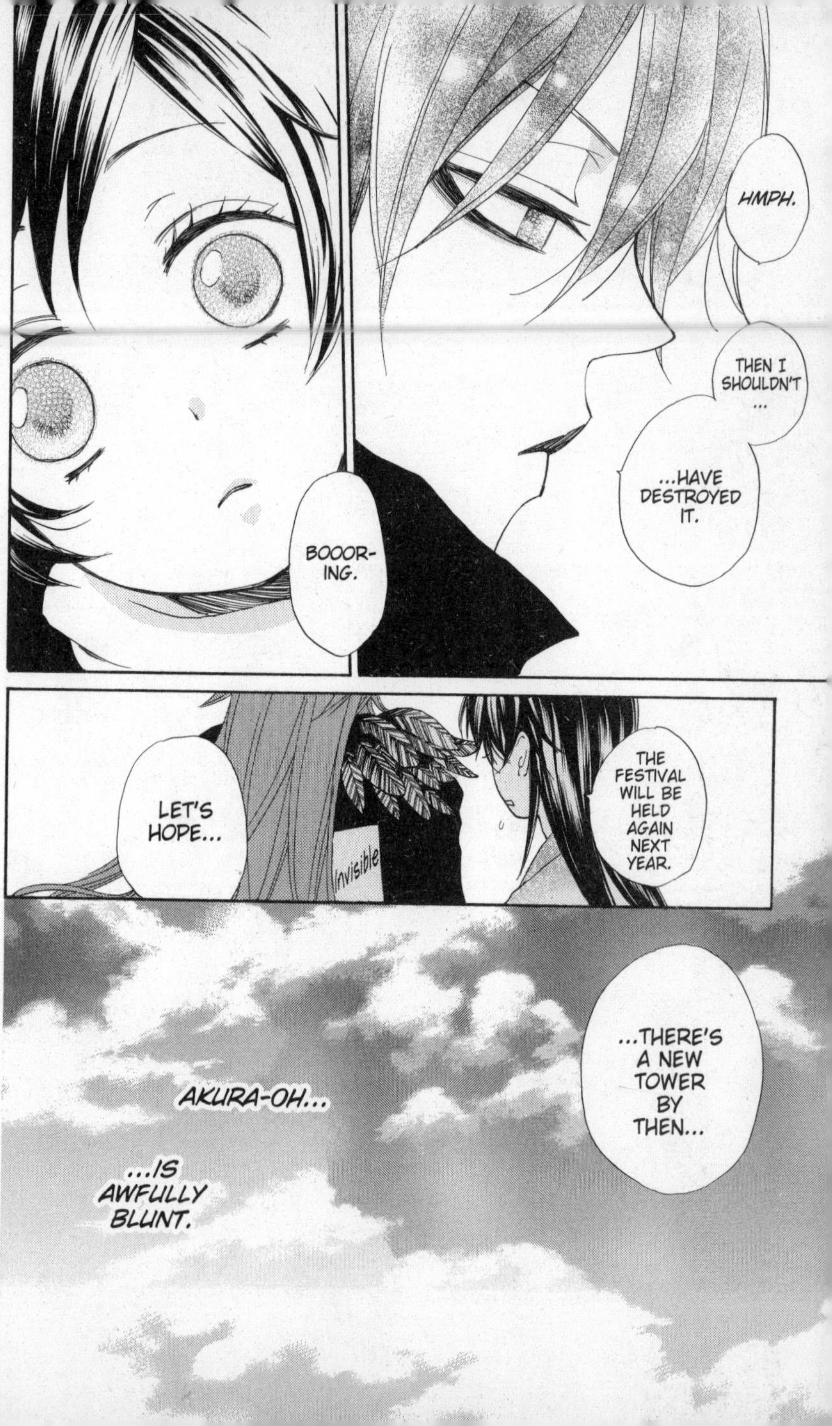
HMPH.
THEN I SHOULDN'T ...
...HAVE DESTROYED IT.
BOOOR-ING.
THE FESTIVAL WILL BE HELD AGAIN NEXT YEAR.
LET'S HOPE...
Invisible
...THERE'S A NEW TOWER BY THEN...
AKURA-OH...
...IS AWFULLY BLUNT.

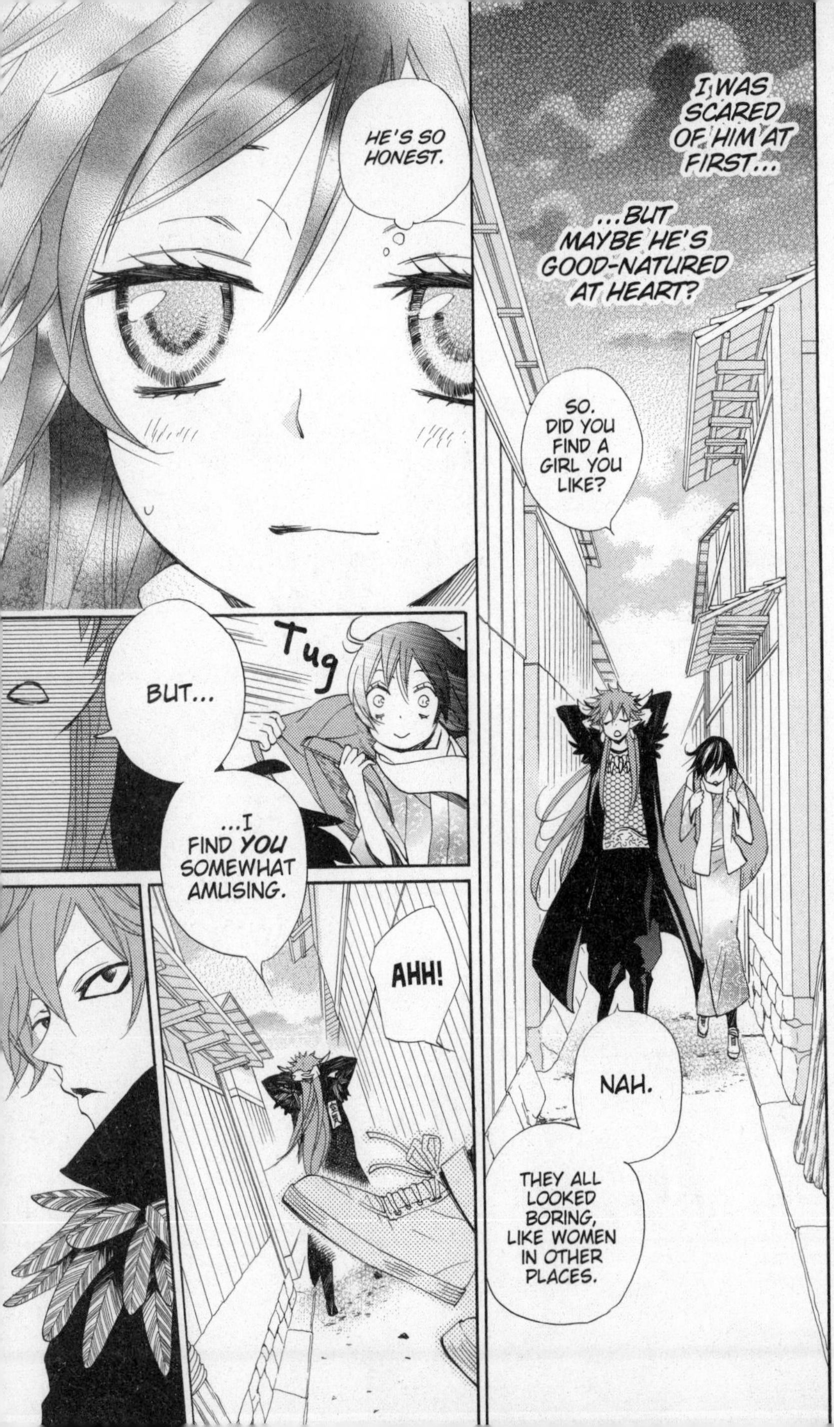
I WAS SCARED OF HIM AT FIRST...
...BUT MAYBE HE'S GOOD-NATURED AT HEART?
SO. DID YOU FIND A GIRL YOU LIKE?
NAH.
THEY ALL LOOKED BORING, LIKE WOMEN IN OTHER PLACES.
HE'S SO HONEST.
Tug
BUT...
...I FIND *YOU* SOMEWHAT AMUSING.
AHH!

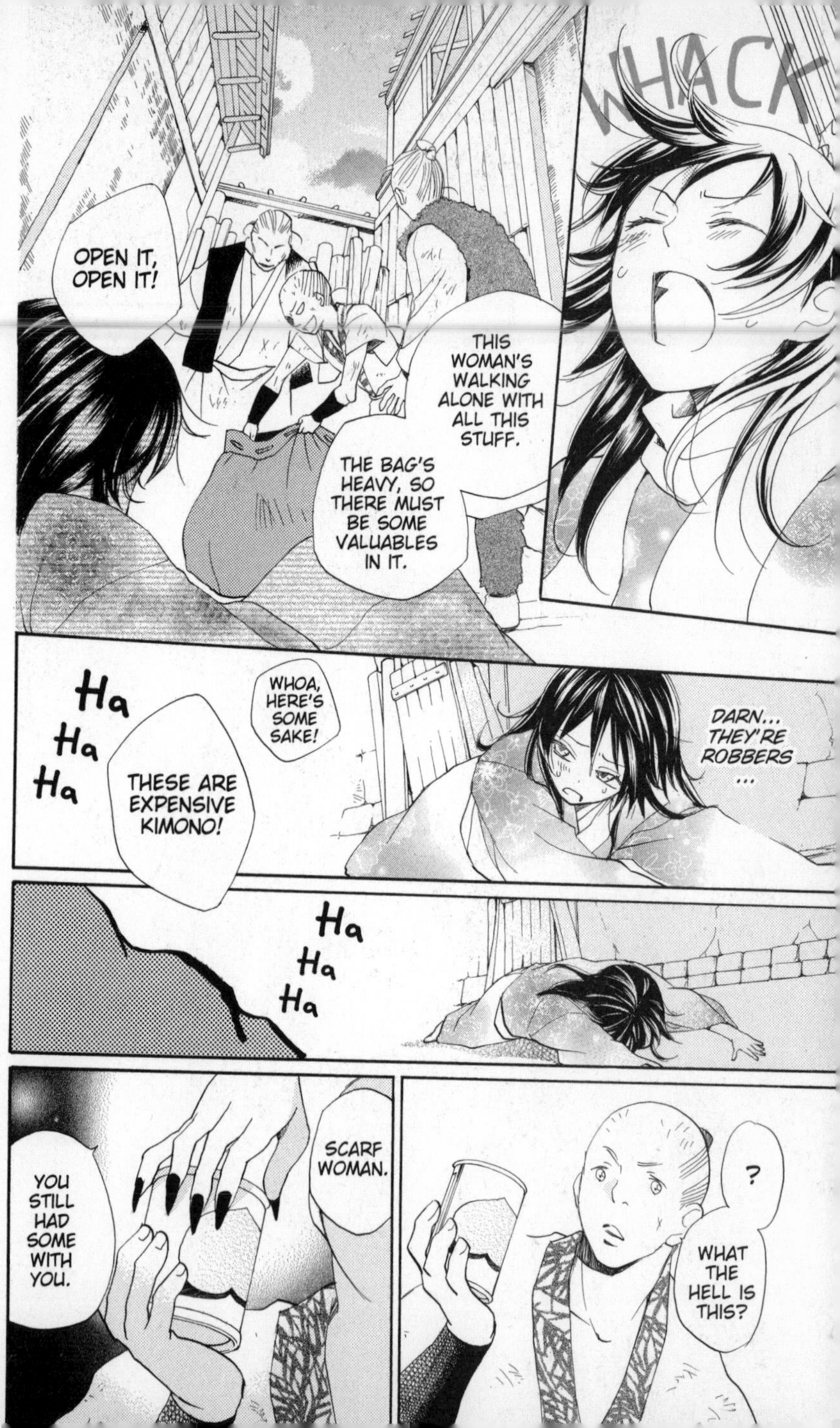
WHACK
OPEN IT, OPEN IT!
THIS WOMAN'S WALKING ALONE WITH ALL THIS STUFF.
THE BAG'S HEAVY, SO THERE MUST BE SOME VALUABLES IN IT.
DARN... THEY'RE ROBBERS...
WHOA, HERE'S SOME SAKE!
THESE ARE EXPENSIVE KIMONO!
Ha Ha Ha
Ha Ha Ha
?
WHAT THE HELL IS THIS?
SCARF WOMAN.
YOU STILL HAD SOME WITH YOU.

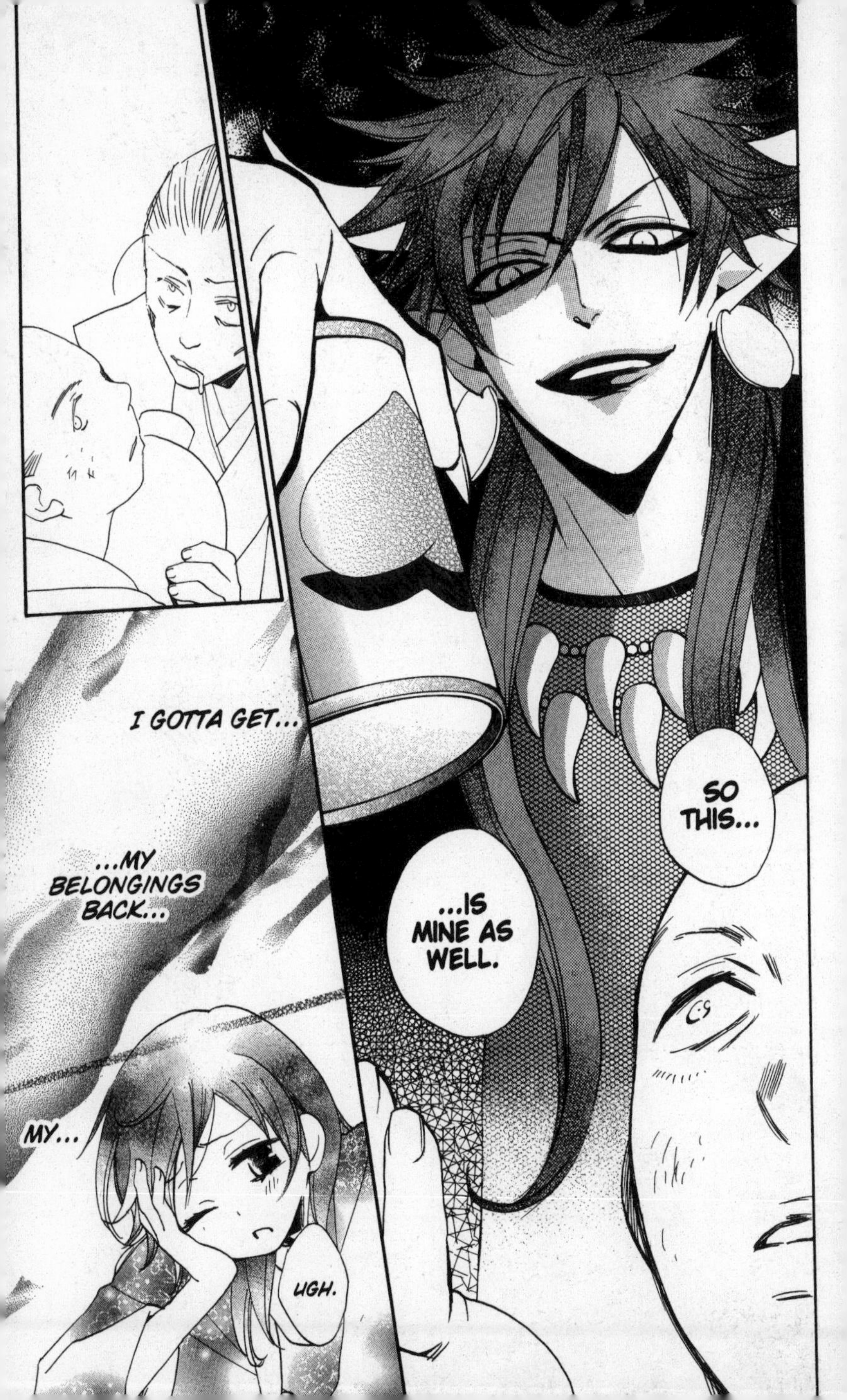
SO THIS...
...IS MINE AS WELL.
I GOTTA GET...
...MY BELONGINGS BACK...
MY...
UGH.

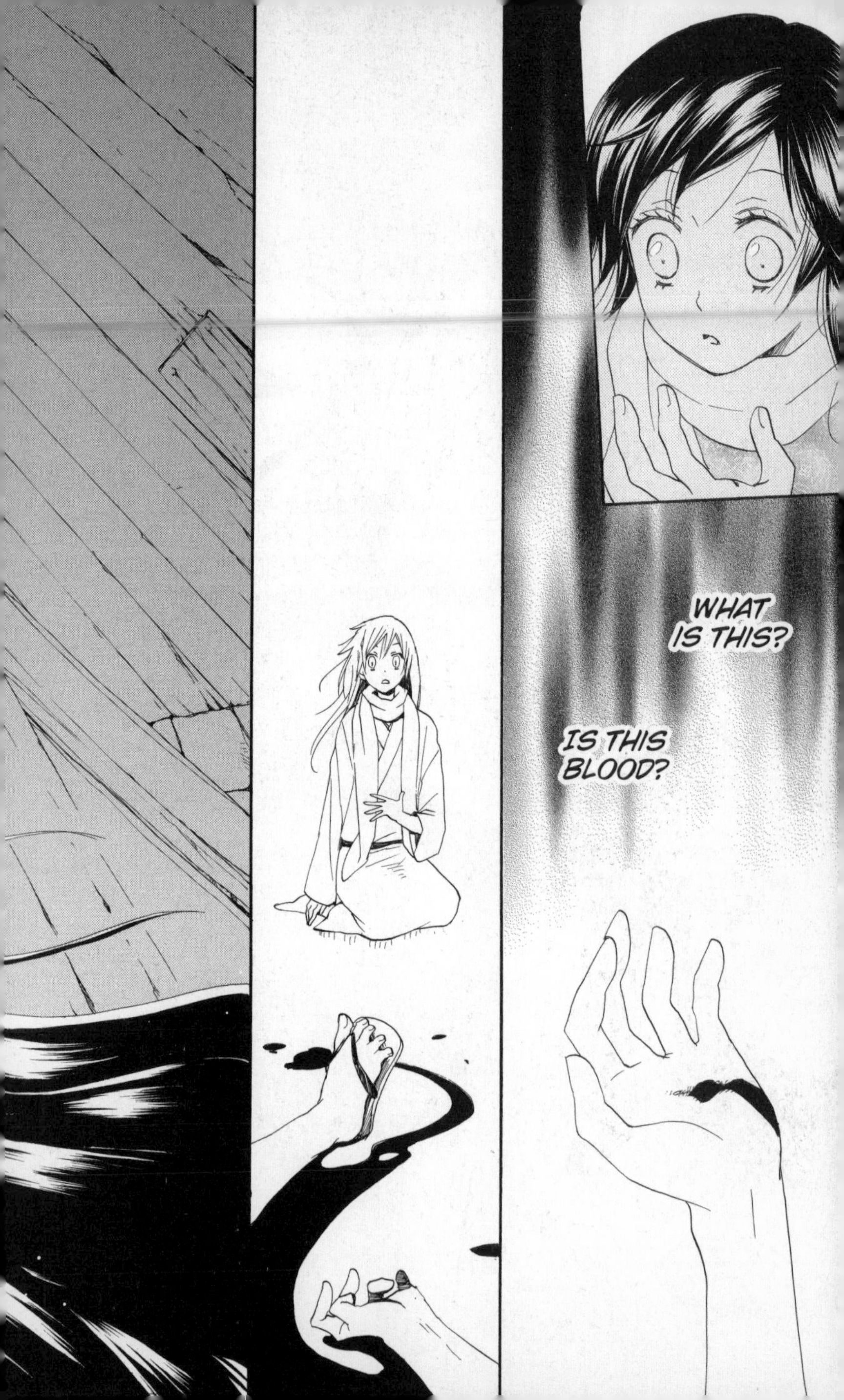
WHAT IS THIS?
IS THIS BLOOD?

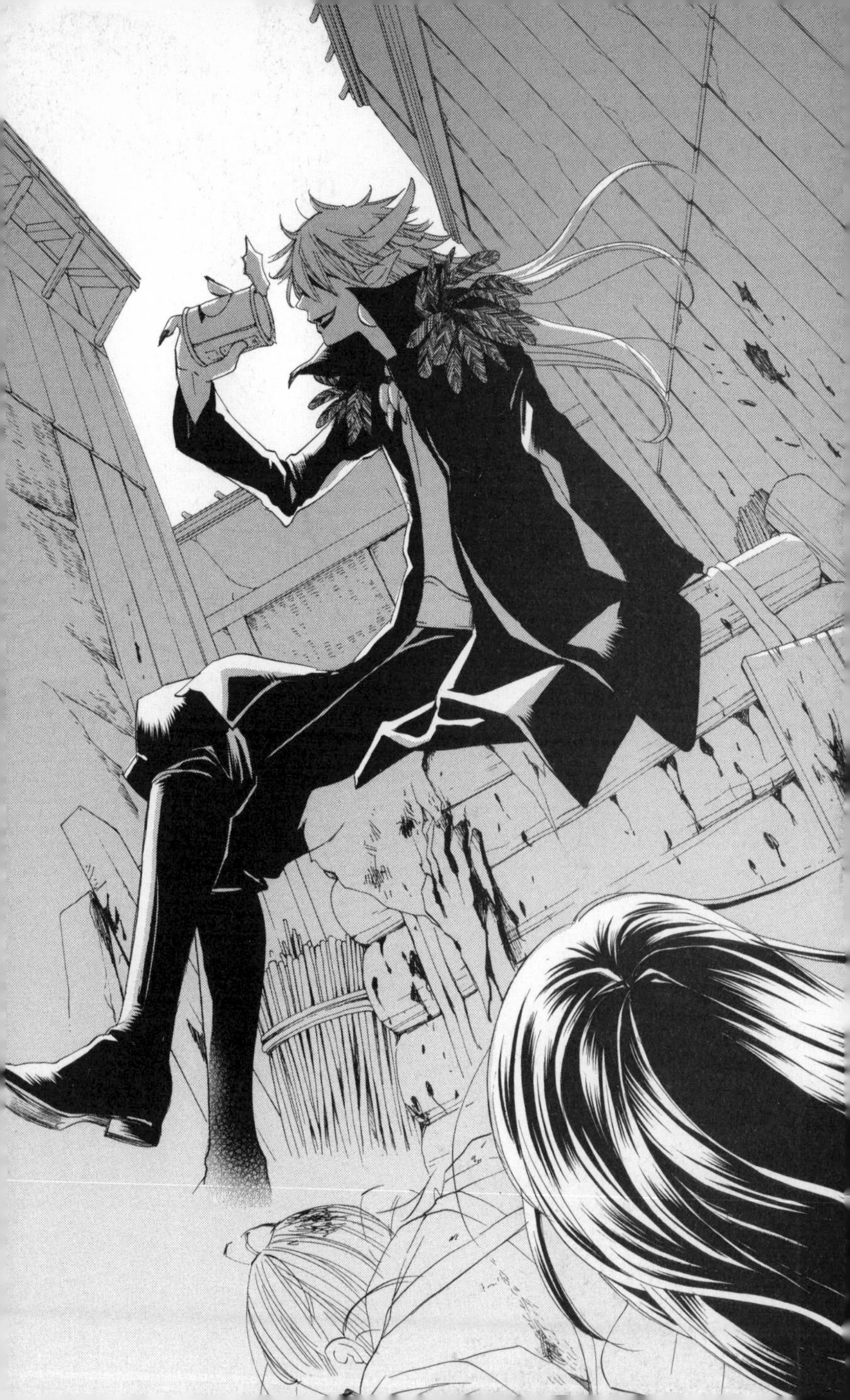

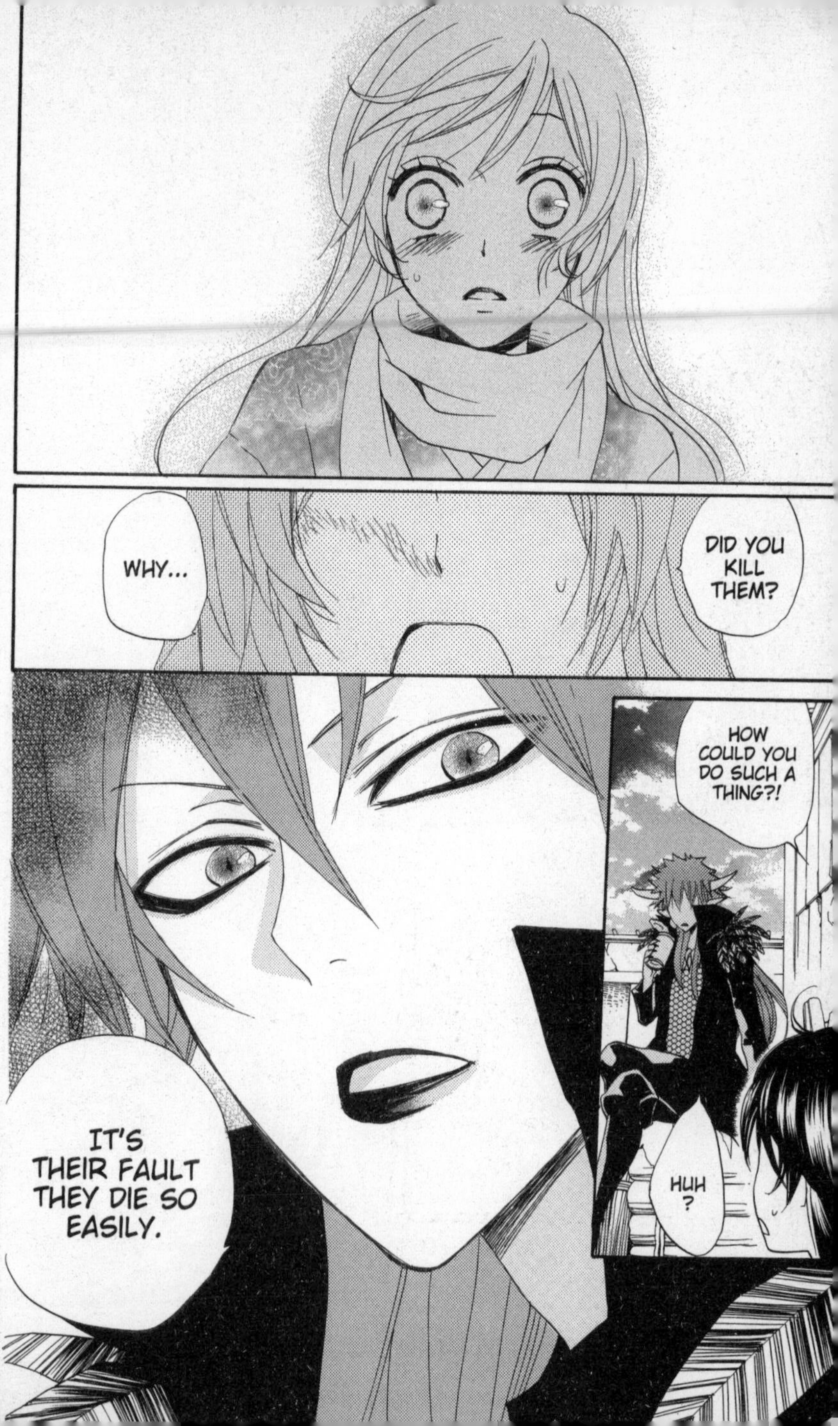
WHY...
DID YOU KILL THEM?
HOW COULD YOU DO SUCH A THING?!
HUH?
IT'S THEIR FAULT THEY DIE SO EASILY.

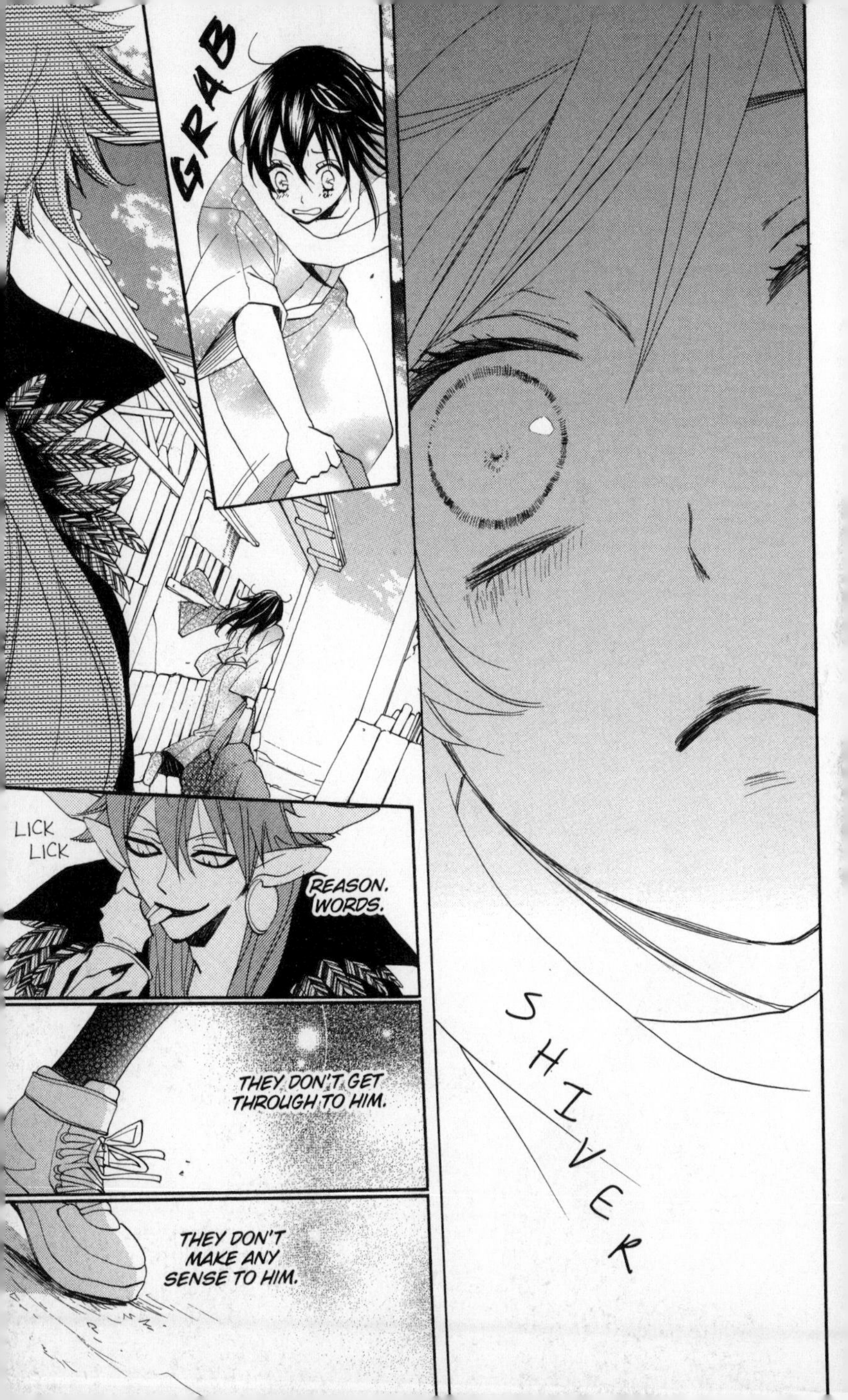
SHIVER
GRAB
LICK LICK
REASON. WORDS.
THEY DON'T GET THROUGH TO HIM.
THEY DON'T MAKE ANY SENSE TO HIM.

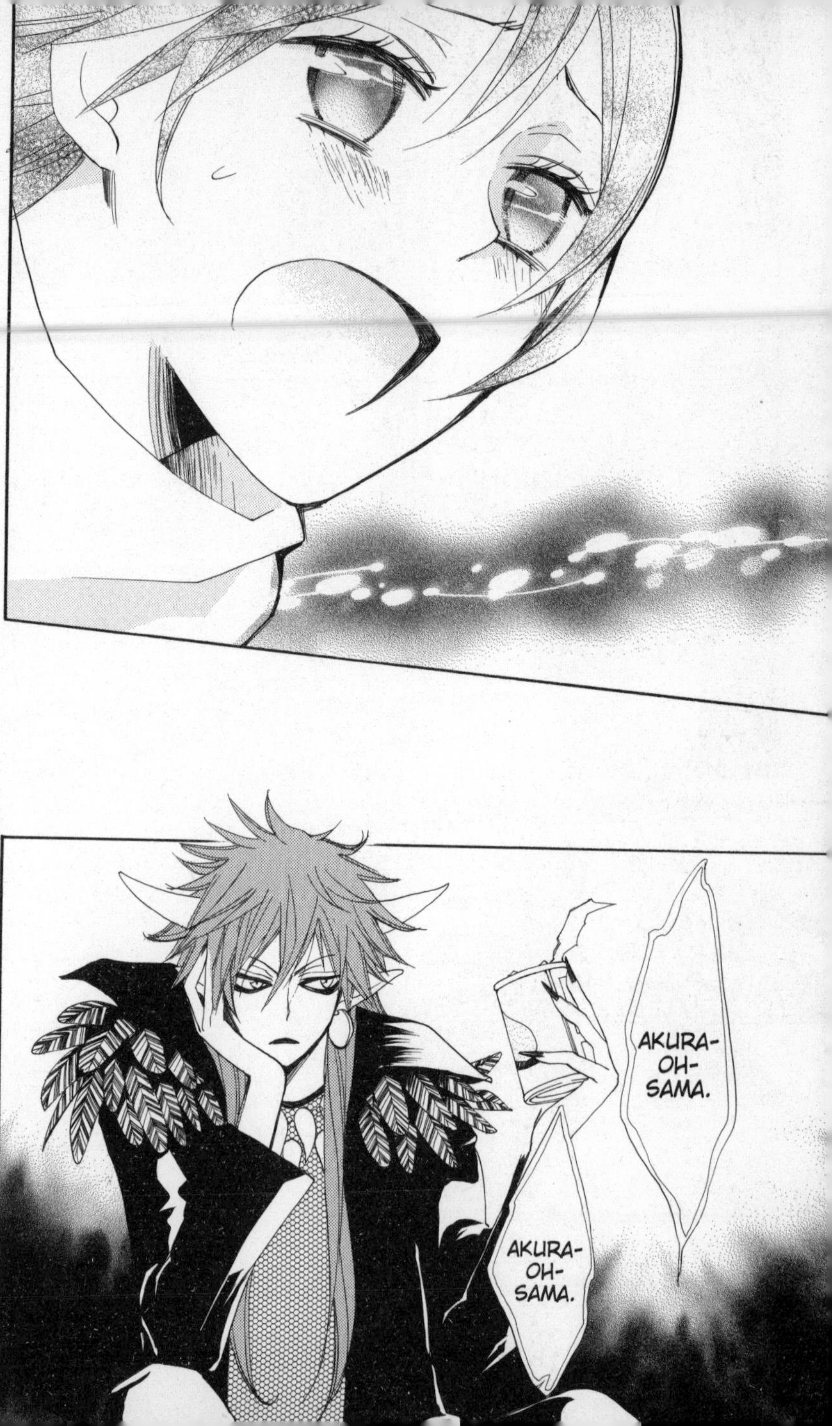
AKURA-OH-SAMA.
AKURA-OH-SAMA.

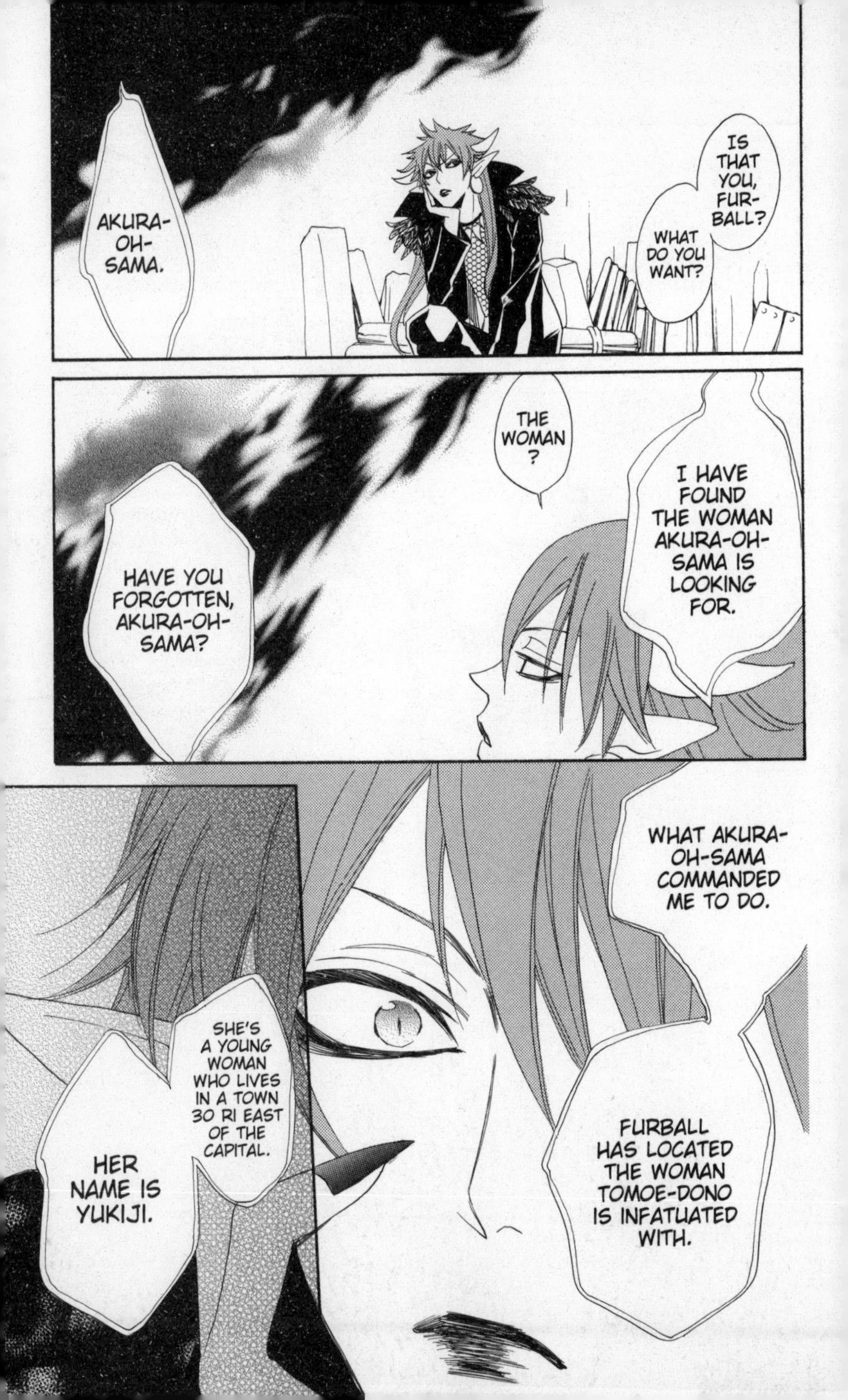
IS THAT YOU, FUR-BALL?
WHAT DO YOU WANT?
AKURA-OH-SAMA.
I HAVE FOUND THE WOMAN AKURA-OH-SAMA IS LOOKING FOR.
THE WOMAN?
HAVE YOU FORGOTTEN, AKURA-OH-SAMA?
WHAT AKURA-OH-SAMA COMMANDED ME TO DO.
FURBALL HAS LOCATED THE WOMAN TOMOE-DONO IS INFATUATED WITH.
SHE'S A YOUNG WOMAN WHO LIVES IN A TOWN 30 RI EAST OF THE CAPITAL.
HER NAME IS YUKIJI.

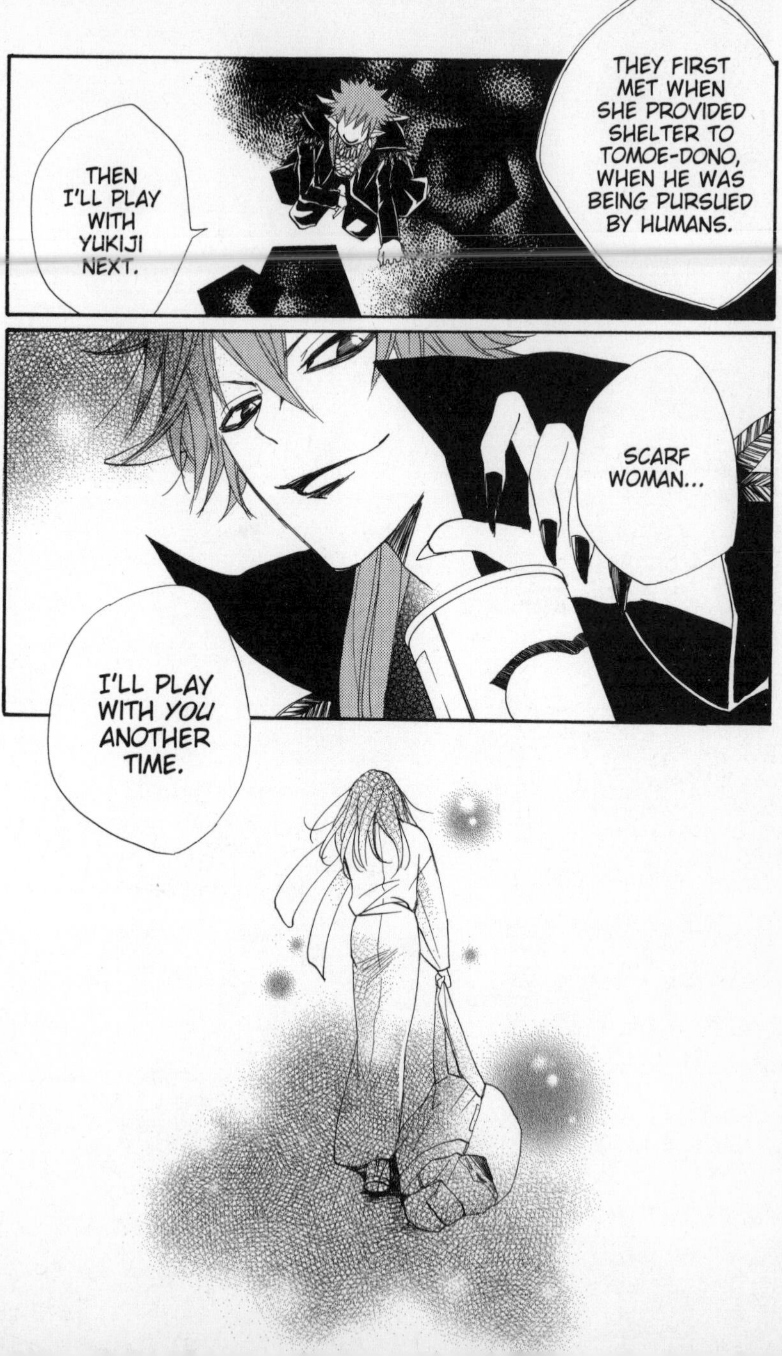
THEY FIRST MET WHEN SHE PROVIDED SHELTER TO TOMOE-DONO, WHEN HE WAS BEING PURSUED BY HUMANS.
THEN I'LL PLAY WITH YUKIJI NEXT.
SCARF WOMAN...
I'LL PLAY WITH *YOU* ANOTHER TIME.

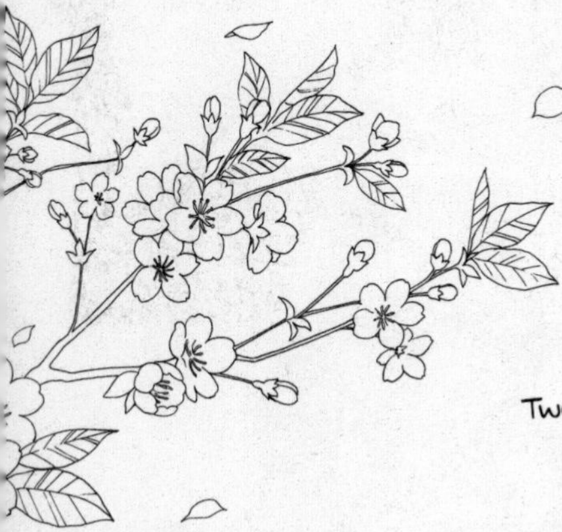

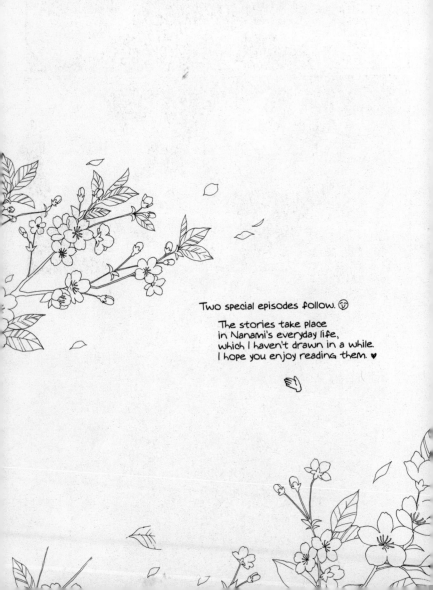

Two special episodes follow.

The stories take place
in Nanami's everyday life,
which I haven't drawn in a while.
I hope you enjoy reading them. ♥

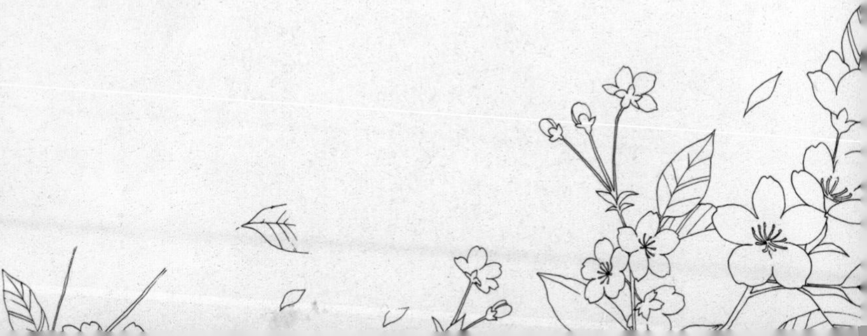

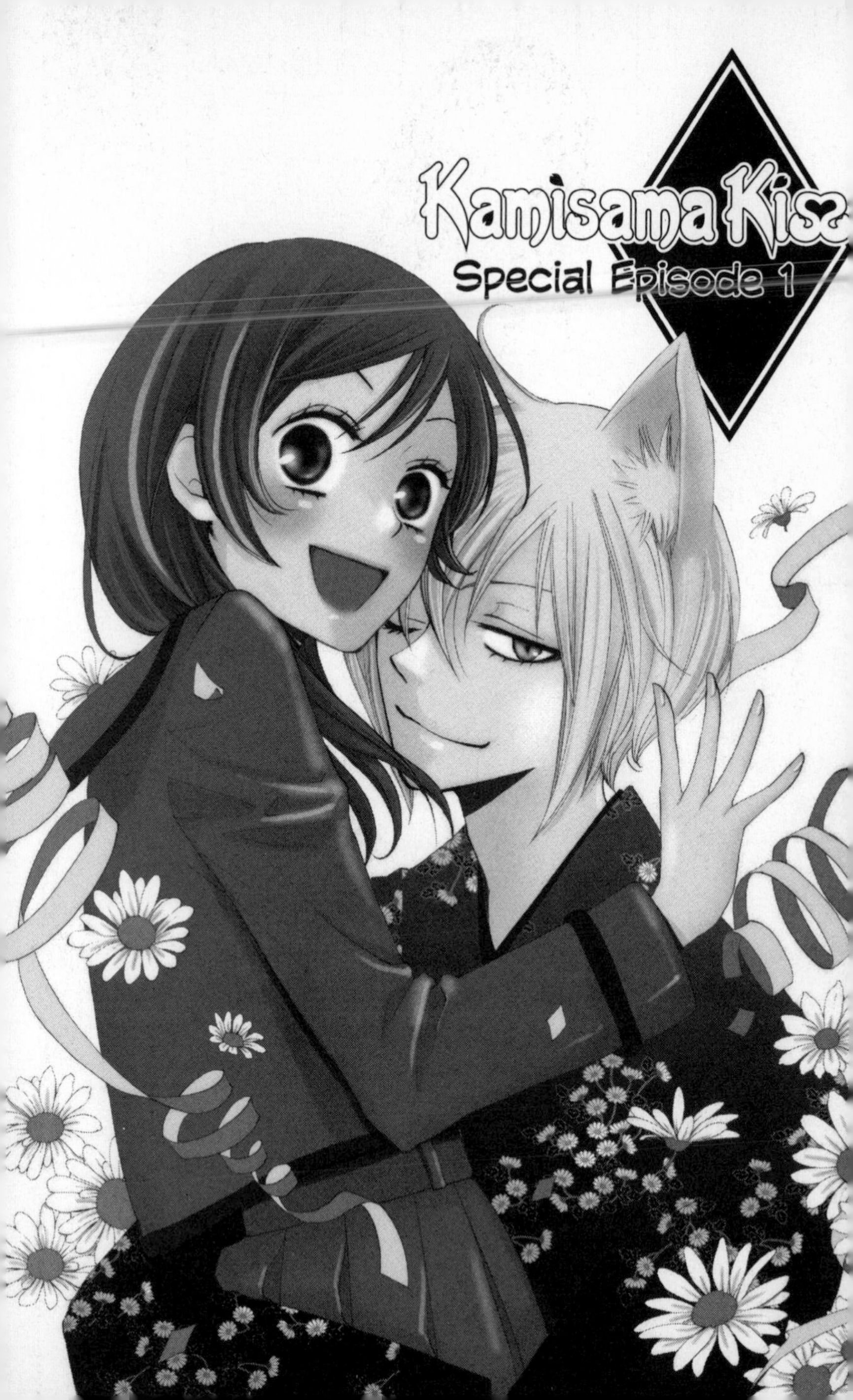
Kamisama Kiss
Special Episode 1

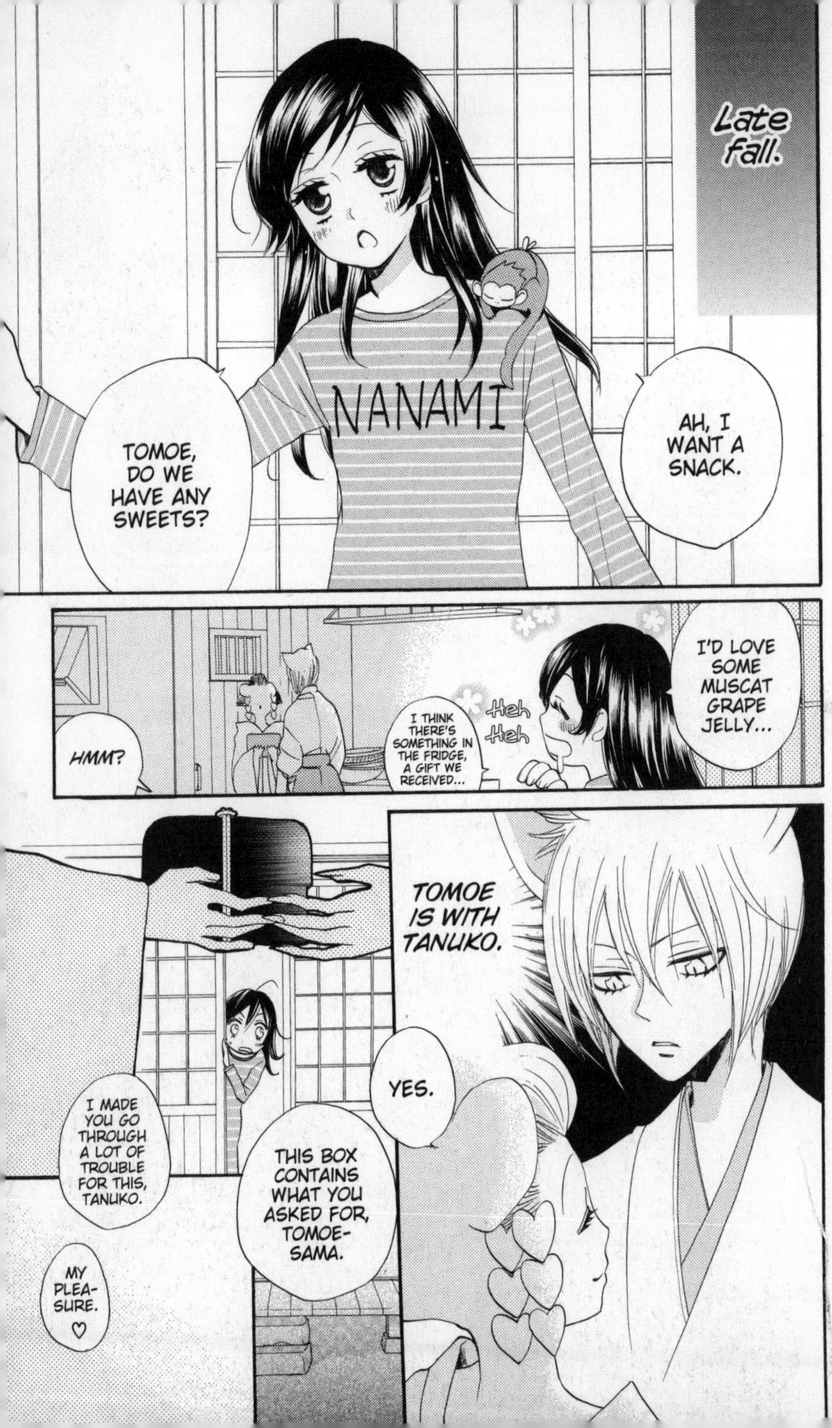
Late fall.
AH, I WANT A SNACK.
TOMOE, DO WE HAVE ANY SWEETS?
I'D LOVE SOME MUSCAT GRAPE JELLY...
Heh Heh
I THINK THERE'S SOMETHING IN THE FRIDGE, A GIFT WE RECEIVED...
HMM?
TOMOE IS WITH TANUKO.
YES.
THIS BOX CONTAINS WHAT YOU ASKED FOR, TOMOE-SAMA.
I MADE YOU GO THROUGH A LOT OF TROUBLE FOR THIS, TANUKO.
MY PLEASURE. ♡

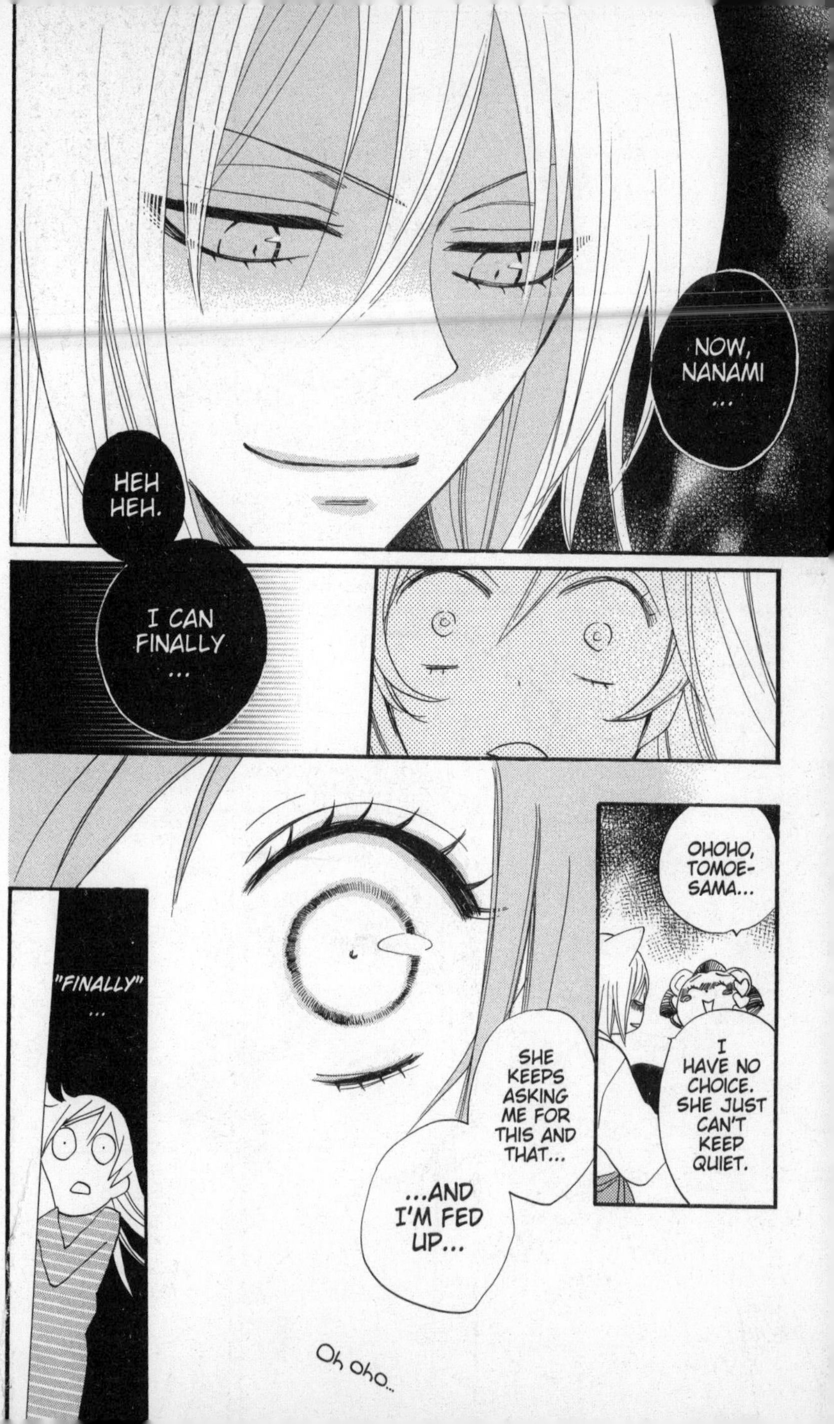
NOW, NANAMI ...
HEH HEH.
I CAN FINALLY ...
OHOHO, TOMOE-SAMA...
I HAVE NO CHOICE. SHE JUST CAN'T KEEP QUIET.
SHE KEEPS ASKING ME FOR THIS AND THAT...
...AND I'M FED UP...
Oh oho...
"FINALLY" ...

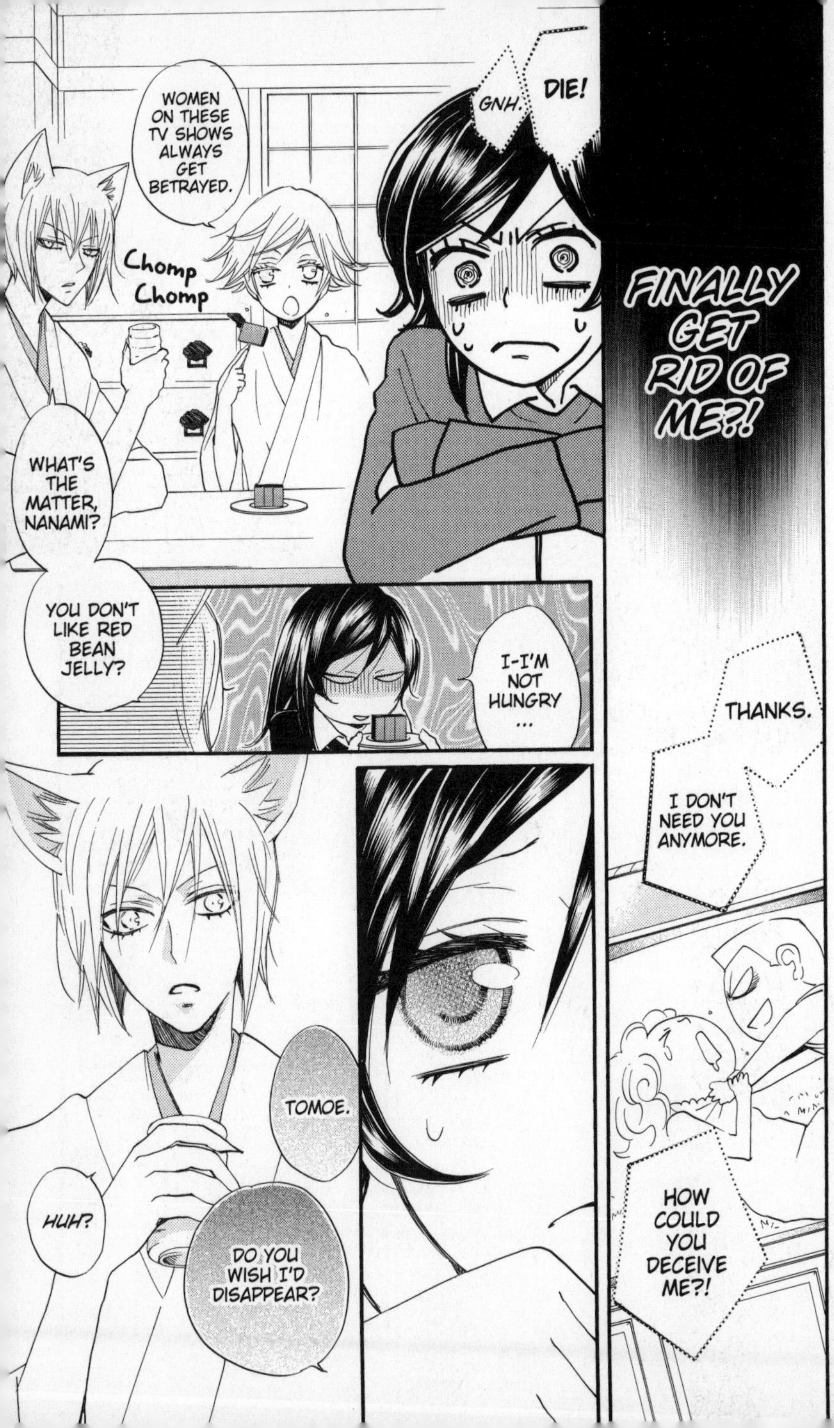
FINALLY GET RID OF ME?!
THANKS.
I DON'T NEED YOU ANYMORE.
HOW COULD YOU DECEIVE ME?!
DIE!
GNH.
WOMEN ON THESE TV SHOWS ALWAYS GET BETRAYED.
Chomp Chomp
WHAT'S THE MATTER, NANAMI?
I-I'M NOT HUNGRY ...
YOU DON'T LIKE RED BEAN JELLY?
TOMOE.
HUH?
DO YOU WISH I'D DISAPPEAR?

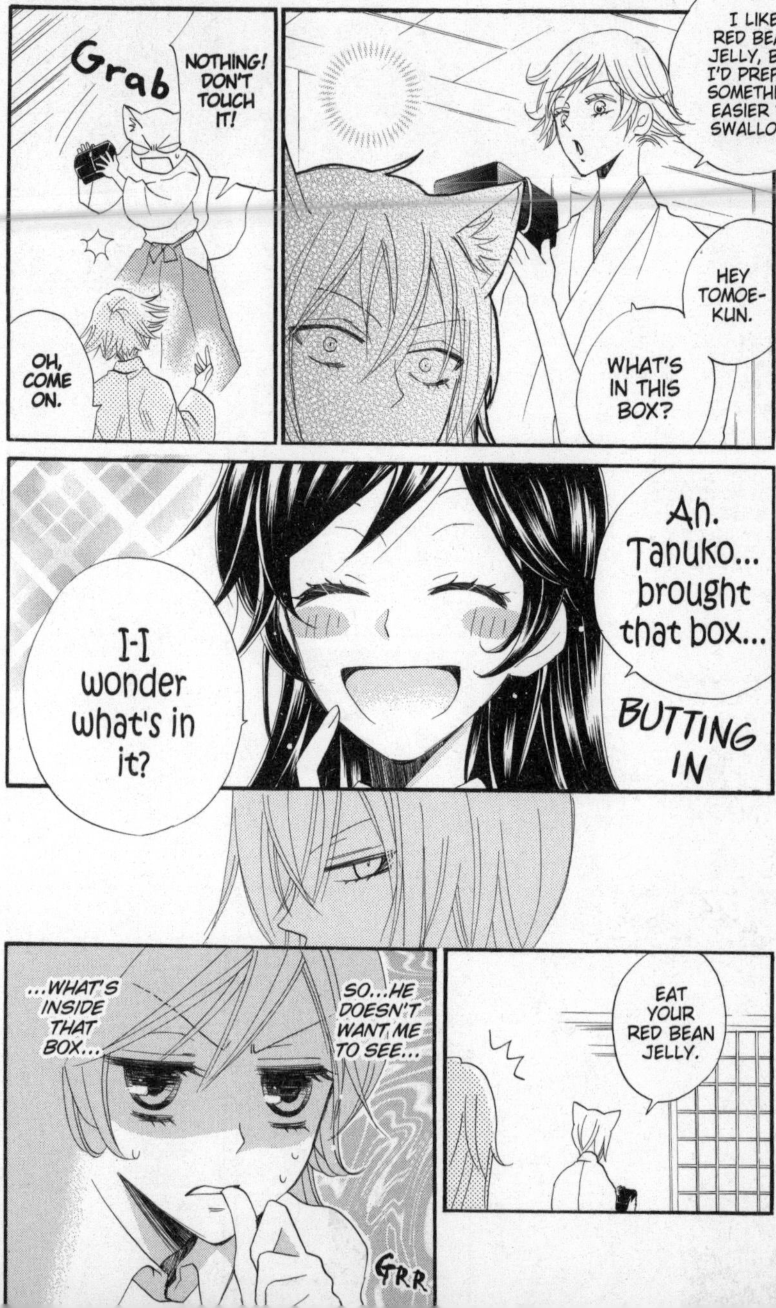
I LIKE RED BEAN JELLY, BUT I'D PREFER SOMETHING EASIER TO SWALLOW.
HEY TOMOE-KUN.
WHAT'S IN THIS BOX?
Grab
NOTHING! DON'T TOUCH IT!
OH, COME ON.
Ah. Tanuko... brought that box...
BUTTING IN
I-I wonder what's in it?
EAT YOUR RED BEAN JELLY.
SO...HE DOESN'T WANT ME TO SEE...
...WHAT'S INSIDE THAT BOX...
GRR

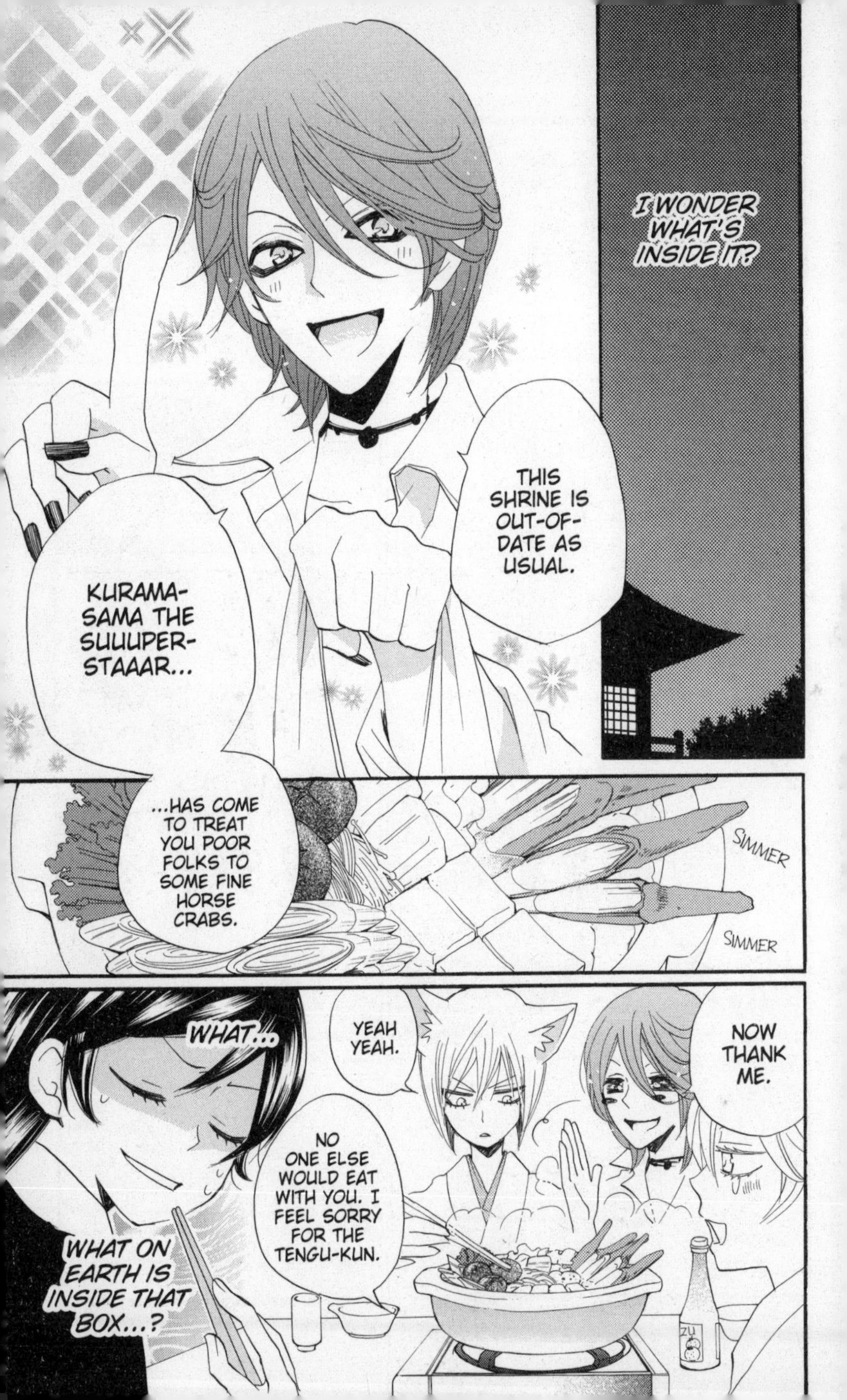

I WONDER WHAT'S INSIDE IT?
THIS SHRINE IS OUT-OF-DATE AS USUAL.
KURAMA-SAMA THE SUUUPER-STAAAR...
...HAS COME TO TREAT YOU POOR FOLKS TO SOME FINE HORSE CRABS.
SIMMER
SIMMER
NOW THANK ME.
YEAH YEAH.
WHAT...
NO ONE ELSE WOULD EAT WITH YOU. I FEEL SORRY FOR THE TENGU-KUN.
WHAT ON EARTH IS INSIDE THAT BOX...?

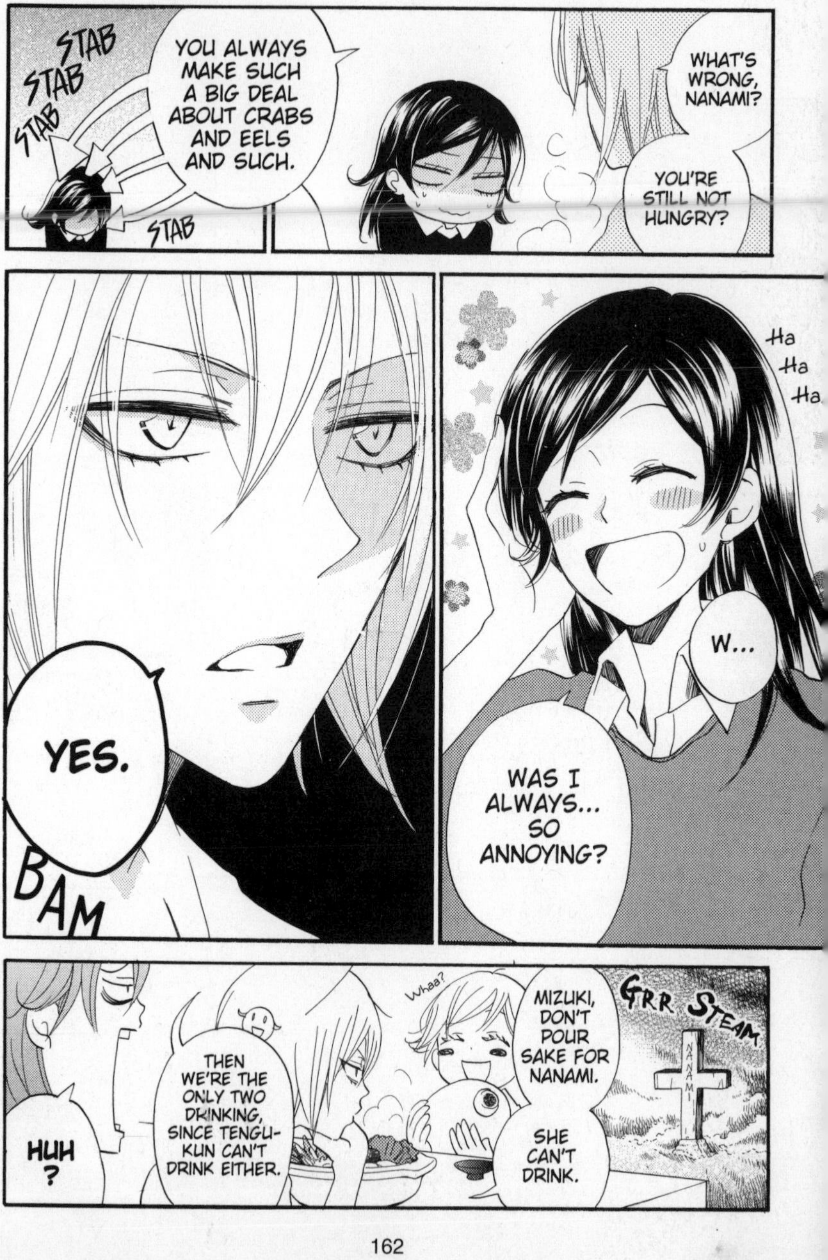
WHAT'S WRONG, NANAMI?
YOU'RE STILL NOT HUNGRY?
YOU ALWAYS MAKE SUCH A BIG DEAL ABOUT CRABS AND EELS AND SUCH.
STAB STAB STAB
STAB
Ha Ha Ha
W...
WAS I ALWAYS... SO ANNOYING?
YES.
BAM
GRR STEAM
NANAMI
MIZUKI, DON'T POUR SAKE FOR NANAMI.
SHE CAN'T DRINK.
Whaa?
THEN WE'RE THE ONLY TWO DRINKING, SINCE TENGU-KUN CAN'T DRINK EITHER.
HUH?

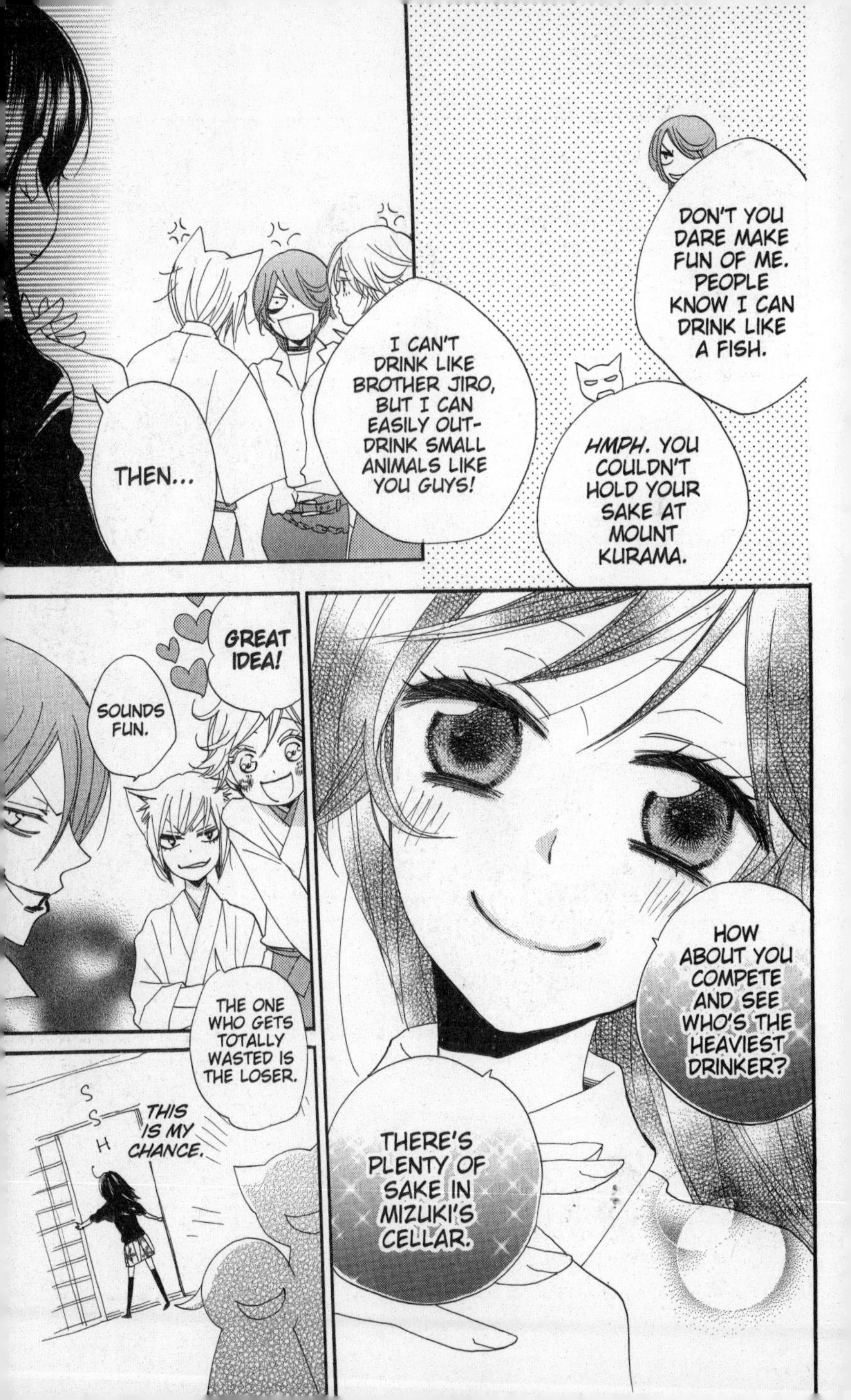
DON'T YOU DARE MAKE FUN OF ME. PEOPLE KNOW I CAN DRINK LIKE A FISH.
HMPH. YOU COULDN'T HOLD YOUR SAKE AT MOUNT KURAMA.
I CAN'T DRINK LIKE BROTHER JIRO, BUT I CAN EASILY OUT-DRINK SMALL ANIMALS LIKE YOU GUYS!
THEN...
HOW ABOUT YOU COMPETE AND SEE WHO'S THE HEAVIEST DRINKER?
THERE'S PLENTY OF SAKE IN MIZUKI'S CELLAR.
GREAT IDEA!
SOUNDS FUN.
THE ONE WHO GETS TOTALLY WASTED IS THE LOSER.
THIS IS MY CHANCE.
SSH

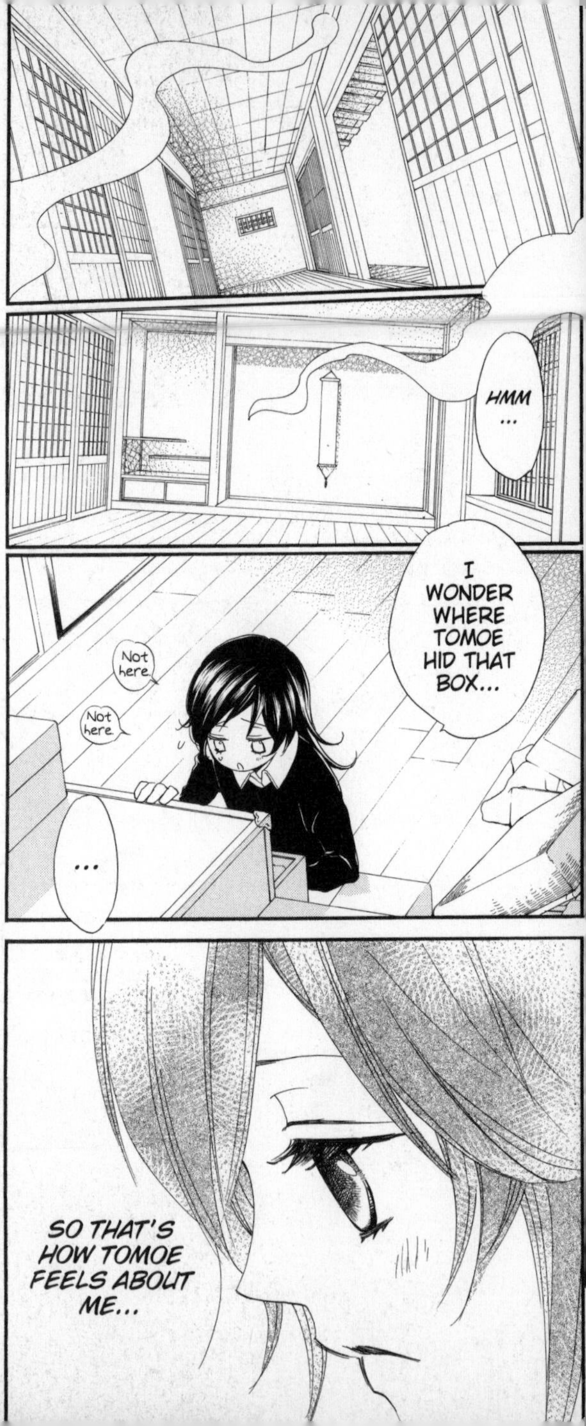
HMM...
I WONDER WHERE TOMOE HID THAT BOX...
Not here.
Not here.
...
SO THAT'S HOW TOMOE FEELS ABOUT ME...

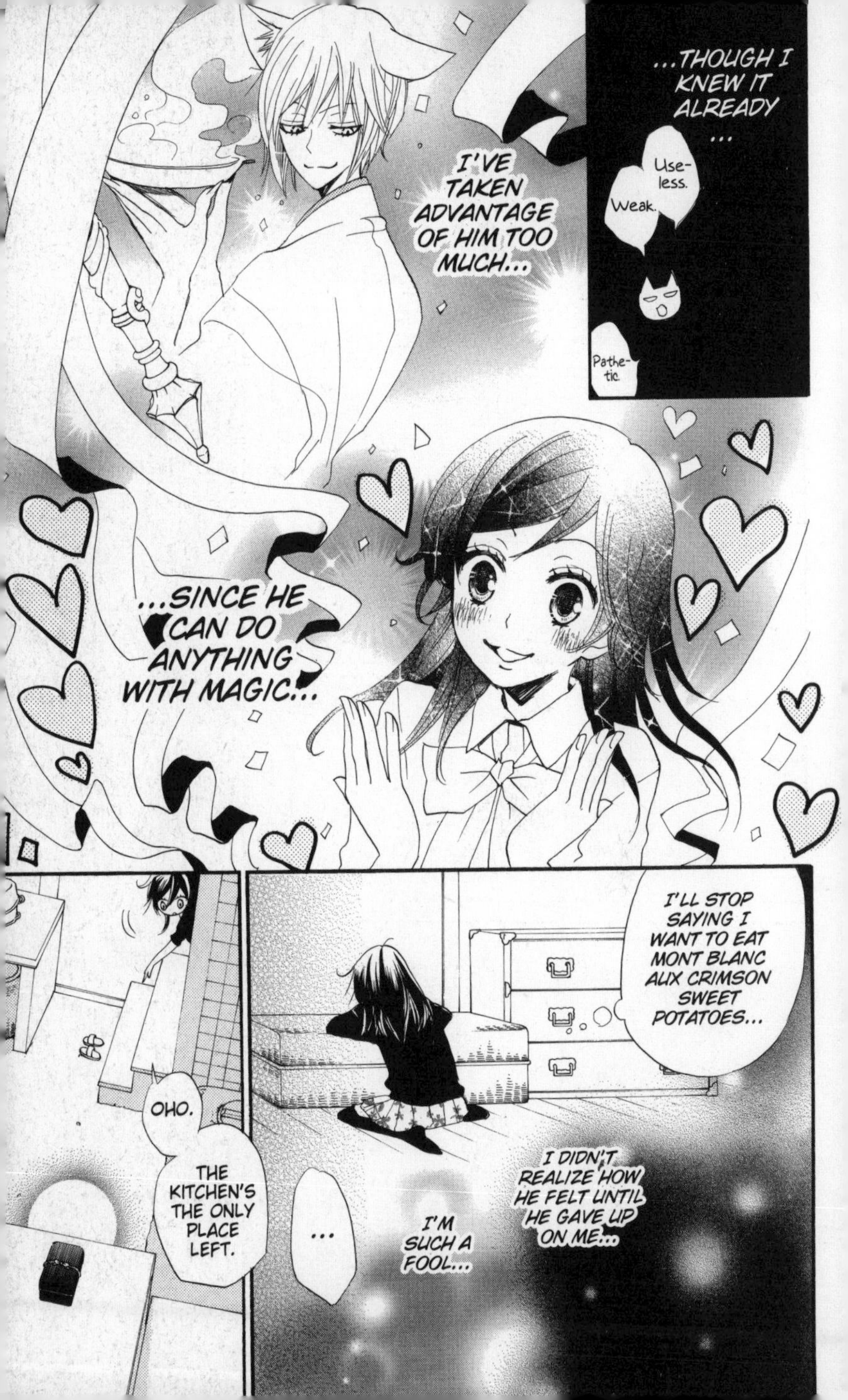
...THOUGH I KNEW IT ALREADY...
Useless.
Weak.
Pathetic.
I'VE TAKEN ADVANTAGE OF HIM TOO MUCH...
...SINCE HE CAN DO ANYTHING WITH MAGIC...
I'LL STOP SAYING I WANT TO EAT MONT BLANC AUX CRIMSON SWEET POTATOES...
I DIDN'T REALIZE HOW HE FELT UNTIL HE GAVE UP ON ME...
I'M SUCH A FOOL...
...
OHO.
THE KITCHEN'S THE ONLY PLACE LEFT.

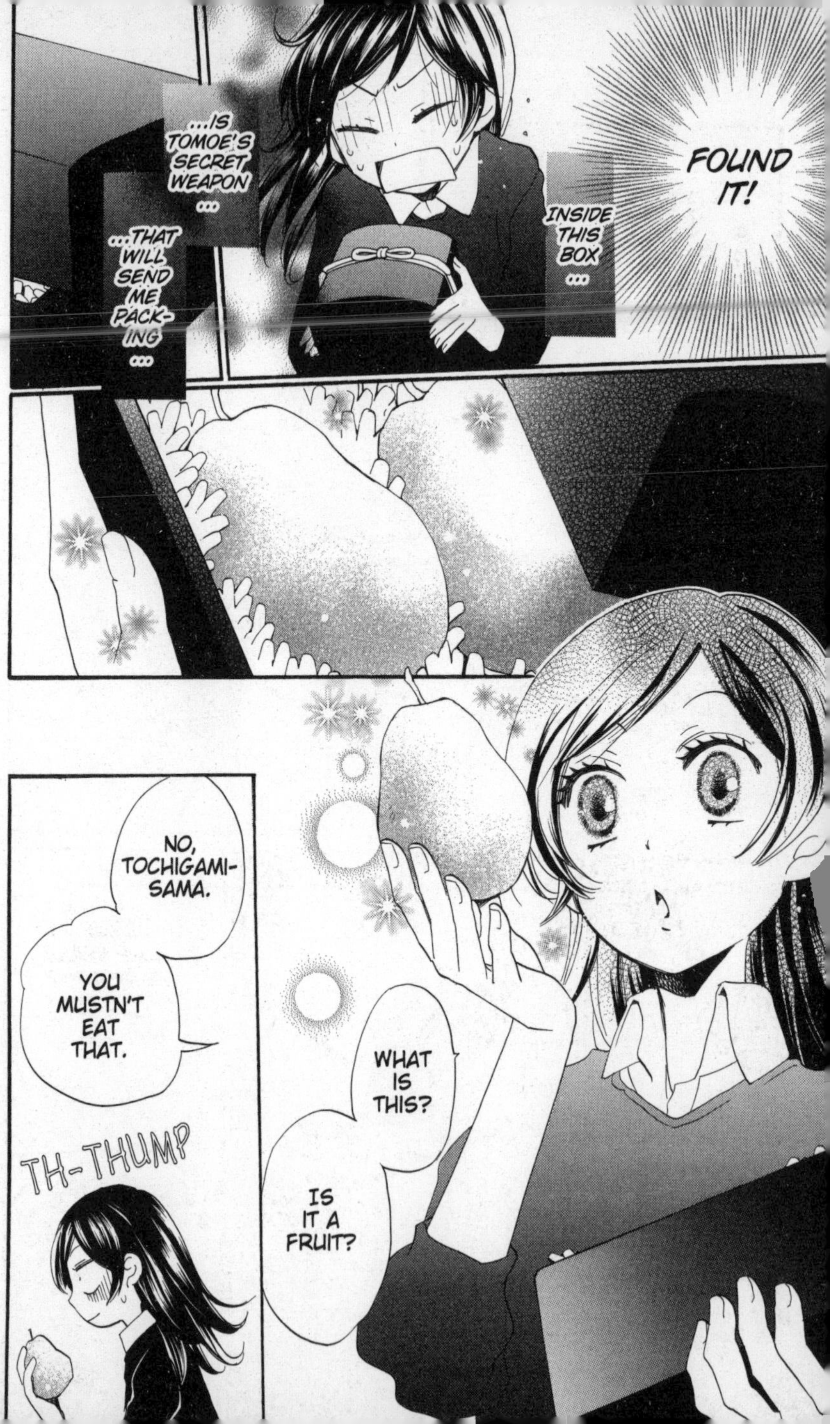
FOUND IT!
INSIDE THIS BOX...
...IS TOMOE'S SECRET WEAPON...
...THAT WILL SEND ME PACKING...
WHAT IS THIS?
IS IT A FRUIT?
NO, TOCHIGAMI-SAMA.
YOU MUSTN'T EAT THAT.
TH-THUMP

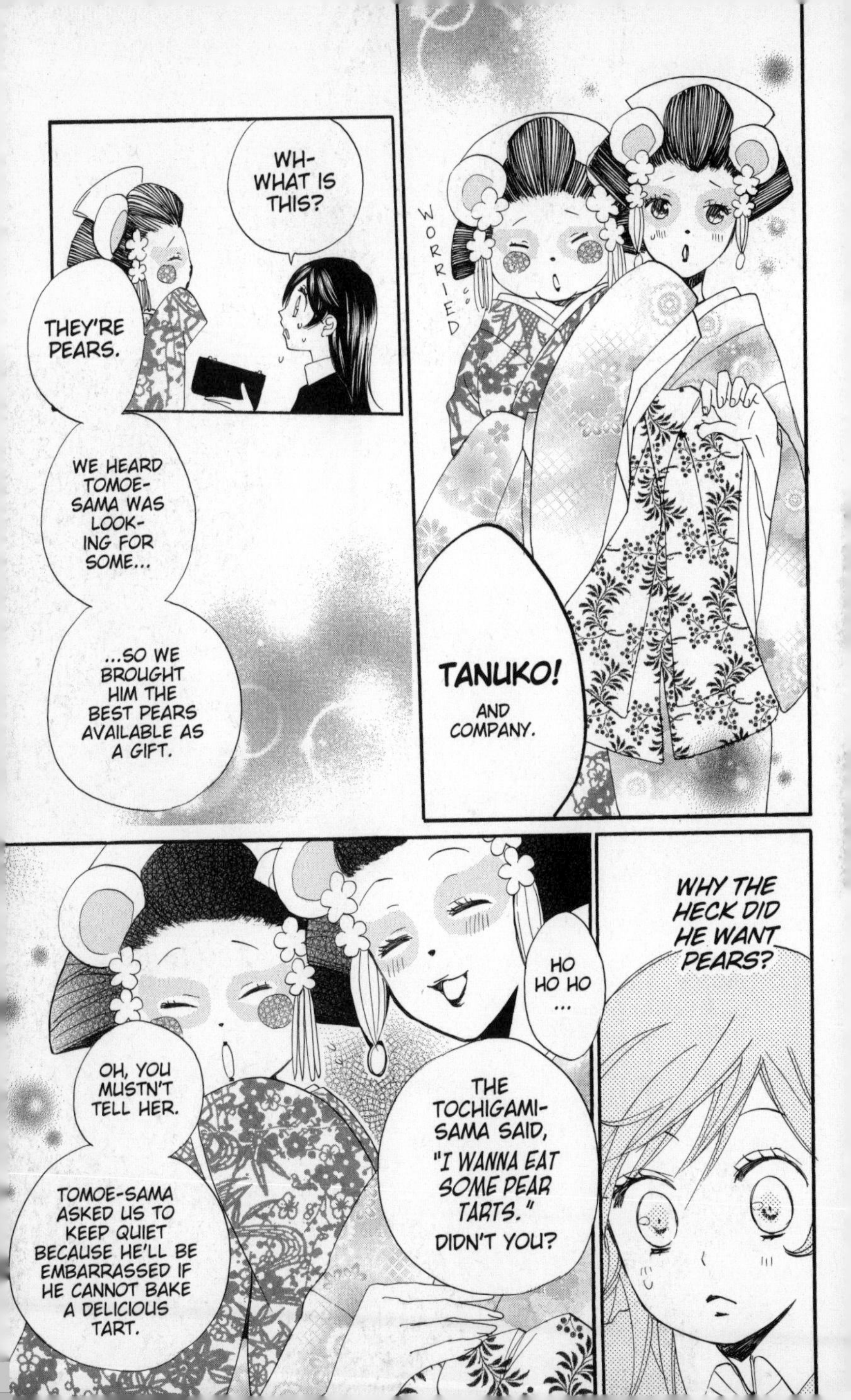
WORRIED
TANUKO! AND COMPANY.
WH- WHAT IS THIS?
THEY'RE PEARS.
WE HEARD TOMOE-SAMA WAS LOOKING FOR SOME...
...SO WE BROUGHT HIM THE BEST PEARS AVAILABLE AS A GIFT.
WHY THE HECK DID HE WANT PEARS?
HO HO HO...
THE TOCHIGAMI-SAMA SAID, "I WANNA EAT SOME PEAR TARTS." DIDN'T YOU?
OH, YOU MUSTN'T TELL HER.
TOMOE-SAMA ASKED US TO KEEP QUIET BECAUSE HE'LL BE EMBARRASSED IF HE CANNOT BAKE A DELICIOUS TART.

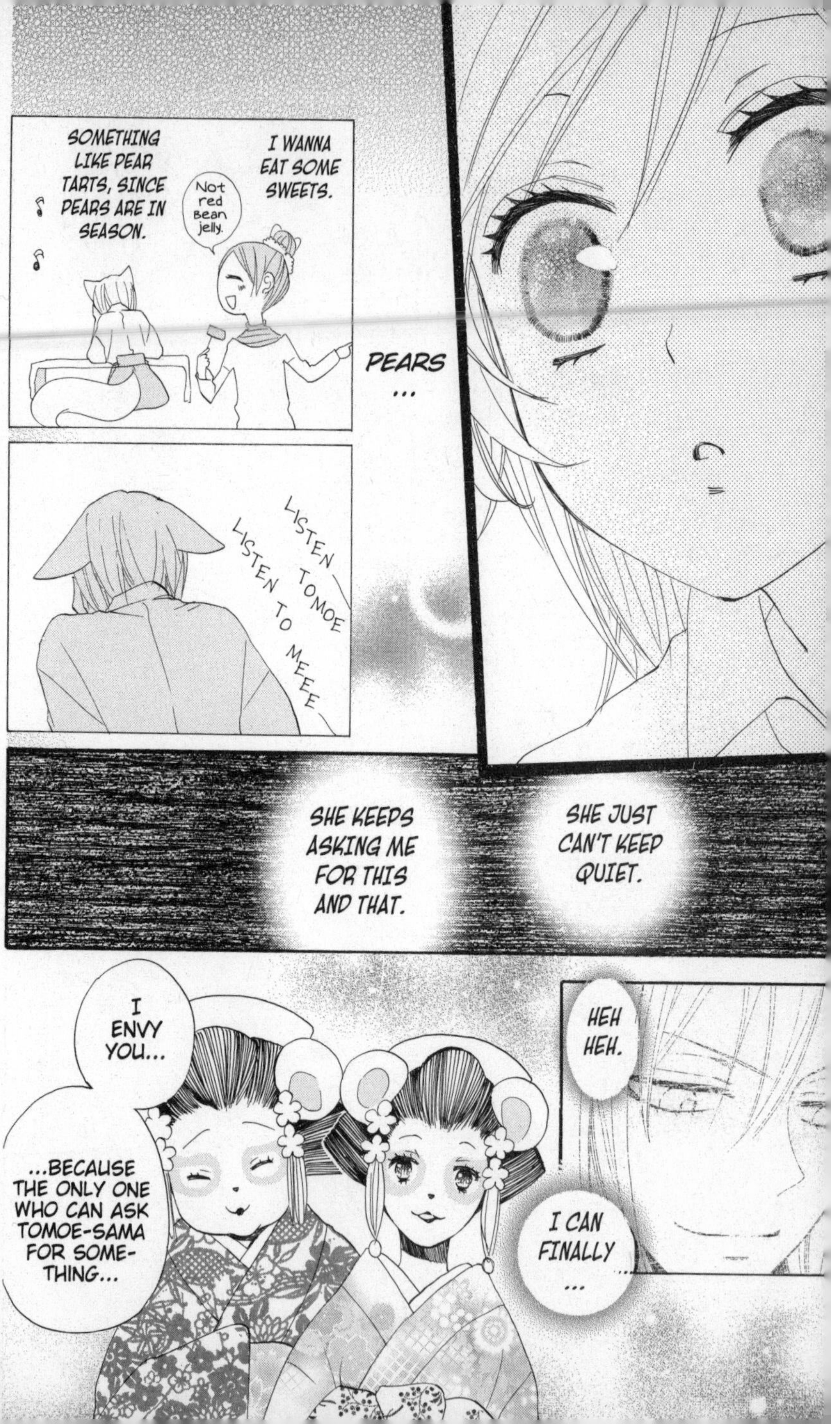
PEARS ...
I WANNA EAT SOME SWEETS.
Not red Bean jelly.
SOMETHING LIKE PEAR TARTS, SINCE PEARS ARE IN SEASON.
LISTEN TOMOE LISTEN TO MEEE
SHE JUST CAN'T KEEP QUIET.
SHE KEEPS ASKING ME FOR THIS AND THAT.
HEH HEH.
I CAN FINALLY ...
I ENVY YOU...
...BECAUSE THE ONLY ONE WHO CAN ASK TOMOE-SAMA FOR SOME-THING...

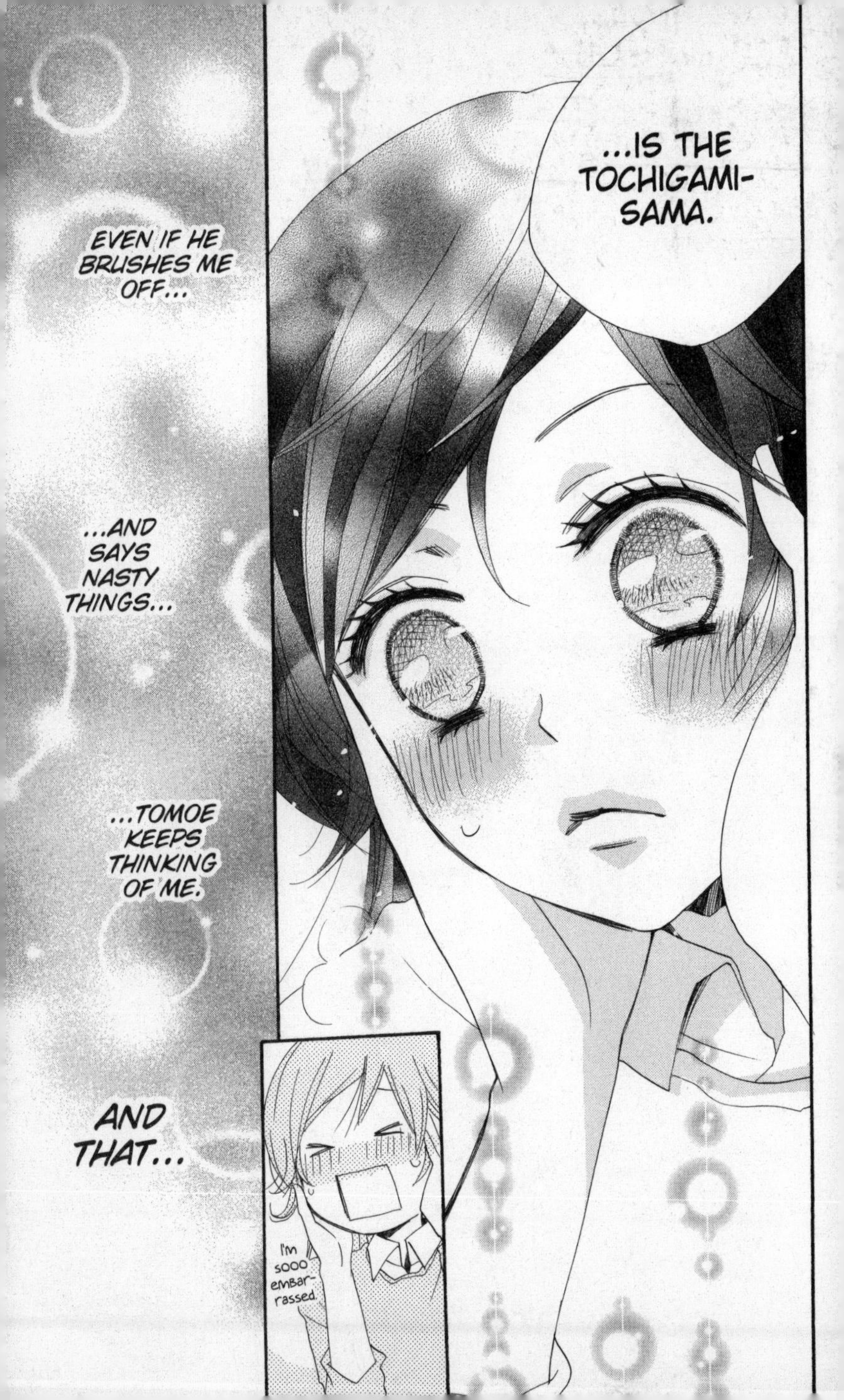
EVEN IF HE BRUSHES ME OFF...
...AND SAYS NASTY THINGS...
...TOMOE KEEPS THINKING OF ME.
AND THAT...
...IS THE TOCHIGAMI-SAMA.
I'm sooo embarrassed.

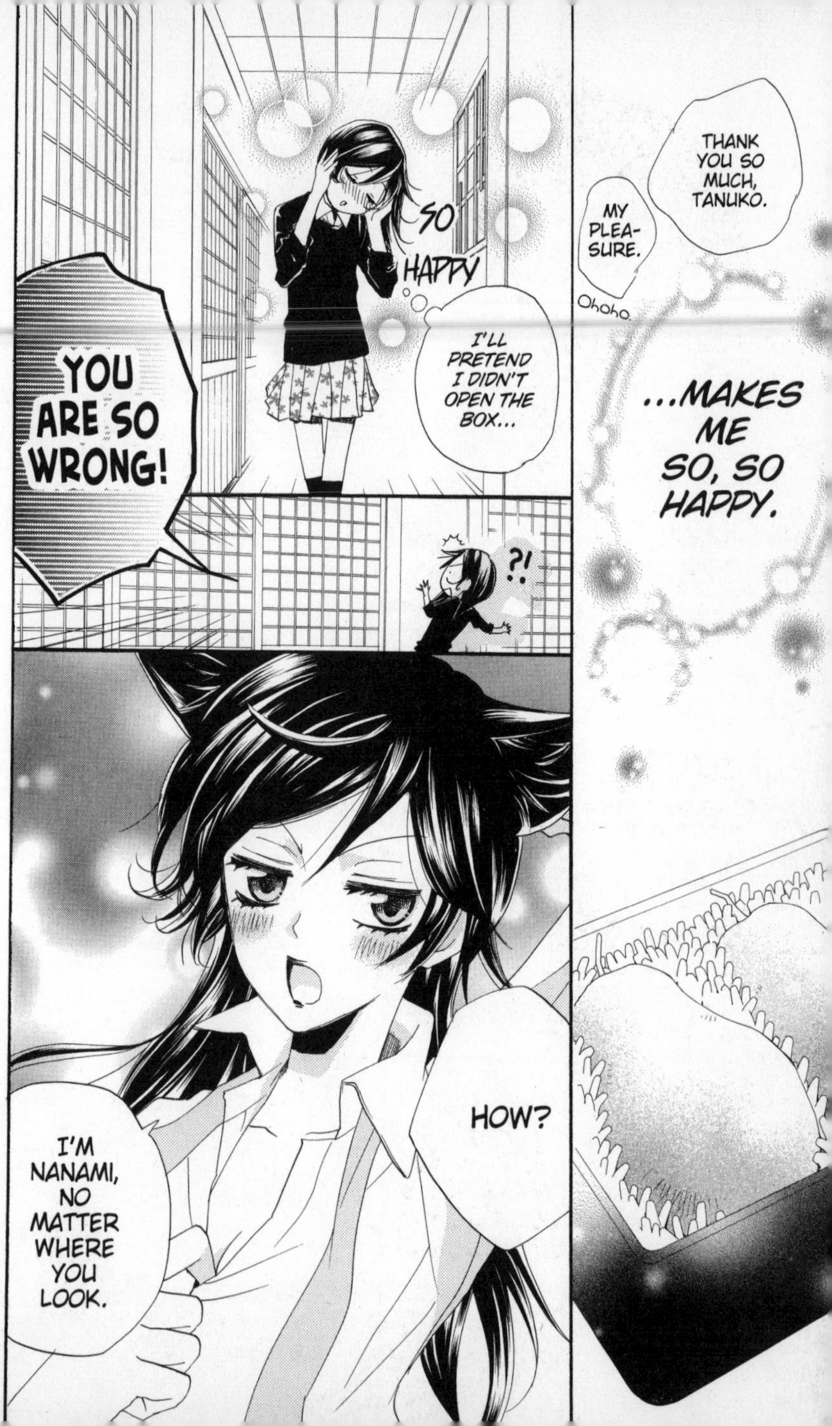
THANK YOU SO MUCH, TANUKO.
MY PLEA-SURE.
Ohoho.
...MAKES ME SO, SO HAPPY.
SO HAPPY
I'LL PRETEND I DIDN'T OPEN THE BOX...
YOU ARE SO WRONG!
?!
HOW?
I'M NANAMI, NO MATTER WHERE YOU LOOK.

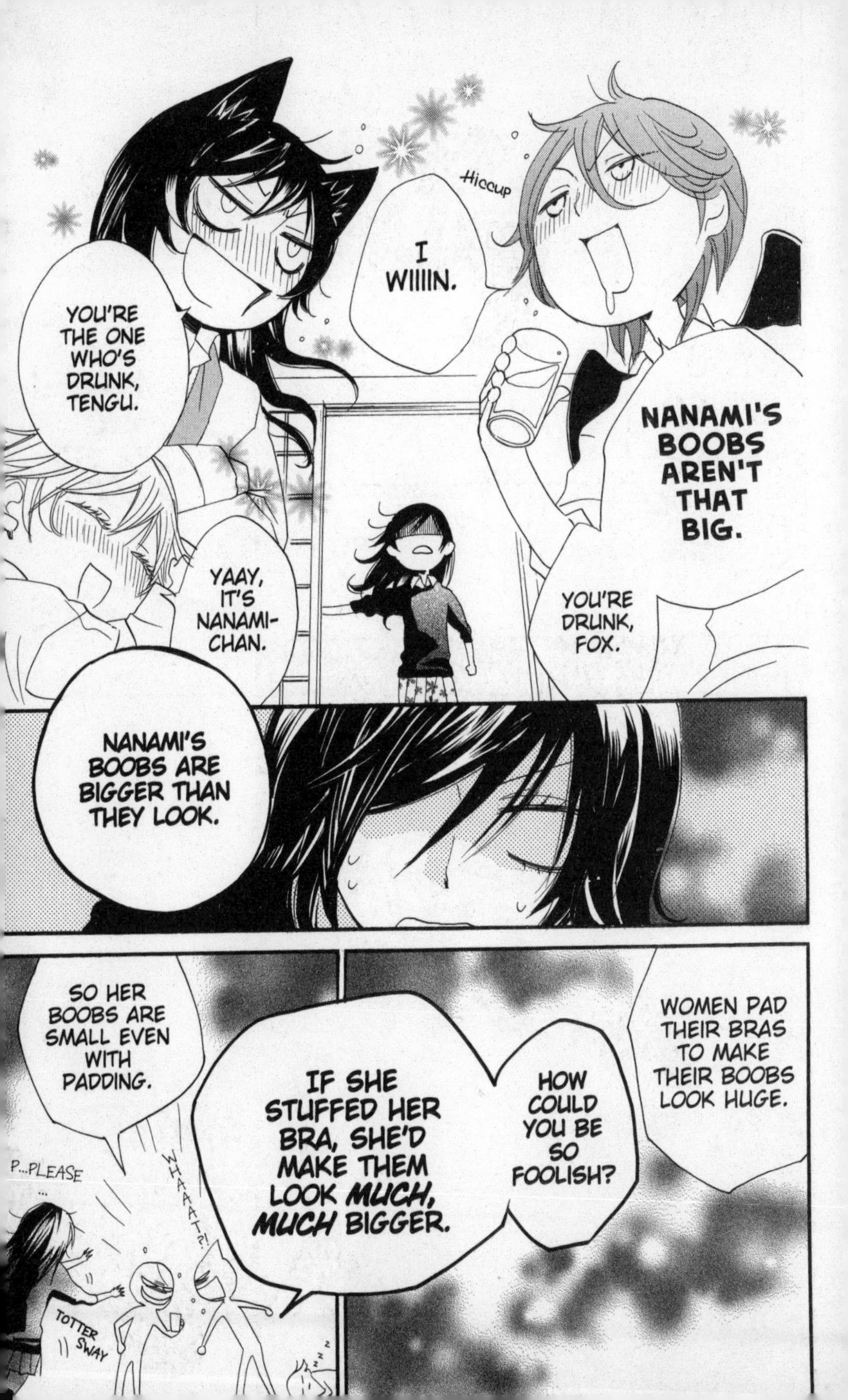
Hiccup
I WIIIIN.
NANAMI'S BOOBS AREN'T THAT BIG.
YOU'RE THE ONE WHO'S DRUNK, TENGU.
YOU'RE DRUNK, FOX.
YAAY, IT'S NANAMI-CHAN.
NANAMI'S BOOBS ARE BIGGER THAN THEY LOOK.
WOMEN PAD THEIR BRAS TO MAKE THEIR BOOBS LOOK HUGE.
HOW COULD YOU BE SO FOOLISH?
IF SHE STUFFED HER BRA, SHE'D MAKE THEM LOOK *MUCH, MUCH* BIGGER.
SO HER BOOBS ARE SMALL EVEN WITH PADDING.
WHAAAT?!
P...PLEASE ...
TOTTER SWAY

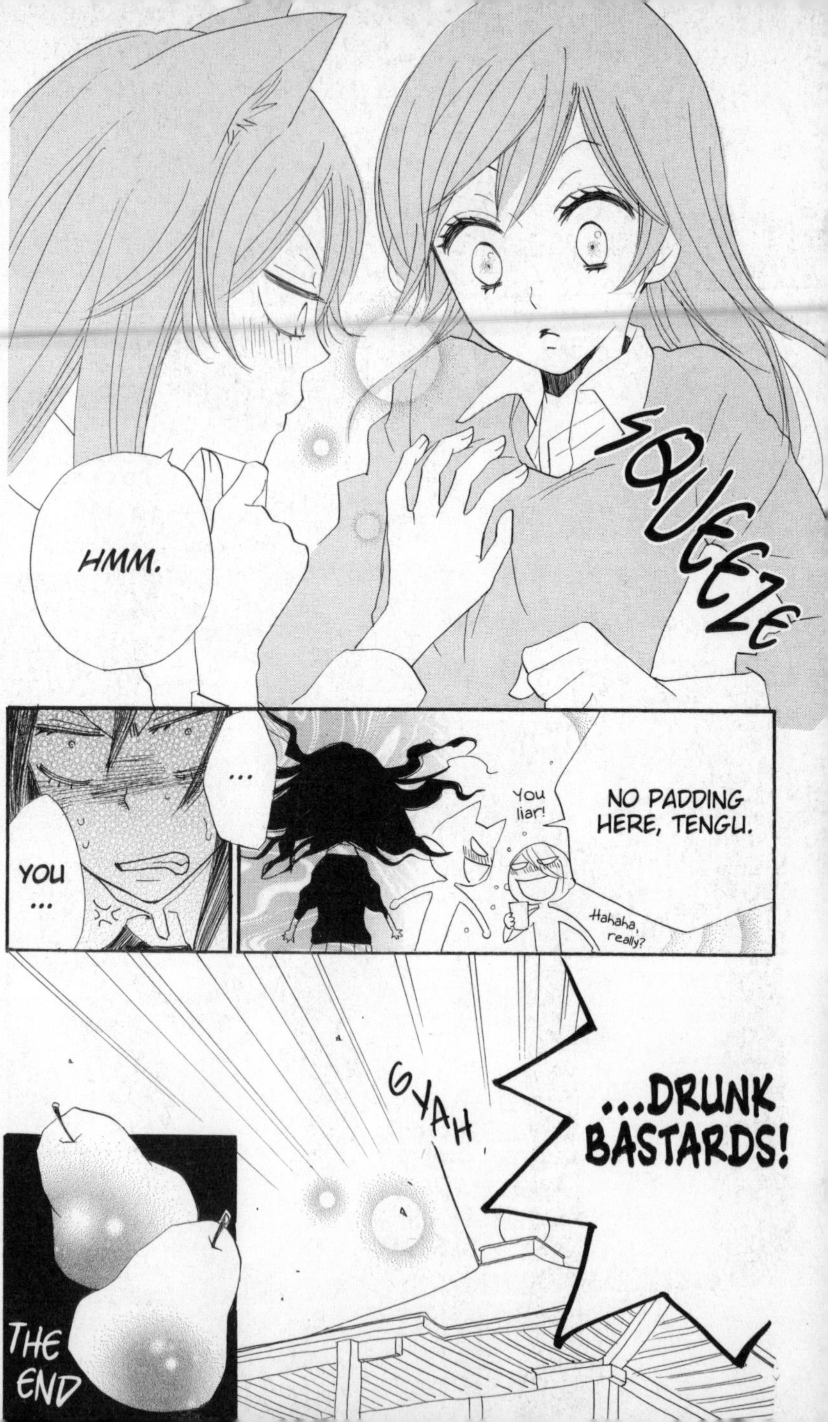
SQUEEZE
HMM.
NO PADDING HERE, TENGU.
You liar!
Hahaha, really?
...
YOU ...
...DRUNK BASTARDS!
GYAH
THE END

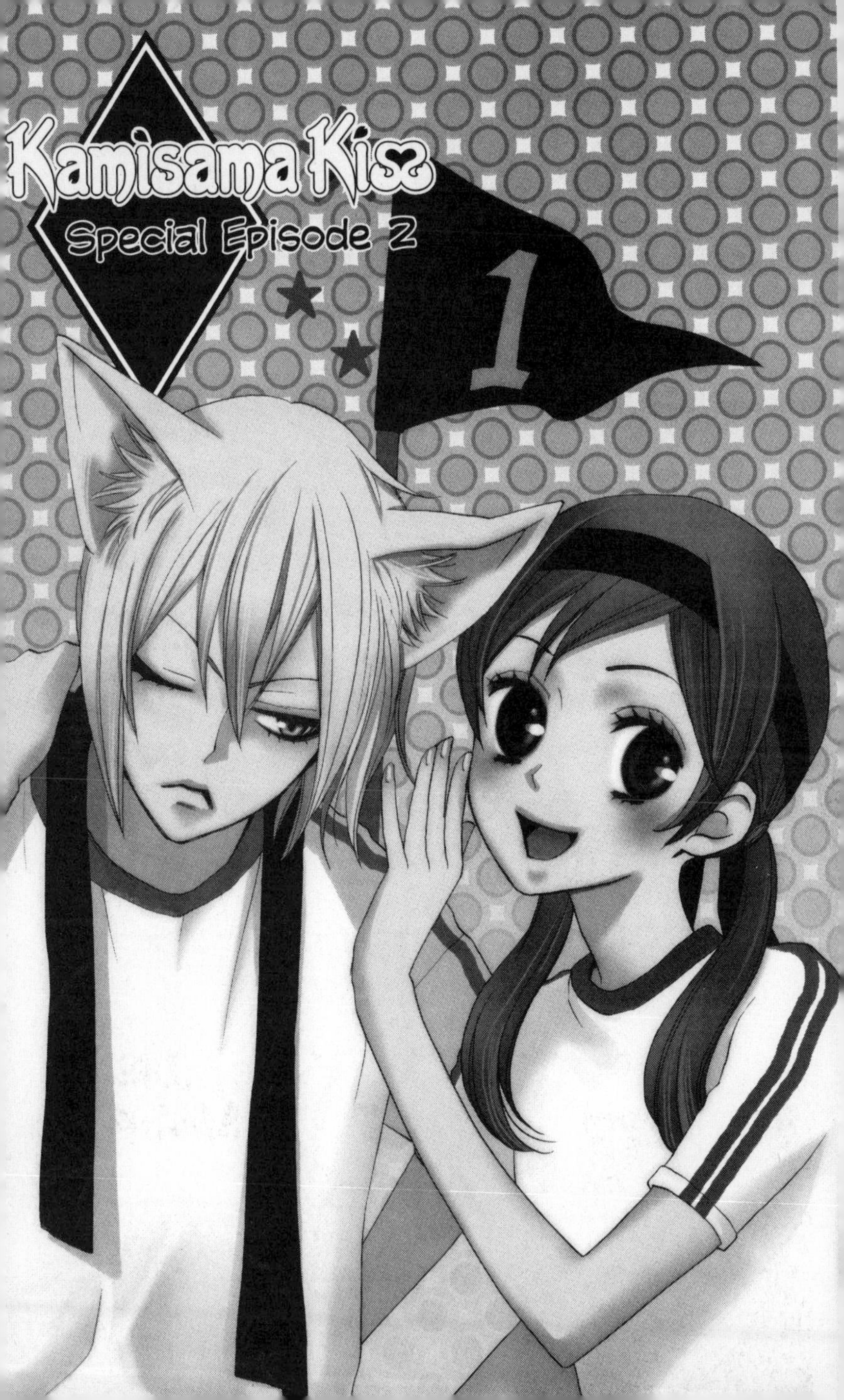
Kamisama Kiss
Special Episode 2
1

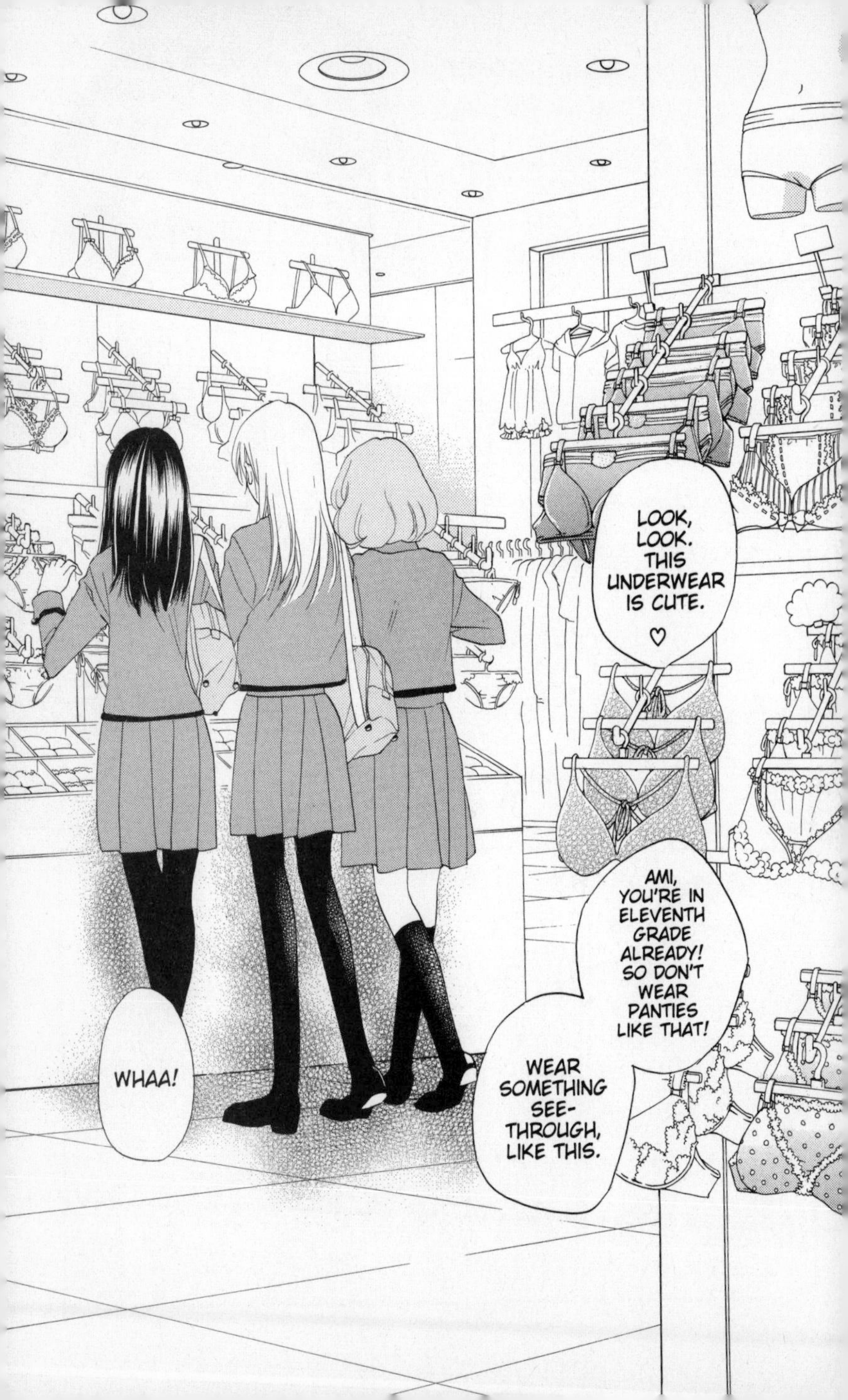
LOOK, LOOK. THIS UNDERWEAR IS CUTE. ♡
AMI, YOU'RE IN ELEVENTH GRADE ALREADY! SO DON'T WEAR PANTIES LIKE THAT!
WEAR SOMETHING SEE-THROUGH, LIKE THIS.
WHAA!

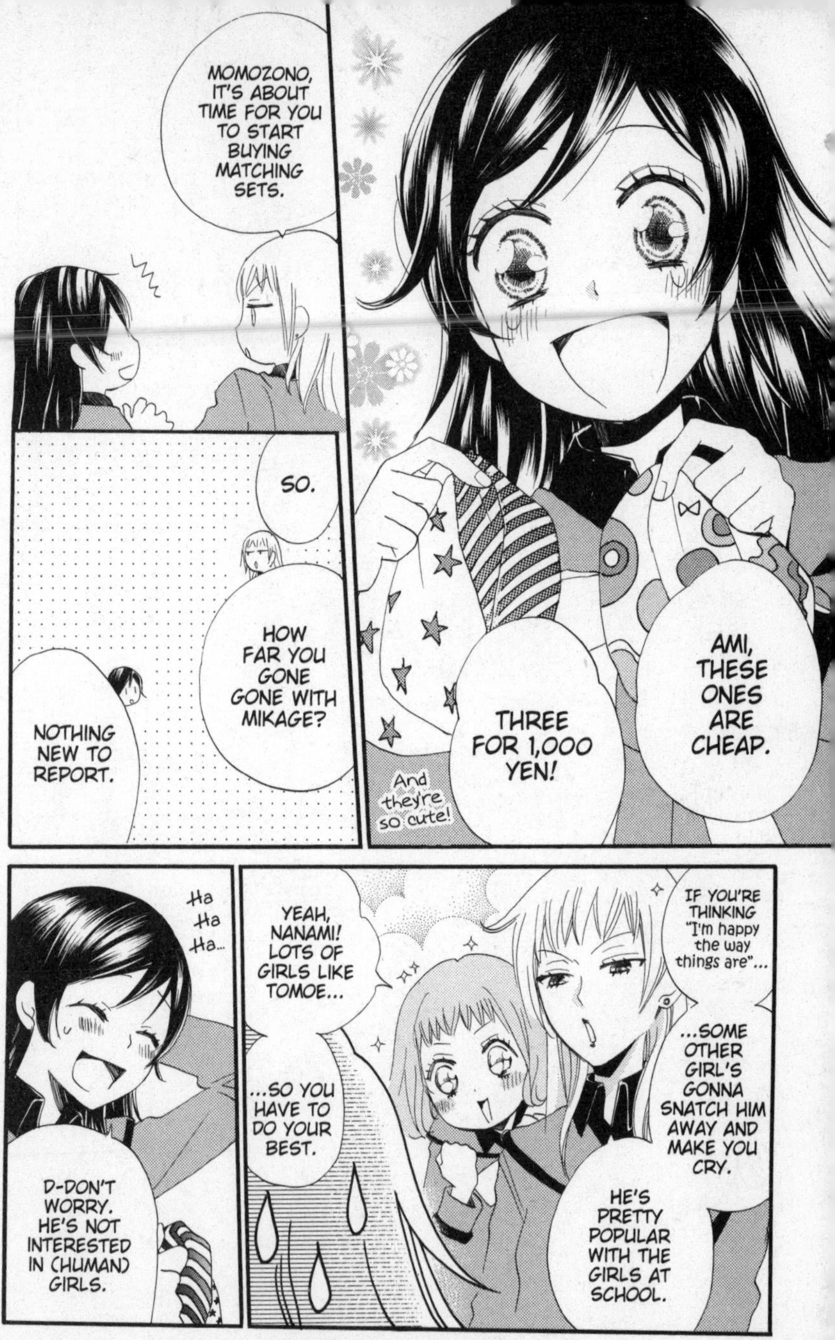
AMI, THESE ONES ARE CHEAP.
THREE FOR 1,000 YEN!
And they're so cute!
MOMOZONO, IT'S ABOUT TIME FOR YOU TO START BUYING MATCHING SETS.
SO.
HOW FAR YOU GONE GONE WITH MIKAGE?
NOTHING NEW TO REPORT.
IF YOU'RE THINKING "I'm happy the way things are"...
...SOME OTHER GIRL'S GONNA SNATCH HIM AWAY AND MAKE YOU CRY.
HE'S PRETTY POPULAR WITH THE GIRLS AT SCHOOL.
YEAH, NANAMI! LOTS OF GIRLS LIKE TOMOE...
...SO YOU HAVE TO DO YOUR BEST.
Ha Ha Ha...
D-DON'T WORRY. HE'S NOT INTERESTED IN (HUMAN) GIRLS.

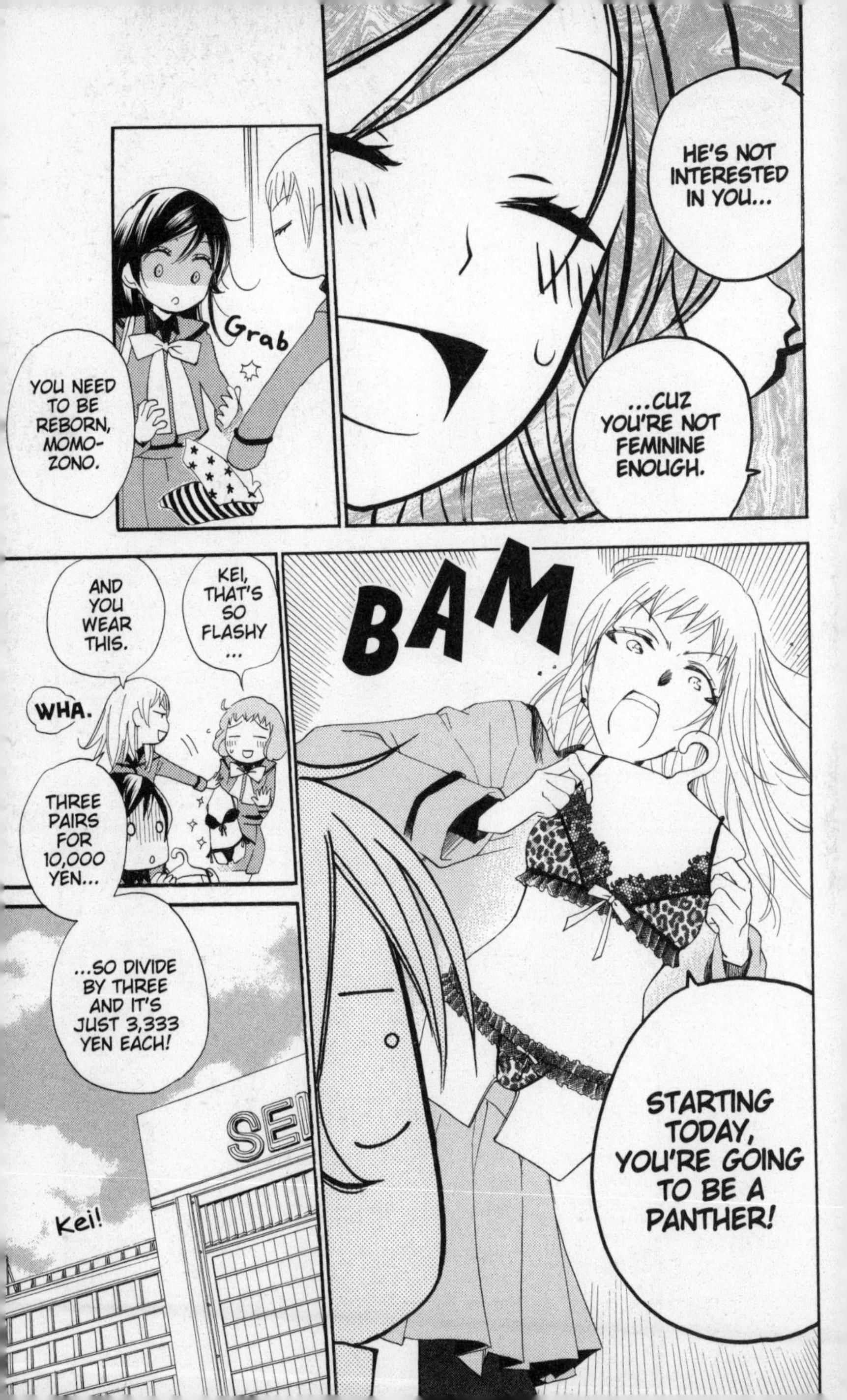
HE'S NOT INTERESTED IN YOU...
...CUZ YOU'RE NOT FEMININE ENOUGH.
Grab
YOU NEED TO BE REBORN, MOMO-ZONO.
BAM
STARTING TODAY, YOU'RE GOING TO BE A PANTHER!
KEI, THAT'S SO FLASHY ...
AND YOU WEAR THIS.
WHA.
THREE PAIRS FOR 10,000 YEN...
...SO DIVIDE BY THREE AND IT'S JUST 3,333 YEN EACH!
Kei!

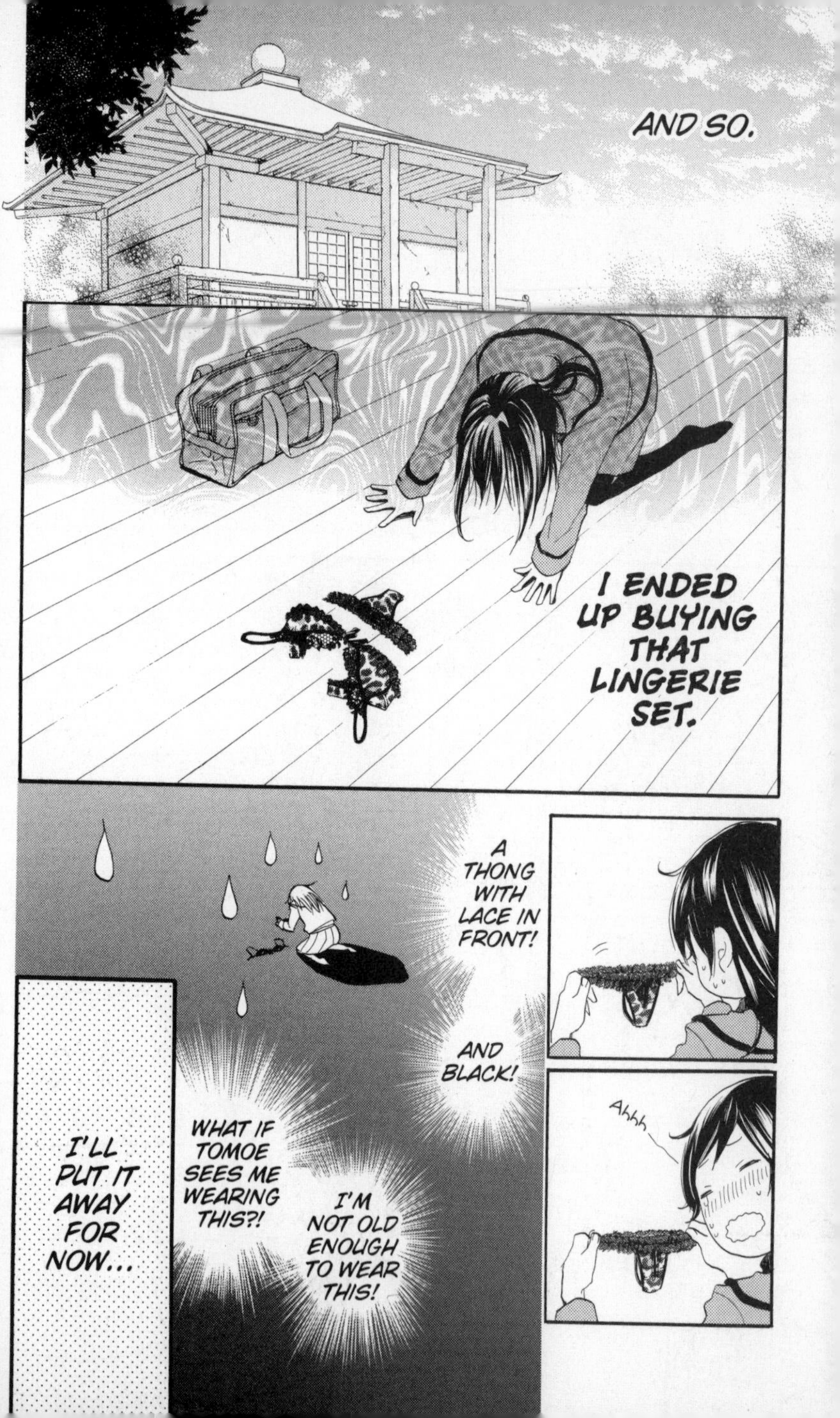
AND SO.
I ENDED UP BUYING THAT LINGERIE SET.
A THONG WITH LACE IN FRONT!
AND BLACK!
Ahhh
WHAT IF TOMOE SEES ME WEARING THIS?!
I'M NOT OLD ENOUGH TO WEAR THIS!
I'LL PUT IT AWAY FOR NOW...

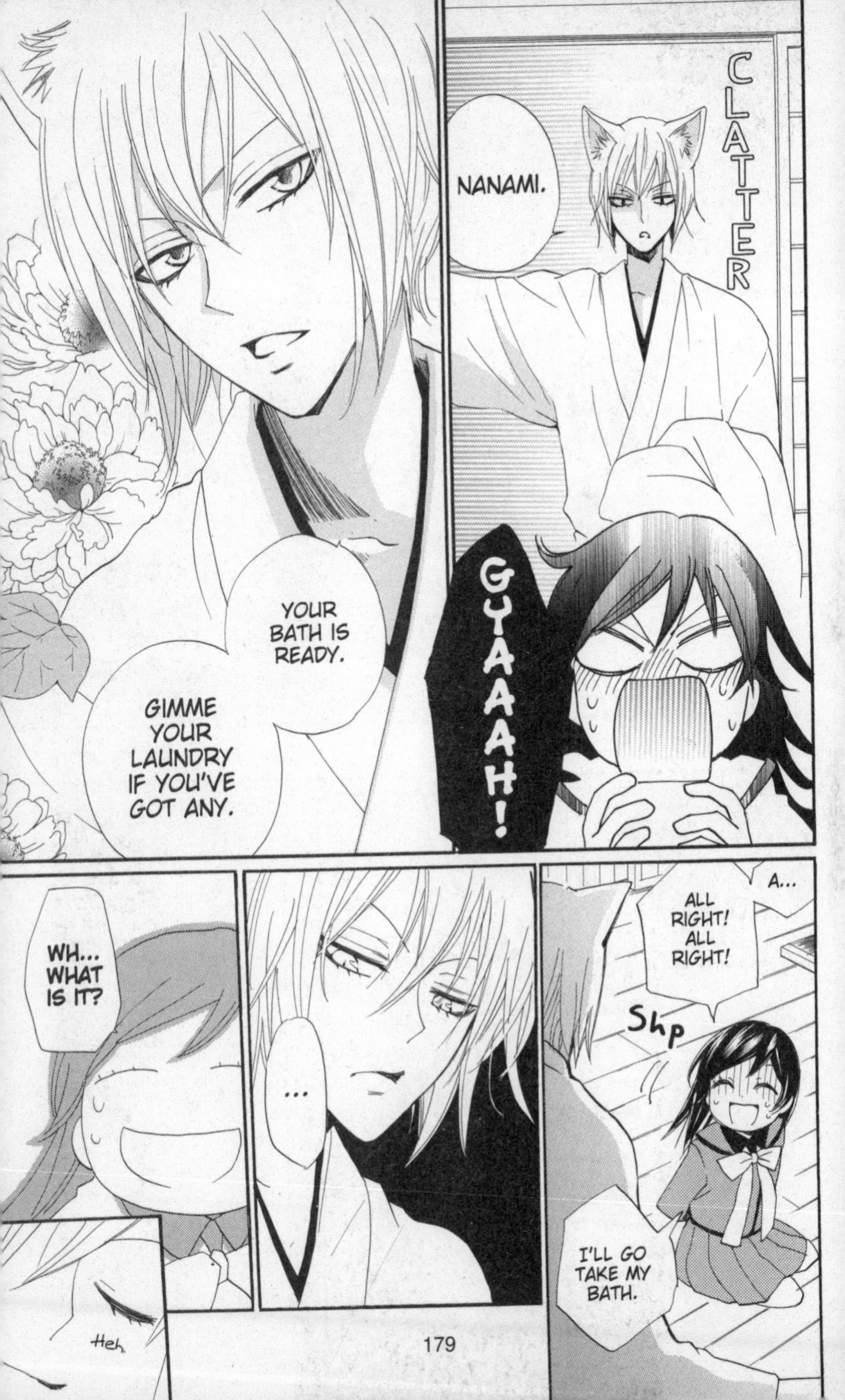
CLATTER
NANAMI.
GYAAAAH!
YOUR BATH IS READY.
GIMME YOUR LAUNDRY IF YOU'VE GOT ANY.
A...
ALL RIGHT! ALL RIGHT!
Shp
I'LL GO TAKE MY BATH.
...
WH... WHAT IS IT?
Heh.

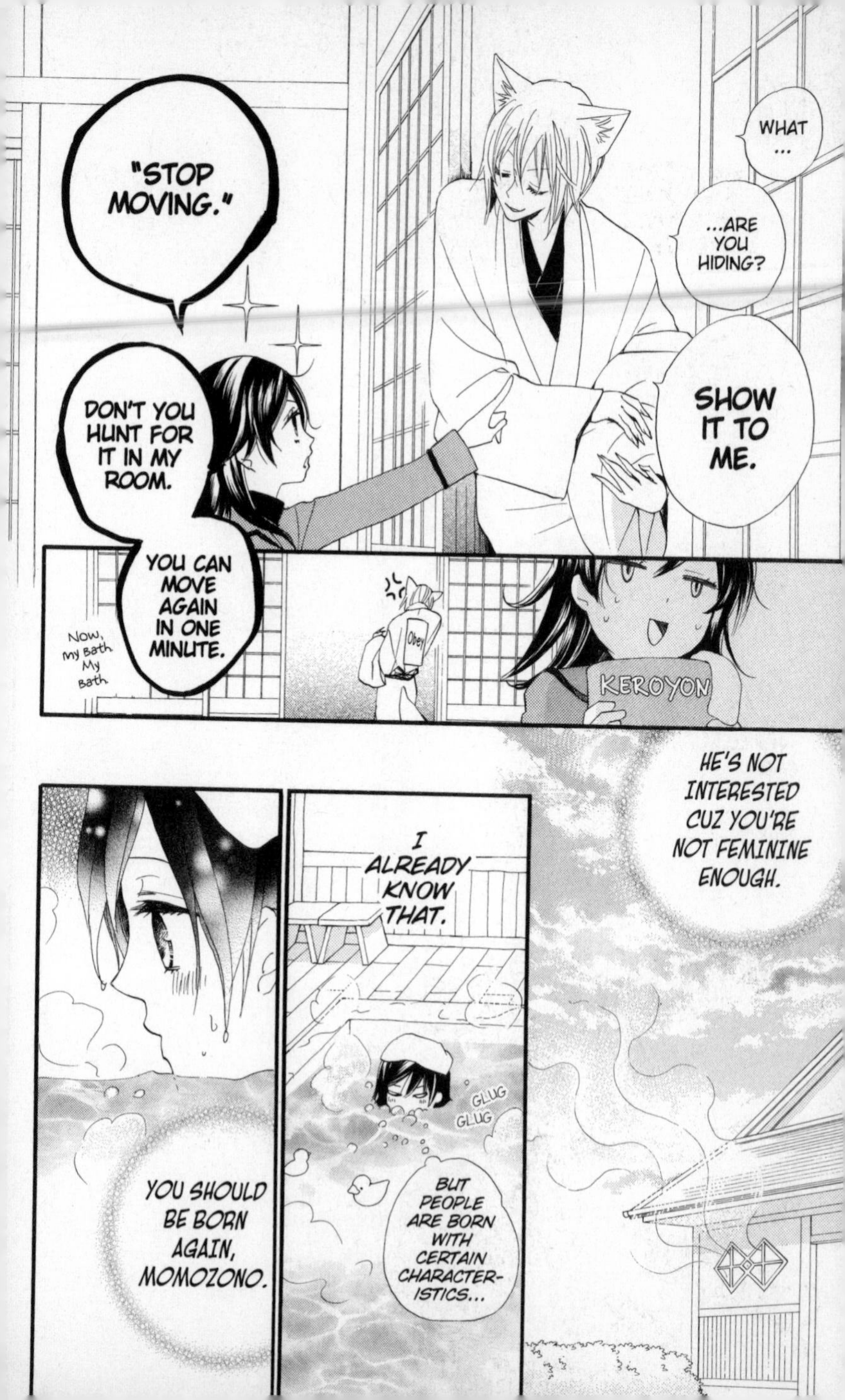
WHAT ...
...ARE YOU HIDING?
SHOW IT TO ME.
"STOP MOVING."
DON'T YOU HUNT FOR IT IN MY ROOM.
KEROYON
YOU CAN MOVE AGAIN IN ONE MINUTE.
Obey
Now, my Bath. My Bath.
HE'S NOT INTERESTED CUZ YOU'RE NOT FEMININE ENOUGH.
I ALREADY KNOW THAT.
GLUG GLUG
BUT PEOPLE ARE BORN WITH CERTAIN CHARACTER-ISTICS...
YOU SHOULD BE BORN AGAIN, MOMOZONO.

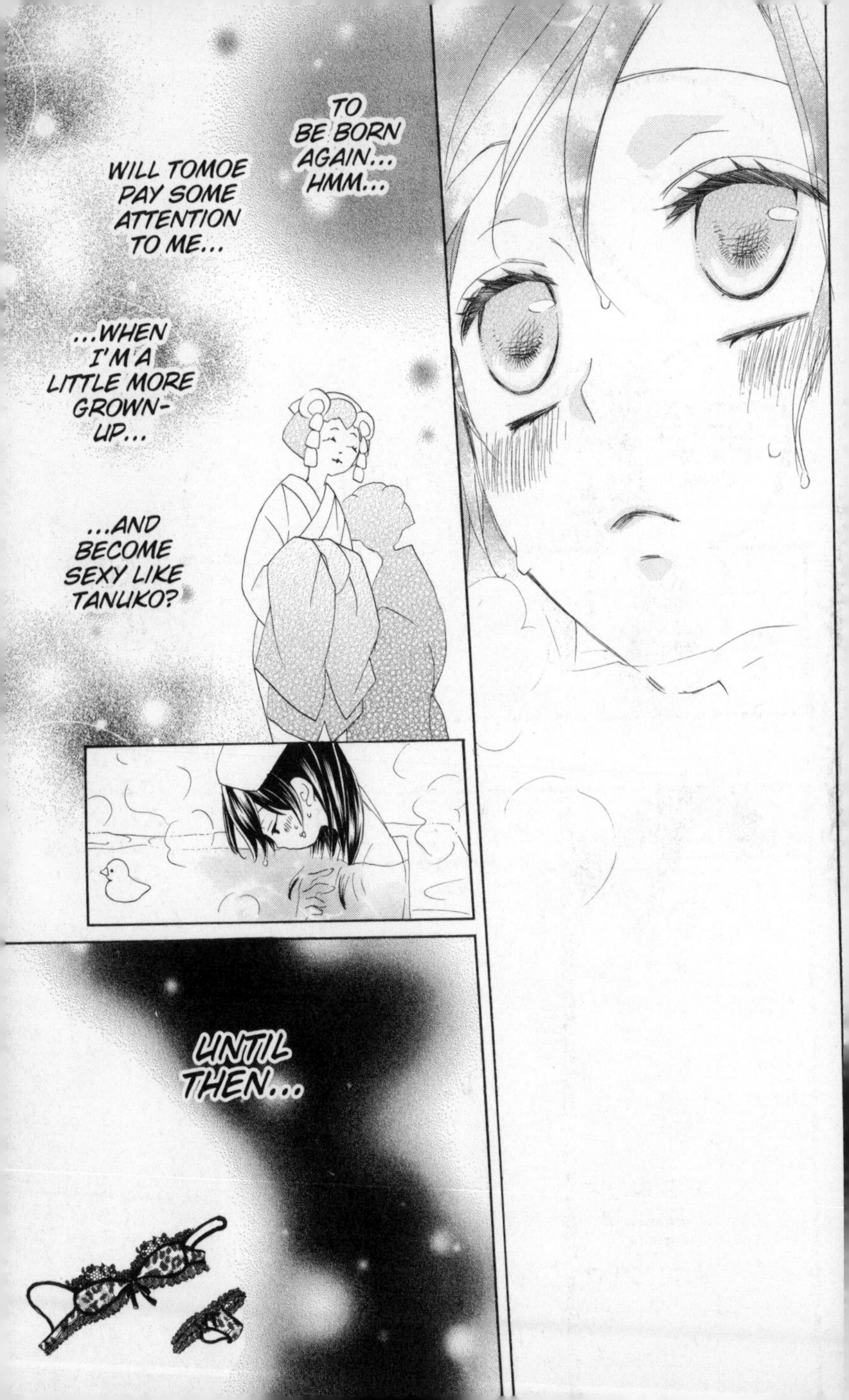
TO BE BORN AGAIN... HMM...
WILL TOMOE PAY SOME ATTENTION TO ME...
...WHEN I'M A LITTLE MORE GROWN-UP...
...AND BECOME SEXY LIKE TANUKO?
UNTIL THEN...

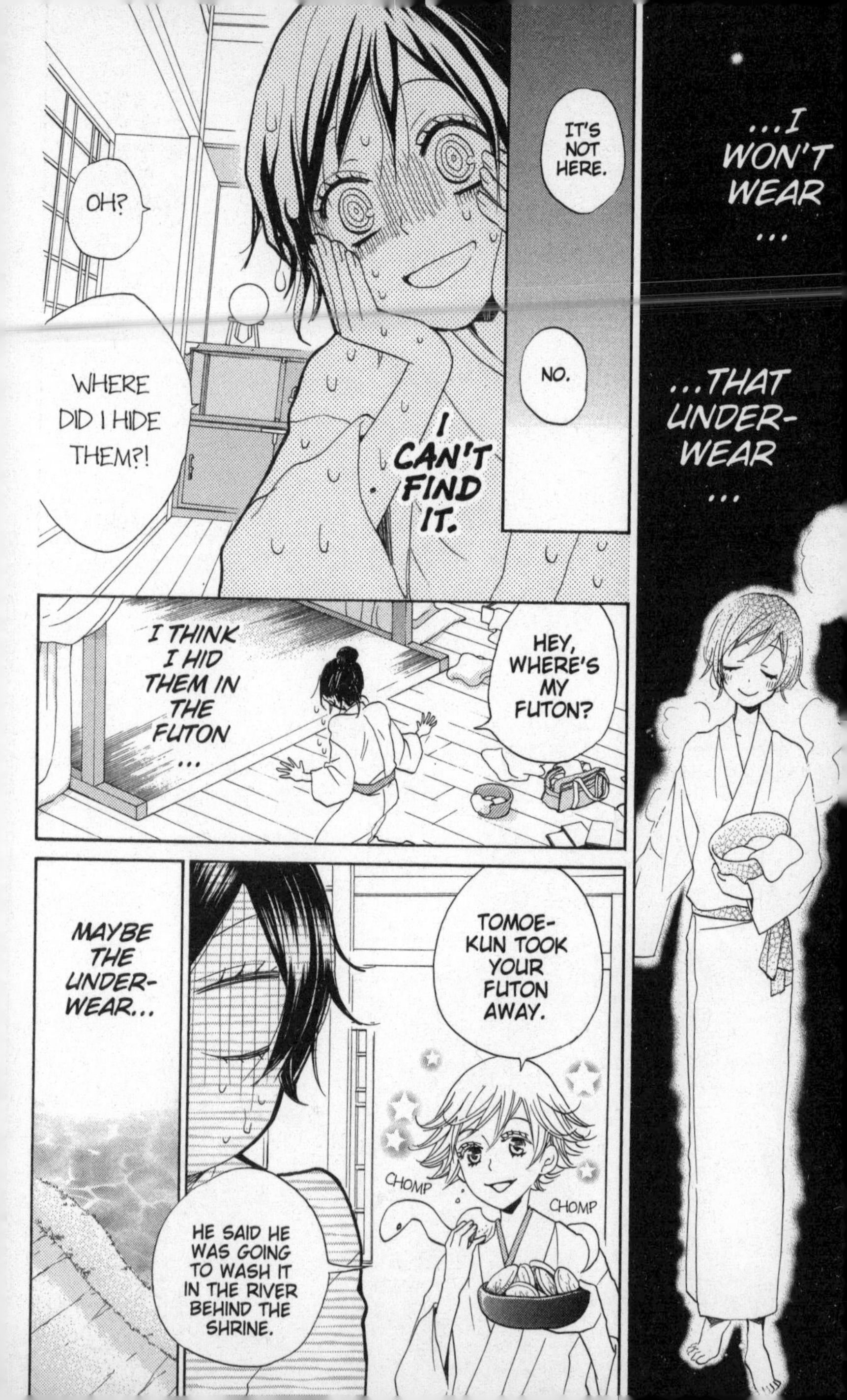
...I WON'T WEAR ...
...THAT UNDER-WEAR ...
IT'S NOT HERE.
NO.
I CAN'T FIND IT.
OH?
WHERE DID I HIDE THEM?!
HEY, WHERE'S MY FUTON?
I THINK I HID THEM IN THE FUTON ...
TOMOE-KUN TOOK YOUR FUTON AWAY.
CHOMP
CHOMP
MAYBE THE UNDER-WEAR...
HE SAID HE WAS GOING TO WASH IT IN THE RIVER BEHIND THE SHRINE.

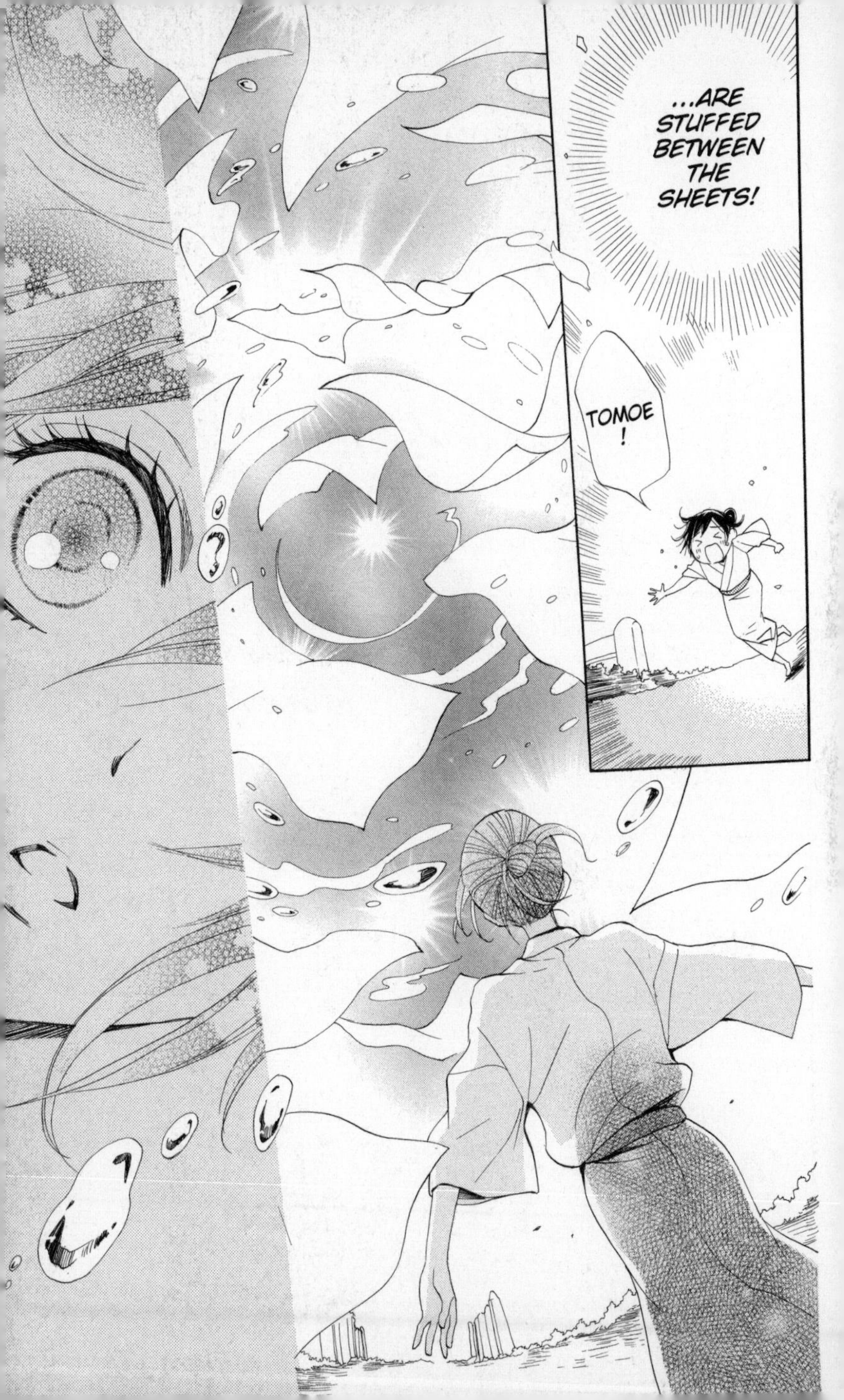
...ARE STUFFED BETWEEN THE SHEETS!
TOMOE!

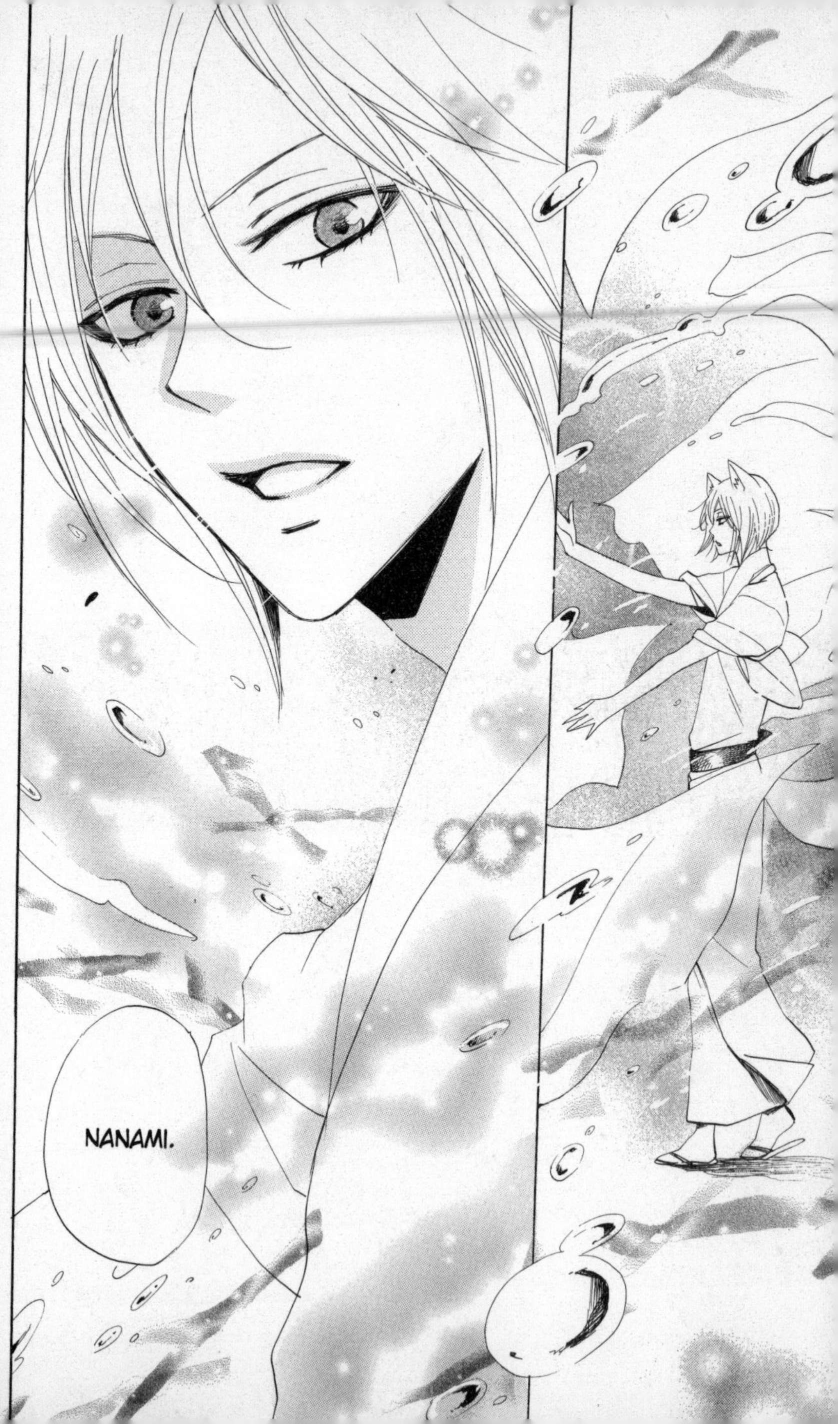
NANAMI.

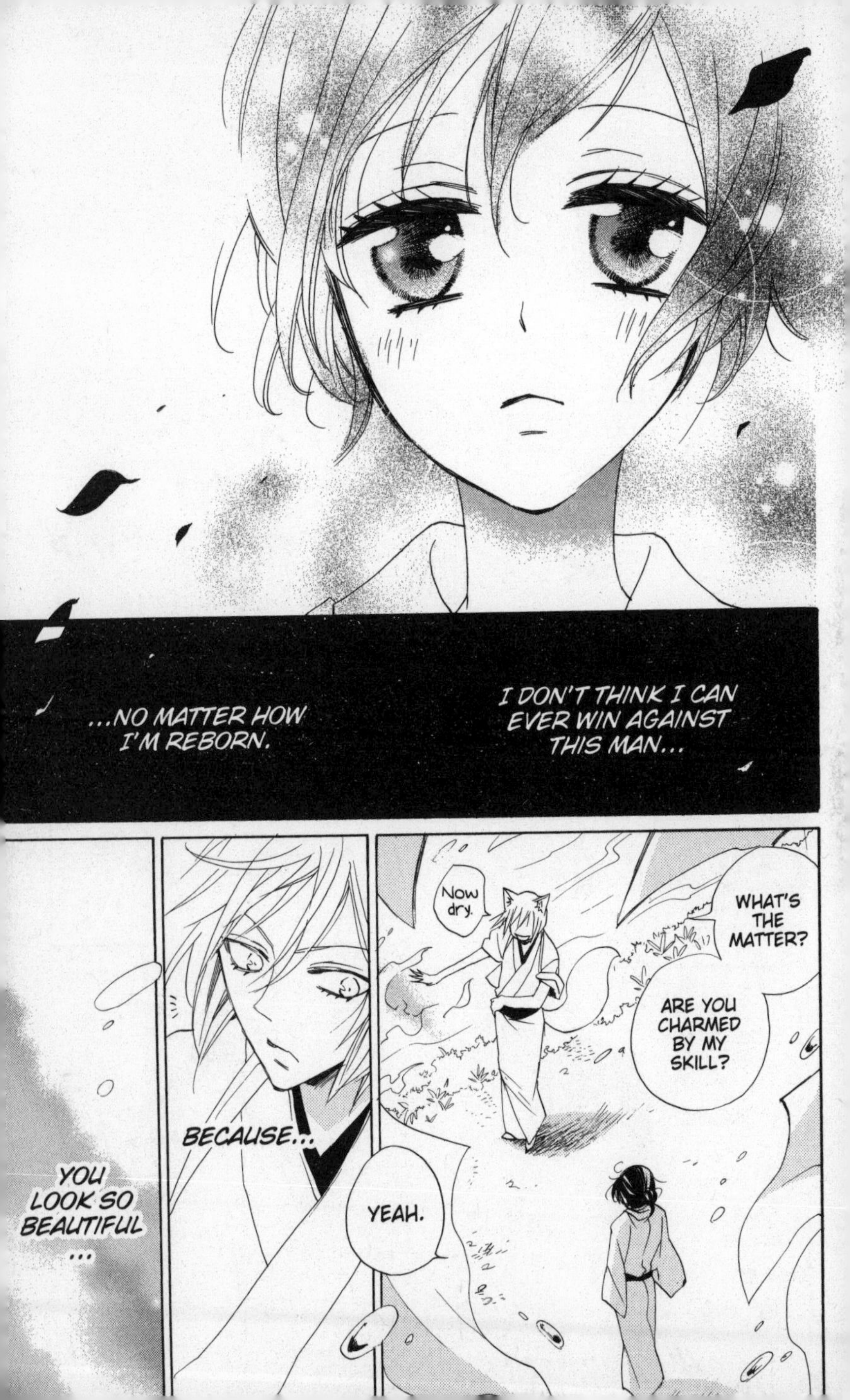
I DON'T THINK I CAN EVER WIN AGAINST THIS MAN...
...NO MATTER HOW I'M REBORN.
Now dry.
WHAT'S THE MATTER?
ARE YOU CHARMED BY MY SKILL?
YEAH.
BECAUSE...
YOU LOOK SO BEAUTIFUL ...

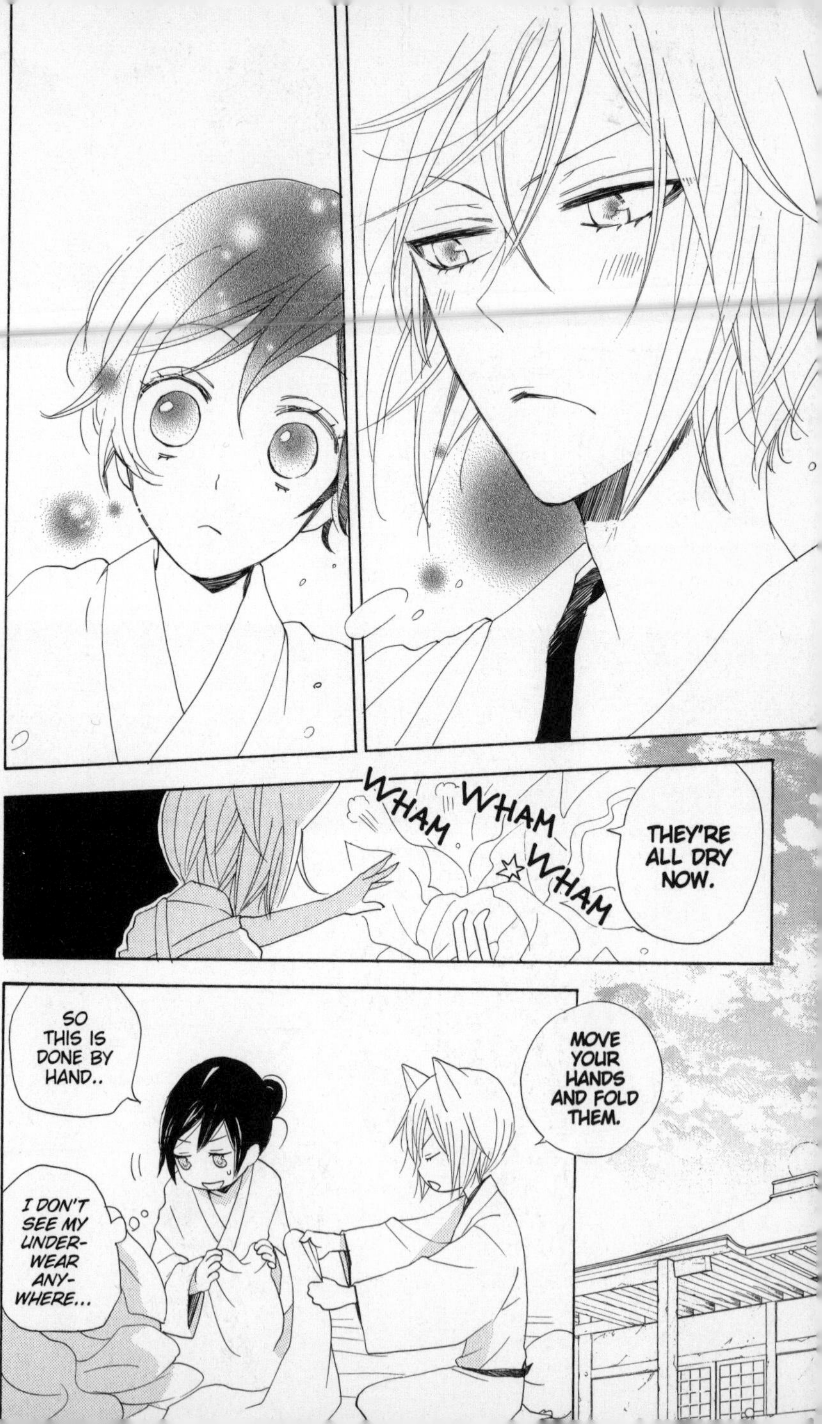
THEY'RE ALL DRY NOW.
WHAM WHAM WHAM
MOVE YOUR HANDS AND FOLD THEM.
SO THIS IS DONE BY HAND..
I DON'T SEE MY UNDER-WEAR ANY-WHERE...

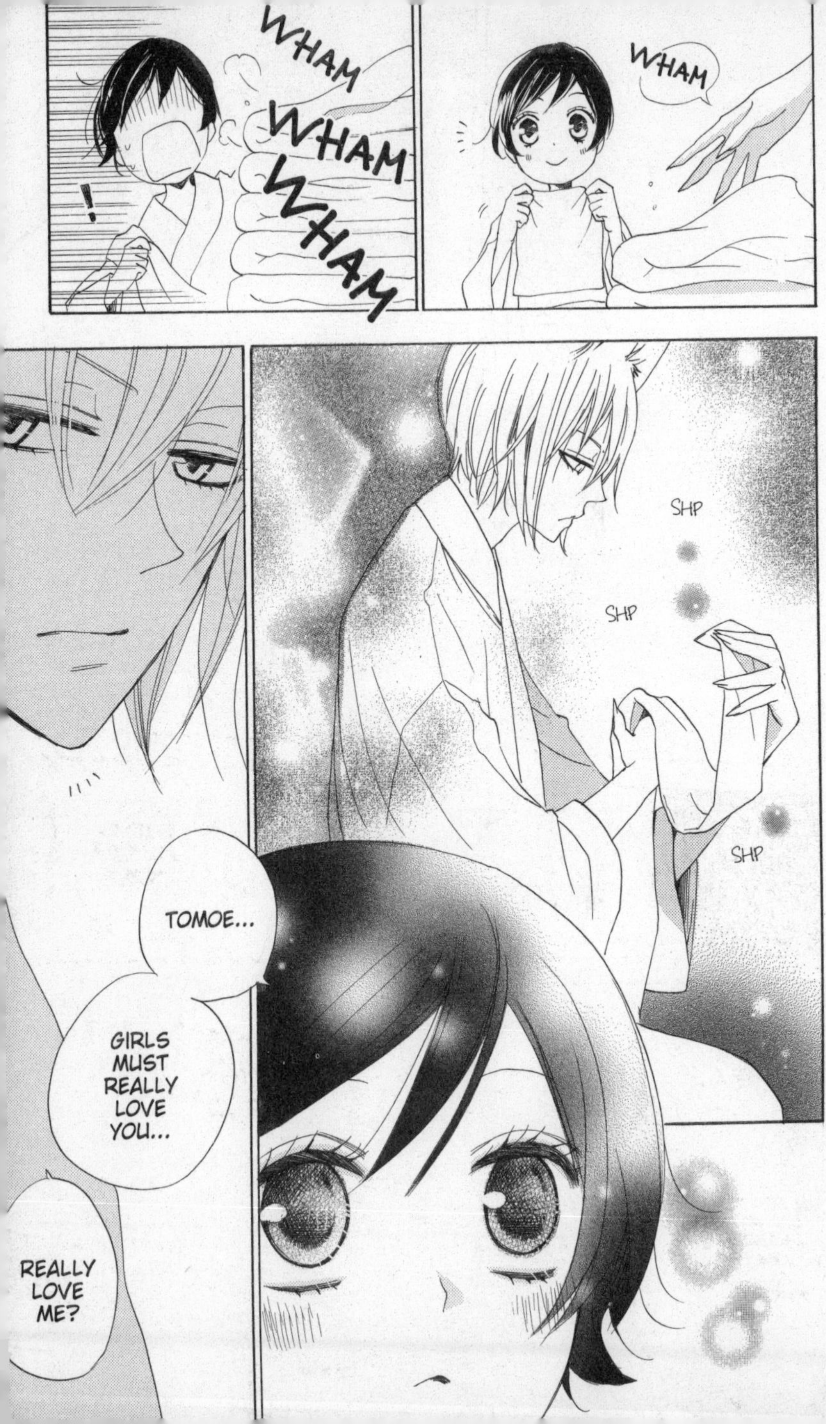
WHAM
WHAM
WHAM
WHAM
!
SHP
SHP
SHP
TOMOE...
GIRLS MUST REALLY LOVE YOU...
REALLY LOVE ME?

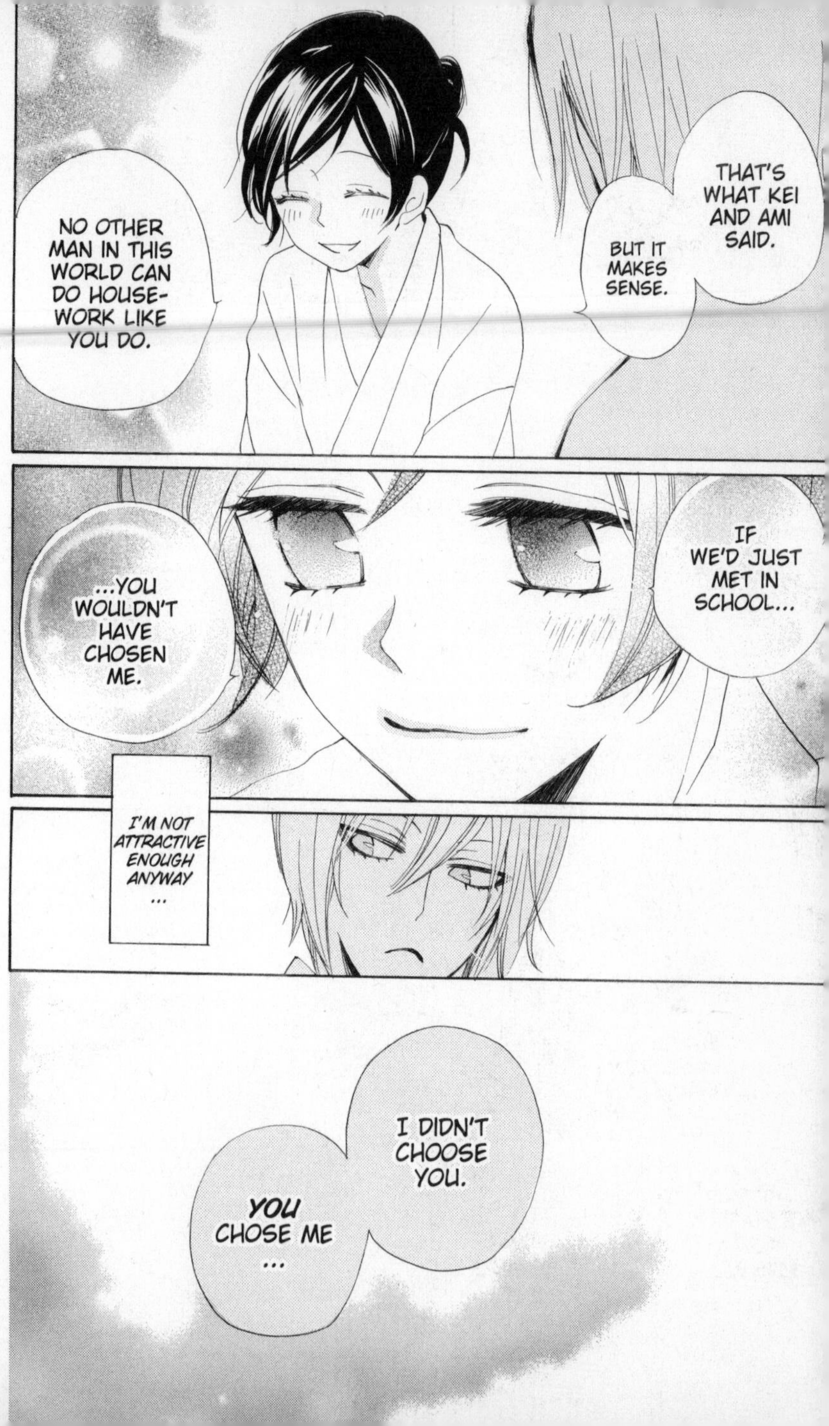
THAT'S WHAT KEI AND AMI SAID.
BUT IT MAKES SENSE.
NO OTHER MAN IN THIS WORLD CAN DO HOUSE-WORK LIKE YOU DO.
IF WE'D JUST MET IN SCHOOL...
...YOU WOULDN'T HAVE CHOSEN ME.
I'M NOT ATTRACTIVE ENOUGH ANYWAY ...
I DIDN'T CHOOSE YOU.
YOU CHOSE ME ...

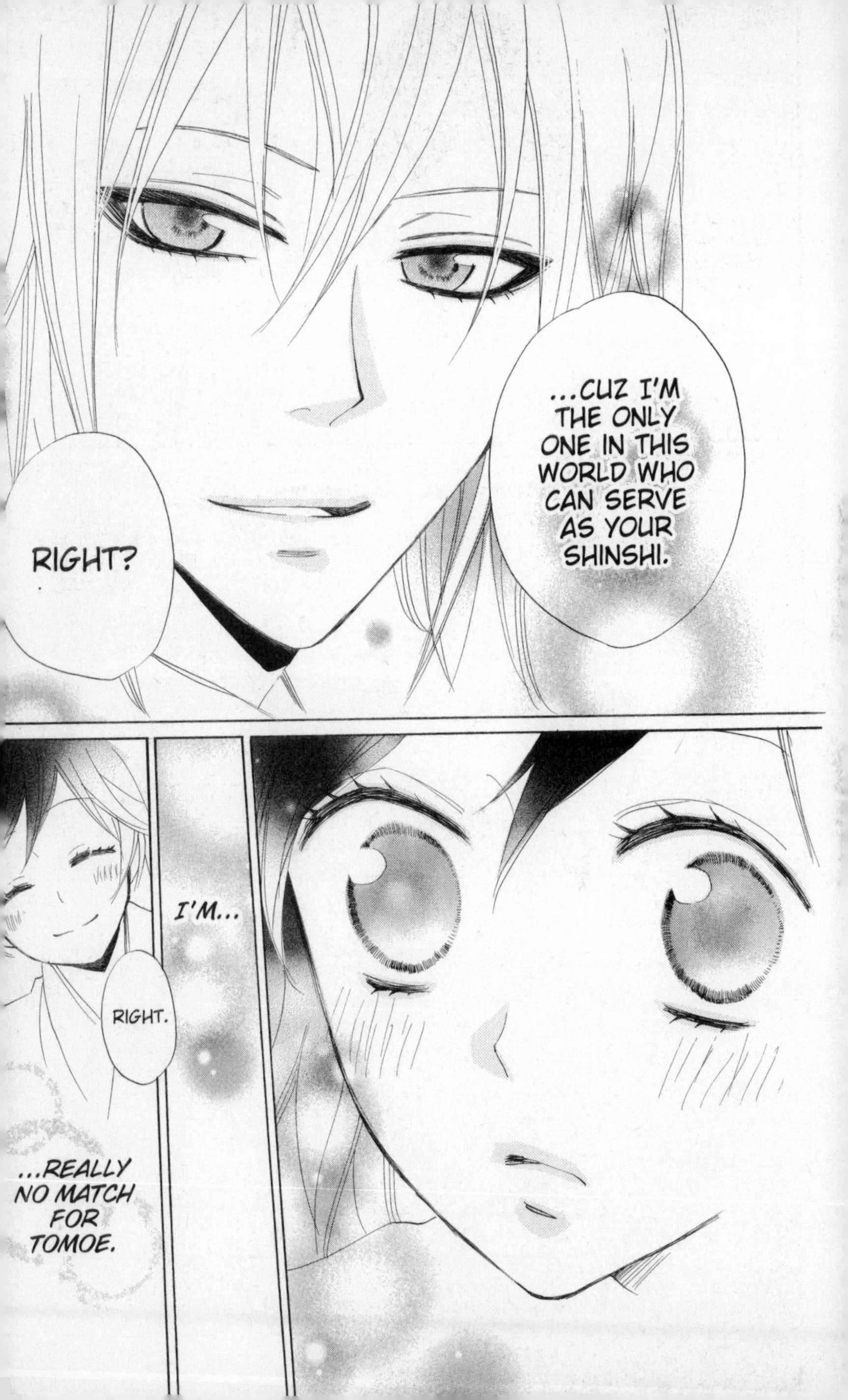
...CUZ I'M THE ONLY ONE IN THIS WORLD WHO CAN SERVE AS YOUR SHINSHI.
RIGHT?
I'M...
RIGHT.
...REALLY NO MATCH FOR TOMOE.

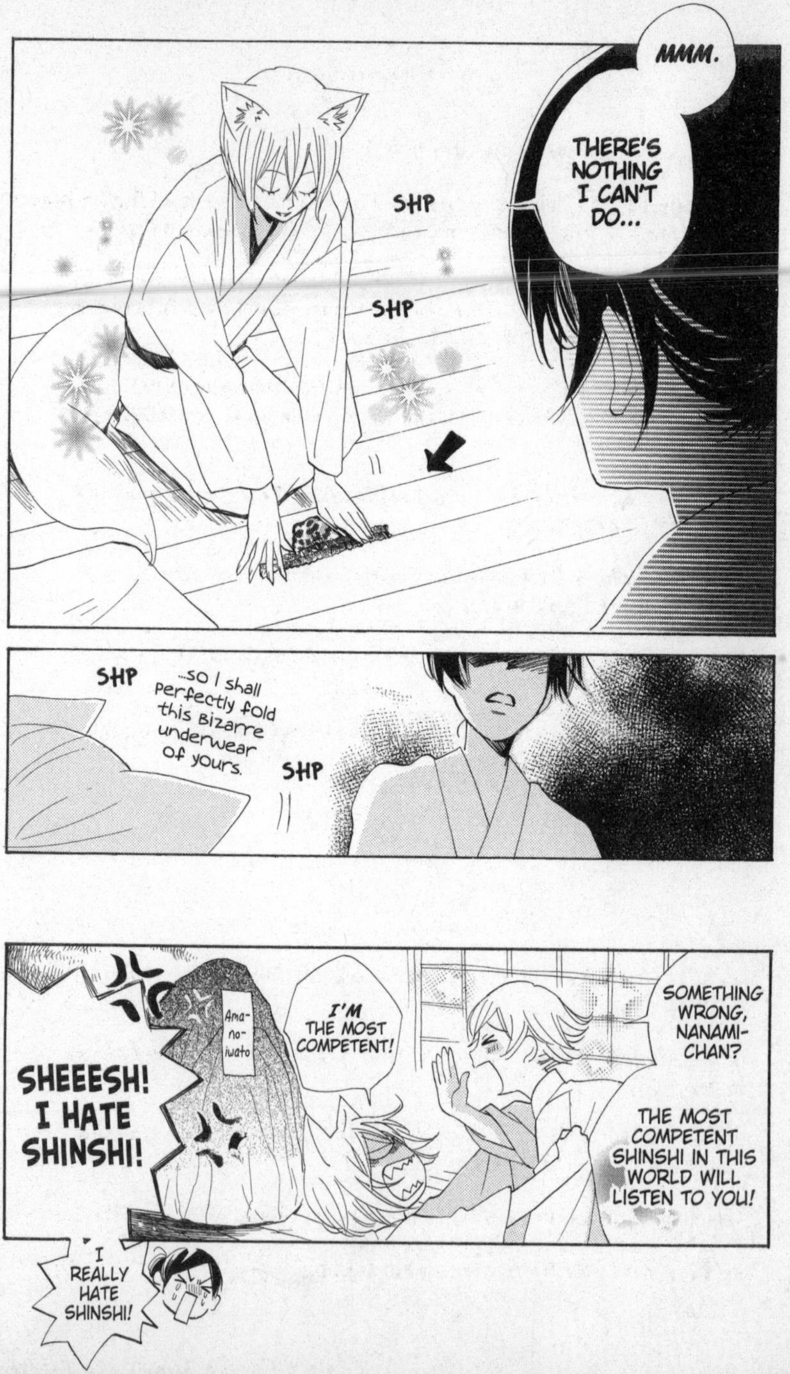
MMM.
THERE'S NOTHING I CAN'T DO...
SHP
SHP
...so I shall perfectly fold this bizarre underwear of yours.
SHP
SHP
SOMETHING WRONG, NANAMI-CHAN?
THE MOST COMPETENT SHINSHI IN THIS WORLD WILL LISTEN TO YOU!
I'M THE MOST COMPETENT!
Ama-no-iwato
SHEEESH! I HATE SHINSHI!
I REALLY HATE SHINSHI!

The Otherworld

Ayakashi is an archaic term for yokai.

Kami are Shinto deities or spirits. The word can be used for a range of creatures, from nature spirits to strong and dangerous gods.

Kirin (or *qilin*) is a mythical Chinese chimera that is believed to appear before saints. It is one of the three most powerful creatures, along with the phoenix and the dragon.

Kotodama is literally "word spirit," the spiritual power believed to dwell in words. In Shinto, the words you speak are believed to affect reality.

Shikigami are spirits that are summoned and employed by *onmyoji* (Yin-Yang sorcerers).

Shinshi are birds, beasts, insects or fish that have a special relationship with a kami.

Tengu are a type of yokai. They are sometimes associated with excess pride.

Tochigami (or *jinushigami*) are deities of a specific area of land.

Yokai are demons, monsters or goblins.

Honorifics

-chan is a diminutive most often used with babies, children or teenage girls.

-dono roughly means "my lord," although not in the aristocratic sense.

-kun is used by persons of superior rank to their juniors. It can sometimes have a familiar connotation.

-san is a standard honorific similar to Mr., Mrs., Miss, or Ms.

-sama is used with people of much higher rank.

Notes

Page 7, panel 2: Momotan
A miraculous cure-all that Nanami got in Izumo.

Page 15, panel 4: Himetaro
The kanji for *hime* means "princess" and *taro* is a common suffix for boy's names.

Page 70, panel 7: ofuda
A strip of paper or a small wooden tablet that acts as a spell.

Page 71, panel 2: The yokai in the pond
This is a *kappa*, a type of water spirit that mainly haunts rivers.
Kappa look like children, are green or red, have plates on their heads, tortoise shells on their backs, and webbed hands and feet.

Page 76, panel 2: Mount Ontake
A mountain in Nagano Prefecture. It is the second highest volcano after Mount Fuji, and is worshipped as a holy site. The way it is normally spelled, the kanji for *take* means "mountain peak" and the *on* is an honorific prefix. But the manga uses kanji that means "grudge peak."

Page 107, panel 1: Suzaku
One of the four sacred beasts that rule over the four points of the compass. *Suzaku* is the red phoenix that rules the south.

Page 153, panel 3: Ri
Ri is an old unit of measurement that was used in Japan, Korea and China. In Japan, it was equivalent to about 2.4 miles.

Page 157, panel 2: Muscat grape jelly
Muscats are a wine grape with a sweet, floral aroma. The jelly Nanami wants to eat is like a very firm jello, rather than a jam you spread on bread.

Page 159, panel 3: Red bean jelly
Called "yokan" in Japanese, it is a traditional Japanese dessert made of red bean paste, agar and sugar. The agar gives it a firm, somewhat gelatinous consistency.

Page 165, panel 3: Mont Blanc aux crimson sweet potatoes
Pureed, sweetened sweet potatoes topped with whipped cream. A variation of the traditional Mont Blanc, made with chestnut puree.

Page 176, panel 1: 1,000 yen
Around $10.60 U.S.

Page 177, panel 4-5: 10,000 yen and 33,333 yen
About $100.60 U.S. and $335.60 U.S.

Page 190, panel 3: Ama-no-iwato
The name of a cave that appears in Japanese myths. Amaterasu, the sun kami, hid there after her younger brother Susano-oh played too many pranks and caused one of her female weavers to die. The world was covered in darkness, and to get the sun kami out the other kami start partying in front of the cave. Amaterasu peeked out, wondering why everyone was laughing. One of the kami grabbed her and brought her out of the cave, and light returned to the world.

Julietta Suzuki's debut manga *Hoshi ni Naru Hi* (The Day One Becomes a Star) appeared in the 2004 *Hana to Yume Plus*. Her other books include *Akuma to Dolce* (The Devil and Sweets) and *Karakuri Odette*. Born in December in Fukuoka Prefecture, she enjoys having movies play in the background while she works on her manga.

KAMISAMA KISS
VOL. 15
Shojo Beat Edition

STORY AND ART BY
Julietta Suzuki

English Translation & Adaptation/Tomo Kimura
Touch-up Art & Lettering/Joanna Estep
Design/Yukiko Whitley
Editor/Pancha Diaz

KAMISAMA HAJIMEMASHITA by Julietta Suzuki
© Julietta Suzuki 2013
All rights reserved.
First published in Japan in 2013 by HAKUSENSHA, Inc., Tokyo.
English language translation rights arranged with
HAKUSENSHA, Inc., Tokyo.

Printed in Canada

Published by VIZ Media, LLC
P.O. Box 77010
San Francisco, CA 94107

10 9 8 7 6 5 4 3 2 1
First printing, June 2014

www.viz.com   www.shojobeat.com